The Cannabis Grow Bible

Second Edition

Also by Greg Green
The Cannabis Breeder's Bible

The Cannabis Grow Bible

Second Edition

by Greg Green

The Definitive Guide to
Growing Marijuana for
Recreational and
Medical Use

**GREEN
CANDY
PRESS**

PUBLISHED BY GREEN CANDY PRESS
SAN FRANCISCO, CA
www.greencandypress.com

First Edition Copyright © 2003 Greg Green
Second Edition Copyright © 2010 Greg Green
ISBN 978-1931160582

Photography © by Andre Grossman, David Strange, Delta-9 Labs, DNA Genetics,
Dr. Greenthumb, Dutch Passion, Ed Borg, Green House Seed Co., Hydro Garden,
KC Brains, Kissie, Mel Frank, MG Imaging, Paradise Seeds, Pepper Design, Sagarmatha
Seeds, Sativa Steph, Sensi Seeds, Serious Seeds, Subcool, Zoe Yonge

This book contains information about illegal substances, specifically the plant
Cannabis Sativa and its derivative products. Green Candy Press would like to
emphasize that cannabis is a controlled substance in North America and
throughout much of the world. As such, the use and cultivation of cannabis can
carry heavy penalties that may threaten an individual's liberty and livelihood.

The aim of the Publisher is to educate and entertain. Whatever the Publisher's
view on the validity of current legislation, we do not in any way condone the
use of prohibited substances.

PRINTED IN CHINA
MASSIVELY DISTRIBUTED BY P.G.W.

Acknowledgments

My deepest thanks go to open-minded and open-hearted people everywhere who understand the need to research and explore our world. I would like to say thank you to Simi and family. I love you. I would also like to say a special thanks to my publisher and editor for their always-welcome words of wisdom and their dedicated effort in bringing you the best presentation of cannabis cultivation methods possible. They have helpfully criticized various chapters for me. Without them this book wouldn't be what it is. I would like to ask that if you smoke tobacco, make a promise to yourself to stop. Trust yourself in the hope that you will quit and enjoy the new lease on life you will get from it.

Publishers Acknowledgements

First I'd like to thank Greg Green who has worked tirelessly on the first edition of the *Cannabis Grow Bible* and was then willing to return to the material and expand it into what became a truly amazing book. He was hugely motivated to get the best possible information out there to all who wanted to learn about cannabis. Then of course, behind the scenes was the Green Candy Press crew of Patrick, Steph and Ian who all contributed in major ways to the book that you hold in your hands. I'd also like to thank some of the other authors who were amongst the earliest pioneers of cannabis education; Ed Rosenthal, Mel Frank and Jorge Cervantes have all contributed a great amount to our knowledge of cannabis. To all the growers and breeders who've shared their knowledge and experience, you have helped the cannabis community take great strides forward. In particular I'd like to thank Delta-9 Labs, DNA Genetics, Dr. Greenthumb, Dutch Passion, Green House Seed Co., KC Brains, Paradise Seeds, Sagarmatha Seeds, Sensi Seeds and Serious Seeds for their years of work on producing amazing new strains. Finally, it would impossible to produce a book like this without the help of amazingly talented photographers; Andre Grossman, David Strange, Ed Borg, Hydro Garden, Kissie, Mel Frank, MG Imaging, Pepper Design, Sativa Steph, Subcool and Zoe Yonge. Overall this book has been a true collaboration and it's been a real joy to work with such a talented group of people and to bring you the second edition of the *Cannabis Grow Bible*.

TABLE OF CONTENTS

xiii	**Preface**
xvii	**Foreword**
1	**Chapter 1: The Cannabis Plant**
1	A Brief History of Cannabis
1	Cannabis Paleobotany
2	Cannabis Geography
3	Landrace Cannabis
4	Nomenclature of Cultigens
5	Cannabis and Modern Law
5	The High
10	Trichome
12	The Plant
14	Cannabis Species
14	The History of the Scientific Classification of Cannabis
14	Species
15	Flowering
18	Varieties
20	Ancient Names
21	Cannabis Taxonomy for Scientists and Researchers
21	Scientific Cannabis Taxonomy
25	Sub Species
26	Strain List
29	Cannabis Reproduction
31	Advanced Sinsemilla Facts
32	Breeding for Desirable Traits
34	Understanding Sex Determination Systems
35	Leaf Types
35	A Word About Male Potency
35	The Life Cycle of the Marijuana Plant
36	Plant Types
41	The Decision to Grow
42	Cycle Times
43	Let's Get Growing
45	**Chapter 2: Seeds: Selection, Banks, and Storage**
48	Selecting Seeds
50	How to Get Seeds
50	Choosing a Seed Bank
51	Transporting Seeds
54	Harvesting Seeds
57	Storing Seeds
59	**Chapter 3: Propagation and Germination**
59	What is Propagation?
59	Propagation Logistics
60	Germination
63	Germination Techniques
63	Seed Soil Propagation
63	Germination Soil
64	Seed Towel Propagation
64	Propagation Kits
65	Cannabis Seeds
66	Cannabis Seed Structure
67	Cannabis Seed Germination
68	Cannabis Seed Functions
68	Dangers When Germinating Seeds

71 | Transplanting Seedlings
74 | Transplanting
80 | Transplant Shock

83 | Chapter 4: The Great Divide: Indoors or Outdoors
83 | Gardening Tools
84 | Planning for Indoor Growing
86 | Outdoor Growing
88 | Planning for Outdoor Growing and Guerrilla Farming
89 | Guerrilla Farming
90 | Security
92 | Indoor Security
94 | Outdoor Security
95 | Guerrilla Growing Security

99 | Chapter 5: Organic Growing
104 | Organic Soil Garden
111 | Organic Growing
111 | Compost
112 | Organic Compost
113 | Composting
114 | Compost Tea
115 | Mulch
117 | Worm Composting
121 | Humus
121 | Organic Weeding
121 | Controlling Pests
121 | Organic Feeding Products
121 | Rules for Organic Growing

123 | Chapter 6: The Indoor Growing Environment
123 | Lighting
124 | Color Bands and Plant Growth
126 | Spectrum of Electromagnetic Radiation
126 | Impact of Light Color on Plant Growth
127 | Basics of Photosynthesis
128 | Common Lighting Types
130 | Wattage and Lumens
133 | HID Bulb Brand Comparison
134 | Questions to Ask When Buying a Lighting Kit
135 | What to Look For When Buying a Lighting Kit
135 | Lamp Efficiency in Lumens
137 | Lamp Efficiency For MH and HPS
138 | Sample Comparison of Wattage and Lumens
138 | How to Get the Most from Your Lighting System
140 | Adjusting Your Lights
141 | 24/0 and 18/6 — The Vegetative Photoperiod
144 | Electrical Costs
144 | Advanced Lighting
146 | How HID Works
148 | How HPS Works
150 | Soil
151 | pH
151 | Nutrients
152 | Composition
152 | Common Soil Types
155 | Mixing Soils and Soil Ratios
156 | Understanding the NPK Ratio
156 | Pots

161 **Chapter 7: Indoor Environmental Control**
161 Nutrient Control
164 Problematic Nutrients
165 Macronutrient Disorders: A Rough Guide
168 Feeding
171 Soil Control
173 Water Control
174 Air Control
174 Odor Control
176 Ionizing
176 Ozone Generating
177 Activated Carbon Air Filtering
178 Ventilation
180 Fans
181 Humidity
181 Temperature
184 Timers
184 CO_2 (Carbon Dioxide)
186 Calculating How Much Carbon Dioxide You Need
188 Climate Controllers
191 Soil Flushing
192 Here is How to Flush Your Soil

195 **Chapter 8: Pre-Flowering and Flowering**
196 Pre-flowering and Early Sexing
198 Checking for Calyx Development
198 First Early Sexing Method: Height
199 Second Early Sexing Method: Calyxes
199 Third Early Sexing Method: Force Flowering
200 Plant Traits
201 When to Flower?
202 The All-Important 12/12!
205 Problems with 12/12
206 Pre-Flowering for the 24/0 and the 18/6 Photoperiods
207 The Male/Female Thing or How to Sex Your Plants
207 Calyx Development
208 The Male Flower
209 Male Flowering
211 Flowering

213 **Chapter 9: Advanced Indoor Soil-Based Grow Methods**
213 Preparing the "Special Clone Mother"
217 Sea of Green (SOG)
220 Screen of Green (ScrOG)
221 ScrOG Growing by Real High
225 Some Notes on SOG and ScrOG Growing
226 Cabinet Growing
227 Closet Growing
228 Perpetual Grow Cycles
228 Customizing Advanced Setups
229 Dutch Passion
230 Delta-9 Labs
232 DNA Genetics
234 Green House Seed Co.
236 High Bred Seeds
238 Paradise Seeds
240 Serious Seeds
241 Sagarmatha Seeds

243 **Chapter 10: A Look at Hydroponics**
243 The Grower and the Growing Medium
244 Hydroponic Systems

244 | Nutrient Film Technique (NFT)
245 | A Manual NFT System
246 | Nutrient Film Technique
246 | Flood and Drain / Ebb and Flow
247 | Ebb and Flow System
249 | Drip Irrigation
249 | Drip Irrigation System
251 | Aeroponics
251 | Aeroponic System
252 | Wick
252 | Wick System
253 | Gravity
254 | Gravity System
255 | Automatic Hydroponic Pots and Manual Hydroponic Pots
255 | Commercial Pot
256 | Ebb and Flow System
264 | Setting up the Hydroponic Environment
265 | The Hydroponic Growing Medium
269 | Preparing Nutrient Solutions
270 | Analysis of Perlite
270 | Analysis of Vermiculite
271 | Hydroponic pH
272 | Algae
272 | Grow and Bloom
273 | A Word About Nutrient Strengths
274 | Trichome Technologies Custom NFT System
276 | Controlling the Hydroponic Environment
276 | Hard Water Problems
277 | When to Add More Nutrients
277 | Affordable Hydroponics
277 | The Bubbler
278 | The Bubble Bucket

283 | **Chapter 11: Outdoor Growing**
286 | Preparing a Plot
290 | Outdoor Soil
293 | Caring for Outdoor Plants
297 | Outdoor Flowering and the Photoperiod

301 | **Chapter 12: Caring for Mature Marijuana Plants**
302 | Thinning
304 | Light Bending (Phototropism)
305 | Pruning for Yield
306 | Topping
308 | FIM Technique
308 | Super Cropping Technique
310 | How to Make Cannabis Bushes
312 | Training
313 | Cloning
314 | Making Clones
322 | How to Air Layer a Clone
323 | Bonsai Clones
323 | Sinsemilla Hermaphrodites
324 | Increasing Yield
325 | Reverting to Vegetative Growth
326 | Increasing Your Chances of Females
328 | End of the Grow

331 | **Chapter 13: Problem Solver**
331 | Domestic Pets
332 | Pesticides, Herbicides, and Fungicides
332 | Pesticides

334 | Pest Index
344 | Pest Predators
347 | Recovering From a Pest Invasion
351 | Fungi
353 | Root Rot
354 | Powdery Mildew
355 | Chemical Burns
356 | Nutrient Deficiencies
356 | 10 Steps to Saving Your Grow
357 | Nutrient Deficiencies
363 | No Cure for Bad Genetics

365 | **Chapter 14: Harvesting and Curing Your Bud**
366 | The Harvest
367 | Quick Bud Samples
367 | Expert Harvest Indication
370 | Indica Harvest
371 | Sativa Harvest
372 | Fan Leaves, Leaves, and Trim
373 | Harvest
374 | Manicuring
377 | Curing
379 | Trichome Tech Bud

383 | **Chapter 15: How To Breed Marijuana**
383 | Making Seeds
383 | Collecting and Storing Pollen
384 | Collecting and Storing Seeds
385 | Simple Breeding
385 | Continuing a Strain Through Seeds
385 | Making a Simple Hybrid
386 | Introduction to Plant Genetics
388 | Green House Seed Company: R & D Laboratory
389 | The Hardy-Weinberg Model of Genetic Equilibrium
390 | Genetic Equilibrium Theory and Application
396 | The Test Cross
403 | Hardy-Weinberg Law, Part 2
406 | Mendel and the Pea Experiments
408 | The First Hybrid Cross (the F1 Generation)
408 | The Second Hybrid Cross (the F2 Generation)
410 | More on Genetic Frequencies
412 | How to True Breed a Strain
416 | Advanced Breeding Techniques
419 | How to Generate a Clone Mother
419 | Selfing
420 | Notes on Selfing by Vic High
423 | Concluding Thoughts on Breeding

425 | **Chapter 16: Top Ten**
427 | Top 10 Indica
429 | Top 10 Mostly Indica
431 | Top 10 Sativa
433 | Top 10 Mostly Sativa
435 | Top 10 Indica/Sativa Mix

437 | **Chapter 17: How to Make Hash**
437 | Gathering the Stalked Capitate Trichomes
438 | Skuff
439 | Screening Basic Methods
441 | Multiple Screening Method
442 | Advanced Screening
444 | Drum Machines

445 | Basic Water Extraction
445 | Advanced Water Extraction
448 | Supercritical Fluid Extraction
450 | Butane Extraction
451 | Tips for Butane Extraction
453 | Pressing Resin into Hash

457 | **Chapter 18: Important Cannabis Issues**
467 | The Truth About Hyer-Potent Cannabis
467 | So, What Has Actually Changed?
469 | How to Avoid Taking Cancer-Causing Agents
470 | Cooking With Cannabis
471 | Vaporization
473 | Cannabis Legalization and Social Issues
474 | The Alcohol vs. Cannabis Debate
477 | Driving While Under the Influence
479 | Cannabis and Brain Damage
480 | Cannabis and the Immune System
480 | Cannabis and Sexual Dysfunction
481 | Cannabis and Pregnancy
481 | Cannabis and Human DNA Repair Malfunction
483 | Medicinal Use
485 | Cannabis and Harder Drugs: The Gateway Theory
485 | Cannabis and Memory

487 | **Chapter 19: How to Enjoy Your Bud**
488 | How to Roll a Joint
489 | How to Make an Apple Pipe
490 | How to Make a Tinfoil Pipe
492 | How to Make a Bucket Bong
493 | How to Make a Light Bulb Vaporizer

495 | **Chapter 20: *The Cannabis Grow Bible* Checklist**
495 | Good Genetics
496 | Proper Lighting
496 | An Ounce of Prevention
497 | Air Circulation and Ventilation
497 | The Right Medium
498 | Optimal Pot/Container Size
499 | Safe Fertilizers
499 | 12/12
500 | Avoiding Plant Stress
500 | Carbon Dioxide (CO_2)
500 | Labeling

503 | **Resources**
507 | **Glossary of Terms**
513 | **Endnotes**
523 | **Index**

Preface

Cannabis cultivation and research continues to take place, and although the amount of care we take is vital, more important is to do things right. In the first edition of this book I proposed the rule, "Never Tell a Soul that You Are Growing Cannabis!" This principle, when examined in practice, turns out to be completely baseless and practically impossible, leaving me hard-pressed to believe it and forced to relegate it to myth. In order to gain good cannabis genetics, you will need to make and cultivate contacts somehow. Don't panic if you have bought this book and suddenly find yourself feeling as if you've done something wrong; you've done nothing wrong, and in fact you've made the right choice for a guide. Writers can write whatever they please, you can read whatever you like, and this book will show you how growing cannabis is done correctly.

his book was written with growers in mind; we listen to and talk with growers. The need for this second edition of *The Cannabis Grow Bible* became clear thanks to questions raised by the first edition as well as *The Cannabis Breeder's Bible: The Definitive Guide to Marijuana Genetics, Cannabis Botany and Creating Strains for the Seed Market*. There is a constant need to revise and update previous systems with new advancements and progress in the world of cultivation. More immediately, there is a need to draw the cultivator's attention to a change in botanical orientation and circumstances that maximize yields. No longer are growers just satisfied by the look of one plant in two-dozen that might be of book- or magazine-publication quality. No longer are they content with half the yield's potency and expectations. The natural cannabis grower is consumed by an urgent and ever-increasing need to generate productive, efficient grows that instantly meet expectations and exceed in results the first time. For these reasons, this second edition contains immediate information to acquaint the reader with the more impressive techniques that result in consistent, verified, high-yielding, potent crops. However, the onus is on the reader and potential cultivator to think everything through before considering buying a single seed. This especially means thinking about the impact on one's own family, which should be put before everything else.

There is also a growing awareness that many sources for quality seed genetics in the West may be facing tougher legal issues, coupled with concern over Internet security and even the worldwide distribution of seeds.[1]

A little know-how, which this book teaches, will immediately allow you to avoid common mistakes and achieve higher rates of success than even experienced cultivators. This book will cover all the groundwork for you.

Claiming to know everything is a strong assertation to make. I believe that a growing manual should try and reference source material as much as possible. I believe growing is a science but I am also aware that it is an art. Every grower has his own point of view, and being critical of another grower's opinion is not the way to improve. The best grower is critical of himself, always.

This book is not about me, it is all about you. This is a circular process of giving out better growing information and seeing better grows as a result, and then writing about them. You are part of that process.

I try to present this data as a case for growing cannabis in the context of the most optimal ways of producing results. Our methods are documented and repeatable, catering to the needs of both the small home-grower and the outdoor breeder. Yet, we recognize there is a greater need to be concerned with the small home-grower (large-scale breeders may prefer to read *The Cannabis Breeder's Bible*) and to this end we offer synoptic plans on how to go about getting the results that you need. Frequently, we include our own brief recommendations, but we do so knowing that the work *you* put in will finally generate exactly what you need. Take this advice.

A good grower is not a grower who knows lots or pretends to know everything, but one who gets into the rhythm of growing the right way. The truth, however, is that there is no right way. Some ways are just better than others. It is your grow. It is your fun. It is your love. Never forget this when people dangle their steroid-pumped-up buds before you. This is about enjoying your time. Remember to grow cannabis without love is to never experience the joys of cannabis cultivation. Some growers with the biggest buds in the world have never grown at all!

Greg Green

Foreword

This book is all about symbiosis. Symbiosis is the relationship between two different living creatures that live in close proximity and depend on each other in particular ways, each getting specific benefits from the other.

I write this book because symbiosis is a very interesting biological phenomenon. In the past century, symbiosis between living things on this planet has merited the attention of leading biologists everywhere. Symbiosis appears to be something much greater, and with more intricacy, than we previously realized.

Throughout everyday existence we take many things for granted. A lot of the time when we stop to examine these things we get a surprise. For instance, the origin of living things was once a mystery, but Darwin and Wallace solved this in the middle of the nineteenth century. The solution to this puzzle was natural selection, a mechanism (essentially an algorithm of non-random mating plus genetic diversity) driving biological evolution from its early primordial molecular form up to all the diversity we see in life today. Biologists continue to confirm this amazing discovery; symbiosis has an important role to play in it.

Cannabis enthusiasts take for granted that they like cannabis, but do they know that cannabis also likes them? That is symbiosis. We, as humans, sometimes have the tendency to see things from our own point of view. Imagine seeing things from another. Describe what the earth would look like from the point of view of the moon. Visualize how a stone would seem from the point of view of a sparrow. Picture what the world looks like from the point of view of cannabis. Think about how cannabis sees you.

Cannabis happens to be one of our earliest symbiotic plant partners with use throughout our ancestry. These relatives, through to us, have used cannabis in a variety of ways. We have bred cannabis by selection. Darwin and Wallace's theory of natural selection was based on environmental pressures influencing genetic variability creating, basically, all of biology. Natural selection promotes fitness, selecting genes that do best in the environment in which they are found. In evolution, gradualism, over long periods of time (at least 3 billion years: 3×10^9 years, or 3,000,000,000) produces the kind of complexity we find in living things, making them appear as if they have been engineered by intelligence. On closer examination of these complexities we find that nature is, in fact, more than capable of this task.

Experimentation is a great thing.

I have been interested in creating the best possible access to cannabis cultivation information for a long time. In 2000, I began to work extensively on compiling a text with a whole new view of cannabis cultivation. This work culminated in the production of the first edition of the *Cannabis Grow Bible*, published in 2003. The importance of its influence can be seen in cannabis cultivation and books that followed in its wake. I put this revolution down to a few things. The first is that I genuinely wanted to present readers with correct information as opposed to pseudoscience. I feel that the *Cannabis Grow Bible* is a landmark correction that separates cannabis cultivation mythology from cannabis cultivation reality. Next, I had to deal with putting forward the best reality possible. That meant rediscovering how cannabis cultivation should be done. Not only that, but I had to present the best way of generating the best results. It wasn't long before I realized that genetics had to play a major role in this.

Explaining genetics to people is not easy, but it is not too difficult either and the rewards for doing so are both intellectually stimulating and very productive. I not only wanted the reader to learn about genetics, I wanted the grower to *feel* genetics. Without electron microscopes we haven't a hope of seeing genes themselves, but we can see and understand their phenotypes (how those genes are expressed in the way an organism appears to us).

It isn't enough just to understand basic genetics though; you have to understand it in terms of how you can get the most from it, learning to work with it as a potter does with clay. I can't say that regular grow books, such as ones about growing tomatoes, have not had an impact on cannabis cultivation; they have. I suspect, however, that the popularity of cannabis cultivation has had a greater impact on tomato growing.

The development of growing is evolutionary, from hunters and gatherers to farmers. Symbiotically, humans have always lived with and worked with cultivated plants. If we didn't, we wouldn't have made it as a race, and we wouldn't be here to read this. I believe we should all have the genes for a green thumb. Anyone who thinks they can't grow only needed better guidance about it. I hope this book will provide that guidance.

Moreover, I believe that reading this book will be a deeply satisfying experience. I want every page to give you something that you didn't know. Returning readers from the first edition will come across equally exciting new material.

I believe that the combination of good genetics and understanding the cannabis plant holds the key to successful cultivation. This is not only true for cannabis, but for any type of cultivation project, and even domestic breeding programs for other organisms.

I hope, as an author, that what I write will have an enduring impression. The first edition of the *Cannabis Grow Bible* has not been short-lived. The second edition is an update with new material. The encouragement that I need to continue this project is found in the results that have been generated. There has been little contemporary criticism of my approach and it seems that the orientation of this book toward genetics has put an end to opposing points of view.

Long live this new direction. It is called the "Gene-centered view". May your fruits be bountiful thanks to this applied gene selection theory.

1 | The Cannabis Plant

A Brief History of Cannabis

Cannabis has been growing on this planet for thousands, maybe millions of years, since quite some time before human intervention. Cannabis can be grown nearly anywhere, as long as the temperature is not consistently cold and there is enough sunlight and food for the plant to flourish. In Asia, you can travel to various regions around Mongolia and visit the cannabis plant growing naturally on hillsides and across vast plains, sometimes covering entire hill faces and spreading across the valley below. The origins of cannabis are not entirely clear, but biologists and cannabis researchers generally agree that the plant first took root somewhere in the Himalayas. The evidence for this conclusion is found in cannabis' paleobotanical record.[1]

Cannabis Paleobotany

Support for the theory that cannabis began its life in the Himalayas comes from historical record. Paleobotany is a branch of paleontology that deals with plant fossils and ancient vegetation. Palynology is the scientific study of spores and pollen. Cannabis fossil evidence is accessible in the form of plant fibers, pollen grains, seed remains, trichome remains, and artificial compounds found at locations of archaeological interest. An abundance of primordial pollen grains have been recovered from many European sites. Asia has lots of cannabis plant impressions on ancient pieces of ceramics, along with seed remains. Africa and Europe have some incinerated residue or ash deposits but the instances are rare. Cannabis trichomes remain the best possible paleobotanical evidence for cannabis' history because they do not decompose quickly. Ancient trichome remnants have been analyzed for cannabinoid content and can be matched with specific cannabis plant populations.[2]

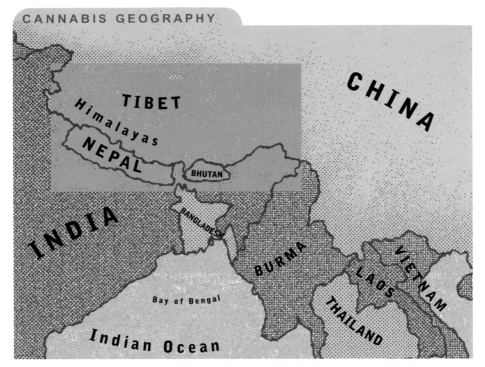

Map of Asia: the square indicates where cannabis is believed to have originated.

Mankind has been using cannabis as far back as we know he existed. The burial shroud of a Celtic chieftain found at Hochdoft (550–500 BC) was made from a cannabis fiber textile. Danish Bronze Age skirt cords made from cannabis fiber have been dated back to 1250 BC. The Gravettians were an industrial culture of the European Upper Paleolithic (the Old Stone Age); considered hunters and gatherers, they also developed human technology such as stone tools. Hunting nets made from cannabis and used by the Gravettians have been dated by researcher H. Pringle from 24,980 to 22,870 BC.[3] Pringle's findings at the Czech Republic sites also revealed more impressions of cannabis fiber in the clay floors of excavated living quarters.

Ancient cannabis breeding is archaeologically recorded by the botanist N.I. Vavilov, who worked with wild cannabis populations to reproduce the first domesticated cannabis cultivar, thought to be first bred some 6500 years ago in Mongolia[4]—although throughout this region and into China pollen was transmitted over long distances by bees to northeast India.[5] Major domestication occurred in northern China and still continues to this day.[6] While the evidence for the Mongolian cultivar origins is good, there is general consensus that the larger center of domestication was probably Pan-p'o, China, around 4500 BC.[7]

The record of pollen evidence for the dispersal of cannabis across Europe and the Middle East shows that it was established in the Balkans during the Greek and Roman Empire, spreading upward and east.[8] Evidence for Roman usage is well documented in their literature, but cultivation was almost nonexistent for environmental reasons. Poland has deposits of pollen evidence in lakebeds that are dated to 3500 BC,[9] with some grains dating back to 5000 BC.[10] Great Britain has provided a wealth of cannabis palynological evidence for early cultivation and usage, dating back to the start of the first century.[11]

The cannabis plant has managed to travel across the globe without the involvement of humans. As we have learned, the seed has been carried by the wind, bees, in bird droppings, and has attached itself to animals that trek over long distances, thus globally dispersing the plant naturally.

Today, human intervention has forced the cannabis plant to be grown under more controlled conditions and in areas where the plant would not have previously existed. That same intervention has also forced indigenous cannabis and foreign cannabis crops to be destroyed.

Landrace Cannabis

Landrace, also known as land race, is an important word when it comes to understanding types of wild cannabis and types of domesticated cannabis. While originally the term was meant to refer to a specific breed of hog, in later times it has been adopted by the scientific community to mean something else—especially in botany. J. R. Harlan defines landrace as having

> a certain genetic integrity. They are recognizable morphologically; farmers have names for them and different landraces are understood to differ in adaptation to soil type, time of seed, date of maturity, height, nutritive value, use and other properties. Most important, they are genetically diverse. They are balanced populations—variable, in equilibrium with both environment and pathogens and genetically dynamic.[12]

Italian botanical glossarists suggest that landraces "are crop populations in balance with their environment, and remain relatively stable over a long period of time."[13] Robin Pistorius records that landraces are "farmer-developed cultivars of crop plants, which are adapted to local environmental conditions."[14] Friis-Hansen and Sthapit state that landraces are

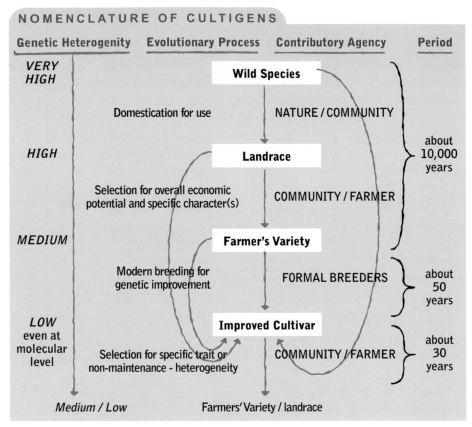

NOMENCLATURE OF CULTIGENS

| Genetic Heterogenity | Evolutionary Process | Contributory Agency | Period |

VERY HIGH — **Wild Species**

Domestication for use — NATURE / COMMUNITY

HIGH — **Landrace**

Selection for overall economic potential and specific character(s) — COMMUNITY / FARMER

about 10,000 years

MEDIUM — **Farmer's Variety**

Modern breeding for genetic improvement — FORMAL BREEDERS — about 50 years

LOW even at molecular level — **Improved Cultivar**

Selection for specific trait or non-maintenance - heterogeneity — COMMUNITY / FARMER — about 30 years

Medium / Low — Farmers' Variety / landrace

Nomenclature of cultigens based on evolutionary process. Here the four categories of nomenclature of Cannabis cultigens would be "wild species", "Landrace", "Farmers' Variety", and "Improved Cultivar."

farmer-developed varieties of crop plants that are heterogeneous, adapted to local environment conditions and have their own local names. In other words, landraces are farmers' varieties, which have not been improved by formal or private/NGO breeding programs. Modern cultivars can be grown by farmers and over a period of time, especially when self-seed is used and selection is practiced, can 'evolve' into a landrace.[15]

More recently, Sanjeev Saxena and Anurudh K. Singh published an article titled "Revisit to Definitions and Need for Inventorization or Registration of Landrace, Folk, Farmers' and Traditional Varieties Published by Current Science." In that article, they produced the following nomenclature of cultigens based on evolutionary process.

The Afghani plant has been used by many modern cannabis plant breeders to create improved cultivars. Kush, Master Kush, and the Hash Plant are well-known landrace strains. Farmers' varieties can make their way back into the wild species populations. In Afghanistan there are several different landrace cannabis along with several farmers' varieties. The improved cultivars of these are mostly found to be bred for modern domestic drug cultivation.

Cannabis and Modern Law

Wild and landrace cannabis plants are rarer in countries that have tried to eliminate the plant by burning fields and conditioning woodlands. In certain countries, the cannabis plant has been identified as a dangerous drug and has been eradicated by government and law-enforcement officials. Highly adaptable, however, the cannabis plant has survived these attempts at eradication in secret indoor and outdoor grow spaces around the world.

The High

THC

Cannabis plants produce psychoactive ingredients called *cannabinoids.* The main ingredient in cannabinoids that gives the high effect is called THC, also known as Tetrahydrocannabinol or δ9-THC, δ9-tetrahydrocannabinol. All strains vary in THC levels and quantities or percentages. There is a difference between THC levels and THC quantities.

THC Levels

THC levels are genetically determined, meaning the grower cannot remarkably influence how potent the strain inherently is. This inbuilt level can only be produced by the grower through the growth of a greater quantity (meaning a bigger yield after harvest). The grower can influence a plant to reach a genetically inherent level of optimal growth to produce the largest quantity of THC the plant is capable of.

THC Quantities

THC quantities are related to bud mass and how much resin can be collected from that bud mass. By way of example: the level of THC found in a single trichome gland when comparing the cannabinoid content of that trichome was 10 percent. That plant produced .5 oz. of resin under average growing conditions. Out of that resin, maybe .05 oz. was THC. This 10 percent level seems to be genetically set in

This is what it is all about. These are the results that every grower
eventually hopes to see: colas deep with resinous trichomes.

Elevation view of trichomes. The density and sizes of trichomes can vary quite dramatically between strains. Note bigger and more does not necessarily mean stronger.

the plant. Under optimal growing conditions, the plant may have the genetic capability of producing .75 oz. of resin. Out of that resin, maybe .075 oz. will be THC. It is the case here that the THC quantity has increased from .05 to .075 oz., but the THC level of 10 percent remained the same.

THC levels correspond to the ratio of THC to other cannabinoids contained in the trichomes of the pistils of flowering female plant. Although this ratio varies depending on the strain, how it is grown, when it is harvested, and how it is cured, under optimal conditions a stable strain should produce a consistent THC level that is genetically inherited. Once the THC level is genetically set in the seed it cannot be increased past this point during the plant's life.[16] Likewise, the maximum quantity of bud that the plant can produce is also genetic and cannot increase past this point during the plant's life. The grower should endeavor to create a growing environment that optimizes both these traits to their full potential. Emphasis should be made here on choosing good genetics. You can't improve on something that isn't there in the first place. This cannot be understated.

An optimally potent plant will have both high levels and quantities of delta-9 THC. Cannabis plants also produce a compound called delta-8 THC. This ingredient is found in low levels but does contribute to the high. When we mention THC levels, we are referring to both delta-8 and delta-9 THC. There are also other ingredients that add to the high, such as CBD, CBN, THCV, CBDV, CDC, and CBL. Since these are minor components compared to THC they will not be discussed in this book.

When examining a strain in a seed bank catalogue you can check the THC levels of that plant to understand the *potency*. Many seed retailers and breeders measure their plants' THC levels and offer accounts of how much THC their plants have. Of course, breeders may be tempted to embellish the THC levels their plants produce. If you want to know more about the THC level of a specific strain, you should consider consulting the seed bank or breeder for details.

Another interesting fact is that some cannabis plants do not produce any THC at all. These plants have been bred to produce very low levels of THC and are mainly used by farmers in countries that permit the growth of cannabis for textile production. This hemp does not produce a high. (These hemp seeds may be found in birdseed.)

Resin

Some female plants produce resin glands that contain lots of resin but are not considerably potent. Other plants may have little resin but be highly potent. Optimal growth gives rise to a plant that has both a considerable amount of resin and is highly potent. Resin glands are produced all over the female flowers and new leaves, and can be seen clearly with the use of a magnifying aid. These resin glands are called *trichomes.*

Trichomes grow on almost all of the bud mass. Notice the slight variations of trichome shapes, sizes and amounts between leaf (bottom) and pistil (right).

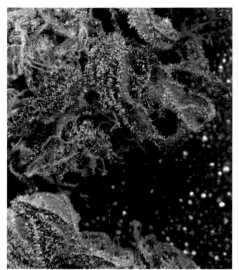 

Flowers change their appearance over time. This freshly manicured bud displays orange pistils that were once creamy colored. Growers can gauge harvesting times by this.

Savour the moment. Feel proud of your efforts and takes notes on what you see, smell, taste and feel. This can help with future changes you may want to make or keep.

Resin can be rubbed off the bud using your fingers and then rolled into the palms to create small balls of hand-rubbed hashish. The main concentration of produced cannabinoids and THC exists within these glands. When a plant is in full flowering, some of the resin glands may explode or break, dropping resin onto the leaves below, giving these leaves an extra-shiny, potent look during flowering. Toward the bottom of the plant are the *fan leaves*. These leaves are generally large, outstretched, and used to collect light for plant growth. Because these leaves are far away from the top of the plant and the furthest away from the light, they produce the least amount of resin glands and collect the least amount of burst resin from the tops. They are not considered to be very potent. It is best to separate the fan leaves from the rest of the plant after harvesting, as these leaves will not provide the best high.

Zero Zero

Cannabis can be cured into various forms. Most popular is hashish, also known simply as hash.

Hashish can also be graded, and one of the most famous grades of hashish is called *Zero Zero*. Hashish making can improve—but sometimes degrades—the overall potency of marijuana. The grades of hashish are as follows: 00 (Zero Zero), 0, 1, 2, 3. Zero Zero is by far the purest form of hashish and comes from plants that

TRICHOME

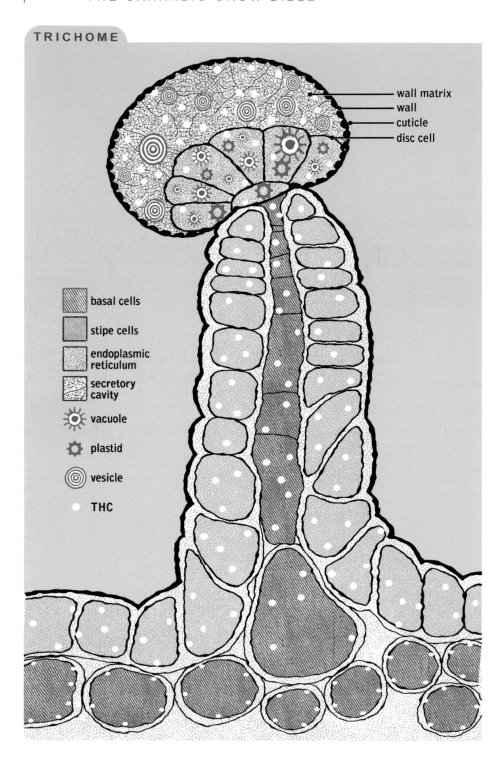

wall matrix
wall
cuticle
disc cell

basal cells

stipe cells

endoplasmic
reticulum

secretory
cavity

vacuole

plastid

vesicle

THC

Powder power. This is a collection of resin and some plant material
that has been screened. This concentrate can be quite potent.

This is the most popular form that hashish comes in. Graded according to
quality and quantity of cannabinoids against plant materials.

This Sweet Purple from Paradise Seeds has been bred for traits that really stand out. Photo Paradise Seeds.

A difficult low-yield strain to grow, but very potent, Neville's Haze is reputedly some of the strongest cannabis around.

have high levels of THC in conjunction with a good hash-making technique. Sometimes the technique may be good, yet the levels of THC in the plant are low. This may produce a hash grade of 2 or 3. The best way you can be sure of actually acquiring a high grade of hashish is by making it yourself.

The potency of a plant depends on a number of factors. It should be the goal of every grower to produce a potent, high-grade product. Hash-making is discussed in greater detail in Chapter 17.

The Plant

When the word *cannabis* is uttered, the image of the famous leaf shape is immediately recalled. Leaves are in fact the least potent part of the plant, next to the stem and the roots. The cannabis plant can be divided into six main sections, the bud, stem, branch, *nodes,* leaves, and main *cola.*

Next, note that cannabis plants have genders. They can be male, female, or a mixed gender (commonly called the *hermaphrodite* condition). There is also a condition of the female plant called *sinsemilla* that growers and breeders alike need to understand.

Male Plant

The male plant contains low levels of THC and does not taste very good, but it can produce a high. Growers only cultivate male plants for pollen so that they can make seeds.

Female Plant

The female plant, when *pollinated,* produces THC but also produces seeds, which prevents larger quantities of bud from growing.

Hermaphrodite Plant

Hermaphrodite plants contain both male and female organs. If the *pollen* is viable, the plant will automatically pollinate itself (selfing), resulting in a crop that can never be sinsemilla. Some plants will become hermaphrodites under poor growing conditions or periods of great stress. Certain strains are more likely to become hermaphroditic than others. In general, growers avoid hermaphrodites.

Sinsemilla Plant

A non-pollinated female, or sinsemilla plant will produce more flowering buds and more quantities of THC than the male plant or a seeded female plant of the same

Males do not have pistils. Males are mostly used to provide pollen for future breeding endeavours to make seeds. Most growers cull them from the garden.

Hermaphrodite flowers, containing both male and female parts, are to be avoided. A stressed plant or unwelcome genetics can produce this undesirable result.

strain. The buds produce resin, which contains THC and can drop down or spread onto the leaves. When fully mature, it should produce a very pleasing high, depending on the grow method, strain of plant, and time of harvest.

It should be the goal of every cannabis cultivator to grow non-pollinated female plants because these produce the best yield. The goal of a cannabis breeder is to produce quality seeds and plants. How breeders and growers achieve these goals is the subject of this book.

Cannabis Species

One of the mostly hotly contested topics in cannabis is the question of species. For nearly two hundred years, cannabis has been the subject of several serious and often contentious studies, including court trials, to determine its taxonomy. There was a legal necessity to make a viable (and possibly universal) statement on a complete scientific orientation for the cannabis species, along with a need to identify lawful and illicit substances.[17] For this reason, the categorizing of cannabis is of immediate scientific concern. Today, we are able to answer many of these questions because of advancements in genetic research.

The History of the Scientific Classification of Cannabis

Older sources, such as the *Encyclopaedia Brittanica*, defines Cannabaceae as

> of the hemp family of the nettle order (Urticales), containing two genera and three species of aromatic herbs distributed throughout temperate parts of the Northern Hemisphere. Older authorities included the two genera, Cannabis and Humulus, in the mulberry (fig) family (Moraceae).[18]

The order of Rosales has replaced Urticales, but cannabis (hemp) is still in the same family Cannabaceae along with Hops (Humulus) and Celtis (hackberries). This means that cannabis is only in the same order of Rosales (Urticales) as nettles but is of the different family Cannabaceae and is more distinctly called cannabis to distinguish itself from Hops and Celtis (including the genera Gironniera, Parasponia, Pteroceltis, and Trema). Proceeding from this formal classification is the question over cannabis species.

Species

The term *species* is hard to define, but it can be referred to as "a fundamental category of taxonomic classification, ranking below a genus or subgenus and consisting of related organisms capable of interbreeding."[19] However, biologists agree that

FLOWERING

Normally a pistil or two will show at first. With a magnifying aid you might even see these sooner with less growth.

There should be more than just one pistil. Look around the node areas of the plant. When one shows more will quickly follow.

This type of flowering development should be plentiful around the plant at all of the node regions. By this time a grower would have flipped to the 12/12 photoperiod.

taxonomy at the species level is not always clear because it is a manmade description with limitations. A species is a classification of a distinct genus into groups that meets the main criteria of a population; the species reproduces itself by breeding within its own population group to produce fertile offspring. Usually, this definition comes with some standards that need to be upheld. If a population group, a species, can breed outside of its group, with another species population, to produce fertile offspring, then this appears to be in violation of the definition. At least one of the two parents seems to have been incorrectly classified as a different species to the other parent. It seems they should be from the same species and classed as such. However, some species can break these standards. Understanding geographical isolation is important because of the role it plays in species classification. Sometimes two separate populations, although considered separate species, can interbreed and produce viable offspring. They are nicknamed a "ring-species" because of these wider reaching breeding capabilities. Some ring-species produce infertile offspring. A common example is a cross between a donkey and horse to produce an infertile mule.

It is important to know that all varieties of cannabis can interbreed, and produce fertile offspring.

The truth is that "species" is just a labelling system. The existence of a species was questioned by Charles Darwin in *The Origin of Species* (1859). Darwin verified through the mechanism of natural selection that all organisms had gradually evolved from a common ancestor. This effect is much like a tree with branches and every branch being the line from which new organisms are evolving. Because of extinction large segments of this tree vanish from the face of the Earth while other segments remain. Even though a gradual evolution of an organism has taken place, these gradual changes are not always seen living among us (for example, the dinosaurs are extinct); however, had all of the history of biological things been present, we would have great trouble with the term "species" because the diversity would seem much less. In fact, it might be no more than the difference of a pimple between creatures. It certainly does expand the mind to envision such a spectacular zoo. However, Darwin's point was clear. The concept of species is a human labelling system that gets in the way of seeing biological evolution as a gradual process of biological diversity. If we don't forget this then we can make some headway.

Linnaeus

1753. The genus (genera) for cannabis is contested. The father of modern taxonomy, Swedish botanist Carolus Linnaeus (May 23, 1707–January 10, 1778) also known as the nobleman Carl von Linné, invented a scheme of nomenclature classification and published it in his *Systema Naturae.* After observing what he called "Cannabis (hemp)," he subsumed all the cannabis varieties he studied under the name Cannabis sativa. The genus is called "Cannabis sativa L." — in the order of Linnaeus.[20]

Since we know that all varieties (strains) of cannabis can interbreed and produce fertile offspring, this means that the species Cannabis sativa L. satisfies an important criterion for a single species orientation.[21]

Lamarck

1785. The French biologist Jean Lamarck immediately challenged this single species orientation by classifying a distinctive second species of cannabis, "C. indica." Lamarck was very precise about the differences:

> This plant, of which Mr. Sonnerat has sent us some samples which he collected in India, appears to us a species very distinct from the preceding. It is smaller, more branched, with a firmer, nearly cylindrical stem, and it particularly is distinguished in that the leaves are all constantly alternate. The leaflets are very narrow, linear-lanceolate, and very acuminate. Male individuals have five or seven leaflets; but those which are female commonly carry only three on each petiole and the upper leaves themselves are quite simple. The calyces of the female flowers are velvety, the long styles are similarly velvety. This plant grows in the East Indies. Its firm stem and thin bark make it incapable of furnishing similar fibres to the preceding species (C. sativa L.) of which so much use is made.[22]

Delile

1849. A. R Delile names a species found in China as C. chinensis Delile. Ind. Sem. Hort. Monst. And in 1851, he names another C. gigantea Delile. L.[23]

Janischevsky

1924. D. E Janischevsky writes the paper "*Forma konopli na sornykh mestakh v yugo-vostochnoi rossii.*" Affiliated with the University of Saratov, in the former Soviet Union, he proposed the species C. ruderalis Janisch, or C. sativa L. f. ruderalis (Janisch.), or C. sativa L subsp. spontanea Serebr.

Vavilov

1929. Nikolai Ivanovich Vavilov and D. D. Bukinich write the paper "*Zemledelcheskii Afghanistan. Trudy po prikladnoi botanike, genetike i selektsii. Prilozhenie*" to approve of the use of C. indica while naming a wild variety of cannabis they studied, C. indica var. kafiristanica.

VARIETIES

Kush

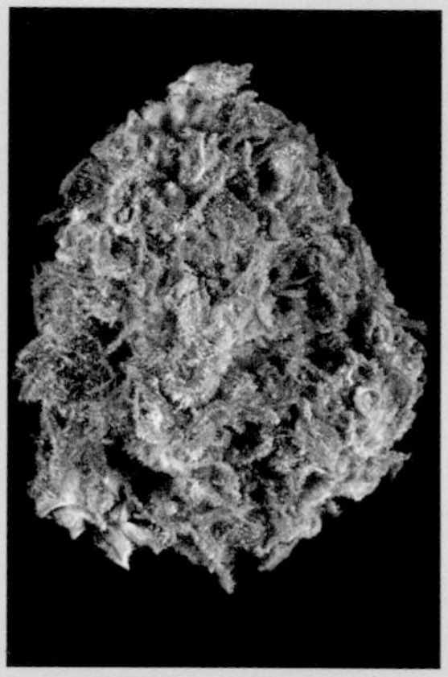

Bubblegum

Chronic

Durban Poison

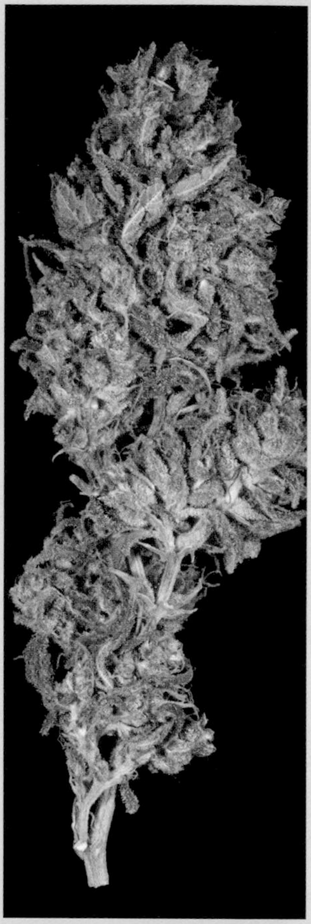

Swazi

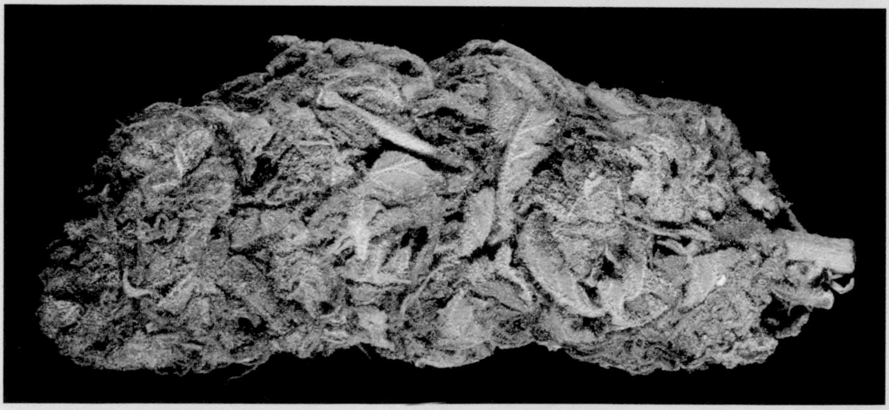

Skunk

Schultes

1974. The botanists Richard E. Schultes and Loran Anderson conducted taxonomic studies of cannabis, concluding that the multiple species model of three species, Cannabis sativa, Cannabis indica Lam., and Cannabis ruderalis, should be used appropriately. These proposed species are simply described: "C. sativa is tall and laxly branched with relatively narrow leaflets, Cannabis indica is shorter, conical in shape, and has relatively wide leaflets, and Cannabis ruderalis is short, branchless, and grows wild in central Asia." [24]

Small

1976. Small and Cronquist revise 223 years of taxonomy to conclude that speciation—the creation of a new species by the division of an old one—has not occurred in cannabis. They forward the original proposal by Carolus Linnaeus for a single species model, Cannabis sativa L., with two subspecies, C. sativa L. subsp. sativa and C. sativa L. subsp indica (Lam) and C. sativa L. subsp. indica var. kafiristanica (Vavilov).

Hillig

2005. K.W. Hillig discovers genetic evidence for speciation in Cannabaceae.

Sample populations of 157 Cannabis accessions of diverse geographic origin were surveyed for allozyme variation at 17 gene loci. The frequencies of 52 alleles were subjected to principal components analysis. A scatter plot revealed two major groups of accessions. The sativa gene pool includes fiber/seed landraces from Europe, Asia Minor, and Central Asia, and ruderal populations from Eastern Europe. The indica gene pool includes fiber/seed landraces from eastern Asia, narrow-leafleted drug strains from southern Asia, Africa, and Latin America, wide-leafleted drug strains from Afghanistan and Pakistan, and feral populations from India and Nepal. A third putative gene pool includes ruderal populations from Central Asia. None of the previous taxonomic concepts that were tested adequately circumscribe the sativa and indica gene pools. A polytypic concept of Cannabis is proposed, which recognizes three species, C. sativa, C. indica and C. ruderalis, and seven putative taxa.[25]

Hillig understood that there was a need to know whether or not speciation had occurred in cannabis. In a follow-up paper Hillig writes,

Botanists disagree whether Cannabis (Cannabaceae) is a monotypic or polytypic genus. A systematic investigation was undertaken to elucidate underlying

ANCIENT NAMES

BC	Qunubu, Konaba[27,28], qěněh bośem[29], κανναβις, kannabis and hemp
AD	hemp, Indian hemp, cannabis, and marijuana[30]
Early Suggestions for Single Species	
1753 by Carolus Linnaeus	C. sativa L. or Cannabis sativa L. subsp. sativa
Early Dispute / Reputed New Species	
1785 by Jean-Baptiste Lamarck	C. indica Lam
1849 A. R. Delile[31]	C. chinensis Delile
Modern Dispute / Reputed New Species	
1924 by D. E Janischevsky[32]	C. ruderalis Janisch. or C. sativa L. f. ruderalis (Janisch.) or C. sativa L subsp. spontanea Serebr
1929 by Nikolai Ivanovich Vavilov[33]	C. indica var. kafiristanica (Vavilov)
Modern Research	
1974 by Richard E. Schultes and Loran Anderson[34]	C. indica
	C. ruderalis
	C. sativa
Modern Dispute / Research Dispute	
1976 by Ernest Small & Cronquist[35]	C. indica Lam to Cannabis sativa L. subsp. indica (Lam.)
	C. indica var. kafiristanica (Vav) to C. sativa subsp. indica var. kafiristanica (Small & Cronquist)
	C. chinensis Delile to C. sativa subsp. sativa var. sativa (Small & Cronquist)
2005 by Karl W. Hillig	Cannabis sativa L. subsp. indica (Lam.) to C. indica

evolutionary and taxonomic relationships within the genus. Genetic, morphological, and chemotaxonomic analyses were conducted on 157 Cannabis accessions of known geographic origin. Sample populations of each accession were surveyed for allozyme variation at 17 gene loci. Principal component (PC) analysis of the allozyme allele frequencies revealed that most accessions were derived from two major gene pools corresponding to C. sativa L., and C. indica Lam. A third putative gene pool corresponds to C. ruderalis Janisch. Previous taxonomic treatments were tested for goodness of fit to the pattern of genetic variation. Based on these results, a working hypothesis for a taxonomic circumscription of Cannabis was proposed that is a synthesis of previous polytypic concepts. Putative infraspecific taxa were assigned to "biotypes" pending formal taxonomic revision. Genetic variation was highest in the hemp and feral biotypes and least in the drug biotypes. Morphometric traits were analyzed by PC and canonical variates (CV) analysis. PC analysis failed to differentiate the putative species, but provided objective support for recognition of infraspecific taxa of C. sativa and C. indica. CV analysis resulted in a high degree of discrimination of the putative species and infraspecific taxa. Variation in qualitative and quantitative levels of cannabidiol (CBD), tetrahydrocannabinol (THC), and other cannabinoids was determined, as were frequencies of alleles that control CBD and THC biosynthesis. The patterns of variation support a two-species concept, but not recognition of C. ruderalis as a separate species from C. sativa. PC analysis of terpenoid variation showed that the wide-leaflet drug (WLD) biotype of C. indica produced enhanced mean levels of guaiol and isomers of eudesmol, and is distinct from the other putative taxa. In summary, the results of this investigation show that a taxonomic revision of Cannabis is warranted. However, additional studies of putative wild populations are needed to further substantiate the proposed taxonomic treatment.[26]

Cannabis Taxonomy for Scientists and Researchers

Reputable government scientific bodies such as the Germplasm Resources Information Network (GRIN), USDA, ARS, and the National Genetic Resources Program would concur with the USDA Plants Database as well as the Integrated Taxonomic Information System (ITIS). They agree with Carolus Linnaeus, Ernest Small, and Cronquist.

Scientific Cannabis Taxonomy

It is important that we also understand the species dispute as it applies to breeder terminology. If a breeder uses the standard set forth by GRIN, the USDA Plants Database and ITIS, then a better standardizing and consensus can be achieved within the scientific community.

Kingdom . . . . . . Plantae

Division . . . . Magnoliophyta

Class . . . . Magnoliopsida

Order . . . . Rosales

Family . . . . Cannabaceae

Genus. . . . . Cannabis L.

Species . . . . Cannabis

Cannabis sativa L. ssp. indica (Lam.)

Cannabis sativa L. ssp. Sativa

Subspecies . . . . . C. sativa L subsp. spontanea Serebr.

Cannabis sativa L. ssp. sativa var. spontanea Vavilov

This photo of Super Silver Haze from Green House Seed Co. clearly shows the pistils growing from the calyx. Photo Green House Seed Co.

Breeders' Strain Type Terminology

For the breeding community, working inside the last part of this last model provides several problems in terms of breeding and marketing. Breeders side with models such as Jean-Baptiste Lamarck, D. E Janischevsky, and especially Richard E. Schultes and Loran Anderson.

Kingdom   Plantae

Division	Magnoliophyta
Class	Magnoliopsida
Order	Rosales
Family	Cannabaceae
Genus	Cannabis L.
Species	C. indica
	C. sativa
	C. ruderalis

The next comparison model shows the cross-reference.

Proposed Breeder's cannabis taxonomy

Division	Magnoliophyta
Kingdom	Plantae
Division	Magnoliophyta
Class	Magnoliopsida
Order	Rosales
Family	Cannabaceae
Genus	Cannabis L.
Species	Cannabis sativa L. ssp. indica (Lam.) as
	C. sativa L. ssp. Indica
	Cannabis sativa L. ssp. sativa as C. sativa L.
Subspecies	C. sativa L subsp. spontanea Serebr

Varieties, Strains, Subspecies, and Hybrids

Adopting the USDA sources for a moment, there are six immediate possible combinations because the offspring can only share two parents.

C. sativa L. ssp. indica.	C. sativa L. ssp. Indica x C. sativa L. ssp. indica.
C. sativa L subsp. spontanea Serebr.	C. sativa L subsp. spontanea Serebr x C. sativa L subsp. spontanea Serebr.
C. sativa L.	C. sativa L. x C. sativa L.
C. sativa L subsp. spontanea Serebr/ C. sativa L. ssp. indica hybrid.	C. sativa L subsp. spontanea Serebr x C. sativa L. ssp. indica.
C. sativa L. ssp. indica / C. sativa L. hybrid.	C. sativa L. ssp. indica x C. sativa L.
C. sativa L subsp. spontanea Serebr / C. sativa L hybrid.	C. sativa L subsp. spontanea Serebr x C. sativa L.

The single species orientation still works. Even a C. sativa L. ssp. Indica / C. sativa L subsp. spontanea Serebr / C. sativa L. hybrid can still be classed as the species Cannabis sativa L.

In cannabis breeding terminology the combinations would have been:

C. indica. . . . . C. indica x C. indica.
C. ruderalis. . . . . C. ruderalis x C. ruderalis
C. sativa.. . . . . C. sativa x C. sativa.
C. ruderalis / C. indica hybrid.. . C. ruderalis x C.indica.
C. indica / C. sativa hybrid.. . . . C. indica x C. sativa.
C. ruderalis / C. sativa hybrid. . . C. ruderalis x C. sativa.

The most commonly found phrases in relation to marijuana species and hybrids are "pure indica," "pure sativa," "indica/sativa hybrids," "mostly indica," and "mostly sativa." "Mostly" is used to mean greater than 50 percent, usually estimated by the breeder. There are some additional hybrids that are not commonly used and so are excluded from the core material.[36] This says a lot about breeds. For example a "mostly indica/sativa" tells a bigger story. It says that at one stage a C. indica parent was crossed with a C. sativa parent to produce indica/sativa offspring which are then crossed with C. ruderalis to produce indica/sativa/ruderalis hybrids (1:1:1) which could be then crossed back to the indica/sativa to create a strain with less ruderalis properties and more indica/sativa properties, hence the phrase "mostly indica/sativa."[37]

Let us see how our scientific taxonomy model can applied to this same paragraph, repeated again.

The most commonly found phrases in relation to marijuana species and hybrids are "C. sativa L. ssp. Indica," "C. sativa L.," "C. sativa L. ssp. Indica / C. sativa L. hybrids," "mostly C. sativa L. ssp. Indica," and "mostly C. sativa L." "Mostly" is used to mean greater than 50 percent, usually estimated by the breeder. There are some additional hybrids that are not commonly used and so are excluded from the core material. This says a lot about breeds. For example, a "C. sativa L. ssp. Indica / C. sativa L. hybrid" tells a bigger story. It says that at one stage a C. sativa L. ssp. Indica parent was crossed with a C. sativa L. parent to produce C. sativa L. ssp. Indica / C. sativa L. offspring, which are then crossed with C. sativa L subsp. spontanea Serebr to produce C. sativa L. ssp. Indica / C. sativa L subsp. spontanea Serebr/ C. sativa L. hybrids (1:1:1) which could be then crossed back to the C. sativa L. ssp. Indica / C. sativa L. to create a strain with less ruderalis properties and C. sativa L. ssp. Indica / C. sativa L. properties, hence the phrase "mostly C. sativa L. ssp. Indica / C. sativa L. hybrids"

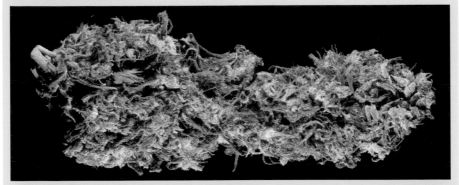

Sativa Bud

Indica Bud

Ruderalis Bud

Breeder taxonomy terminology

Pure Indica . . . . C. sativa L. ssp. Indica

Pure Sativa . . . . C. sativa L.

Indica Sativa . . . C. sativa L. ssp. Indica / C. sativa L. hybrid.

Mostly Indica . . . Mostly C. sativa L. ssp. Indica hybrid

Mostly Sativa . . Mostly C. sativa L. hybrid

"Subspecies" is a very good category for two groups of pure species that come together, when a barrier is removed, to create fertile offspring of a new species group, called a subspecies. It is "a taxonomic subdivision of a species consisting of an interbreeding, usually geographically isolated population of organisms."[38] In our single species model the phrases pure indica and pure sativa indicate species (also sometimes called a pure species in this context), while phrases like indica/sativa hybrids, mostly indica, and mostly sativa indicate a subspecies.

Specific breeds of cannabis species or subspecies are called "strains." For example, Afghani #1.

Strain list[39]

C. sativa L. ssp. indica landrace strains

- Afghani
- Iranian
- North Indian
- Tajikistani
- Arab
- Lebanese
- New Zealand Sativa
- Turkish
- Chinese
- Moroccan (Kif)
- Pakistani
- Uzbekistani

C. sativa L. landrace strains

- African (Durban Poison, Swazi Red, Congolese, Malawi Gold, Angolese, Lesothan, Nigerian)
- Colombian (Columbian Red, Santa Marta Colombian Gold)
- Japanese (Hokkaido)
- Mexican (Acapulco gold, Oaxacan, Zacatecas Purple, Guerrero Gold, Michoacan)
- Swazi (Swazi Gold, Swazi Red "redbeard," Swazi)
- Vietnamese
- Brazilian (Manga Rosa, Santa Maria)
- Burmese
- Cambodian
- French (reunion island: Zamal)
- Indian
- Laotian
- Nepalese
- Panamanian (Panama Red)
- Paraguayan
- Thai (Juicy Fruit Thai, Chocolate Golden Triangle Thai)
- Pakistani

C. sativa L. ssp. indica hybrid strains

- Afghani #1
- Celtic Stone
- G-SUS
- Mango
- Northern Lights #1
- Southern Daze
- Millennium Bud
- Romulan
- Sour Bubble (ahx1)
- Taste Bud (SeediSm.nl)
- Bella ciao
- Celtic Cross
- Kush
- Mazar
- Oasis (Northern Lights #2)
- Mongolian
- Matanuska Tundra (a.k.a. Alaskan Thunderfuck)
- Butterscotch Hawaiian
- Early Girl
- Lightstorm
- Newberry
- Manghani (a very resinous Mango x Afghan)
- Mother of Mercy
- Mad Shad
- Superglue (SeediSm.nl)

C. sativa L. ssp. Indica / C. sativa L. hybrid strains

- John Newsom x Skunk
- Blue Velvet
- Consequence Kush
- Fruity Thai (Ceres; Thai Sativa x Dutch Indica)
- Humboldt Select
- Kushage
- Mistletoe
- Northern Lights #2 (Hindu Kush x Northern Lights)
- Sour Romulan
- Pakalolo
- Skunk Red Hair
- White Smurf (Ceres)
- White Widow (Green House; Brazilian x South Indian)
- Terry Parker
- Matanuska Tundra (a.k.a. Alaskan Thunderfuck)
- Bubblegum (from Indiana)
- Full Moon
- Greece Coat
- Juicy Fruit (Golden Triangle Thai x Afghani)
- Northern Lights (Thai x Afghani)
- Northern Lights #5
- NYC Diesel (Soma; Sour Diesel Afghani Hawaiian)
- Skunk Passion
- Silver Pearl (Sensi; Early Pearl x Skunk #1 x Northern Lights)
- Yumboldt (Sagarmatha; Afghan x x Himalaya)

Mostly C. sativa L. ssp. Indica hybrid strains

- Aurora Indica (Nirvana; Afghani x Northern Lights)
- Blueberry (DJ Short; [Oaxacan Gold x Chocolate Thai] x [Highland Thai x Afghani])
- Bubblicious (Nirvana)
- Celtic Stone (Celtic Stone Seeds; Stonehedge x Dixie Crystal)
- Holland's Hope (Dutch Passion; Big Bud x Skunk #1)
- Lemon Stinky (crazy x seeds; sensi star x chronic)
- Northern Berry (Peak Seeds, Hygro; Northern Lights #5 x Blueberry)

- BC Purple Star (BC Bud; Purple Star [Holland] x BC Purple Indica)
- Shanti Devi (Tikiseedbank)
- Shulam (Tikiseedbank)
- Skunk Kush (Sensi; Hindu Kush x Skunk #1)
- Snow White (Nirvana)
- White Indica (Ceres Seeds; Afghani x Afghani x Skunk #1)
- White Rhino (Greenhouse Seeds; White Widow x Unknown Indica)
- Yarkoum (Tikiseedbank)

Mostly C. sativa L. hybrid strains
- AK-47 a.k.a Special-K (Serious Seeds; Colombian x Mexican x Thai x Afghani)
- California Orange a.k.a. "Cali-O" [Thai x (Afghani x Acapulco Gold)]
- Celtic Cross "CC" Celtic stone x F420
- Choco Diesel "Choco D"(Chocolate Trip x Sour Diesel)
- Cinderella 99 a.k.a. "C99" (Mr. Soul; Princess x Princess 88)
- Citrus Skunk (Skunk #1 x California Orange)
- Early Pearl
- Early Skunk (Sensi; Skunk #1 x Early Pearl)
- Euforia (Dutch Passion; Unknown Skunk x Unknown Skunk)
- FourWay (Head Seeds; [Cinderella 99 x Apollo 11] x [NYC Diesel x G-13])
- Flo (DJ Short; Purple Thai x Afghani)
- Floater (Flo x Jacks Cleaner x Blueberry)
- Green Devil (Tikiseedbank; Bambata x Shulam)
- Hawaiian Skunk (Seedsman; Hawaiian Indica x Skunk #1)
- Hempstar (Dutch Passion; Skunk x Oasis x Haze)
- Jack Herer (Sensi; Skunk #1 x Northern Lights #5 x Haze)
- Lambsbread Skunk (Dutch Passion; Jamaican Lambsbread x Skunk #1)
- Lemon Skunk (Jordan of the Island; Citrus Skunk x Skunk #1)
- Lifesaver (BOG; Jack Cleaner x DJ Short's Blueberry x BogBubble)
- Life Star (BOG; Lifesaver x Sensi Star)
- L.S.D (BOG; Lifesaver x NYC Diesel)
- Neon Super Skunk (Subcool; Super Skunk x Black Russian)
- Neville's Haze (Thai x Colombian, with a 1/4 NL#5)
- Orange Crush (AE77 Cali-O x DJ Short's Blueberry)
- Purple Skunk (Dutch Passion; Purple #1 x Early Skunk)
- Royal Hawaiian (Reeferman; Hawaiian Indica x Hawaiian Sativa)
- SAGE (THSeeds; Big Sour Holy x Afghani)
- Shaman (Dutch Passion; Purple #1 x Skunk)
- Shiva Skunk (Sensi; Skunk #1 x Northern Lights #5)

- Skunk #1 (Dutch Passion; Afghani x Thai x Colombian Gold)
- Skunk #5 (Effettoserra; [Afghani x Acapulco Gold x Colombian Gold] x Dutch Skunk)
- Skunk Berry (Peak Seeds; Skunk x Blueberry)
- Skunk Haze (Seedsman; Skunk #1 x Original Haze)
- Strawberry Cough (Dutch Passion; Strawberry Fields x Haze)
- Super Silver Haze (Mr. Nice; [Northern Lights #5 x N. Haze] x [Skunk #1 x N. Haze])
- Super Silver Sour Diesel Haze (Reservoir; Super Silver Haze x Sour Diesel)
- Super Skunk (Sensi; Skunk #1 x Afghani)
- Turtle Power (Amsterdam Marijuana; Purple Power x Early Girl)
- White Skunk No.1
- Ultra Skunk (Dutch Passion; Swiss Skunk x Skunk)

Cannabis Reproduction

Cannabis reproduction is botanically similar to other plants, and yet unique. All flowering plants, such as cannabis, have a structure designed for reproduction in the form of developing imperfect flowers with the male staminate formed separately from the female pistillate (carpellate), except for instances where perfect hermaphroditism is observed, where staminates form next to or from pistillate with calyx formation.

Dioecious, Monecious, and Hermaphrodites

It is unwise to use the term "mainly" to support one sexual description of cannabis. While we find "dioecious" populations having the male and female reproductive organs borne on loose panicles and racemes "separately" as individuals (having the male and female reproductive organs borne on separate individuals of the same species), we also find populations or members within dioecious populations bearing "both" male and female organs that are "monecious." Likewise, we can say that we find dioecious members within monecious populations. For monecious members, the respective organs can be found within the same floral cluster: the inflorescences. Sexually, we can describe any cannabis member as:

Hermaphrodite . Only hermaphrodite plants.
Monecious . . . . . Only monecious plants.
Dioecious . . . . . . Only dioecious plants.
Gynodioecious . . Both female and hermaphrodite plants present.
Androdioecious . Both male and hermaphrodite plants present.
Trioecious / Subdioecious Male, female, and hermaphrodite plants are all in the same population.

Some colas have short twisted sticky buds but the resin and taste
produced by these plants is something to behold.

While all dense clusters of female flowers produced by cannabis are loosely referred to as "bud," all unfertilized female flowers are called "sinsemilla"; however, the nature of members of plant populations that are hermaphrodite, monecious, gynodioecious, andridioecious, or subdioecious will tend to produce pollen that fertilizes the female flowers, producing seeded buds. While in general seeded bud is regarded as low in quality, this is not because of potency factors—as long as the pistils have time to mature to the point of optimal potency—but because it is harder to work with bud that has seeds. Seeds are sought afterwards in breeding programs, but usually only healthy ones from dioecious parents.

Advanced Sinsemilla Facts

Sinsemilla is a term for a type of "marijuana" first used by the American Spanish-speaking cannabis cultivation community and means "without seeds." It occurs in cultivation where male plants are removed from the population, leaving only the female plants as part of a plan to promote optimal yields and results. However, with this type of technique there is a chance that fertilization can occur because it produces stress-related sexual change where some dioecious females will express gynodioecious sexuality by bearing male organs. For this reason, great care is taken in choosing a mother plant for a perpetual clone sinsemilla system that will push the female's genetic capacity for pistil gland production to the maximum. This is undertaken while under the supervision of a grower who will manually remove the presence of any and all male reproductive organs where gynodioecious occurs. Sometimes it is better to remove a whole plant rather than let it pollinate the other sinsemilla-conditioned females. If the gynodioecious sex is too profuse, the grower will usually terminate cultivation of that clone population while trying to find a more suitable mother plant that can be tailor-made for a sinsemilla environment. Here we cannot overemphasize the need for good genetics if the sinsemilla grower wishes to generate the results that he needs.

While there can be some sustainable evidence to support a case for more psychoactive "cannabinoids" in sinsemilla produce, there is little evidence to support that the cannabinoid levels in the glands secreted by the pistils are of higher value. Rather, there is an optimal production of the number of glands.

There is a claim that a female in a sinsemilla environment is being stressed to receive pollen by generating more resin. This image, however, is distorted once more by the presence of high calyx and resin gland counts on some low potency strains and the low calyx low resin count of very high potency strains. The main concern for the cultivator here is to watch males in the flowering cycle of a sinsemilla crop.

These leaves are covered in trichomes and can be used to make hash or for cooking.

Federal research shows that the average potency of cannabis in the United States has increased very little. According to the Federal Potency Monitoring Project, in 1985 the average THC content of commercial-grade marijuana was 2.84 percent, and the average for high-grade sinsemilla in 1985 was 7.17 percent. In 1995, the potency of commercial-grade marijuana averaged 3.73 percent, while the potency of sinsemilla in 1995 averaged 7.51 percent. In 2001, commercial-grade marijuana averaged 4.72 percent THC, and the potency of sinsemilla in 2001 averaged 9.03 percent.[40]

Breeding for Desirable Traits

Because of the large-volume, high-yielding, resinous, potent, high calyx-to-leaf ratio, and high trichome production of a dioecious population of female-only plants for sinsemilla there is accordingly an increase in and refinement of the strains available to the cultivator—although tried and tested clones are maybe far more appropriate for those who want to get going immediately. For this reason, most growers are concerned with obtaining gynodioecious-resistant clones that meet the standards the grower wants from the genetic material. The grower will

After harvesting growers manicure their bud. This is a tight cut that even ends up revealing some stem.

probably not want to be concerned with breeding for cannabis seeds (nuts or achenes) but is interested in C. indica species or subspecies indica/sativa hybrids; they will probably exclude most sativa because it is an expert plant to work with and unsuitable for anything less than a very sizeable growing area with longer flowering times. The cultivator will automatically stay away from hemp or from "autoflowering" ruderalis in order to have sinsemilla results, although there is consideration for outdoor ruderalis/indica hybrids where the grower can only grow an auto-flowering cannabis strain because of short flowering seasons.

Working with dioecious populations is the common practice. A high calyx to leaf ratio of female flowers is the telltale sign of useful drug cultivars, if potent. Taste, smell, observable attractive traits, yields, and ease of manicuring are usually secondary appreciations after potency. The existence of the monecious types is for the production of hemp-related products, while dioecious types include both recreational and medical drug uses, and are also used in textile production for fiber. Note that there is a danger of casually associating some de-drugged hemp with normal cannabis hemp. We do not want to deal in detail with monecious individuals or populations.

Understanding Sex Determination Systems

Cannabis has been widely studied with regards to its sexual systems because of observable and repeatable sex reversal conditions.[41] The usual expectancy of an XY sex-determination system was confirmed in 1924 by K. Hirata,[42] but was disputed by J. H. Schaffner in 1925, who found through his own sex reversal studies in hemp that an X:A system was present and highly influenced by environmental conditions.[43] There is doubt over how the XY system occurs in cannabis, with statements that the Y chromosome is slightly larger than the X being difficult to distinguish.[44] What is important to understand is that cannabis may be stressed to express all forms of sex within the same population.

Most strains that you will come across are the result of human intervention. Breeders try to produce strains that are tasty, smell good, and give the user different types of highs. Good strains are widely sought after by growers because you can be guaranteed that the seller of the seeds knows a great deal about the plant and its particular history.

Sativa
Height — Tall, averaging between 4 and 15 feet
Nodes — Long internodes between branches, 3 to 6 inches
Leaves — Thin, long, and pointy leaves with no markings or patterns
Blades — Usually between 6 and 12 blades per leaf

Indica
Height — Small, averaging between 6 inches and 4 feet
Nodes — Short internodes between branches, 3 inches and less
Leaves — Wide, short, and rounded leaves with marble-like patterns
Blades — Usually between 3 and 5 blades per leaf

Ruderalis
Height — Small, averaging between 6 inches and 4 feet
Nodes — Very short internodes with much branching
Leaves — Small and thick
Blades — Usually between 4 and 6 blades per leaf

Ruderalis is hardly used today. Sativa and Indica are extremely common and these two species will be the main focus of this book. Indica and Sativa species produce different forms of high. The high of each species can be controlled by the time at which you harvest. In addition, they can be crossed to produce Indica/Sativa hybrids. This may sound confusing, but it is in fact quite simple and will be further explained in Chapter 15.

LEAF TYPES

Indica   Mostly Indica   Indica / Sativa

Mostly Sativa   Sativa   Ruderalis

A Word About Male Potency

In general, the male plant is considered inferior. This, however, may not be true in all cases. Male plants from some strains can produce more THC or be more potent than females from weaker strains. Most male plants from good genetics are stronger than the Ruderalis female. Males can also be smoked[45] (not advised) or made into *hash oil.*

The Life Cycle of the Marijuana Plant

The marijuana plant grows in three main stages: *germination, vegetative growth,* and *flowering.* There are also three additional sub-stages in the marijuana plant's life cycle. Here we describe the complete life cycle of the cannabis plant in brief.

Germination

Germination is the initial stage of growth and occurs when the seed's *embryo*

Sativa

Ruderalis

Indica

Germination in the initial stages as the plumule (seedling root) pushes through the seed shell.

The seed shell is still attached to the cotyledon (first seedling leaf). Photo Paradise Seeds.

breaks through the shell, the *testa,* and the seedling produces its first initial root, the *plumule.* This root fixes itself into the germination *medium* and pushes the newborn seedling up and over the surface. Following surface contact, two embryonic leaves, the *cotyledons,* open outward to receive sunlight, pushing the empty testa away from the seedling. It takes anywhere between 12 hours and 3 weeks for seeds to germinate.

Sometimes the shell can be removed by hand if it appears to be obstructing the seedling's growth. In nature the wind helps to shake the seed shell away. Since artificial wind is not initially used in the germination environment, some seedlings find it harder to shed their shell, although most do not have a problem doing so. Care should be taken not to damage the seedling when removing the shell.

Seedling

After the first pair of embryonic leaves receives light, the plant will begin to produce another small set of new leaves. These leaves are different from the first two and may have some more noticeable marijuana characteristics, such as the three-rounded, finger-shaped points. As the seedling grows, more of these leaves are formed and bush upward along with the stem. Some stems are very weak at this sub-stage and need the support of a small, thin wooden stake tied to the seedling with some fine thread. The seedling sub-stage can last between one and three weeks. At the end of the seedling sub-stage, your plant will have between four and eight new leaves while some of the original bottom leaves and cotyledons may have dropped off.

This is a seedling that is approaching vegetative growth. It is around this time that growers may move these plants to the main grow room.

This is a cutting, or clone, that is being prepared for propagation. You can tell the difference because the cutting looks more like a branch than grown from seed.

This is a mother plant that is kept as a clone donor. You can identify mothers by their many branches, created by the grower to provide lots of areas to cut from.

Here we have a range of plants in vegetative growth in the grow room. Notice the healthy upward pointing leaves.

This is a good example of how a high trichome count can undermine the principle that a high calyx to leaf ratio is a desirable trait in marijuana plants. Here the trichomes almost seem to be covering the plant in a balm.

Vegetative Growth

The plant now begins to grow at the rate that its leaves can produce energy. At this stage the plant needs all the light and food it can use. It will continue to grow upward and produce new leaves. It will also develop a thicker stem and thicker branches, as well as its maximum finger (blades) numbers on the leaves; it will eventually start to show its sex, when mature enough to do so. Then it is time for the plant to enter pre-flowering. The vegetative growth stage can last between one and five months.

Pre-flowering

At this sub-stage, the plant's upward growth slows. Instead of growing taller,[46] the plant starts to produce more branches and nodes. The plant fills out during this stage and will start to show a calyx where the branches meet the stem (nodes). This calyx is the ultimate indicator that the plant is in the pre-flowering phase of growth and is mature enough to flower. Pre-flowering can last anywhere from one day to two weeks. During this sub-stage, plants start to exhibit signs of their sex and more calyx development takes place at other node points.

Seeds grow within the calyx of the flowers. Usually they are not visible being covered by the calyx but growth bursts eventually produce what you see here. Photo Paradise Seeds.

Flowering

Here, the plant continues to fill out. The plant's sex is now clearly evident. The male plant produces tiny, creamy, yellow sphere shapes that are clustered together like grapes. The female plant produces little white pistils that look like oily tentacles coming out of a pod. Each of the plants will continue to fill out and their flowers will continue to grow. It can take between 4 and 6 weeks for the plant to fully develop its flowers, depending on the strain. During this time the male's pollen sacks would have burst, spreading pollen to the female flowers.

Seed Production

The female plant will produce seeds at this point if she has received viable pollen from a male plant. The seeds grow within the female bud and can take anywhere

THE DECISION TO GROW

Important issues to bear in mind before you decide to grow cannabis:
- What do you hope to achieve—high potency, high yield, one or many plants?
- Which species/strain best meets your needs?
- Are you willing to spend over $100 for 10 seeds?
- Will you grow indoors or outdoors?
- How do the people you live with feel about this?
- Do you have time to take care of your plants?
- Do you have someone you trust to take care of your plants in your absence?
- How secure is your grow area?
- Are people going to walk past your grow site?
- Can you hide the smell when the plants start to flower?
- Do you have the patience to wait a few months before sampling what you produce?
- Are you prepared to spend money on lights and other grow items?
- Are you prepared to pay the costs of a higher electricity bill?
- Are you aware of the risks for the amount you plan to grow?
- Are you sure you really want to do this?
- Can you afford a good attorney if you think there could be legal consequences to your grow?
- Have you any previous convictions which could be used as a legal prejudice against you if you are charged with growing cannabis?
- Do you know what your legal rights are?
- Can gun ownership be used against you if you are caught growing cannabis?
- Can other drug possession in your home be used against you if you are caught growing cannabis?
- Can your children be taken from you and put into social care if you are caught growing cannabis?
- Is your home safe to grow in?
- Are there any pets around which can damage your crop or start a fire?
- Can you deal with a fire?
- Are you a relaxed tight-lipped person?
- Do you really want to be another dull cash-cropper who wastes their lives just selling cannabis, or do you want to be a new wave frontier grower who grows to rid themselves of the connection to the black market in order to enjoy their favorite herb?
- Do you want to grow?

If you are hesitant on any of the points above, I suggest you resolve those issues before growing. Reading on should help you answer most of these questions.

between 2 and 16 weeks to grow to full maturity. The female pistils may change color before finally bursting the seedpods, sending them to the soil below. Breeders like to collect seeds before the seedpods burst.

If, during the flowering stage, there are no males present to pollinate the female plants, the buds will grow larger and develop more resin glands. Resin may drop down on to the leaves, making the plant very sticky. The pistils on the buds will begin to thicken and cluster. The reason for the high increase in bud growth is that the female plant is trying her best to attract male pollen. This is the sinsemilla condition. Toward the last days of flowering, the pistils may change color, indicating that the plant is ready for harvest.

Cycle Times

Given different breeds and the various stages of growth, it can take between 10 and 36 weeks for a plant to grow from a seed to full maturity. The most common grow time is three to four months. All this is dependent upon the strain that you have selected. Pure Sativa can run anywhere into the six to nine month bracket.

This is Sensi Star from Paradise Seeds. There are many strains out there with many different flavors, colors, potencies, morphology, smells and flowering times. The varieties of cannabis are immense. Photo Paradise Seeds.

How much of this strain is green? Look again and you can see that there are many other colors at work and green may not be the majority.

Indica can flower in six weeks. As you can image, a Sativa/Indica hybrid plant will fall into the two to four month flowering period.

Let's Get Growing

You should now have a general idea of what to look for in a plant to produce a good-quality smoke. We are looking for non-pollinated female plants that have flowered, producing lots of buds with resin glands containing high levels and quantities of THC. We are also looking for plants that have been well cured and processed in a way that allows us to sample the full flavor, smell, and potency of the plant. Some people prefer plants that provide a high but do not cause drowsiness. Other people like plants that give a down effect and cause the body to become less responsive to stimuli.

Another thing to note is that street cannabis may contain added drugs. For example, animal tranquilizer is a popular adulterate used to make black market hashish more potent. People who add other drugs to cannabis are not doing the cannabis community a favor. This is a good reason to grow your own pot.

2 | Seeds: Selection, Banks, and Storage

There are approximately 450 seed varieties of cannabis on the market today.[1] Out of the 450 seed varieties, 200 are worth considering, and out of the 200 about 50 are truly outstanding.

A hybrid is the offspring of two animals or plants of different breeds, varieties, species, or genera, especially as produced through human manipulation for specific genetic characteristics. Stock lines with common parents are loosely referred to as a "cannabis strain" by cultivators. Stable strains have stable genetic traits, which means that the offspring will all be very similar. In fact, most cannabis strains are called cannabis strains because of their uniformity in growth and reduced variations in the offspring. Hybrids tend to be unstable, or genetically unpredictable, because of their "newness." A good stabilized hybrid eventually goes on to become a strain.

Out of the 450 seed varieties, we said that 200 were good. This leaves 250 that we have disregarded. Those 250 are usually very unstable hybrids. These hybrid plants are so unstable that their description is difficult because of the extent of the variations in the population.

Most unstable hybrids do not find their way into the market and are found only among breeders who are experimenting with plant genetics. Seed producers tend to only produce strains in the following categories (bearing in mind the discussion in Chapter 1):

- Pure Sativa
- Sativa (mostly Sativa species with some Indica)
- Pure Indica

- Indica (mostly Indica species with some Sativa)
- Indica/Sativa (50/50 cross between an Indica and a Sativa species)
- Ruderalis

Ruderalis is a problematic plant. It does not produce large quantities of THC or flower like the others. Ruderalis is considered substandard by most growers because it flowers according to age, not according to the photoperiod. This means that the Ruderalis cannabis plant will flower when it is mature enough to do so, and this flowering action of the Ruderalis plant is out of the grower's hands, so to speak. Ruderalis is grown in countries that experience cold weather conditions— Russia, Eastern Europe, and Alaska are places where Ruderalis grows wild. It is an extremely sturdy plant for outdoor growing, however, the autoflowering properties of this plant make it hard to control. Trying to clone a Ruderalis plant is nearly impossible because it is extremely hard to force the clone to remain in the vegetative growth stage of the plant's cycle. Photoperiod manipulation—the way growers control cannabis flowering with Indica and Sativa plants—does not work with Ruderalis plants. Photoperiod, an extremely important part of cannabis cultivation, is further explained in Chapter 8. One reason to grow Ruderalis is if you must grow outdoors, where the photoperiod is of no concern to you.

Seeds develop in the calyx. Here you can see seeds coming out from the calyx while others have not yet emerged. Photo Paradise Seeds.

Seeds that have just begun to germinate sandwiched in wet cheesecloth.

This stash of seeds from Paradise Seeds is enough to create several gardens for the next season. Photo Paradise Seeds.

Pure Sativa is a total head high. Pure Indica is a total body stone / couch-lock. A 50/50 cross will give a 50 percent head high and a 50 percent body stone. If an Indica plant is crossed slightly with a Sativa plant it will give a 60 percent body stone and a 40 percent head high. A Sativa plant that is crossed slightly with an Indica plant will give a 60 percent head high and a 40 percent body stone. The 60/40 ratio is the most common but breeders can also alter the ratio.

Equipped with this knowledge, you are now ready to choose a plant that fits your needs in terms of height, potency, and high. Your choice of seeds will also depend on whether you will grow indoors or outdoors. It will also depend on other characteristics of your grow space. There is no point trying to grow an eight-foot Sativa indoors if you don't have the space, and a two-foot Indica plant may not survive outdoors if other plants compete with it for light. As a rule, we can always shorten the plant through pruning, but it is impossible to double the plant's height if the plant's genetics only allow two or three feet of growth. Indoor and outdoor grow spaces will be discussed more in later chapters. The rest of this chapter will focus on selecting, acquiring, and handling quality seeds.

Selecting Seeds

Now you have an idea of the species and strain of plant you want. The next step is to verify if the seeds are for indoor or outdoor use. There is a saying that all cannabis seeds can be grown indoors and outdoors. This is true, but for the best results, growers should consider what the breeder intended. If the breeder created a plant that does well indoors, then it is suggested that you only grow these seeds indoors. If you grow outdoors and the plant does not produce that well, then you know that you should have followed the breeder's advice. Of course, there is nothing stopping you from experimenting, and some growers have produced excellent results this way, but if you are new to growing it is best if you follow the advice you're given.

When selecting a seed, check to see what kind of strain it is. Most seed sellers will have this listed along with their seed type. Keeping in mind the species debate issue, when you look at strains that are crossbreeds you must foresee which type the plants lean toward. Some Sativa plants may be shorter because of their Indica genetics and some Indica plants may be taller because of their Sativa genetics. In Chapter 15, we will see that as breeders, we can control the plant's appearance and growth and can influence height and particular features. We can also harvest the plant in a specific way to produce a different high. The later you harvest the plant, the more you'll help produce a couch-lock effect. Harvesting just before peak growth will induce a more cerebral high. If you are working with strains that

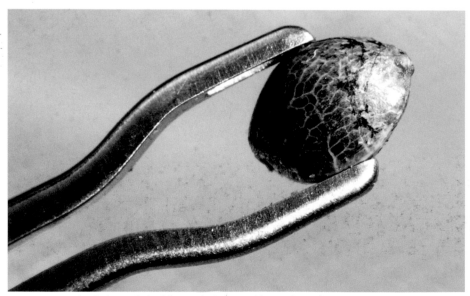

Analysing and checking seeds that you either gather or buy is important.
This is not a damaged seed. The markings including the dark patch are natural.

Notice the purple and yellow coloring of the leaves on this strain. Reasons for this could be natural genetics, missing nutrients, pest attack or a finishing harvest flush.

are for either cerebral or couch-lock highs then you can use harvest time to augment these properties.

The next thing to look at is the flowering period. Each strain's flowering period can vary. It is toward the last days of flowering that you should begin your harvest. If the seed bank says Skunk #1, flowering time seven to nine weeks, then you should be able to know roughly when your plant will be ready for harvest. In this case, it will be seven to nine weeks from the time your plant starts to flower.[2]

You may also find that a number of similar strains have been produced by different breeders. When you look at the seed bank list you may see as many as four or more listings for the same strain. Take Skunk #1 for example. Skunk #1 is a mostly Sativa plant, but there are about seven breeders who have provided a certain seed bank with Skunk #1 seeds. Each breeder tries to develop the best plant possible from that strain, but some breeders are better than others. Make sure that you check with the seed bank and confirm which strains are the best. The reason for choosing the best is that later on you can produce your own seeds from that optimal strain.

How to Get Seeds

The best way to get seeds is from another grower who has developed a plant that you enjoyed. This, by far, is the best way because (1) you may get the seeds for free and (2) you know what the high will be like because you have already sampled it.

The next best way is through seed bank catalogues on the Internet. The Internet is full of seed banks that want to sell you seeds, but you may encounter problems. Firstly, some of these seed banks are not legitimate and will rip you off. Secondly, some of these seed banks do not ship worldwide and their products may be unavailable to you. Thirdly, some of these seed banks misrepresent their stock. Finally, seeds can be very expensive. Some seed banks charge anywhere between $80 and $300 for 10 to 16 seeds. There are rip-off artists out there. So, how do you choose a seed bank?

Choosing a Seed Bank

After locating a seed bank, the first thing you should do is to research what people have to say about that particular seed bank. The best way to find this information, apart from word of mouth, is to check one of the more popular sites on the net, like Greenman's www.seedbankupdate.com, which is the most useful seedbank review site on the internet. It was one of the first review sites ever established and still remains the most popular to this day.

This is a harvest drying. This washing line setup is very common but what is most important is that this is done in a dark environment without light and with some airflow.

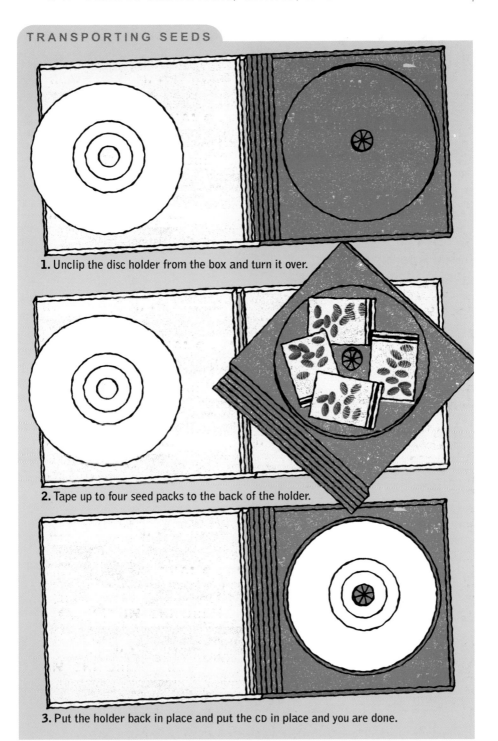

1. Unclip the disc holder from the box and turn it over.

2. Tape up to four seed packs to the back of the holder.

3. Put the holder back in place and put the CD in place and you are done.

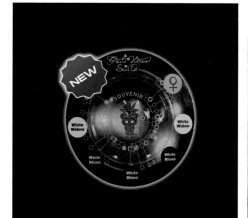

Good seed banks sell seeds in their original professional packages with logo and brand name.

Confirm that the web site you are buying from has a registered URL, like a dot.com site. If they use a free web-site service then consider avoiding it because it could disappear overnight.

Next, check out the reviews on each seed bank by the public. Then, visit the URL of each seed bank and check out their prices. Make sure that the seed bank has a quick turn-around time. It should only take up to 30 days for delivery. Some seed banks have been known to create back orders that take over two to three months to clear. I have personally witnessed Christmas seed orders arrive in the following March. This is a problem usually associated with counterfeit goods.[3] However, there can be circumstances where a breeder simply doesn't come up with viable stock for that season. The general rule is to avoid seed banks that have a large turn-around time gap. You want a snappy service and delivery within 30 days is the norm. Some seed banks have a 1 to 2 day shipping policy as soon as your money has cleared. These seed-banks are generally very popular with most growers.

Some seed banks offer deals on seeds and you will also find that prices fluctuate from bank to bank. Before buying anything, send them an email and inquire about their services, the seeds you like, delivery options, postage, packaging, and security arrangements. Wait until you receive a reply. If you do not get a reply then do not use that seed bank. These individuals are salespeople and should communicate with you and answer your questions.

Most seed banks sell their seeds in batches of 10 to 20, but anything can happen in transit. A misplaced foot in the postal office can kill the seeds, making them not viable. Quality seed banks should provide good protective packaging.

Communication with your seed bank is important. If your seeds do not arrive in a reasonable amount of time, you need to be able to ask the seed bank what happened. This will improve your communication with the seed bank the next time you purchase seeds. If you do not have access to the web, then you will have to write to the seed banks to request more information.

Always consult the seed bank about your strain—you never know, they may even be able to recommend something better to suit your needs.

You should receive your seeds in a stealth package. You will probably find them inside a clear, heat-sealed and labeled plastic bag. Check your seeds to make sure

HARVESTING SEEDS

Teasing seeds from the bud. Here a calyx containing a seed is being lightly squeezed between the thumbs at its base so as not to damage the seed.

The calyx opens and the seed comes up. Be careful doing this because is quite easy for the seed to fly out, drop or become lost.

This is the seed. It is not pale and so is likely viable. However, some pale seeds can be viable, depending on the strain.

A collection of some strains and the variation in their morphology. This strain is called strawberry.

This is a skunk strain. Skunk is very popular and is considered one of the old timer strains.

This is a skunk hybrid that has been crossed with Northern Lights. Hybrids are very popular although sometimes not as stable as old timer strains.

This is a haze strain. Notice the longer internode lengths? Haze type strains are considered some of the hardest to grow.

A collection of healthy viable seeds shows their various natural patterns. These are all from the same strain and this usually means that the patterns will be largely uniform.

Clearly labeled vacuum sealed bags are the best solution for long term storage.

that none are crushed. If some or all of the seeds are crushed, send them back to be replaced explaining to the seed bank that this particular package was damaged. Do not open the bag if you are sending them back.

Storing Seeds

If the seeds appear to be in good condition, then the first thing you should do is to remove them from the bag. Make double sure that these seeds do not come in contact with anything damp or wet or they may start to germinate. Once you have removed them from the bag you should place the seeds in a small, clean, and very dry film canister. (You may find that film canisters are less popular because of digital cameras; you can always switch to plastic vitamin containers or plastic medicine containers). Seal the canister and make sure that you *label it*. I can not stress how many times I have heard of people storing seeds only to forget what they were and when they were stored when the time came to use them.

The film canister is a short-term solution to seed storage. It will prevent your seeds from coming in contact with light, bacteria, moisture, and air—all of which can cause either germination or damage to occur. If you are going to store your seeds for more than a year, you should store them in an airtight container in a freezer.

3 | **Propagation and Germination**

What is Propagation?

1) The action of breeding or multiplying by natural processes: procreation, generation, reproduction.

2) The action of spreading an idea, practice, etc., from place to place.

3) Increase in amount or extent; enlargement; extension in space or time.

Propagation is The Grow; however, some growers treat propagation only as the time span between the planting of the seed and the transplanting of the seedling to the main grow environment. We will correctly treat propagation as the entire process of growing, from seed to harvest, including the logistics of the grow: in short, propagation represents the events that occur over the entire life cycle of the plant. This chapter focuses on the first stage, germination, but first we'll discuss propagation logistics. You will hear the term propagation used to describe elements of the grow that may be seen as one-time actions, like seed towel propagation, but we ask you to bear in mind that propagation is the continuous growing process.

Propagation Logistics

So, what are you going to do? Are you going to buy a batch of 10 seeds and grow them all in one go? Are you going to then remove the males and just use the females? Are you going to keep the males and produce more seeds from the females? How many seeds can a female plant produce? What can you do to guarantee that all your seeds will grow? This is where propagation logistics come into play. The answers to these questions depend largely on the size of your grow area and your budget.

GERMINATION

Seeds can be germinated in cloth. Cheesecloth is the most popular type of cloth used in the process but even paper towels will do.

The size of cloth to use depends on how many seeds you want to germinate. It is important to keep the cloth damp and not to let it dry out.

This is a seed in cloth that has not yet germinated. Seeds can be checked daily for new growth.

This seed is starting to germinate. It must remain moist, as a dry environment causes damage.

This seed has been germinating for a few days. Care must be taken to keep the environment slightly wet and to avoid breaking the root (radicle).

These two radicles are around three times the length of the seed and suggest that they should be transplanted to a medium very soon.

If seeds are not harvested from flowers they will eventually disperse naturally.
This is part of the life cycle of the plant.

Let's say you have about $200 to spend on seeds. You can buy an expensive strain, like a G13 cross, grow the G13, and produce more seeds from it. You could get between 100 and 2,000 seeds, depending on plant size and grow conditions. If you produce lots of seeds in one season, you may never need to buy seeds for this strain again.

There is something else you can do to prevent the need to ever buy or grow from seeds again: cloning. Cloning is a technique whereby you first grow a number of plants and select a quality plant; in the case of cannabis cultivation, a female is selected. You then take cuttings from that female plant, and grow these cuttings into new plants. Clones always retain the same sex and vigor as the mother plant, so it is possible to create a garden of plants through cloning that will last for decades from a single mother plant. Cloning is described in detail in Chapter 12.

For the new grower, it is advised that you buy 10 seeds and only germinate three the first time, followed by another three, and then the last four. This will allow you some degree of experimentation, as you may fail on your first attempt to germinate the seeds.

For people who have germinated seeds in the past, it is advised that you germinate five, followed by another five the next week. Only if you are a long-time grower with a good amount of growing experience should you germinate all the seeds at once. In this way, you can reduce the risk of spoiling some, or all, of your seeds because of bad germination methods.

During your plants' growth you may decide to pollinate only a few of your females. You will need two grow areas to do this: one for growing all your female plants as sinsemilla, and another for growing one or more females mixed in with males. As stated before, this depends on the size of your grow space and your budget. It is important that your pollination room be kept well away from your all-female sinsemilla grow room because pollen can travel by air. Bees and other insects can spread pollen, and so can you. Always wash your hands and face after handling a male plant to prevent pollen from getting onto a female that you wish to keep.

This male is beginning to produce pollen. Without males it is not possible to make seeds. Breeders cultivate males so that they can make seeds.

This harvested male is carefully taken to the breeding room to make seeds. Do not have any fans on in the room as they may blow the pollen away.

So, now you have 10 seeds and your goal is to achieve 100 percent germination results. The following section on germination will help you achieve an optimal success rate.

Germination Techniques

Seeds can be germinated a number of ways. Some guarantee more success than others. It is recommended that you consider the rockwool SBS (single block system) propagation tray method.

A germinated seed can be transplanted by simply placing it in the soil, covering it up and keeping it moist.

Seed Soil Propagation

In this method, seeds are placed in moist soil about 3 mm, or the length of the seed, from the surface. The soil is kept moist (not soaking wet), by sprinkling water over it once a day. This has a moderate success rate: out of 10 seeds, you can expect 7 to 8 to germinate.

The seed while germinating will push the cotyledons to the surface. Sometimes the shell may still be attached. Let it fall off naturally if you can.

Germination Soil

There are many soils advertised as germination soils.[1] They are basically the same as other soils, except that they contain special blends of micronutrients and are kept somewhat clean (the soil is sifted and no compost is added). Ordinary loam soil with a pH of 7 and an NPK (nitrogen, phosphorous, potassium)[2] of higher or equal amounts of N than P or K is good for starting seeds. Even NPK ratios of 5:1:1 or 8:4:4 are good. Just make sure that the N is equal to or higher than each of the P and K factors on the label.

After the next few days the first set of leaves will appear. Don't let your medium get dry and try to get your plant some light.

Some substrates are actually developed with seedlings in mind (low or absent in nutrients). They are usually called seed starters.

Seed Towel Propagation

Seeds are placed either on a damp towel or on damp cotton balls (cheesecloth may also be used). Cover the seeds with more damp cotton balls or a damp towel. If the material dries out it may damage the seeds, so keep it moist at all times. Every day, check to see if the seeds have started to produce roots. If they have, immediately transfer the seedlings to a grow medium, such as soil, using a pair of tweezers. Do not touch the roots, as this can kill your seedlings. This method has a moderate-to-high success rate. Out of 10 seeds, 8 to 9 may germinate. The problem with this method is that sometimes the transplant can cause the seedling to go into shock. This can terminate the germination process, leaving you with nothing. With practice you can get all your seeds to germinate using this method.

Propagation Kits

Seeds are germinated in small units inside a seed or clone propagator: a tray, of sorts, designed to help plants germinate. One such kit is called a rockwool SBS propagation tray.[3] At the bottom of the tray is a small area where water or germination hormones can be poured. Small grow cubes called rockwool cubes are placed into slots in the tray, which automatically dip the rockwool into the solution. The seeds are placed into tiny holes in the cubes (the holes are filled with rockwool particles to prevent the seeds from being directly exposed to air in the environment) and the cover is replaced. Some propagation kits are even heated and look like miniature greenhouses.

This method has a very high success rate, however a disadvantage is the cost of the tray, rockwool, and grow fertilizers. You should note that, although some seedling fertilizers contain growth hormones mixed into the nutrients in order to promote plant growth, it is recommended that you not use fertilizers or growth hormones with your seeds unless you have experience. Even the slightest amount of overfeeding can kill your seeds or burn your seedlings. In fact, you are better off just using water in your propagation kit to germinate your seeds. I have yet to find a cannabis strain that needed growth hormones or fertilizer to germinate properly. The price of the tray is about $10, the rockwool cubes $5,

You do not have to use soil as a medium to start seeds. There are many seed starter kits out there like this rockwool seed kit.

the grow fertilizers $5. If you have spent upwards of $50 on good seeds, why not spend the extra $20 on getting a small kit like this together and increase your chances of achieving a 100 percent success rate? The kits offer the added advantage of being able to root your clones.

Cannabis Seeds

Cannabaceae is part of the Angiosperm Phylogeny Group.[4] Cannabis seeds are created by the angiosperm mechanism. Seeds are small embryonic plants sheltered by a casing, called the seed coat, and are commonly found containing nutrients for food in store. A seed is a product of the fertilization of a plant, specifically the female flower gymnosperms' and angiosperms' ripe ovules. A fully formed seed is the completed process of a plant's reproduction. The formation of the seed, from zygote to embryo, and the seed coat completes the process of reproduction in the plant. It cannot occur without the development of flowers and pollen and the mechanisms of pollination.

This is a good example of a seed that while germinating and pushing the cotyledons to the surface still has the shell attached.

The first part of the process involves the angiosperms, which are fertilized twice with the union of the egg and sperm nuclei into a zygote. The polar nuclei unite with the second sperm cell nucleus, creating a primary endosperm. This endosperm divides into endosperm tissue, which becomes a source of nutrition. The source terminates shortly after the root and stem form. Gymnosperms have two sperm cells relocated from the pollen. Only one sperm fertilizes the egg. The seed is made up of the embryo and some tissue from the parent plant, which forms a covering around the seed. Seeds are formed in plant structures called fruits.

Another, more basic, definition of a seed is that it is a biological organism that is sown. However, seeds are not the only form of plant propagation. Ferns, for example, reproduce spores and an intermediate plant stage called a gametophyte.[5] Seeds are the main reason why plants can successfully take over as much land as is available for sowing.

Cannabis Seed Structure

Seed shape and structure differ from plant to plant and will vary even within cannabis varieties. The cannabis plant embryo has two cotyledons (dicotyledons),[6] also known as the seed leaf. The cotyledons take root by the radicle, which is the

For seedlings or clones fluorescent lights are a good way to keep the internode lengths short so that the young plants don't grow too tall.

root in embryo—both of which are at either end of the plumule, the shoot that acts like an embryonic plant stem. The epicotyl is the embryonic stem above the site of attachment of the cotyledons, while below this site is the hypocotyl.

In cannabis seeds, nutrition in the form of stored food starts with the endosperm containing oils, proteins, or starches produced in seed reproduction. The cannabis seed is albuminous, meaning that it is made up of simple, water-soluble proteins that can be coagulated by heat; an egg white is another example.[7] The actual seed, though, is physically recognized by its outer layer, a tissue called the integument that covers the ovule. The cannabis integument is of the hard type.

Cannabis Seed Germination

There are two main initiators of cannabis seed germination. "Imbibing" is the process whereby the seed soaks up water, which eventually results in the seed coat splitting. Seed coat hardness is variable with cannabis seeds. Ripe seeds should germinate but immature seeds are often not viable (usually a soft whiteness of a cannabis seed is attributed to immaturity, although some strains have this natural density and color). The second initiator of germination is light, which can penetrate the shell of seeds that have a weak or permeable coat. If the coat is not

The seeds are a lot darker than many of the seeds we have shown so far. Seeds can have lots of variation.

A close-up of a seed out of soil that is nearing shedding its shell.

permeable by light or water, the seed may not be viable at all. Other inhibitors may include bad soil, incorrect pH level, seed exposure, seed depth, weeds, rich nutrient content, physical damage from animal or environmental causes, and fungi. Germination can take 12 hours to several weeks, depending on the seed structure and germination conditions.

Cannabis Seed Functions

The inherent nutrient food substances in seeds allow the embryo to grow quickly. Cannabis seeds are heavy, meaning that wind travel is usually limited to a close area. Animals, birds, and man are the primary vehicles by which cannabis seeds are distributed over long distances.[8] Cannabis produces resin along with seeds which means that when the opportunity presents itself, the seeds will stick to almost anything with which the resin come in contact. Cannabis seeds have a historical record of being edible, although for growers their value is not in being a source of food.

Dangers when Germinating Seeds

During germination and transplantation, your plants are at their most vulnerable. Here are some tips to help you protect your future crop during germination.

A close-up of a seed out of soil
that has shed its shell.

A comparison of seedling with shell,
without and after first leaves.

Drafts can stunt germination. Always make sure you keep your germinating seeds away from any open windows or fans. Also ensure that the room is warm. A cold room can inhibit your germination rates.[9]

Take care when using germination fertilizers or hormones to ensure that your mix ture is correct. Do not use high doses of fertilizers with seedlings. Water is all seedlings really need. You do not need to add anything. Some people use germination solutions, but these solution strengths should be low. An incorrect mixture can burn your seedlings and cause them to fail.

Leave your seeds alone to grow.[10] You may be tempted to check on your seedlings and could run the risk of disturbing the soil. This is a bad move as too much tampering and shifting of the seeds can break and damage the young roots.

Some strains produce seedlings with weaker stems than others. In these cases, the seedlings may tend to lean to the left or right. If you find that your seedlings need support then use a small stick to brace your seedling. Tie the stem to the stick using a piece of thread. Never tie the thread above a growing shoot or the seedling will push up against the thread and may rip itself. You may continue to use a stick to support your plant as it grows. Never bring a stick in from outdoors as bugs, like spider mites, may go undetected inside the wood. If your plant still has a weak stem during vegetative growth it is recommended that you give the base of the stem a gentle shake every morning and evening. This will help the plant to develop a more solid stem. Outdoors, the wind shakes the plant and causes it to develop more solidly. You can simulate the effect of wind by gently prodding the plant every morning for two or three seconds. Indoor fans also help and are described in more detail in Chapter 7.

Seeds must be viable if they are going to germinate. Never use white seeds. They are immature. Find seeds that have white and gray markings or another color apart from white. Crushed seeds will not germinate. Old seeds may have trouble germinating. Always try to use the best seeds you can find.

A collection of seedlings in pots. These can go either indoor or outdoor.

Transplanting Seedlings

During the stages between germination and vegetative growth the grower may find that plants outgrow their pots. Transplanting to bigger pots should be done as early as possible.

Here is an example. When your seedlings are ready, simply lift them from the propagation tray along with the rockwool cube and place the cube and seedling into a bigger container full of another grow medium, such as soil or a hydroponic setup (more about hydroponics can be found in Chapter 10). There is not much of a problem when transferring a cube and seedling to soil. Just dig a small hole in the soil for the cube and place the cube in the hole. Cover the cube with soil. The cube will not affect your plant's growth and will provide additional support as it grows into its larger container.

It is always a good idea to label your seedlings so you know which strain it is. This is Jacky White from Paradise Seeds.

Even if you have started your seedlings in soil, transferring them to bigger pots need not be a complicated process. The problem you'll encounter is that, in order to move the soil and roots from one pot to another, the plant must be lifted out gently, with the soil in place. The most important objective of any transplant is to keep the roots intact while avoiding as much material spillage as possible. How is this done? There are three basic ways:

The first way is to simply cut away the base of the smaller pot and place it inside the bigger pot of soil. The roots will grow down through the hole in the bottom of the smaller pot and into the larger one.

The second way involves making sure that the soil is very dry. Delay watering your plant for a couple of days and let the soil settle until hard. You can then use a

First fill the container with the new medium. In this case, a soil mix.

clean knife to cut around the inside edge of the pot. Cut deep, but not so deeply that you risk damaging the roots. Push your fingers down into the sides and lift the plant and soil out. Some soil will break away but this shouldn't affect your plant. Quickly place the plant into the larger pot and cover with soil. Give your plant some water so that it will take to the new soil. Although you can lift some plants out of their pots by pulling on the stem, this can cause problems down the line. You should always maintain a firm grip on the soil when transplanting.

If your soil is very compact, you may be able to turn the pot upside down and gently tap the whole medium out as one solid mass. This transplanting method — turning the pot upside down and tapping it out—is a very professional way of transplanting but you should try it out first on a plain pot of dry soil. A bit of practice will pay off in the long run. Simply move your hand to cover as much of the top of the pot as possible. The stem should be resting at the base between your fingers. Lift the pot and plant up with the other hand. Turn the plant upside down and use your free hand to pull the pot away from around the soil. You can also use the remains of an indoor harvest (if the cut stem is still in the soil in the pot) to practice.

The transplanted clone in its rockwool cube
is then placed in the soil mix.

Extra soil mix is added to cover
the rockwool cube.

The soil is then patted down, leaving about an
inch of space between the top of the container
and the soil mix.

Two weeks later, the transplanted plant is growing
vigorously. It is important to label plants,
including the variety and transplanted date.

Transplanting

This section is about a premeditated transplant. If you need to make an emergency transplant because of overfeeding, then consult "soil flushing."

Transplanting is the procedure of taking something from one location and then moving it to another location. Technically, transplanting can occur over any conceivable distance. The primary concern in all instances throughout the method is plant health and avoiding unnecessarily damage. Transplants can be as simple as moving a germinated seedling from its incubation cube to some soil in a simple, swift pickup and bury, and as advanced as moving multiple fully grown plants from one location to another over long distances. Transplanting is all about pre-planning and executing the plan carefully. It can be challenging but experience makes it easier and will give you more confidence.

Clean your tools and containers. Many cultivators consider the digging of the plant to be the most difficult part of the process. For small plants, a simple hand-held trowel with a pointed, scooped metal blade is used to break up the soil. Plant nurseries can sell specialized transplanting trowels if you are interested in high volume work. The trowel may also be used for preparing a hole in the plant's new medium.

Transplanting if done correctly shouldn't put your plant through too much stress or fail to produce a bounty. Transplants can still generate some amazing nuggets of dankness like this Kush bud.

The base of some plants can get very big and thick. This is
one of the thickest cannabis bases I have ever seen.

Preparing the new medium before working on the transplant is an absolute essential for success—as is working with healthy plants. Working with damaged plants or an emergency transplant always reduces the rate of success. If you need to do an emergency transplant because of a problem, consult Chapter 7. Weather conditions

Propagation determines the outcome. The more control and planning you put into propagation the better your results and grow will be.

should be factored in if the transplant will take place outdoors. A cold, windy day is not the best environment to carry around an exposed plant. Plants moving into different environments, going from good conditions to bad, are more susceptible to problems than plants going into similar or better-quality environments. If you must choose from a selection for successful reproduction of a garden, then vigorous plants are better suited to relocation procedures.

Estimation of the root ball size comes with experience and is variable from strain to strain and growing conditions. Hydroponics growers can usually see the root mass and do not need to dig because the plant can be removed from the hydroponics unit directly. Roots produced in water are usually very different, being more fragile, from those produced in soil. Other substrates can cause the roots to grow differently. Roots growing in liquid tend to be weaker than roots growing in soil.

Plants that are near maturation, with a trunk size of 3-4" and over, may require two people to hold the root mass and the plant for transport. A canvas spread (which can be used when harvesting) can carry the plant as though on a stretcher. Transplanting at these late stages is uncommon, as transplant shock may cause sexual dysfunction in the flowers. Transplants can be successful for any size plant over any distance, as long as the preparation is good and care is taken. The reason for the care is to not only avoid bad transplants or plant damage but to prevent the plant from going into shock. This type of shock is called "transplant shock."

Transplant shock can be caused by a number of factors, most commonly root damage, plant damage, or overexposure of the roots. Plants that are being transplanted may be more susceptible to contamination by pests and disease. Transferring plants in or to the wrong medium may cause transplant shock, overcrowding may cause undue stress and transplant shock. Plan the move well. Protect your plants by handling them carefully, and make sure that you are moving them to a safe, secure site with plenty of room to grow.

Digging a tree or shrub in preparation for transplanting involves several steps. Various digging techniques can be employed, but no matter what approach is used, these steps must be attended to. The information covered here includes just the bare essentials. There are many factors which should be taken into account if one is to realize the best possible results. These considerations include the species of plant being moved and its condition, the soil conditions, climate, season of the year, and accessibility of the site.

Transplanting can occur anytime from seedling stages to flowering. Here a seedling in a rockwool cube is being transplanted.

Plants that have undergone several transplants can be just as good as plants that have not if the transplants are done properly.

This giant wall of bud will produce a giant harvest.

For potted plants, the whole soil will come up with the plant and go directly into a new medium (unless the plant is being treated for transplant shock) and so digging it up will not be necessary and instead the trowel will just be used to make the hole in the transplant medium. If the pot has the capability, it should be lifted and checked for any visible roots. If any are exposed, a quick check for any blackening will reveal if the plant has suffered any cold damage already. If the roots have grown out of the drainage holes and are small, then check to make sure they are free enough to go back through the holes again as you pull the plant up, or else you may tear the roots along the way. If they are tangled, then you will need a knife to cut these small roots so that the plant can move freely through the pores. Big roots protruding from the drainage holes can be a problem because avoiding main root damage is essential to a stress free and successful transplant. It is far better to saw or cut a cheap plastic pot to free a large root in the drainage system than to cut the root. Protruding roots are usually a sign that the plant may already be going through some pot-bound stress. A pot-bound plant cannot find space to produce roots and so creates a winding wall of roots around the inside rim of the container. If the container is particularly small and the plant is big, then this pot-bound wall chokes the plant's roots and can stress the plant to failure if left untreated.

Check the plan in your head. Work through what you will do with the plant after it has been uprooted. Once you are certain that you have a transportation route without obstruction, then you should start to prepare the transplant medium well before you dig up the plant. The transplant medium is entirely up to you.

Cannabis has a tendency to produce lots of root in vegetative growth if growing under optimal conditions. Measure the trunk diameter and multiply it by 20. This is a general formula for estimating how far the roots will extend out under the soil. After you find out how big they actually are, you can use this experience for next time. This same figure is also how far the root penetrates down into the soil.

Use the trowel to cut 1/6 of the way around the estimated root ball size—do it slowly. Use your hands to part the soil gently and observe any roots, if you can. If you have gone through roots or can see roots on both sides of the soil, then make the cut bigger until you find no roots. Roots can, and do, grow unequally and unevenly so care should be taken in cutting and checking that you do not slice roots. Slitting a smaller root does not mean that you will kill the plant but the more roots that get damaged, the greater the chances of inducing stress and limiting the chances of recovery.

Once you have cleanly cut through medium so you can lift the root ball out, you are ready to transplant. Clear away any roots attached to anything that can obstruct a clean uprooting. Plants that have intertwined roots because of crowded spaces will have this problem. If you can't loosen the roots slowly, then you can either cut directly down halfway or salvage one plant's roots more than the others by cutting away more roots from one to keep the other plant's roots intact and intermingled with the separated ones. If you have done all these things, you are prepared for the lift.

Depending on the root ball size, the plant can be lifted without aid and the root ball stabilized with one hand and the stem with the other. It is possible and advised to bag larger root masses that are to be moved over longer distances. Canvas is always helpful.

Root pruning before transplanting is a debatable topic. There are two schools of thought: leave the roots alone and transplant, or clean them and prune them to fit

Why not recycle? Old products may have some use if
you are inventive enough with them. Keep it green.

the transplant medium. There are circumstances where restricted transplant space means that pruning is necessary. Simply plant into the new medium and clean your tools after.

Transplant Shock

During some transplants, the cannabis plant may go into shock, even if your transplant was done cleanly and quickly. If your plant is otherwise healthy, it should survive. If the plant hasn't been looked after it may fail quickly. Transplant shock results in delayed or slowed growth and is caused by damage to or a disturbance of the roots. This is why you must always make sure to keep a firm hold of the soil during transplants. Also, refrain from feeding plants suffering from transplant shock for one week. The reason for not feeding the plant is because shocked plants cannot use fresh nutrients properly. The plant's poor health, coupled with its inability to uptake and use the fresh nutrients, usually results in plant burn, which can be fatal to a shocked plant.

While there has been some criticism that normal growing temperatures or high humidity can have an adverse effect on transplants that find it hard to recover in a dry environment, it appears that many of these plants were not healthy to begin with prior to the transplant and suffering from heat drought in their original environment. It is essential to work with healthy, well watered plants.

Some growers like to clean down their roots before transplanting. Although this can be done with some plants, cannabis does not like it unless the root mass is small and undemanding. Cleaning cannabis roots is not needed, but should you wish to attempt it then it is best to do it between the first and second weeks of vegetative growth. Root size and complexity is very strain dependent. Since cannabis mostly produces a complex root system, it is nearly impossible to avoid some root damage when cleaning the roots, and in most cases where root damage has occurred, plant growth will be stunted. If the damage is severe, the plant could die.

There are some transplant feeding products available. One popular brand of growth hormone called Superthrive is used extensively by cannabis growers to help the plant through the transplant process and recovery from shock. Superthrive contains the vitamin B1, better know as the hormone "thiamine"– a proven root and growth hormone.

For step-by-step information on THC extraction, please refer to Chapter 17.
For more information about breeding cannabis, refer to Chapter 15.
For more information about soil, pH, and NPK, refer to Chapters 5 and 6.

4 | The Great Divide: Indoors or Outdoors

We now come to the core divide in marijuana growing. At this stage, you should know something about the history of cannabis, how it is smoked, its various species, the high, its seeds, the life cycle of the plant, not to mention propagation, germination, and transplanting. With the exception of transplanting, all these things are generally pre-production methods. Now, you are ready to start growing: you're about to take your seedling and put it into your main grow area. This means that for the next three to nine months your plant is going to be located in a certain environment. That environment will be either indoors or outdoors. So, let us talk about each environment in brief for a moment and also discuss the important issue of security before moving on to a more detailed description of indoor and outdoor grow spaces, environmental control, and basic and advanced growing techniques in the chapters that follow.

Gardening Tools

Here is a list of the basic items used to grow cannabis plants, both indoors and out.

- Light source
- Nutrients
- Soil/medium
- Rockwool cubes (Oasis cubes or Jiffy cubes are just as good)
- Small shovel or trowel
- Support sticks
- Water source and delivery system
- Fertilizers
- Propagation trays
- Pots
- Scissors and/or a sharp knife
- Pest control
- Thread

As we advance to the latter sections of this book we'll see that growers can equip themselves with many more items to help them on their quest for bigger buds. The above list of tools represents the basics.

Some places are remote enough and big enough to allow for several hundred plants to grow indoors.

Planning for Indoor Growing

Next to choosing a strain, lighting is the most important factor that must be considered when growing indoors. The first thing you should know is that indoor lights produce bigger flowers (more bud) than natural light coming in the window (the

It is very important to plan ahead and envisage the final harvest in order to space your plants accordingly.

A grower pulls up a fistful of top colas from an indoor grow room. There are several ounces here and loads more to come.

process of utilizing natural light indoors is often called a window grow). This means you get more THC quantity with artificial lights than you will with natural sunlight indoors. Even in countries that have relatively hot sun for six months of the year, it is still hard to produce big buds indoors under natural light. Some people have grown plants under an attic window that's open during the dry days. This will grow you bud, but not as much as an artificial lighting system will produce. The other side of the coin is that natural light is free, electricity is not, and grow lights can be expensive to buy and run.

When using a window grow, try to place your plant near a window that receives the most sunlight throughout the day and the seasons. If you plan on a window grow, remember that you want your plant to get most of its light during flowering. If July is the best month for sunlight, then you may consider germinating your seedling back in April or May or even as early as early March. Try to estimate when you'll get the best weather and coordinate this with the flowering times directed by the breeder.

A single light, large reflector and lots of mylar can spread enough light to
expand the parameters of a grow by several additional plants.

Also remember that people might be able to look up and see your plant if it is
growing near the window. People washing your windows can also see in. Also, if
you have a Sativa plant it will get big and very conspicuous. Take all these factors
into consideration when you are growing your plants with natural sunlight indoors,
but keep in mind that even low wattage indoor grow lights will improve your yields
tenfold compared to a window grow. Window growing can result in a vain attempt
to grow bud and is one of the top reasons why first time cannabis growers discontinue growing cannabis. A window grow by no means reflects the cannabis
plant's true potential.

If you are growing indoors, then you may have a room or part of a room that you
wish to use, such as an attic, closet, basement, or spare bathroom. These locations
nearly always require artificial light. There are many ways to set up an indoor
grow room. We will discuss this in Chapter 6.

Outdoor Growing

Throughout the discussion that follows, we define outdoor growing as growing on
your own property and guerrilla farming as growing away from your property,
either in public areas or on someone else's property.

A trailer full of clones on their way to an outdoor grow. These babies will eventually cultivate into some very nice mature bushes.

Outdoor clones planted in rows can grow into every cannabis farmer's dream.

This sativa-heavy T.N.C. from K.C. Brains grows tall and yields a lot of bud. Photo K.C. Brains

Your grow patch, whether on your own property or public property, must be pre-treated and tended to regularly. Leaving seeds in the soil and coming back four months later is generally not going to produce the best results. Two things must be done to the patch before the grow—weeding and digging.

Planning for Outdoor Growing and Guerrilla Farming

The biggest problem with outdoor growing is keeping your grow area secure and private. Some people will rip off your plants in a second if they see what you have. Others will just create trouble for you. The risks are high and security is vital. I once heard about a small community that lived near a forest and grew their marijuana near a stream. They eventually had to stop growing as their plants were being ripped off by the locals from the town nearby. The thieves were not just teenagers, adults will also steal. Some rippers are professionals, using other people's grow as their main supply.

Perhaps the best, most affordable, and low-key way to conceal an outdoor garden is to grow your cannabis plants among other plants that will mask the cannabis. If you have the advantage of living out-of-town and have a garden in which this kind of stuff can be constructed, you could also grow plants inside a brick cubicle with sheets of glass on top. This is much like a very small greenhouse without the

This K.C. Brains greenhouse has cannabis as far as the eye can see. Large populations are a breeder's delight. Photo K.C. Brains

glass sides and can be camouflaged to look like a small shed. The problem with enclosed outdoor grows like this is that light only really gets to the canopy of the plants and very little bud is produced under this canopy. The advantage is that this setup does not look like a greenhouse or anything that is housing plants. If you want to use a greenhouse instead, then it is suggested that you paint the sides of the greenhouse white to prevent anyone from looking in. The white will also help reflect the sunlight that enters in above through the glass around the grow area, promoting growth on lower leaves and bud areas.

Whatever method you choose: hide your crop well. Not everyone can easily spot marijuana, but someone who is trained to watch out for the plant will know it right away for what it is.

Guerrilla Farming

Guerrilla growing is hard work and often prone to rip-offs. By planting in a forest or in someone else's field or property, you are not in any danger of being caught with the plants on your property. However, the person's property you plant on is put at risk. Be a good grower and do not plant on someone else's private property. It is not nice and reflects badly on the cannabis-growing community. Find a public area, such as a forest or a hill slope. Look for an area that is away from the public eye,

A garden, an unused patch, a high enough wall and Paradise Seeds' Sensi Star: the end result will be the proof that this space went to very good use. Photo Paradise Seeds

It's never a good idea to camp right next to your grow.

but will receive plenty of light. There are lots of places for this sort of thing, but spend time finding the right spot. Finding a good patch is the key to successful guerrilla growing. A patch near a river is ideal because it offers ready access to water and can help your crop survive a short drought.

Most guerrilla farmers prefer to keep it simple and favor the following method. They start their seedlings in small plastic pots indoors. When the seedlings have developed, and the plants are ready to enter the vegetative growth stage of the life cycle, the grower cuts the bottoms of the pots away and tapes a small piece of cardboard to the bottom of each pot. The plants, in their pots, are then taken to the grow patch where the grower digs holes in the ground, removes the cardboard and places the pots and plants in the earth. Then the holes are filled in with soil. This way the grower has germinated the plants and only needs to worry about secondary factors such as light, security, and pests. The roots will find their way out of the bottom of the pots and into the soil below. Don't worry about the roots not finding a way out of the pot. They always do, that's their job.

Security

The old saying, "Never tell anybody that you grow cannabis," is extremely difficult

Growing plants in with others reduces the conspicuousness of cannabis.

to commit to and seems extraordinary for growers to employ. The truth is that there are many ways you can be discovered without saying a word. Keeping your mouth closed about growing reduces the probability of raising security issues. There are many reasons why a growing operation will reveal itself, from obtaining equipment, to obtaining seeds or clones, to actually growing smelly plants. However it is true that loose lips cause 99.9 percent of all security-related issues. The remaining 0.1 percent of security breaches are due to poor preparation and growers neglecting to take the time to conceal the area well enough. If you intend to share your crop with friends do it by other means.

This outdoor cola is as long as a human arm and still has more to grow. Outdoor bud can get very big.

Security is always an issue, whether you are an outdoor or indoor grower. We have learned that to secure your grow area you must prepare yourself for any future eventuality. Pre-production security arrangements are very important. A sudden peak in your electricity bill may attract unwanted attention from certain authorities that look for these things. This may seem odd to you, but it does occur.[1]

It is now common practice in most countries that support cannabis prohibition to set up special task forces to track down growers. The most frequently used technique is tracking purchasing orders. Many agencies keep tabs on grow shops and the items being sold to customers. Tracking requires special court orders, but law enforcement agencies can obtain these with ease. If someone has been identified as buying suspicious grow products, the agency will also try to find out what other items have been bought using the same credit card or other accounts. Many growers have been caught this way. The best way to avoid this trap is to always pay with cash.[2]

Seed banks are also sometimes tracked by agencies that watch for incoming mail with certain stamps and envelope headers. Sometimes it isn't the agency that does the tracking but people in the post office. To get around this, most seed banks don't head their mail anymore. If your seed bank does, it is best to keep away from that seed bank in the future.

If you have done the right thing, then you should have all your growing tools and kits bought using cash and your seeds purchased from a seed bank that offers good seeds and a safe, secure way of sending you their product. Many seed banks use great stealth to get you your seeds. It is advised that you never have seeds sent directly to your grow area.

Indoor Security

When growing indoors, try to consider certain short-term security factors, like visits from service people. Some growers have a grow room that can be swept clean in under a minute. They have a closet nearby where they can quickly move their plants if visitors do drop by.

Always keep your security closet near your grow area. It's no good walking around your house with five or more plants in your arms. It's a bad idea to use a bathroom as a backup security area unless you have another one that guests can use.

Another thing you must consider with indoor security is odor. Now Super Skunk and Skunk #1 are very smelly plants, especially during flowering, hence the name

Even growing in a cage can break up the image of an obvious outdoor cannabis plant. Boards can be placed around it and the top left open when the plant grows tall enough.

Skunk. If you live in an apartment complex, there's no way you'll be able to hide the smell unless you have some form of extraction fan or an ozone generator.

In some indoor setups, fans can be used to extract unwanted smells away from corridors and high-traffic areas. Air can be pumped through a window or filter to another area where the smell will not be noticed. Not only that, but plants love fresh air and wind, so the fan can do two things at once for you. An ozone generator is a device that helps to get rid of cannabis odor problems and can be purchased from most grow shops.

Fire is another major security issue for growers. Some people growing indoors use second-rate lights and/or fixtures, creating a very real fire hazard. Never use any lighting kit or fixture that is either damaged or unsuitable for indoor use. Taking shortcuts with lighting and electricity is a big no-no—you could be risking your home, and everything and everyone in it. I have heard of and met people who have come home only to find the fire department outside just finishing putting out the fire that engulfed part of their house. The same thing happens in every case: the grower approaches and sees a number of police officers looking around the area. The fire officer points to the cause of the fire—a half-melted light fixture with burnt-out sockets. They all know what this is all about because they have seen it all before.

New marijuana growers nearly always make the mistake of creating inferior lighting setups. Needless to say, this is because of three factors: either they don't have the right information, they don't have the money to invest in a proper lighting system, or they just want to grow their pot quickly and cheaply. Proper lighting systems are discussed in Chapter 6.

Outdoor Security

As previously stated, the best way to secure your outdoor garden is by using a shelter. You must also remember that some outdoor plants do smell and this can carry over a short distance, given the right wind conditions and climate. Most people won't know what the smell is, but some will! Many growers get around this problem by growing cannabis plants that have very little smell during flowering. Ask about these strains when you contact your seed bank. They should be more than happy to recommend a less smelly strain for you. All cannabis plants smell to some degree, however, during flowering.

The other thing to make sure of is that you can harvest your crop as quickly and as privately as possible. Standing over a small shelter putting cuttings of cannabis into a big black bag is not exactly the most secure way to go about this. Some people go to their garden with black plastic bags and drop the bag over the plant before pulling it up. This way you won't expose your crop to anyone. Some people do their harvesting at night. This is not recommended though, as it can draw unwanted attention to you and your setup. A flashlight rummaging around in the darkness is not very stealthy at all. Also, during the day you have a clearer view of what is around you. It is much wiser to do your harvesting during the day unless for some reason there is less activity in your area at night.

If you are growing your plants outdoors without shelter and away from the general public then you may want to create a pen for your plants. A pen made from chicken wire will prevent any unwanted predators, such as deer or rodents, from eating your plants. Predators are a big problem for outdoor growers and will be further discussed in Chapter 13.

Guerrilla Growing Security

Tracks left behind from your ventures to and from your grow area are the worst giveaway for any guerrilla farmer. People just love to walk through the woods and say: Oh, look a nice track, I wonder what's down there? Do not create a track when you go to your grow area. Even by visiting the same spot once every two weeks you will leave a trail, which hikers might see and use. Try to access your grow area through several different routes.

As a guerrilla grower you probably don't want to hack through 100 feet of brambles to access your grow site. When choosing a spot, look for an area that is neither too dense nor too sparse. Some guerrilla growers have even created small grow baskets that hang from trees away from the public eye. If the baskets are well camouflaged then you can get away with loads.

Hanging baskets are easy to make. You need a three-gallon wire-hanging basket, a plastic garbage bag to fit inside the basket, and some wire. Simply line the inside of the hanging basket with the garbage bag and lightly perforate the bottom of the bag to allow water to drain through. Fill the basket with soil and transplant your seedling to the basket. You can then suspend this basket high up on the branch of a tree. Hanging baskets need to be used in conjunction with slow release fertilizers—types like granular foods. All the plant's nutrients should be stored in the soil throughout the plant's grow. Slow release feeding products do this. A popular brand of slow release food is Fish, Blood, and Bone. Slow release foods are not as controllable as

Living in remote places in the right environment allows some growers to enjoy all the glory of having hundreds of plants quietly developing where nobody knows.

normal feeding products because the nutrient break down in the soil occurs over weeks and months in different quantities, but the foods permit the grower to feed the hanging plants less often. Although hanging baskets are a stealthy way to grow, they can be hard to access and maintain. Watering is also a consideration that must be taken into account. It is advised that if you try growing cannabis in hanging baskets that you have a little experience with growing cannabis beforehand.

As a guerrilla grower you should always wear gloves when handling your grow and tools. If you have buckets nearby don't leave fingerprints on any of these. Also, you will want to consider having a good excuse for being in your grow area. Imagine that you're walking back from your path with nothing incriminating on you and someone jumps out and asks what you are doing here? Of course, you know that there's a river nearby so you show your fishing rod or your binoculars and bird-spotting book. There are many things you can take with you to make you look like somebody other than a cannabis grower. I have heard cases of grow sites being staked out by people you would definitely not like to meet. Always check the area around your grow site for suspicious-looking people.

The worst security time for any guerrilla grower is during the harvest. This is when you must go from your grow area to your home or another location with your growing rewards. Always do this in the morning, as early as possible. Double-check the area for any suspicious-looking people. Pack your buds and plants into bags (brown paper bags are better or, alternatively, use black plastic bags) and then put these into a backpack. Before you approach your vehicle, drop your bag against a bush and cover it up. Walk toward your vehicle and look around again. You may even want to drive for about five minutes and look out for anything suspicious or anyone who might be following. Remember, you can always leave the bag and go to a nearby town (not home—leave that until the situation is well under control again). If things look okay, you can drive back to where you left your bag, pick it up, stow it out of sight (the trunk for example) and drive home carefully.

Some people can get away with guerrilla farming lots of pot. This is commercial growing on a risky scale but still occurs in various parts of the world where cannabis is banned. The growers usually live deep in the forest miles away from the nearest town. They may spend up to seven months on their own, cultivating the crop. Recent grow busts by the police have identified several tons of bud being grown by as few as three people living in a remote region of British Colombia.

There isn't much more to guerrilla growing than this. Most of the elements that you need to complete your outdoor and guerrilla grow site are in the indoor growing chapters of this book. Read through this and it should give you ideas about how to treat your outdoor grow patch.

Guerrilla growing is so popular in some places around the world that it has become competitive and dangerous. Remember that not all growers are nice people. Some of them don't even smoke cannabis and just want to make money. Check your local news media for information relating to seizures of guerrilla grows and if those arrested were armed. This is a huge problem associated with cannabis prohibition.

5 | Organic Farming

Organic farming is any form of agriculture that does not use synthetic nutrients, synthetic fertilizers, pesticides, hormonal regulators, and synthetic additives and does not have any type of association with artificial genetic modification. Organic farming uses crop surplus, animal waste, compost, weeding, and natural pest and disease controls in combination with the theory of the mechanisms of organic farming. The leading global standard in organic agriculture is the International Federation of Organic Agriculture Movements (IFOAM). It is important to note that organic farming is a scientific, practical "movement" based on sound scientific principles. The ideology has profoundly altered many laws governing the commercial farming sector as the ideas also Implicate synthetics additions in farming crops as a cause for immediate concern. Organic farming, when regulated, usually results in a crop that is government-approved organic, which by demand traditionally acquires a higher price tag—except in places that have flourishing organic farming activity.

While modern organics is well grounded in a practical movement with a wholesome approach for the benefit of mankind, the roots are entirely different, stemming from religion, to industrialization, to chemical experimentation, to the War efforts and genetic research. The historical record for organic farming theory and practice stems mainly from advances in biochemical engineering of the early 1900s as a result of industrialization. Mechanical engineers also sought actively to produce machinery capable of the lowest economical cost for the highest rates of efficiency.

Breeders experimented with hybrids, artificially selecting donors to the best possible gene pool for adaptation to a local environment which included organics.

A dozen or so plants organically cultivated in a garden can produce
a nice bounty whilst still meeting our green ambitions.

While there are countless examples of the entire planet cultivating organically before the introduction of synthetics through industrialization and chemical engineering, organics cultivation was also actively improved during this era. Many religious farmers are scientists who find moral and ethical compatibility with their belief and organics. In 1924, Rudolf Steiner used religion to promote organics, which he termed "biodynamic" in his book *Spiritual Foundations for the Renewal of Agriculture*. The text led to the popularization of biodynamic agriculture.[3]

The term biodynamic is still used today[4] although it is recognized by the majority of growers now as organic agriculture. Organic farming is closely linked to the concept of biodynamic agriculture in that the entire process is a self-contained organism. This idea was first elaborated on by Walter James, 4th Baron Northbourne, who called it a "farm as organism."[5] Northbourne would then go on to write *Look to the Land* in 1940, which also contributed to the movement.

World War II efforts forced scientists to concentrate on chemical engineering, which extended all the way to organic crops and synthetic experimentation. It is during this era that scientific advances in organics boomed. Salesmen took the idea and sold it, building a broader consumer base. The International Federation of Organic Agriculture Movements (IFOAM), organized in 1972, had become the central nerve center for data collection, analysis, and dissemination. IFOAM helped propose that governments should take a critical approach to synthetics and promote an increase in certified organic produce. The proposal worked and organic agriculture is constantly on the rise. It has already reached a capacity where organic produce is abundant.

Natural processing, recycling, time, soil enrichment, and release systems are important parts of organic growing. Natural processing includes mixing minerals and organic substances, either separately or together. Beneficial or friendly pests are used to combat unfriendly pests.

The viability of organic growing when compared to artificial must take into account factors other than yield (after all, we can produce a gigantic harvest that costs a hundred times what it is worth). Safety, health, and environmental reasons should be factored in. Artificial growth hormones and boosters

Trichome Technologies Ultra Violet.

Famous for its dark color and unique flavor.

A pure Indica with over 16% THC.

are capable of yields that are much higher than organics grown under similar conditions. Comparisons should only be made where the artificial methods exclude growth stimulators. There is a general scientific consensus that organics will in general not produce more than artificial cultivation. There is also a consensus that organics can produce the same quantity as artificial cultivation. A typical 10% difference is considered minor when the organic method used less energy and no pesticides.[6]

Organic pest and disease control is mainly done by improving genetic integrity through selective breeding. The introduction of friendly pests is considered the last way to solve a pest problem. There are many organic pesticides on the market, however, not all are considered harmless. Organic pesticides may also be toxic!

In 1998 IFOAM declared that organic agriculture should be GMO-free. GMOs are Genetically Modified Organisms. The main argument against GMOs is that we simply do not know enough about its impact on the environment and how much it could possibly alter the way we live. While there are obvious benefits to creating a strain that is pest resistant, high yielding, energy efficient, and has all the other bells and whistles by genetic modification, there still remains the problem that there are possible criticisms of specific instances where GMOs have been defective. Proponents would suggest that they would get all the criteria right for introduction into the wild.

There is also always the general fear that a "Frankenstein science" could destroy us all, but there is a scientific consensus that GMOs are trying to improve our world, not destroy it. Organic supporters say that we can do just fine farming with what we have, without any need for GMOs. Yet to say we should not genetically modify crops would be an error, as natural selection and selective breeding by humans has caused crops to change their genetic code over time. Crops evolve whether we use GMOs or not.

Nonetheless, there is the problem of releasing GMOs into the wild. GMOs may breed with non-GMO crops, creating "GMO/non-GMO" hybrids. This point must also be factored in to the release of GMO crops into the wild. IFOAM still maintains a non-GMO stance.

Organic cultivators argue that there is an imminent necessity to go organic now, not tomorrow. They point to the fossil fuel exhaustion problem and pollution as an example. Chemical factories create waste in producing synthetics. There is no hotter topic today than how much we contribute to the facts of global warming and global pollution. There is a scientific consensus that man contributes to global warming.[7]

Growing outdoors is an excellent way to explore organic gardening.

ORGANIC SOIL GARDEN

Organic growers take great care and know that preparation is everything for maintaining what may be a challenging growing technique.

To have made it this far with a healthy seedling going into vegetative growth and looking healthy will be an enormous achievement for beginner organic growers.

It helps to clip the edges of the leaves if they are drooping downwards and making contact with the soil. If they do touch this will probably cause the tips to undergo cellular necrosis.

Vegetative growth means the organic
grower has come a long way.

The development of new leaves
occurs at the nodes.

Plant stress is the enemy of every grower but organic growers need to be extra vigilant for signs of
stress. Stressed plants increase the probability of producing hermaphrodites.

ORGANIC SOIL GARDEN

This is a critical time for the organic grower to pay extra attention. Flowering plants generally require more P than N and K.

How the grower delivers more P is one of the topics in this chapter. It can be added to the medium in a number of ways.

Grows like this are testimony that organics doesn't mean weak results. Anyone should be proud of this garden.

This strain has a fairly high calyx to leaf ratio, but is still producing a fairly thick amount of bud. It's already towards the later stages of flowering.

Approximately 50% of the pistils here have changed color indicating that harvest time is approaching or here already.

As we can see organic grows are capable of producing pistils in abundance.

ORGANIC SOIL GARDEN

This is one plant after harvest that has been trimmed with the leaves removed. This will hang upside down in a dark place until dry.

This dried organic plant is being prepared for manicuring by being placed into a frame with a white base so that trichomes can be gathered.

First of all the plant is chopped up so that it can be managed easily. Each piece can then be worked on independently.

The plant is then broken down: the stem on the right, the bud at the top, branches in the middle, and the remaining trimmed leaves at the bottom.

This organic plant has produced 0.7oz after manicuring. Most growers like to try and get at least 1oz per plant or better but 0.7oz for an organic grow is a good harvest.

This substrate is made from sheep manure. It is balanced because the NPK values of 0.5 are all the same.

This substrate has the same balanced NPK values as the other but is made from cattle manure and not sheep.

Organic farming does have some drawbacks. One predicament is the problem and cost of creating independent chemicals. Organics try to maintain the right balance, but includes additional organic chemicals that are not often necessary. Organic farmers recognize that organic growing, especially with manure, has the potential to cause water pollution—but then again, so do conventional methods. There is still a debate over whether global organics is actually economically and environmentally feasible, but organic growing continues to grow in popularity.

Conventional growers argue that even though the artificial supplements they use in agriculture are synthetic, there is less chance of exposing the crop to potential hazards, while there does remain a chance that organic bacteria and unwanted diseases can be introduced with the organics. It is possible for organics to contain unwanted toxins. This is one of the reasons why organic farmers are advised to get certified and monitored.

Since the government approves and promotes organic foods, they actively promote it as better. However, the real question is if there is any conclusive evidence to support the claim that organics produce healthier foods. The answer is that there is a body of evidence that can go either way. There are more than several important comparisons which suggest that organic food healthier.[8]

Organics are not limited to simply the "healthy soil, healthy food" claim, so even if the results have not been as persuasive as its critics would like, organics still continues to have almost universal support because organic growers generate a lot of enthusiasm which drives research and development in the agriculture sector as a whole. There is also an independent movement within organics to complete with big business. These smaller organic farms are ultimately the best example of the traditional farming methods that we had before synthetics.

Organic Growing

Starting organic growing requires that we dispose of all synthetic products and develop a basic scheme to prevent them from being introduced to your garden again. Any and all soil should be obtained organically and treated organically.

Compost

Compost is a major component of organic farming. In fact, most organics are types of, or become, compost. Compost forms with the aerobic decomposition of organic material. Compost is a natural state for all organisms. All living things decompose. Since living things eat, what they eat is vital to the quality of the organics they produce, either through natural decay or waste materials. It is essential to understand

Natural homemade compost.

Compost bought from the store.

that animals eating synthetics may have an effect on the quality of the waste material. These types of waste can be treated, but only by professional compost systems that take the compost to a high temperature and so kill the pathogens.

Compost can be made or bought certified. Compost can be made from bark, biodegradable substances, coffee (used grounds), grasses, green waste, hay, humus, leaf, manure, microorganisms, mulch, sawdust, straw, wood, wool, and worm compost. These are all good organic mulches. Cardboard and newspaper should be treated as a mulch rather than as a compost, even if it is sometimes found in composts. They are usually there to allow airflow or to act as a covering.

Aerobic decomposition is important. Nature has its own way of allowing air to enter the soil by means of living things active in the soil, such as worms and ants. There are some conditions that can prevent aerobic decomposition from occurring, like very dry conditions combined with tightly locked compost. In general, organic growing enforces a much quicker breakdown of the organics than in nature. Air, carbon, nitrogen and water are required for the microbes to live actively. Decomposition does not have to be aerobic. If air is restricted, then anaerobic decomposition can occur. Anaerobic decomposition produces a foul, sour-smelling odor, a sign that some of the compost has become potentially toxic for plants.

Organic Compost

Organic composts try to achieve a rate of decomposition in which there are 30 parts carbon to one part nitrogen, or 30:1. This is a standard organic mix ratio. It is much easier to buy organic compost and to mix known ratios than to discover the exact ratio of a homemade organic compost mix. Most organic growers rely on formulas, experience, and trial and error experiments in order to estimate this ratio. Having samples analyzed is expensive, but not impossible. The idea here is to stay clear of compost or compost ingredients that could contain unwanted synthetics or toxics. Some degree of compost toxicity will always exist in amateur organic mixes, but it generally dissipates quickly if the compost is well maintained through aeration.

Carbon has cellulose, which creates sugars during aerobic decomposition. Nitrogen has protein, which promotes higher activity in the microbes. Carbon-high organics include leaves gathered from the autumn to winter period (usually during clearing for compost preparation), sawdust, and straw. Nitrogen-high organics include coffee (used grounds), fruit (used), manure, plants, seaweed, and vegetables (used). Nitrogen only includes manure from chickens or other poultry.

LAYERS IN A COMPOST HEAP

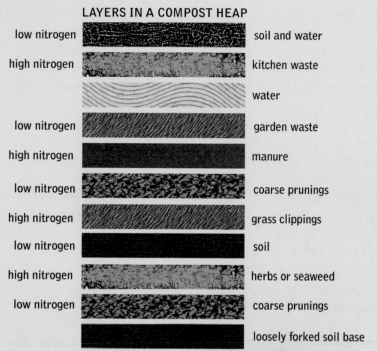

low nitrogen	soil and water
high nitrogen	kitchen waste
	water
low nitrogen	garden waste
high nitrogen	manure
low nitrogen	coarse prunings
high nitrogen	grass clippings
low nitrogen	soil
high nitrogen	herbs or seaweed
low nitrogen	coarse prunings
	loosely forked soil base

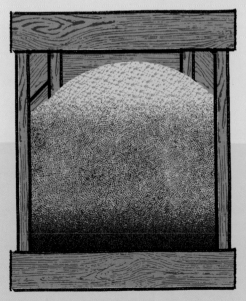

compost heap

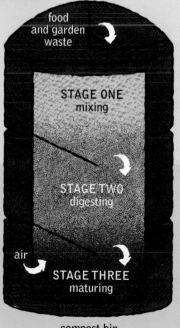

food and garden waste

STAGE ONE
mixing

STAGE TWO
digesting

air

STAGE THREE
maturing

compost bin

Horse manure contains carbon and nitrogen. Horse and poultry manure breaks down more quickly than cattle or sheep manure. Avoid using dairy products or meat in organic compost because they attracts unwanted pests. If you want to use dairy or meats, then you are better off buying prepared organics that have already broken down and have the oils removed. A good example is organic eggshells.[9]

Compost bins are excellent. They allow temperatures to soar to 50 °C–60 °C (122 °F–140 °F). Insulation wraps can increase the temperatures even further. This is called active composting. Any compost that stays under 30 °C (86 °F) is referred to as cold compost. Compost should be kept somewhat damp, as if the compost has had any excess water pressed out of it. Add more water if you think it is not breaking down fast enough. Again, experience will guide you. Watch out for the high temperatures in the middle of the compost heap. It can get quite hot. Wear gloves. Turning and leaving the organics in open air is a good idea if you need to cool it down. Compost is ready when it stops changing color, becomes dark, and feels brittle.

The more control the organic farmer has over the compost, the better the results will be. Reactive organic growing (only doing something when the environment alerts you) is a passive means of maintaining an organic garden, one in which the least amount of attention is paid. Proactive organic growers pay attention to their garden and check it even without prompting.

Product compost is compost bought from the store. Most versions can be used alone or combined with a home compost system.

Compost residuals are found in the fluid drained from soaking compost. If the compost is new, then the residue is usually high in nutritional value. Dispersion of the organic nutrients to other areas of the medium occurs with watering.

Compost "leachate" is made by rinsing compost, straining it, or crushing it to release nutritional fluids. The percolation, however, is significantly different from modern methods, which activate more microbes to higher states, are more manageable, less messy, and produce higher quality results.

Compost Tea

Compost "tea" is prepared in dechlorinated water by adding compost and unsulfured molasses and then using an air pump and distribution to aerate the mixture. Compost tea can be prepared especially to create a fluid solution as organic feed.

Go to the local aquarium store and buy a gang valve system (either brass or plastic) and now you have multiple air lines to aerate the compost tea container. You will also need an aquarium pump (don't worry about owning one of these; you can experiment with it later, too, for hydroponic bubbling buckets) and some hose to pump air through the gang valve. The aquarium shopkeeper can measure the valves and hoses for you. The valve sits at the bottom of your bucket to mix the tea. If you don't have dechlorinated water, then you will need to bubble your water for at least one hour to try and cause as much chlorine evaporation as possible. Add compost and pour about 1 oz. of unsulfured molasses to excite the microorganisms. Bubble it for 2 to 3 days and stir every so often to make sure that the mix is breaking up properly. The results are strained through a cloth into a watering can for immediate use.

If the organic tea mix is not breaking down fast enough, then balance it by adding less compost and more unsulfured molasses. Again, experience is everything. If this doesn't work, then the chloride in that water supply was too high to get rid of through aerating and it has killed the microbes. Either bubble for longer next time or get dechlorinated water. If the tea smells bad, then something has gone wrong and the process needs to be checked through again, from the quality of the compost, to the mixing itself.

You can ferment compost tea on a very basic scale by just leaving compost and water to mix in a container for a week. However, compared to the above method this system is hardly considered viable anymore.

Mulch

A mulch is a covering used to protect the soil. Since organics are sometimes loosely left on top of the ground, they need to be held down to prevent the elements from shifting them; mulch does this. Mulching also helps to control soil temperature, prevents water evaporation, reflects light from the ground to the plants, kills weeds by preventing photosynthesis, stops pests from going into the

A bag of mulch.

A bag of worm casting.

ground, and prevents pests from coming up. You can prevent environmental rain from being added to the soil.

Compost is a popular form of mulch. The composted material tends to be heavier and stays down. Bark, cardboard, grass, hay, leaf, newspaper, sawdust, straw, wood, and wool are all good organic mulches.

Organic mulches can also be bought prepared at organic supply outlets. They are usually made from recycled rubber and plastic. Rocks and stones can also be used for mulch. In fact, anything organic that can be placed over the soil as a covering can be considered mulch.

Mulches can break down depending on what they are made from. The rate of decomposition depends on the environmental conditions that influence the rate of increase in decomposition. Mulches can become a hindrance in the later stages of decay and their worth should be judged in terms of their effectiveness versus interference. Once the losses start outweighing the benefits, replace the mulch.

Mulching can be applied at any time. Organic mulches should be above five inches per plant; it will sink in time. Rubber mulch comes from recycled rubbers such as tires. There are traces of wire, but usually less than 5%. Some organic mulch may turn toxic during decomposition, producing a sharp sour smell. Mulching needs to be aired by moving or rotating the mulch to allow for air to circulate. If your mulch smells, it indicates that anaerobic decomposition is talking place.

Airing mulch and removing the infected parts solves this smell problem. Mulch toxicity that seems to have seeped into the soil can be solved by either emergency transplanting or over watering; however, both of these remedies can shock the plant—which is already in a shocked state. Mulch pH maintenance is important and is performed in the same way as regular pH maintenance. High acidic pH levels are a sign of possible anaerobic toxicity.

Worm Composting

Vermicomposting, or "worm composting," is very popular because it usually doesn't have an odor and yet is abundant in nutrients. Its origins lie in the tradition of keeping worms in your garden. Vermicomposting uses worm castings, a type of humus manure that results after the breakdown of organics left by the worm.

The most common type of worm used is the "red worm" (*lumbricus rubellus*), also called the red wiggler. Brandling worms (*eisenia foetida*) are also popular. Unless you know a natural supplier, these worms are best bought from organic stores or fishing bait shops.

Vermicomposting bins vary drastically depending on the desired kind of system. Smaller bins may be made from wood, but normally plastic or even stainless metal are the material of choice. All bins will have an airflow system with a drain.

"Undivided" vermicomposting bins are simply based on building layers according to the instructions. The layers usually consist of bedding, organics, compost. These bins are easy to use, but when it comes to preparing the vermicompost the worms must be taken out from the compost by hand.

Forced migration of the worm from one part of the bin to another is done in "continuous" systems, named so because the system continuously provides vermicompost. Continuous vermicomposting bins or vertical bins use vertical stack layering which cause the worms to rise through the compost towards newly added organics to create a layer free of worms that is easier to work with. Continuous vermicomposting bins can also be horizontal.

Larger systems use rows or lines of hay raked together to dry before being raked into heaps. These heaps are called "windrows." The sheer size and wealth of organic material of the rows prevents the earthworms from leaving.

Start with a bin and add a bedding, consisting of damp newspaper, some soil, cardboard, sawdust, or moss—or better yet, a combination of all. This is a mostly carbon bedding. Carbon in these forms takes longer to break down. This bedding acts as a foundation which helps deal with smells from food atrophy in the organics. Bedding should be kept damp if accessible in your system. The idea is that this is a near pure carbon base.

This greenhouse grow is organic and the grower is doing incredibly well, but you can see some problems; nutrient disorders, longer internode lengths and lower bud production than might be expected. This is actually typical of what many organic growers experience.

The more worms the better. Get as many as you can. There is a saying that you can never be short of them in vermicomposting and this is true. Obviously, use the maximum you think your system can take. Weigh the amount of worms used. Worms can deal with half their weight per day, so naturally, the worms are able to use half their weight in organic feeds per day. Your scraps can fuel them. If the worms are really active then they can consume their own body weight per day or more. Shade the bin. Do not add more scraps until the old scraps have been used up.

Vermicompost bins work best at temperature between 55–80 °F. Red wigglers will survive in temperatures from 40–90°F. Less than 40°F can be enough to kill vermicomposting worms. Bring the bin inside if the temperature drops below 40 °F.

Generally, bedding layers are put down before the organic feeds are added. This feed is then covered with another bedding layer. As the older organics break down, new organics are added to the bedding and more organic feeds are placed on top with another bedding layer. Some growers prefer to just keep the top bedding layer recycled by either lifting or opening it up and inserting the new organic feed in underneath.

Added vermicomposting organics should be balanced with the consumption rates of the worms. This is to prevent a rotting decomposition of the added organics before the worms reach them. Fruit skins are not recommended for vermicomposting unless you know the fruit has been grown organically without insecticides. Introducing insecticide residues to the bin will exterminate the worms. Fruit skins are generally acidic and so are only to be used in smaller quantities and with other organic feeds. Vermicomposting pH is maintained exactly as you would when growing an organic plant, adding and subtracting pH levels with other organic foods to create a balanced pH of 7.

Worms will not reduce bone or anything artificial. Meats are fine but if not balanced correctly will only attract unwanted pests outdoors. Avoid adding as much oil as possible.

Make sure aeration is good and that the bin does not become anaerobic.

Some bad odors are not from anaerobic decomposition but from high levels of nitrogen. Adding carbon should reduce this. Flies should not be allowed to propagate in the container; get rid of them if they do. Ant infestations are hard to deal with without moving the compost elsewhere and getting rid of contaminated materials.

Natural pest control is very green. These are ladybugs in action. If you
have problems with aphids then ladybugs will consume them.

Humus

You might come across the term "humus" in organic growing or in the grow shop. Humus is essentially organic vegetable compost. Humification of organic matter in the soil occurs naturally all the time. It can contain carbohydrates, lignin, organic acids and compounds, proteins, resins, starches, sugars, and waxes.

Organic Weeding

No synthetics are used to control weeds in organic cultivation. Weeds are hand pulled or obstructed. Mulch can be effective, as can anything that prevents light from getting to the weeds. Tilling soil also helps to remove weeds.

Controlling Pests

In Chapter 13 we examine the various natural and friendly pest predators that can be used to combat unwanted garden infestations. Organic cultivators use exclusively predators to control pests. Farmers may rely on crop rotation, interplanting, and other plants to repel pests.

Organic Feeding Products

The range of organic feeding products vary from liquids to semisolid compounds. Fish, blood, and bone type granules are very popular mixtures. The liquids tend to be aimed at organic hydroponic growers, but any type of grow can use them. Along with worm vermicompost and compost there are organic soil stimulators available to help boost microbial activity.

Rules for Organic Growing

Rule #1 Throw away all synthetics and never buy them again
Rule #2 Conserve
Rule #3 Monitor your organics
Rule #4 Throw away toxic decomposition
Rule #5 Proactively work the garden
Rule #6 Excavate existing soil and replace with organics
Rule #7 Organic systems should be kept moist
Rule #8 Hand pull large weeds

6 | The Indoor Growing Environment

There are many ways to grow cannabis plants indoors. The two core methods are soil growing and hydroponics. The next three chapters deal with soil growing: from basic setups, to controlling the environment, to tending your plants throughout the life cycle, to advanced techniques. Although these chapters focus on indoor soil grow, the hints and tips provided can be used to improve plant health and growth in any growing environment. Chapter 10 is dedicated to hydroponics.

There are many ways to grow an indoor soil garden, ranging from basic setups to advanced setups. The most common basic indoor setups are:
- Soil growing
- Hydroponic growing

The most common advanced indoor setups are:
- Sea of Green (SOG) growing
- Screen of Green (ScrOG) growing
- Cabinet growing

The common advanced indoor setups are discussed in detail in Chapter 9. First, we will look at what all indoor growing setups have in common.

Lighting

Your choice of lighting is the second most important growing decision you will make next to selecting your strain. Lights come in all shapes and sizes, with varying levels of wattage and lumens. A full indoor lighting kit should contain the following items: bulb, reflector, ballast, timer, and electrical inputs/outputs.

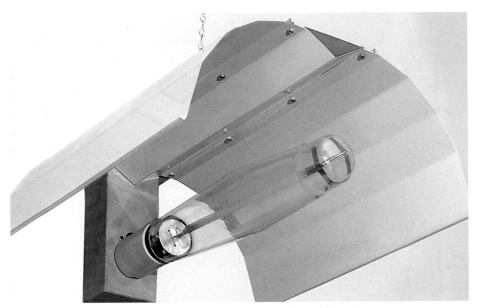

This is a typical HID light. There are three main parts
shown here; the reflector, the bulb and the socket.

Most lighting kits are open, meaning they have no glass cover or hood to shield the bulb. Instead, the bulb is fixed into a socket that is attached to the inside of the reflector and hangs directly underneath the reflector. That socket is in turn connected to the ballast, which can be either internal or external.[1] If external, there will be a cord leading to the ballast from the bulb's socket. If internal, the ballast will be attached directly to the bulb socket and may even support the reflector. The ballast plugs into a domestic light socket like the ones in your home. Some ballasts have built-in timers.

When purchasing a lighting system it is recommended that you look for a complete system and buy an extra bulb. Check to make sure that the lighting system meets safety regulations and has some sort of guarantee or warranty.

Color Bands and Plant Growth

When a beam of light is split by means of a prism or diffraction grating, it produces a number of color bands which represent the colors of the rainbow: red, orange, yellow, green, blue, indigo, and violet. The bands correspond to the frequencies emitted by the heated light source.

The electromagnetic spectrum is a term used to describe the distribution of electro-

This is the fourth and generally most expensive
part of an HID light system: the ballast.

magnetic radiation by reference to energy. The table on the next page roughly gives wavelengths, frequencies, and energies for different regions of the spectrum. You may want to refer back to these later if you are interested in analyzing your bulb's qualities. The bulb's packaging should have data on the bulb's use of the electromagnetic spectrum. Your bulb should mention wavelengths and frequencies somewhere between the infrared, visible, and ultraviolet regions. Each bulb manufacturer has different specifications with regards to the bulb's abilities to cast artificial light.

Light color depends on the light source. Light color is also a visual indicator that a number of different factors important to plant growth are present in the light. Artificial grow lights are designed to provide an intense and clean white light that meets certain color and temperature requirements so that the bulb can be classified as a "grow bulb."

The Correlated Color Temperature (CCT; the thermal temperature) of a light source is usually expressed in degrees kelvin (K). When certain basic elements that are used in light bulbs are heated, they start to glow. As the elements get hotter, they change color. This occurs within a certain range and peaks when the bulb is fully heated. At this peak, the color holds and this is the CCT rating of the bulb. Bulbs that have a CCT rating of 3,000 are referred to as "warm" bulbs. A CCT rating of 4,000 is a

SPECTRUM OF ELECTROMAGNETIC RADIATION

Region	Wavelength (Angstroms)	Wavelength (Centimeters)	Frequency (Hz)	Energy (EV)
Radio	109	>10	<3 x 109	<10-5
Microwave	109-106	10-0.01	3 x 109-3 x 1012	10-5-0.01
Infrared	106-7000	0.01-7 x 10-5	3 x 1012-4.3 x 1014	0.01-2
Visible	7000-4000	7 x 10-5-4 x 10-5	4.3 x 1014-7.5 x 1014	2-3
Ultraviolet	4000-10	4 x 10-5-10-7	7.5 x 1014-3 x 1017	3-103
X-rays	10-0.1	10-7-10-9	3 x 1017-3 x 1019	103-105
Gamma Rays	0.1	<10-9	>3 x 1019	>105

IMPACT OF LIGHT COLOR ON PLANT GROWTH

CCT in Kelvin (K)	Light Color	Effect
5000 to 8000	Deep Blue	Encourages excellent leaf and stem growth
4000 to 5000	Light Blue	Encourages good leaf and stem growth
4000	Neutral White	Promotes normal growth
3700 to 4000	Warm Neutral	Promotes rapid growth
3000 to 3700	Warmer yellow neutral	Highly active photosynthesis for all stages of growth
1500 to 3000	Hot orange or red	Promotes flowering

"neutral" bulb, and a 6,000 CCT bulb is a "cool" bulb. The color of the bulb at CCT is a combination of the many different colors being emitted by the hot elements in the bulb.

Although the CCT gives us an indication of the bulb's color temperature, it does not tell us much about how well each of the color bands are represented. For this we need to refer to the lamp's Color Rendering Index (CRI). This is done under laboratory conditions by comparing the bulb's CCT with a darker material at the same CCT. It is generally understood by the growing community that the higher the CRI rating of a bulb, the better the quality of color distribution.

Natural outdoor light measures around 5,500K for most of the daylight hours.

The next table shows the colors you will come across most often when using artificial light sources and the effect that each one has on cannabis plant growth.

Plants are green, which means they reflect green light. This is because cannabis, and most other plants, do not use green light for photosynthesis. This has to do with chlorophyll. High intensity discharge (HID) bulbs are designed to cast as much useable light as possible. There are two different types of HID grow lights that we will discuss in a moment. Each type is designed to lean towards casting a warm or a cool type of light. HID grow lights are the most common type of indoor lighting used by cannabis growers.

Basics of Photosynthesis

It is important for us to understand the basics of photosynthesis because it is at the heart of the cannabis plant's energy system. Plants are the only organisms with the biological ability to synthesize complex foods for themselves from simple substances.

Chlorophyll

Plants naturally produce chlorophyll, which gives them their green color. Chlorophyll is a group of magnesium-containing green pigments that act as an absorber of light energy for specific wavelengths. The plant converts this light energy into chemical energy.

The Process of Photosynthesis

Photosynthesis means "combining with light." Photosynthesis is a "reactant–product" process which occurs wherever chlorophyll is found in the plant, which is mostly in the leaves. The symbolic equation for photosynthesis is:

$6 CO_2 + 6 H_2O$ - sunlight & chlorophyll $- C6H12O6 + 6 O2$

If there is no light, there is no photosynthesis. At night, plants cease photosynthesis. If there are not enough nutrients then the plant will not produce chlorophyll and photosynthesis will cease. Temperatures are also important for photosynthesis. If the temperatures go out of the normal range for

Light will impact bud size with a strain that is cultivated under similar conditions. Your bud size will increase with better lights.

A cheaper solution may be to use fluorescents. You will still get results, but they may be of a diminished quality. These lights, however, are good for keeping clones or starting seedlings.

good cannabis plant growth then photosynthesis will slow down or even stop. See Chapter 7 for more on temperature.

Common Lighting Types
Domestic Lights

These are the lights you find in use around your house. They come in all sizes and generally range from between 15 and 150 watts. These lights are unsuitable for growing because of their low light intensity and poor CRI rating. Standard domestic bulbs have a CCT rating of about 2,700 K.

Fluorescent Tube Lights

These lights are the long, tube-shaped, lights commonly used in industrial and commercial buildings. They come in a variety of lengths and sizes, but 2 to 10 foot-long bulbs are the most common. They also range from between 10 and 300 watts. These lights are okay for growing but they provide a low light intensity and are difficult to set up properly. They are also not in the best light spectrum for the growth of cannabis plants because, like domestic lights, fluorescent tubes have poor CRI ratings.

Halogen Lights

Halogen lights are small and often used for flood lighting during the night. These lights can range from anywhere between 75 and 4,000 watts. Halogens get extremely hot and this creates a completely unsuitable condition for growing cannabis. They are not recommended because they can be dangerous for indoor growing use. They also have a low CRI rating. Halogens have a CCT rating of about 3,000 K.

Fluorescent White Tube Lights

Similar to fluorescent lights, fluorescent white tube[2] lights have a higher CRI rating. These lights do not range much above 100 watts and are only recommended as "cheap to buy and run" grow bulbs. They can, however, be invaluable for rooting clones and starting seeds. Fluorescent white tube lights are usually found in the following wattage levels: 10W, 30W, 60W and 100W. You should aim for 30W and above if you want to induce some form of floral development. Less than 30W lights are only sufficient for rooting cuttings and starting seedlings. Cool white fluorescents have a CCT rating of about 4,200 K.

Horticultural Lights

Commonly called HID (high intensity discharge) lights, professional horticultural lights are designed to promote indoor plant growth. These lights are available in kits complete with bulb, reflector, ballast, and timer. They also come in different wattage levels, shapes and sizes. If you want to grow good bud, you should use HID lighting. HID lights have three distinct subcategories: metal halide (MH), mercury vapor (MV), and high-pressure sodium (HPS).

Metal Halide (MH) and Mercury Vapor (MV) Lights

MH lights are HID lights that are used for the seedling and vegetative growth stages of your plant. They can also be used for flowering. They come in all shapes and sizes and range from 75 to 4,000 watts. These lights are very commonly used kits and are ideal for the indoor cannabis grower. MH lights mostly lean towards a blue color, meaning that the bulb is a "cool" type. Daylight MH lights have a CCT rating of about 5,500 K. Standard clear MH lights have a CCT rating of about 4,000 K. "Warm" MH lights also exist and have a CCT rating of about 3,200 K. Opt for the daylight halide, as it provides the best possible type of MH light for cannabis.

MV lights have been almost replaced by MH lights. If you have a choice between the two it is best to opt for the newer MH kits. MV has a tendency to be slightly out of the optimal spectrum range, being too blue.

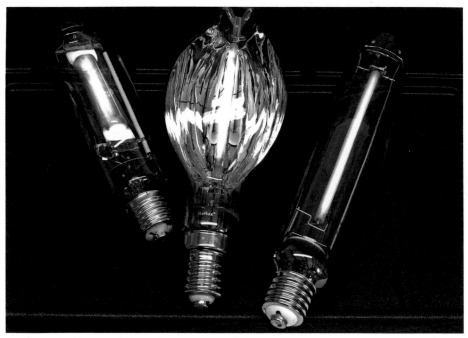

HID bulbs come in different shapes, sizes and wattages.
Here are a few of the different types.

High-Pressure Sodium (HPS) Lights

HPS is the lighting choice of many a cannabis cultivator. HPS lights come in all shapes and sizes and range from 75 to 4,000 watts. They are in the perfect spectrum for growing cannabis and come highly recommended, particularly for the flowering stage of the life cycle. HPS lights lean towards a blue color, meaning that the bulb is a "warm" type. High-pressure sodium bulbs have a CCT rating of about 2,200 K.

Wattage and Lumens

HID lights can range from anywhere between 75 and 4,000 watts.[3] In general, the stronger the wattage, the more light the bulb will produce. However, we must also consider another factor—lumens. Lumens are the correct way of measuring how much light per square foot a bulb emits. Lumens and wattage go hand in hand, but can vary to a large extent between systems. In general, the better the lighting kit, the more lumens it will cast. Lumens have more to do with the design of the light than the wattage of the light itself. Some 600-watt lights may emit the same lumens as a 400-watt light. The sample comparison table on page 138 shows the lumens emitted by four different lamps. Of note, the two HPS lamps both use the same wattage, but cast different levels of lumens.

Lumens and Marijuana Growing

You are probably wondering: How many lumens do I need? This depends on three things:

1. How much you want to spend
2. How many plants you have
3. The size of your grow area

You never want to use less than 2,500 lumens, even for one plant. In general, one light that casts 45,000 lumens is enough to cover a grow space of about 3 feet by 3 feet. This is quite an average space and you'll probably get anything between one to 12 Indica plants in that area. Again, we must keep in mind the strain that we're growing. One large Sativa plant can cover a nine square foot grow area in no time. Short Indica plants are different. If you really want to pump up your plants, then you could consider a lamp that casts 100,000 lumens or more. If you have a big grow area then you might consider two lamps that cast 100,000 lumens each. It's all relative to how much you want to grow and the size of your grow room.

Let's say that you would like to grow four Indica/Sativa hybrid plants. What you should aim for is a light that casts 45,000 lumens. This means you should buy a 400-watt HID system. If you want to pump up your available light to around 60,000 lumens, you should buy a 600-watt HID system. If your area is bigger still, you might need two or more 600-watt HID lights to achieve this.

HIDs are usually suspended from the ceiling by chains, or fixed to a light rail. This one is hanging from chains. Securing your HID is very important; don't skimp on it.

Reflectors come in many shapes and sizes. This reflector allows the
light to be cast very widely over the garden.

HID BULB BRAND COMPARISON

Brand	Make	Category	Watts	Initial Lumens	Par Watts*	CCT
Argosun	Classic	MH	1000	117,000	581	~3K
Hortilux	Super HPS TM EN	HPS	1000	145,000	535	~2K
Sunmaster	Warm Deluxe	MH	1100	133,000	505	~3K
Sunmaster	Warm Deluxe	MH	1000	117,000	470	~3K
Sunmaster	Warm Deluxe	MH	1000	117,000	470	~3K
Sunmaster	Natural Deluxe	MH	1000	117,000	442	~4K
Sunmaster	Warm Deluxe	MH	1000	110,000	441	~3K
Sunmaster	Natural Deluxe	MH	1000	110,000	416	~4K
Sunmaster	Cool Deluxe	MH	1000	80,000	340	~5K
Hortilux	Super HPS TM EN	HPS	430	58,500	220	~2K
Sunmaster	Super HPS Deluxe	HPS	600	85,000	205	~2K
Hortilux	Super HPS Deluxe	HPS	430	58,500	220	~2K
Sunmaster	Super HPS De;uxe	HPS	600	85,000	205	~2K
Hortilux	Super HPS TM EN	HPS	400	55,000	205	~2K
Sunmaster	Warm Deluxe	MH	400	40,000	159	~3K
Sunmaster	Natural Deluxe	MH	400	40,000	151	~4K
Sunmaster	Cool Deluxe	MH	400	32,500	138	~5K
Sunmaster	Natural Deluxe	MH	400	36,000	136	~4K
Sunmaster	Super HPS Deluxe	HPS	400	55,000	132	~2K
Sunmaster	Warm Deluxe	MH	250	22,000	87	~3K
Sunmaster	Natural Deluxe	MH	250	23,000	87	~4K
Sunmaster	Warm Deluxe	MH	250	21,500	85	~3K
Sunmaster	Cool Deluxe	MH	250	19,000	81	~5K
Sunmaster	Natural Deluxe	MH	250	21,000	80	~4K
Hortilux	Super HPS Deluxe	HPS	250	32,000	77	~2K

This chart was compiled by a grower called Nietzche.
*Photosynthetically active radiation (PAR)

The General Illumination Formula

You need roughly 50 watts of HPS or MH light per square foot of your grow area. The simple formula looks like this:

250W HID = 2' x 2' area
400W HID = 3' x 3' area
600W HID = 3.5' x 3.5' area
1kW HID = 4' x 4' area

This simple watts-per-square-foot calculation assumes that each square foot of space receives the same lumens, but in reality bulbs do not cast lumens equally to all areas. We need to include depth in our calculation. As light travels away from its source, its intensity diminishes by a factor of one quarter each time the distance traveled doubles.

There's nothing wrong with using a 1,000-watt HID light on a few plants, or even one plant—they will grow bigger and better for it—but you need to make sure that you choose genetics that can use all the available light. Lighting overkill occurs when a single strong HID light is used to grow a genetically poor yielding plant. You will find that a single 400-watt HID may have been more than enough to grow the plant to optimal maturity. Most strains available from reputable breeders are high-yielding plants, which is why growers can sometimes use a single 1,000-watt light and pull two pounds or more of bud from the one plant.

The other issue is cost. Do you really want to spend all that money on lighting and electricity? HID lights range in price from anywhere between $220 and $700 for a full kit. A 600-watt HPS kit should cost about $250: money well spent if you want great plants with big buds.

Over time, you will understand more about grow rooms and how to light them properly. With experience, you should be able to tell intuitively which light suits your needs. As a general rule, when in doubt buy a 400-watt HPS or better. Even a 250-watt HPS can get you good-size buds, but going below that mark will yield you less than average results. Most growers use a 600-watt HPS for better results. 1,000-watt lights provide the best yields indoors but consume more electricity.

Questions to Ask When Buying a Lighting Kit

What type(s) of HID/horticultural light will you use? Some growers will use a MH setup for seedlings and vegetative growth and an HPS setup for flowering. If you can only afford one setup, we recommend HPS lighting since it is best for flowering—the stage when cannabis produces the all-important bud.
Is the light kit certified; does it come with a warranty?
Is the light kit air-cooled?[4]

Remember that your plants can burn if placed too close to your lights. How will the system be supported? Will you use a light stand or suspend your lighting from the ceiling?

Do the electrical fittings suit your needs? Will they plug straight into your system or will you need an adapter or an extension cord? What wattage and lumens can you use with the kit?

What to Look for When Buying a Lighting Kit

Water-cooled light system—these inventions have been around for a while but have not caught on because they require a bit of work to maintain. A constant pump of cool water must be circulated into and out of the light system.

Good lights should be air-cooled. Some may even have built-in fans. Lights that are air-cooled tend to last longer and do not heat up your grow area as much. If your light is not air-cooled, then you will have to include an air vent and fan in your grow room to keep the temperatures under control.

LAMP EFFICIENCY IN LUMENS

Brand	Make	Category	Watts	Initial Lumens	Par Watts	CCT
Hortilux	Super HPS TM EN	HPS	1000	145,000	535	~2K
GE	Lucalox® Standard	HPS	1000	140,000		~2.1
Sunmaster	Warm Deluxe	MH	1100	133,000	505	~3K
Philips	Son Standard	HPS	1000	130000		~1.95K
Philips	Son T	HPS	1000	130000		~1.95K
Osram Sylvania	Lumalux®Standby	HPS	1000	127,000		~2.1K
Sunmaster	Warm Deluxe	MH	1000	117,000	470	~3K
Sunmaster	Warm Deluxe	MH	1000	117,000	470	~3K
Sunmaster	Natural Deluxe	MH	1000	117,000	442	~4K
ArgoSun	MS	MH	1000	117,000	581	~3.2K
GE	High Output (HO)	MH	1000	115,000		~3.8K
Osram Sylvania	Super Metalarc®	MH	1000	115,000		~4K
Sunmaster	Warm Deluxe	MH	1000	110,000	441	~3K
Sunmaster	Natural Deluxe	MH	1000	110,000	416	~4K
GE	High Output (HO)	MH	1000	110,000		~3.4K
GE	Multi-Vapor® Standard	MH	1000	105,000		~4K
Philips	Son T Plus	HPS	600	90,000		~1.95K
Sunmaster	Super HPS Deluxe	HPS	600	85,000	205	~2K
Sunmaster	Cool Deluxe	MH	1000	80,000	340	~5K
Hortilux	Super HPS TM EN	HPS	430	58,500	220	~2K
Hortilux	Super HPS TM EN	HPS	400	55,000	205	~2K
Sunmaster	Super HPS Deluxe	HPS	400	55,000	132	~2K

Chart continues on next page

LAMP EFFICIENCY IN LUMENS *CONTINUED*

Brand	Make	Category	Watts	Initial Lumens	Par Watts	CCT
Philips	Son T Agro	HPS	400	55,000		~2.05K
Philips	Son T Plus	HPS	400	55,000		~1.95K
Philips	Son Plus	HPS	400	54,000		~1.95K
GE	Lucalox® Standard	HPS	400	51,000		~2.2K
Philips	Son Standard	HPS	400	48,000		~1.95K
Philips	Son T	HPS	400	48,000		~1.95K
Osram Sylvania	Lumalux® Standby	HPS	400	47,500		~2.1K
GE	Extra High Output (XHO)	MH	400	44,000		~4K
GE	High Output (HO)	MH	400	41,000		~4K
Osram Sylvania	Compact Super Metalarc®	MH	400	41,000		~3.8K
Sunmaster	Warm Deluxe	MH	400	40,000	159	~3K
Sunmaster	Natural Deluxe	MH	400	40,000	151	~4K
ArgoSun	MS	MH	400	40,000		~3.2K
Sunmaster	Natural Deluxe	MH	400	36,000	136	~4K
GE	Multi -Vapor® Metal Halide Standard	MH	400	36,000		~4K
Sunmaster	Cool Deluxe	MH	400	32,500	138	~5K
Hortilux	Super H P S Deluxe	HPS	250	32,500	138	~5K
Sunmaster	Natural Deluxe	MH	250	23,000	87	~4K
Sunmaster	Warm Deluxe	MH	250	22,000	87	~3K
Sunmaster	Warm Deluxe	MH	250	21,500	85	~3K
Sunmaster	Natural Deluxe	MH	250	21,000	80	~4K
Sunmaster	Cool Deluxe	MH	250	19,000	81	~5K

This chart was compiled by a grower called Nietzche.

Most HID kits can only accommodate a specific wattage of bulb and a certain type of bulb. If you have a 600-watt HPS system, then you should only use 600-watt HPS bulbs. Some lighting kits include a switchable ballast. This means that you can use both MH and HPS lights with the system.

Also, there is such a thing as too much power. A 4,000-watt HID is overkill for any small grow room. A 1,000-watt bulb is the maximum wattage you should purchase for a small space. Use several 1,000-watt bulbs if you need more light. A 4,000-watt bulb can bleach cannabis and is very hot.

LAMP EFFICIENCY FOR MH AND HPS

Brand	Make	Category	Watts	Initial Lumens	Par Watts	CCT
Argosun	Classic	MH	1000	117,000	581	~3K
Sunmaster	Warm Deluxe	MH	1100	133,000	505	~3K
Sunmaster	Warm Deluxe	MH	1000	117,000	470	~3K
Sunmaster	Natural Deluxe	MH	1000	117,000	442	~4K
Argosun	MS	MH	1000	117,000		~3.2K
GE	High Output (HO)	MH	1000	115,000		~3.8K
Osram Sylvania	Super Metalarc®	MH	1000	115,000		~4K
Sunmaster	Warm Deluxe	MH	1000	110,000	441	~3K
Sunmaster	Natural Deluxe	MH	1000	110,000	416	~4K
GE	High Output (HO)	MH	1000	110,000		~3.4K
GE	Multi-Vapor® Standard	MH	1000	105,000		~4K
Sunmaster	Cool Deluxe	MH	1000	80,000	340	~5K
GE	Extra High Output (XHO)	MH	400	44,000		~4K
GE	High Output (HO)	MH	1000	110,000		~3.4K
GE	High Output (HO)	MH	400	41,000		~3.4K
Osram Sylvania	Compact Super Metalarc®	MH	400	41,000		~3.8K
Sunmaster	Warm Deluxe	MH	400	40,000	159	~3K
Sunmaster	Natural Deluxe	MH	400	40,000	151	~4K
Argosun	MS	MH	400	40,000		~3.2K
Sunmaster	Natural Deluxe	MH	400	36,000	136	~4K
GE	Multi-Vapor® Standard	MH	400	36,000		~4K
Sunmaster	Cool Deluxe	MH	400	32,500	138	~5K
Sunmaster	Natural Deluxe	MH	250	23,000	87	~4K
Sunmaster	Warm Deluxe	MH	250	22,000	87	~3K
Sunmaster	Warm Deluxe	MH	250	21,500	85	~3K
Sunmaster	Natural Deluxe	MH	250	21,000	80	~4K
Sunmaster	Cool Deluxe	MH	250	19,000	81	~5K
Hortilux	Super HPS TM EN	HPS	1000	145,000	535	~2K
GE	Lucalox® Standard	HPS	1000	140,000		~2.1K
Philips	Son Standard	HPS	1000	130,000		~1.95K
Philips	Son T	HPS	1000	130,000		~1.95K
Osram Sylvania	Lumalux® Standby	HPS	1000	127,000		~2.1K
Philips	Son T Plus	HPS	600	90,000		~1.95K

Chart continues on next page

Brand	Make	Category	Watts	Initial Lumens	Par Watts	CCT
Sunmaster	Super HPS Deluxe	HPS	600	85,000	205	~2K
Hortilux	Super HPSTM EN	HPS	430	58,500	220	~2K
Hortilux	Super HPSTM EN	HPS	400	55,000	205	~2K
Sunmaster	Super HPS Deluxe	HPS	400	55,000	132	~2K
Philips	Son T Agro	HPS	400	55,000		~2.05K
Philips	Son T Plus	HPS	400	55,000		~1.95K
Philips	Son Plus	HPS	400	54,000		~1.95K
GE	Lucalox® Standard	HPS	400	51,000		~2.2K
Philips	Son Standard	HPS	400	48,000		~1.95K
Philips	Son T	HPS	400	48,000		~1.95K
Osram Sylvania	Lumalux® Standby	HPS	400	47,500		~2.1K
Hortilux	Super HPS Deluxe	HPS	250	32,000	77	~2K

This chart was compiled by a grower called Nietzsche.

SAMPLE COMPARISON OF WATTAGE AND LUMENS

Lamp Type	Watts	Lumens
MV	175	8,000
MH	400	55,000*
HPS	600	85,000
HPS	600	55,000*

* The 400-watt MH system and the 600-watt HPS system both cast the same lumens. The 600-watt HPS lamp casting 85,000 lumens is by far the best of the four options for cannabis cultivation.

How to Get the Most from Your Lighting System

Reflectors do exactly what their name implies—they reflect light. Growers use reflectors to ensure maximum lumens coverage over their plants. Basically, when light bounces off a reflector it is directed towards your plants, which absorb most of this light. Reflectors should be either white or made of polished metal. Some reflectors have a green plastic film covering the insides. Remove this, if possible.

Some grow guides mention aluminum foil as a useful material to aid grow room reflection. Some have even mentioned using it to cover up anything that isn't reflective like electrical cords, sockets, reflectors, and pots. Aluminum foil is

Light height will have to be adjusted as the plants grow taller. This will depend largely on genetics so you need to get plants that can grow in your space.

actually a very poor reflector, highly heat conductive, and very dangerous to use in a grow room. Aluminum foil only has 30 to 60 percent reflectivity at best, raises the temperature of the item on which it is used (the reflector, pot lid, electrical cord, wall, etc.), and can burn easily. It is also hard to keep clean and tears easily. Avoid using aluminum foil. Growers who line the walls with aluminum foil will eventually find the place falling down around them. If you have no option but to use aluminum foil, then it is suggested that you use the dull side rather than the shiny side. In the meantime, make sure that you place an order for a cheap can of flat white paint that will give you almost 99 percent reflectivity for a couple of years.

There are many lights available for sodium bulbs that do not necessarily need to come from a grow shop and they are just as efficient.

White-colored material is best for reflecting light: not shiny, glossy white, just plain matte white. A white wall will reflect more light than a mirror or foil. Many growers paint the walls of their grow space white. Others line their grow areas with Mylar, a substance that looks like a thick tinfoil sheet. Mylar is, in fact, very popular in cannabis grow rooms. Most DIY and hardware stores sell Mylar in sheets.

It is also recommended that you keep a spare bulb on hand at all times in case the other bulb dies.[5] It's no good going to the local hardware store only to find that they are out of the bulb you need. You risk leaving your plants without light for a long time.

It is also wise to remember that plants need water and lights use electricity. When mixed, these factors can be extremely dangerous. Be safe and wise and keep your plants and any liquids away from all electrical outlets.

Adjusting Your Lights

If you have a good stand or light support, you should be able to lower or raise your light to accommodate your plants at various stages of the life cycle. You should note that the closer your lighting is to the plants, the more light they will receive. However, get too close and you risk burning your leaves. To see if you are too close, try this simple, common sense test: if you can hold your hand under the light and not feel discomfort, then your plants should do okay. If you feel discomfort, so too will your plants. Use common sense and adjust your lights accordingly.

Some cannabis plants can grow as much as an inch a day. Pure Sativa varieties in particular can triple in height between the start and end of flowering. A four-foot Sativa bush can suddenly turn into a twelve-foot monster in a few months. You need to monitor growth carefully to ensure that your plant doesn't get too close to the light. If your plants do suffer a burn, use clippers to remove the burnt areas and either adjust your lights or cut back your plants to maintain a safe, healthy distance. Tying your plants back may be another option if you have out-grown your space and don't want to clip the plants because of flowering.

Your plants need all the light they can get during the vegetative growth stage. Leave your lights on 24 hours a day and enjoy watching your plants as they grow. During the flowering stage you will shift to the 12/12 light cycle, which is discussed in detail in Chapter 7.

24/0 and 18/6—The Vegetative Photoperiod

Cannabis is a light-demanding plant. Professional growers keep the light on their plants using the 24/0 photoperiod for this reason. Plants that grow under 24/0 flourish and do not need a quantity of darkness in order to rest and perform photosynthesis properly. Plants that are grown in optimal conditions under the 24/0 light regime grow vigorously and the benefits of a 24/0 photoperiod can be seen actively in the results. More nodes are formed, more branches are created, leaf numbers increase, and the plant is growing at its finest.

The walls of this grow space are lined with mylar to reflect the light from the walls. This is a very dense cluster of bud without any visible internode gaps developing on the colas.

Some growers opt to use 18/6 as their photoperiod. This is an 18 hours of light, six hours of darkness light regime. Under these conditions the plant will grow quite naturally but not as vigorously as the 24/0 photoperiod.

The 18/6 photoperiod expels 3/4 the amount of light that a 24/0 photoperiod does. Although this does not mean that a plant produces 1/4 less leaves, branches, and nodes under the 18/6 photoperiod, it certainly does show the correlation between light and cannabis growth. As we have said already, cannabis is a light-demanding plant. There are no problems associated with 24/0 and although some have attributed cannabis sexual dysfunction (the hermaphrodite condition) to the 18/6 photoperiod, these problems are actually the result of heat stress.

A 24/0 photoperiod requires that your grow room temperature be kept well-monitored. The 18/6 option is cheaper to run. You use a quarter less electricity and this will have an impact on your electricity bill. Also the 18/6 photoperiod will generally extend the bulb's lifespan. During the 6 hours of darkness the grow room is allowed to cool down for this period but a well maintained, good grow room setup should not require a cooling down period.

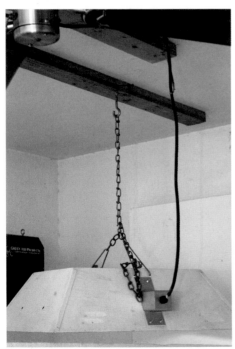

This is a single chain suspended light. You can use two chains for extra security.

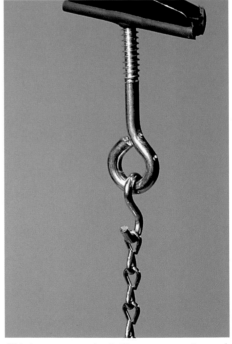

This is a screw eye hook. There are many types of hooks: Cup hooks, S hooks, double hooks, etc.

This is an automated light rail that moves two lights around an entire grow. The advantage of this is that this grow would require four or more lights but here they are just using two.

Light rail combined with air-cooling means the lights can be moved closer to the plants.

24/0 and 18/6 both share the same problem, though. Once you start the photoperiod you should keep it that way, especially when the plants near maturity—the pre-flowering phase. An irregular photoperiod can cause more males than females to develop. It can also cause sexual dysfunction to appear.[6] Whether you choose 24/0 or 18/6 as your vegetative photoperiod, try to keep that photoperiod until your plants are mature enough to express their sex.

Electrical Costs

Everyone who starts out using indoor grow bulbs will probably ask how much they cost to run. The answer to this is—it depends on how much your electrical supply company charge per watt or unit of electricity used. There are also times in the day when electricity is cheaper or more expensive to use. In general, one unit of electricity is measured at about 1,000-watts per hour. 1,000-watts per hour usually works out at about 10 cents, but can be cheaper or more expensive than this. Check your electricity bill for the correct price per unit. So, in our example:

1kW x 24 hours = 1kW x 0.10 x 24 = $2.40 per day = $16.00 per week or $67.20 per month.

A four month, 1,000-watt grow could cost up to $268.00. Average growers using the right genetics yield about 20 ounces from a 1kW single bulb. Experienced growers can go as high as 40 per 1kW bulb. Even though the cost of electricity may seem high, the end results easily justify the cost.

Advanced Lighting

For those of you who do not wish to pursue lighting in greater detail—including the mechanics and physics of how lighting works—then you can move on to the next chapter, as this section will focus on more sophisticated concepts that are relative to growers who maintain several lights or who wish to cultivate a deeper understanding of electromagnetic energy and how to handle it.

Technology has taken growing to new levels. This is a water-cooled light. Water is being pumped around the light to keep it cool so that plants can be closer to it.

The physicist James Clerk Maxwell (1831–1879) successfully unified electrical currents and the effects of magnetism together as a single force called electromagnetism, which can be described as a field throughout all of space-time that can apply force to matter. This field is subject to disturbances like ripples in a pond. These disturbances, depending on the different forms of the waves in space-time, can produce artifacts such as light waves, radio waves, or gamma rays.

By heating a flammable substance to combustion, we produce light waves. By encasing these flames in a clear container that could withstand the heat we have produced our first type of ancient, man-made lighting.

This type of man-made lighting has improved. Machinery can generate light from electricity. These mechanisms can be constructed on the small scale so that the needed components fit into smaller spaces such as a domestic incandescent light source or even a light-emitting diode (LED). Any type of man-made lighting that uses electricity is called a lamp.[7]

The two most common types of modern grow lamps are HIDs and fluorescents.

This is an air-cooled light. The entire bulb is enclosed in the light so that heat can be extracted from the light completely. Plants can get really close to this light.

How HID Works

HIDs are regulated by ballasts. The ballast can be internal or external. Ballasts utilize, convert and run electrical power to the HID lamp.

The Ballast Efficacy Factor (BEF) is used to gauge the light output from power input. The efficiency of the system is measured in lumens per watt (LPW). The Ballast Factor (BF) is a ratio based on measuring the output between different ballasts using a similar lamp. High BFs usually reduce bulb life when compared to average BFs, but low BFs are also known to reduce bulb life. The three main types of ballasts are electronic, hybrid, and magnetic ballasts.

A HID lamp is designed to create an electrical arc discharge inside an arc tube made from fused quartz or fused alumina that contains a gas, housed inside the bulb and electrically regulated by a ballast. One could imagine a bulb inside a bulb without a closed loop filament, but with two tungsten electrodes that will allow an arc of electricity to occur between them. Some HID types only have a single glass tube while others have also an inner glass tube.

The glass tube in the HID, usually made from translucent aluminum oxide (alumina), is flooded with gas which is used to ignite the lamp while metals are heated to produce a specific band of light, evaporate, and become glowing plasma. HID systems include high pressure sodium (HPS; CRI 22-75), low pressure sodium (LPS; CRI 0), mercury vapor (MV; CRI 15-55) and metal halide (MH; CRI 65-90).

The HID manufacturing process. Notice the glass torches in the bottom left.

The lamp is powered by a continuous AC from the ballast. The light from the lamp is mercury sodium emitted light. The sodium light is the strongest release in a HID. This is called the D-line emission.

HID lights, when faulty or damaged, but still working, can cause problems such as sunburn or injury to the eye. For this reason, lamps should checked regularly for damage.[8] This problem can easily be solved by ensuring that you buy a HID of the self-extinguishing type. These bulbs will turn off either instantly or within 15 minutes of fracturing.

LPSs are not efficient for growing. MV lamps are essentially replaced by HPS or MH lamps.

How HPS works

The sodium in HPS does not mean that mercury has been completely replaced, as HPS lamps contain amounts of mercury, sodium, and xenon gas for starting, which produces a white blue or dim pink radiance, later turning orange, as the lamp's heat increases. What is happening here is that some gases are heating up more quickly than others before they reach their maximum temperatures, producing the intended consistent spectrum of light.

How you shape your garden and suspend your lights is up to you.
This is a fairly standard HID to plant distance.

This photograph demonstrates how the inverse square law applies to light dispersal. You can almost see how the light creates a projected shape onto the flowering canopy below.

This photograph demonstrates the same dispersal only this time onto plants in vegetative growth. Look at how these plants are virtually climbing upwards in real-time.

HPS lamps are very efficient light sources. Outside of growing, you may recognize them from street lamp lighting. Their photopic lighting conditions range between 100 lm/W and 150 lm/W.

In the 1980s, some HPS lamps underwent a newer form of high pressure sodium called White SON. White SON's Correlated Color Temperature is 2,700K. White SON has a Color Rendering Index of 85.

Mercury, when blended with an alloy (a substance composed of two or more metals, or of a metal or metals with a nonmetal, intimately mixed, as by fusion or electrode-position) or another metal, produces an amalgam (an alloy of mercury with another metal or metals) of sodium and mercury that produces the vapor for the arc. The power provided determines the temperature of the amalgam. Higher temperature correlates to higher pressure. This process results in a stable operational lamp.

Unstable conditions result from catastrophic failures. If there is no electrical power, then there is no current and the lamp will extinguish slowly. If the vapor is used up, then the amalgam has evaporated and the lamp is running at an extremely low level of intensity and will eventually extinguish. If too much power is used, the lamp will blow in this high-current state due to the runaway effect of the increase in current and the decrease in the lamp's resistance to this higher current.

Soil

Soil comes in many types and varieties. As you gain growing experience, you will learn to add various ingredients to your soil in order to improve plant growth. The cannabis plant will grow long, winding roots into the soil. These roots absorb water and other minerals from the soil to promote plant growth. The soil also goes through dry periods when you don't water your plant or when the plant has absorbed most of the water. During these dry periods, air is allowed to creep between the soil particles, allowing the roots to breathe.

Please note that you should NEVER bring natural outdoor soil into an indoor grow space. This is because the soil will contain bugs and pests that could compromise your grow. Always buy your soil from a gardening shop. Soil should be the cheapest part of your grow.

There are three main factors to consider when selecting the right soil: pH, nutrients, and composition.

A handheld digital pH and
EC reader combined.

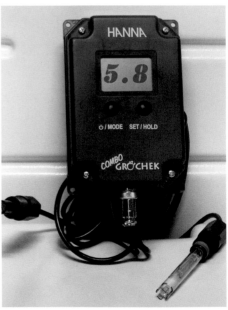

This reader monitors both pH and environmental
control or temperature.

Many nutrients come in packs, such as A and B formulas. Instructions for mixing are usually on the label.

pH

pH measures the levels of acidity and alkalinity in the soil. The pH scale runs from 1 to 14, with 7 being neutral, 0 very acidic, and 14 very alkaline. Cannabis plants like a neutral pH of 7. When choosing your soil you should be looking to achieve a pH of 7 (it should be clearly marked on the bag). Going above or below this mark can create problems for your plant during growth. Small pH meters can be also bought in most gardening shops and used to measure and monitor the overall pH of your soil.

Nutrients

The three major plant nutrients, or macronutrients, found in soil are nitrogen, phosphorous, and potassium: NPK, for short. NPK can come in two forms—either premixed into the soil or as a stand-alone fertilizer (usually in a bottle). The percentage of each nutrient should be clearly labeled on the packaging, in the following manner: 20:20:20. This indicates 20 percent N, 20 percent P, and 20 percent K. The remaining 40 percent are other elements that make up the soil. This ratio can vary among different nutrient and soil brands, so you need to understand which nutrients cannabis requires, and in what amounts, during the various stages of the life cycle.

Cannabis plants like high levels of N and moderate level of P and K during vegetative growth. You should select a soil that that has all three. When choosing a chemical fertilizer you need a mixture with high N, and P and K levels that are equal to or lower than N. Any of the following combinations would be suitable: 12:12:12, 20:20:20, 12:6:6, or 18:4:5. The 12:12:12 and 20:20:20 are best.

During flowering, cannabis needs a higher level of P so you should choose your soil and/or fertilizers accordingly. Since the plants are usually not transplanted between vegetative growth and flowering, you must plan to adjust the nutrient levels for flowering.[9]

Composition

Ideally, your soil will have a balanced consistency: not too moist, not too dry. This will allow the roots to absorb the required amounts of both water and oxygen. The packaging should indicate whether the soil is wet or dry, and you should aim for a balance between the two. Wet soil will sometimes cause plant damage by blocking off airflow to the roots. Dry soil may dry out too quickly, starving your roots of moisture. Try to find a soil that is loose and feels fine, but slightly heavy in your hands. Do not buy anything that is hard and bulky or soft and weightless. Aim for the middle ground: a balanced composition using a mix of the soil types below.

Common Soil Types

There are many types of soil mediums available and we will briefly describe the more common types. Marijuana can be grown in most of these soil types. We have indicated where potential problems could occur.

Clay

Clay is a stiff, tenacious, fine-grained earth consisting of hydrated aluminosilicates that become flexible when water is added. Marijuana roots don't really like clay. Clay can rarely be used on its own to grow cannabis. It is commonly mixed with other soil types to create a medium suitable for cannabis growth.

Humus

Humus is the organic constituent of soil, formed by the decomposition of plant materials, and can be bought in bags at local gardening stores. Most of these products claim to be free of bugs and other living matter, but sometimes this is not 100 percent true. Don't be surprised if you find a worm or green fly in the package. Humus is also sometimes known as compost, but compost is the final mixture of manure (which is of organic origin), loam soil, and some other media, with added organic matter. Humus is that added organic matter.

Sand and Silts

Sand soils can be pure sand or a mixture of sand and soil. The problem with sandy soil is that it drains water and minerals out too quickly. It is a very dry soil and is not suitable for the cannabis grower's needs.

Silt soils are nearly the same as sand soils, except they have a consistency more like clay and are darker in color. Silts hold nutrients well but do not hold water very well. Like sands, they are prone to quick drainage. Sands and silts are rarely used on their own to grow cannabis and are mostly mixed with other soil types.

Loam

Loam tends to be a mix of all of the above. The composition of the mix should be stated on the bag. In fact, in most cases, normal soil purchased in shops has humus, sand, silt and clay already mixed in. When you buy a bag of soil it is nearly always going to be a loam. Loam is a very fertile soil composed chiefly of clay, sand and humus, and is highly recommended for your grow.

Perlite and Vermiculite

One type of artificial medium on the market is called perlite. It's a good medium but doesn't come with any nutrients and generally needs to be mixed with

This is a typical bag of soil found in most grow stores. The contents are written on the front. Check the contents as well as the NPK values.

There are many brands of soil out there. Choose one with a balanced NPK unless your requirements are more specific.

Perlite is distinguishable by
its color and texture alone.

A bag of peat moss.

another soil type. vermiculite is another product that should be treated the same
way. Perlite and vermiculite are also called "inert" soils because they do not contain any nutrients. In fact, vermiculite is processed mica—a naturally occurring
mineral. Mix them well with soil if it's your first time using them. Begin with one-
part substrates for every four parts of soil. With a bit of experience, you should
be able to control the mixture ratios, as high as a 1:1 ratio. Pure vermiculite
mixtures or pure perlite mixtures do not retain moisture very well and thus can
only really be used in pure format as a substrate support for hydroponic systems,
which we will explain in Chapter 10.

Moss
Sphagnum and peat moss are the two most common moss type substrates that
you will come across on the market. This moss is gathered in bogs and dried
out into green, gray, brown, and black masses. It is then compressed into blocks
and is used as a substrate by gardeners for its ability to absorb and retain
nutrients. Moss tends to break down very quickly after successive watering
though, and this may require you to add more moss to your mix before the end
of harvest.

Buying a substrate is often the best way to be sure that your soil does not contain any parasites and is clean to use. Most soil substrates are heated to kill bacteria and parasites.

Mixing Soils and Soil Ratios

There is no perfect soil mix for cannabis plants. This is because all strains are different. Some cannabis strains prefer lots of nutrients. Others do not because they burn easily. Obviously, a less nutrient-holding soil mixture is preferable for the plants that burn easily. Here is a list of loam soil mixes to suit different plant needs.

Strains that require high levels of nutrients:
      1. NPK loam soil (20:20:20)
      2. Moss
      3. pH up

Mix the soil and moss at a 3:1 ratio. Add pH to balance soil to 7. The high NPK ratio of the loam and added moss makes this a strong nutrient-retaining soil mixture.

Strains that require normal levels of nutrients:
      1. NPK loam soil (10:10:10)
      2. Perlite or vermiculite

Mix the soil and perlite/vermiculite at a 4:1 ratio. The average NPK ratio of the loam and added perlite makes this a good nutrient-retaining soil mixture.

Strains that do not require high levels of nutrients:
1. NPK loam soil (5:5:5)
2. Sand
3. Perlite or vermiculite

Mix the soil, sand, and perlite/vermiculite at a 1:1:1 ratio. This soil mix does not hold minerals or water very well. This is good for a plant that does not need lots of nutrients, but will require more frequent watering.

All soil mixtures can be changed to suit your plants' needs. In this section, we have looked at soils without focusing much on nutrient ratios or how the nutrients themselves work. Even though the above soil mixtures contain nutrients, they should never be counted on to feed your plants throughout the life cycle. To maintain the nutrient balance over time you must add nutrients to our mix. We will look at this in detail in Chapter 7.

Understanding the NPK Ratio

It is important to understand the NPK ratio that appears on soil packs, fertilizer packs, and nutrient bottles. Consider a soil mixture like the following:
1. NPK loam soil (20:10:10)
2. Vermiculite

You would mix 4 parts loam to 1 part vermiculite to create a medium for a plant that needs just above normal amounts of nutrients. Instead of using a balanced 10:10:10, we have gone for the 20:10:10 because we need that little bit more nitrogen. Again, 20:10:10 simply stands for 20 percent N, 10 percent P and 10 percent K. If we add them we get 20+10+10, or 40 percent nutrients. The remaining 60 percent is made up of soil particles, or, in bottle foods, water, unless otherwise stated on the packaging.

Pots

Pots come in all shapes and sizes. Marijuana plants are best kept in large pots (1.5 to 3-gallon pots) because cannabis grows long roots. You are better off buying a pot that has perforations (holes) at the bottom. Perforated pots should rest in small dishes (you should be able to buy these at the same time you purchase your pots). When you water your plants, some of the water may drain down through the soil

A collection of plastic pots of various shapes and sizes.

and come out through the perforations into the dishes. The dishes should be emptied to avoid water spills, which can happen if you add too much water. Keep in mind that water on the floor can also be an electrical hazard.

Instead of using dishes you could use trays. Trays are more professional and can hold reserve water that is later soaked up by the roots, but are a lot harder to empty if you have a spill. Although perforations help to prevent over-watering, you should note that water can wash away some of the nutrients in your soil. Over-watering can cost you time, waste nutrients, and may even kill your plants. Water responsibly.

More advanced growers use pots that don't contain perforations. This is because experienced growers don't overwater or overfeed their plants.

Before you bring a pot into your grow space, make sure you clean it thoroughly to get rid of any unwanted chemicals or dust that may have gathered in the shop or factory. Pots are very cheap to buy. Use only one pot per plant so that if there is a problem with the soil, watering, or nutrients, only one plant will feel the effects.

Wide pots permit wider plant growth. This is because the roots are allowed to stretch out further, offering the plant more support for side growth.

Why not be creative and have some fun sometimes?

At this stage, you should have the best soil you can get your hands on. You take a seedling, make the transplant and fill in the empty areas of the new pot with more soil. Pat down the top of the soil lightly and apply a stake if support is needed. Add a small amount of water to your pot and place the pot and plant under the light. You'll leave the light on for 24/0 or 18/6 hours a day and watch as your plants grow over the coming weeks.

By now, you should know how to set up your grow area and make your security arrangements. You will have your lighting kit set up to hang down over your grow area. You will also have some form of light reflection around your plants to help conserve and direct light. You will have obtained seeds, germinated them on a tray, and started preparing to transplant them into larger pots. The larger pots will house the plants throughout the rest of the life cycle, during which time you will provide the best medium possible in which your plants will grow. In the next chapter we will explore how to fine-tune aspects of the indoor environment to maximize your yield and get the most from your plants.

7 | Indoor Environmental Control

By now you have the knowledge you need to set up the basic environment for your indoor plant. As the grower, you have total control over that environment and you need to make sure it meets all of your plant's needs. This chapter deals with controlling four important environmental factors for plant growth: nutrients, soil, water, and air. The most important environmental factor, lighting, was covered in detail in Chapter 5. With the right amount of care in all five areas, your plants with thrive.

Nutrient Control

Remember nitrogen, phosphorus, and potassium (NPK)? These macronutrients are the primary ingredients needed in soil to ensure a healthy marijuana crop. In addition, the secondary supplements calcium (Ca), magnesium (Mg), and sulfur (S), or CaMgS for short, can be used to promote plant growth and health, and are also part of the macronutrient group. Secondary supplements are generally found in soil, but not always in sufficient amounts. There are eight additional plant micronutrients: iron (Fe), boron (B), chlorine (CI), manganese (Mn), copper (Cu), zinc (Zn), cobalt (Co), and molybdenum (Mo). These eight micronutrients are less important for good plant health than NPK and CaMgS. Check your soil bag to see if it contains micronutrients.

The nutrients and nutrient levels in your soil can be monitored using either electronic or manual nutrient testers. Most growers, however, do not have the luxury of such expensive items and have to control everything by hand, using judgment. Don't despair! Growers the world over have successfully tended to plants long before the invention of electronic readers. The key to nutrient control is to plan your feeding in advance of growing your plant. This way, everything else you feed to your plants is simply a supplement to the plan. You can always adjust your plan for future grows of the same strain based on what you learn the first time around. Remember, though, that each strain is different and will probably require changes to the following basic routine.

1. For seedlings, use a soil with an even NPK ratio, such as 10:10:10 or 5:5:5. No nutrients should be added, but if you do find that need to add some, add them in very small doses (no more than 1/8th of the strength of what it says on the bottle).

2. After germination, do not feed for three weeks, unless seedlings show signs of yellowing. In either case, feed them a dose of NPK with an even ratio (10:10:10) or a higher N than P and K ratio (20:10:10) at 1/4 of what is recommended on the label for the first week, and continue this once a week until calyx (pre-flowers) show on the plant.

3. If your plant shows any yellowing, increase the feeding strengths until yellowing stops. Increase in small steps from 25 to 33 percent before trying 50 percent or higher. If plant health does not improve, consult Chapter 13 on problem solving a nutrient deficiency.

4. In the second week of growth you should be adding secondary nutrients to your plants. Mix secondary nutrients at 1/4 strength of what it says on the bottle. Continue adding secondary nutrients once every other week.

5. Once every second week, add micronutrients at 1/4 strength of what it says on the bottle.

6. As soon as calyx development shows, switch to a food with a higher P than N and K ratio (10:20:10). Continue to feed your plants as usual, exchanging the older vegetative food for this new flowering food.

Remember that cannabis burns easily and does not need full strength nutrients. It is better to increase the frequency of your feeding rather than the strength of your foods if you discover that your plant needs more food. This may be more time consuming, but it immensely reduces the risk of plant burn.

Some plants require more foods in higher doses than others do. The frequency of your feeding and food strengths will vary from strain to strain; however the basic elements of these foods and their composition will not. Your plants need NPK as the basic building blocks of their diet. You need to know how to select for these in soil and you need to know how to keep them in your soil type. Some soils also diminish in nutrients more quickly than others do because of the soil's composition and its nutrient- and water-retaining qualities. Whenever you select a soil type for cannabis, try to find one that has an even NPK balance such as 10:10:10. It is easier to maintain this balance if you use a balanced NPK vegetative growth feed. If your soil is higher in P or K then it is hard to balance it using other foods.

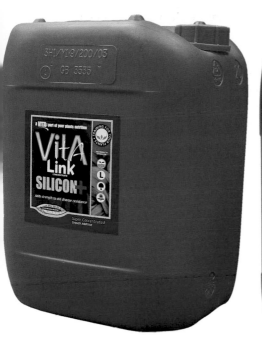
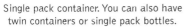

Single pack container. You can also have
twin containers or single pack bottles.

Twin pack. You can also have single
pack bottles or twin containers.

For example:

A soil type of 10:20:10 needs to be balanced back to 10:10:10, or else the high
levels of P will cause the plant problems in accessing the other N and K nutrients
that it also needs for vegetative growth (a condition known as "nutrient lockout"). In order to balance it back, you need to wait until the next time you feed
and only add 10:0:10 to the soil. This is because you would expect the remaining
nutrients in the soil to be already high in levels of P. The hard part is finding a bottle of nutrients that has 10:0:10 on the label. In order to avoid this problem, we
select a balanced soil in the first place.

Growers mainly have four types of nutrients at their disposal: vegetative primary
nutrients, flowering primary nutrients, secondary nutrients, and micronutrients. The
list below contains classic examples of food types that you may find or work with.

1. N10:P10:K10—An example of a balanced vegetative primary nutrient pack.
2. N10:P20:K10—An example of a flowering primary nutrient pack.
3. N0:P20:K10—An example of a flowering food without N.
4. N10:P0:K10—An example of a vegetative food without P.

5. N10:P20:K20—An example of a flowering food that is not suitable for cannabis because of its equal P and K values but lower N values.

6. Ca1:Mg1:S1—An example of a balanced secondary food.

7. Ca2:Mg3:S4—An example of a secondary food.

8. N10:P10:K10:Ca1:Mg1:S1—An example of bottle of food that contains both primary and secondary nutrients.

9. N10:P0:K0—This is a pure N supplement.

10. N0:P10:K0—This is a pure P supplement.

Micronutrients are sometimes listed in ratios like NPK values, but it is more common to just find micronutrient measurements. One good brand of micronutrient that is used by nearly every grower is called Formulex.

Growers should ensure that at least some secondary nutrients are added to the soil mix or put in with feeding routine because some secondary problems are hard to find. Ca problems are awkward to detect because a Ca deficiency only stunts growth and does not appear to display anything else usually associated with a nutrient disorder, such as: leaf discoloring, rusting, blotching, leaf curling, or any other chlorotic condition that one would expect. To solve problems like this, growers always try to prevent instead of cure. Ensure that your soil or feeding routine has some sort of secondary nutrient plan incorporated into them.

Professional growers get their supplements in separate packs of N, P, and K. That way, they have total control over their primary macronutrients. Using these separate packs, they can mix vegetative foods, flowerings foods, pure N, pure P, and pure K supplements—whatever they want and in whatever strengths they want: 20:10:10, 20:5:5, 5:20:5, etc.

Problematic Nutrients

Recalling that some strains may require more of a certain nutrient than others, we know that a balanced food might not have enough of that nutrient to allow the plant to grow without expressing a nutrient disorder. You may have to first identify the strain's "problematic nutrient(s)" before finding a suitable feeding product. Mg is a common problematic nutrient, which means that many strains are more likely to experience an Mg nutrient disorder. In order to correct this, you would have to use either pure Mg, a secondary nutrient feeding product, or preferably a secondary nutrient product with higher Mg to Ca and S ratios.

Problematic nutrients are on the increase with stabilized plant breeding. As breeders develop strains for certain characteristics—flowering times, potency, yield, colors, etc.—they sometimes accidentally stabilize other traits like nutrient requirements, smell, or taste. Some breeders point out when their strains need more K or Mg, and this is worth taking into consideration when choosing your strain and feeding products. However, be suspicious of breeders who claim that you should lower doses of a specific nutrient or range of nutrients. They could be telling you to do this in order to justify the floral and leaf color display that was published in the seed bank catalogue. Nutrient disorders can bring out nice colors in your plants, but you may be sacrificing yield and potency in favor of "an image" by not allowing the plant to thrive in optimal conditions. Lack of K can bring out red hues all over your plant. With some strains this can even turn the bud purple. A few common CaMgS problems and treatments are described next.

Macronutrient Disorders: A Rough Guide

Most micronutrients are used by the cannabis plant in such small quantities that the role they play in plant functionality is quite limited. Also, micronutrient disorders are extremely rare with cannabis plants unless you are using a completely neutral substrate with no added nutrients. Most loam soils already contain micronutrients, so you do not need to add much, if any. Good growers, however, will always top up on low doses of micronutrients because they know that prevention is better than cure.

Macronutrients, on the other hand, are very important plant nutrients used widely by the plant throughout its grow. This guide will explain how these macronutrients work and how to spot macronutrient disorders in your garden.

Nitrogen (N)

Like most plants, cannabis uses N more than any other nutrient—especially during the vegetative growth stage of the life cycle. N directly helps the plant to create chlorophyll, which is used in photosynthesis for the production of plant energy. Without sufficient levels of N, cannabis plants turn a pale yellow-green, starting with the bottom leaves and gradually moving up to the top of the plant. Eventually, the leaves wither and fall off. Lack of N also stunts plant growth.

Phosphorous (P)

Like most plants, cannabis uses P during photosynthesis to create chemical compounds essential to plant growth, especially floral development during the flowering phase of the life cycle. Lack of P causes plant veins to turn red and also stunts plant growth. Foods that are high in P are also called "bloom" foods.

Here a nutrient deficiency looks likely as some leaves are pale and collapsing, though pest attacks can cause plants to have a similar appearance. Both potential problems need to be investigated to determine the real cause.

Potassium (K)

K assists the plant's chemical synthesis and overall metabolism. Some chemical synthesis processes are used to help fight disease, so lack of potassium can make your plant vulnerable to plant diseases like mold, fungi, and wilt. K also assists in seed and stem development. Without sufficient K, stems and branches become weak and break. Necrotic patches develop on leaf tips at the base of the plant and in blotchy patterns in the middle of those leaves. Red stems are signs of a K problem, but red stems can be a genetic trait in some plants, especially in equatorial strains, and cold temperatures can cause stems to turn red as well. Be careful not to misdiagnose these symptoms as a K deficiency and risk overfeeding your plant.

Calcium (Ca)

Plant cells use and store Ca for cell development. Ca problems are rare and the symptoms are almost undetectable in cannabis, but if left untreated they will stunt growth and eventually cause the plant to wilt. If your plants display stunted growth yet do not display any symptoms associated with another nutrient disorder, then adjust the amount of Ca that you are adding to your plants in the feeding plan. To prevent secondary nutrient problems like our Ca problem here, which are hard to detect, you should top up on all of the secondary nutrients together.

Sulfur (S)

Like K, S assists the plant's chemical synthesis and metabolism. It is also used in the creation of amino acids and proteins. Without S, new growth is yellow and pale looking. The rest of the plant will also eventually yellow from lack of S. It is important to catch S and N deficiencies early, before they advance to the stage where it is difficult to detect the actual cause of the problem. N disorders run from the bottom of the plant upwards. S starts at new growth formations and spreads from there. A severe case of an S deficiency looks exactly like a severe case of an N deficiency, so check your plants regularly to increase your chances of early detection.

Magnesium (Mg)

Chlorophyll is a group of magnesium containing green pigments that occur in plants, giving the characteristic green color to foliage and acting as absorbers of light for photosynthesis. Since Mg is central to chlorophyll production, the plant needs it to carry out photosynthesis. Plants with Mg problems exhibit both yellowing and leaf curl, especially leaves that curls upwards at the base of the plant. This is where the saying, "the plant is praying for magnesium," comes from.

Mg problems are the most common secondary nutrient disorder you will come across.

To correct this, feed your plant 1/3 of a tablespoon of Epsom salts per three gallons of water every three to four weeks. You should choose Epsom salts from your grow shop instead of Epsom salts from the drugstore because the grow shop version is designed for plant use (and is thus easier to break down in water). You also get a lot more Epsom salts for your money if you buy it in a grow shop. If your soil does not contain Mg, you will need to use a feeding product that contains Mg. You should be able to buy secondary feeding products from your local grow shop. They come either in liquid, powder, or granular format. Avoid using granules because they take more time to break down in the soil. Granule-type foods tend to be "slow release" foods. "Formulex" is a good secondary food product that can be used to correct Mg problems.

Micronutrient problems rarely occur unless there is a problem with lockout. Lockout is a chemical reaction that takes place with the nutrients in the soil and can occur if a large amount of one single nutrient is added or if salt gets into your mixture. Old nutrient formulas can also cause lockout. It is simply a chemical reaction similar to a precipitation, which results in the combining of nutrients to form new chemical compounds that the plant cannot use. Lockout is hard to detect. If you have problems with a disorder that you cannot seem to solve by adding more of the missing nutrient, then you need to consider that this nutrient is locked out. If lockout does occur you will need to flush your soil. Soil flushing is described later in this chapter.

Feeding

Feeding is the process of adding nutrients back into your growing medium that the plant has removed. We mentioned that you would need a maximum of four feeding solutions throughout your plants' growth. The first is to be used during vegetative growth, the second during flowering, and the third and fourth only as needed. Plant food comes in all different forms—solids, liquids, sprays, powders, and granules. The most common form is liquid and this comes in either bottles or large containers.

You should only feed your plants when they need increased nutrition, or risk burning them. What this means is that you need to be able to judge when cannabis plants need food. In the previous section we looked at certain nutrient formulas and feeding routines, for example, one feeding every seven days at 1/4 strength of what it says on the label during vegetative growth.

Some cannabis strains will need N more than others. You can detect this if your plants start to yellow at the base in first few weeks of vegetative growth. If this happens, reduce your feeding schedule from seven days to five days, then three, and so on until you solve the yellowing. This will tell you how often you need to

Blood meal is a popular organic feed for vegetative growth. The NPK values are clearly seen on the front of this bag. Note the big N value.

Bone meal is also a popular organic feed for flowering. Note the big P value. Organic growers will use bone meal to promote root growth.

feed your plants at 1/4 strength. Instead of watering at 1/4 strength[1] more frequently, you could feed your plants a higher-strength nutrient mixture, but you increase the risk of burning your plants this way. Even though plant burn does not usually kill a plant, if you solve the problem quickly, it can stunt and stress growth.

The amount of feed that you'll use is relative to your growing conditions and strain. You should never have to feed cannabis daily. In fact, the most nutrient-consuming cannabis strains should only need to be fed once every five days at 3/4 strength. Marijuana plants burn easily so never mix your solution at full strength. (We will note some exceptions to this rule below, but they are very uncommon. In all other situations you should abide by the rule.) If the instructions say to use one capful of feed per gallon of water, then aim for 1/4 strength by using one cap to every four gallons. If the instructions say to use one capful of feed per two liters of water and you know that your plants need lots of nutrients, then go for 1/2 strength by using one cap to every four liters of water.

Try not to reduce the cap size in your feeding equation because 1/4 caps tend to be only enough to feed a plant or two. When you mix plant food you will want to be able to feed as many of your cannabis plants as possible. Three-gallon watering cans are best for the job if you have six plants or more. It is possible to burn plants even at half strength, so take care when feeding and observe the behavior of your plants after feeding. If any of the leaf edges crumple up and appear dark green or brown and flaky, then you have probably burned your plants. The only way to solve plant burn is with a soil flush. We will discuss this procedure later in this chapter.

There are some situations that call for mixing nutrient solutions at full strength but these are not common. They are:

1. If you are using "special" cannabis nutrients. These are manufactured and sold in some European countries and can be legally imported into many other countries. You should still take security precautions when buying and storing these items, however, and make sure that it is not illegal to purchase or own them where you live. Special cannabis nutrients are simply normal nutrients mixed at lower strengths so that they will not burn cannabis.

2. If your solution contains nutrient values of less than 5 percent. Doses of values lower than 5 percent on the bottle need to be mixed at higher ratios for some plants. An NPK value of 5:5:5 contains only 15 percent nutrients in the solution; the other 85 percent is usually just water. At 25 percent strength this nutrient solution will contain low nutrient values, so a more nutrient-hungry strain should be fed a higher-strength mixture. Some strains can use a 5:5:5 solution at full strength but this is not recommended because of potential plant burn.

3. If your individual plants are extremely large and flowering. Large, outdoor hybrid strains can consume lots of water and nutrients daily. In Australia, there are hybrid Sativa strains that grow to near tree-like proportions. Even though growers take care to ensure that the soil around the plant is rich in nutrients they may need to feed these plants more often to improve bud growth during flowering with a strong bloom mix. A 100 percent solution may help boost the plant, but only if the grower is certain that the mixture will be spread evenly around the base. By watering in a circle, starting from the base of the plant and moving outwards, the grower can ensure that the strong solution has been distributed evenly to the area surrounding the plant. The soil around the plant will absorb the new minerals at full strength and the roots will find these as they grow outwards. This kind of 100 percent boost can be good for large plants.

As a final note to this section, it would be wise to point out that you should never put food directly from the bottle into your plant's soil. This will probably kill your plant. Always mix it with water first or you could end up having to perform an emergency soil flush.

Soil Control

As your plant grows through its life cycle, it absorbs minerals from the soil and deposits waste material of its own. We have already stated that cannabis plants need a steady pH level of 7. The removal of nutrients and addition of waste material can cause soil pH levels to fluctuate.

pH

You should check the pH level of your soil at least once every week and one or two days after feeding. A pH test kit can be purchased from most grow shops. Be aware that the electronic test kits can be expensive. pH test kits are unfortunately the only way to test your mixture's pH. If you find that your soil's pH has shifted out of the 6 to 8 range you need to bring the level back to 7. Recall that below 7 is acidic, and above 7 is alkaline. There are two ways to adjust the pH of the soil, and these are described below. You can also perform a soil flush. Soil flushing is not recommended except for in extreme circumstances, such as serious pH fluctuations or chemical burns, and is described in detail later in this chapter.

pH—Bringing Back to Neutral from Acidic

If your soil's pH is too acidic you will want to bring it back to a neutral 7. You can do this using lime (alkaline calcium oxide), a brittle white caustic solid obtained by heating limestone. Lime can be bought in small containers from any grow shop and added to your soil the next time you water your plant. Only add small amounts each time, testing the pH the next day to monitor the effects. You'll find that, over time, you will get to know your soil and what it needs. Advanced growers know by trial and error how much lime they need to use to push acidic soil back to a pH level of 7.

pH—Bringing Back to Neutral from Alkaline

If the pH of your soil is too alkaline then you will want to bring it back to a neutral 7 by adding small amounts of any of the following:

- Cottonseed meal
- Lemon peels
- Coffee grounds
- High-acidity fertilizer

Always introduce small amounts of the substance, checking the pH level the next day and readjusting as necessary. Over time, you'll know what measures to use for different pot sizes and soil mixes.

pH up / pH down

Chemical pH products are growing in popularity among professional growers. They essentially act as a chemical agent for adjusting your soil pH and are available in most grow shops. They come in two forms: up and down. There is also a third type of pH solution called a buffer. The buffer solution is always a neutral 7 and is used to calibrate instruments so that they read correctly when you use them to test pH.

Both pH up and pH down come in liquid form. pH down contains nitric acid at roughly 38 percent strength and pH up contains potassium hydroxide at roughly 50 percent strength. Always check the label to make sure. The rest of the solution is usually just water. It is not a good idea to use your pH caps as measuring devices as this could result in foreign elements being introduced into the pH solution.

To adjust pH, read the instructions on the bottle carefully. It is wise to use a clean syringe for measuring how much of the pH up or down formula you need to use, but a beaker or plastic measuring jug will do. Carefully add the recommended amount to water and mix well. Then add this to your soil mixture and check your pH level with a reader. In general, 0.5 ml of pH up or pH down will move the solution by +/- 0.1 pH per three gallons of mixture. A normal-sized syringe will usually drop out anywhere between 0.1 ml and 0.5 ml at a time.

For example: say you have a three-gallon pot system and your soil tests at a level of 5.6 pH. You need to move this up to a stable 7 so you need to go +1.4 pH by using pH up. Here's how to do it. Simply fill a watering can with three gallons of water and test it using a pH meter to get the reading of the water. If it is 7 then all is fine. If not, then you need to balance the water to 7 before adding the +1.4 pH up. So, if your water has a pH of 6 then you need to add 2.4 pH up (1.4 pH up + 1.0 pH up) to bring the soil mixture back to 7 after watering. 2.4 pH up roughly translates to about 12 ml of pH up. Use a pH reader to test the end results, which should be +8.4 pH. Simply add this pH-treated water to the soil, which has a pH of 5.6, and it should balance back to 7 again. Check your soil's pH a day or two after treatment to confirm this.

pH is important because low or high pH levels can cause nutrient lockout to occur. pH irregularities can also cause growth stunting, leaf spots and wilting. Always check the pH level of your soil before treating a nutrient problem. Another thing to note is that nutrient formulas have their own pH levels and you can use your pH reader to check a nutrient solution's pH level. You may need to balance the nutrient pH using the method of control we have outlined above. Serious pH irregularities occur in cannabis either when the pH drops below 5.5 in soil or goes above 8. The normal level of 7 induces optimal growth. It must also be noted at this point that the pH level and treatment of hydroponic solutions is very different to soil and is covered in Chapter 9.

Water Control

Water your plant at least every second or third day, or, better still, as needed. Never let the soil dry out completely for long periods of time. The following method works well with good-sized three-gallon pots:

- Day 1: water
- Day 2: let dry
- Day 3: let dry
- Day 4: check soil and water if needed

Your watering schedule will really depend on the size of your pots and soil type. If you pick up your pot when it's dry, then try to pick up the same pot when it has been watered, you will feel the difference in weight. This is one way to judge if your pots need watering.

There are many watering devices out there. This is a watering wand, which has a variety of nozzles to control the watering spread.

A fan strengthens plant stems by bringing out their natural adaptation to wind resistance. It also creates import airflow.

You can detect signs of underwatering and overwatering simply by observing your plants' leaves. Watch your plants for two to three days after you have watered them. Do the fan leaves point outward to receive more light or do they wilt downward? Wilting leaves can be a sign of either underwatering or overwatering. Check your soil. Is it dry? If so, then add more water. You may find that you need to water every day because your lighting discharges a lot of heat and your soil is a quick-draining kind. If your soil is wet, then leave the soil to dry out until your leaves pick up again. You'll eventually establish a pattern for your plants' watering needs.

Be aware that overwatering will eventually kill your plants. If this happens, you can only let the soil dry out and hope for the best. Using a fan near the surface of the soil is the single best way to help solve an overwatering problem. Transplants are difficult to do with wet soil. If you think you need to perform a transplant because of overwatering, then do so—but remember that the soil will be wet and break up easily in your hands. Try and do the transplant quickly and neatly over a short working distance.

Air Control

During the vegetative growth and flowering stages, cannabis plants love to get fresh air. Bearing in mind security, if you have a window in your grow leave it open for a while and let your grow room refresh itself every day. Also, during the dry periods in between watering, the roots like to breathe. The fresher the air, the better. During winter you may want to reduce the time that the windows are open as the cold may stunt growth. Just refresh the air in your room for 15 to 20 minutes during winter and close it again. If your grow is enclosed, without windows, then use fans to extract the old air outside and another fan intake to refresh the system.

Odor Control

To say that we smell with our noses is like saying we taste with our lips. The nose channels air to our olfactory epithelium, a patch of cells which reside at the end of the nasal cavity. The olfactory epithelium senses the different compositions in the air and detects odorous molecules which give us the effect of smell.

Cannabis plants continue to release odorous molecules into the air throughout their life. In vegetative growth the cannabis plant has a detectable odor which starts around the 1st week of vegetative growth and gradually increases until the end of the grow. This scent is very unique to the cannabis plant and can be

Carbon filters control all odor problems and smells.

Carbon filters are attached
to extraction fans.

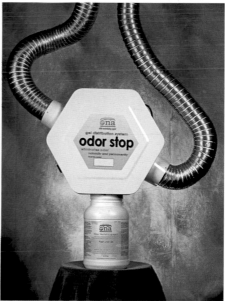

There are many types of odor control devices
available like this odor stop.

described as a sharp, pleasingly pungent, freshly cut grass type of smell. In the flowering stages the plant tends to release numerous odorous molecules into the air in very large amounts. These scents are like freshly cut grass coupled with fruity, forest, hash, skunk, or chemical type odors. Cannabis naturally has a diverse range of smells and odors as the result of recombining its genetic material through natural selection and breeding (see chapter 15).

You must deal with odorous molecules before they leave the grow room if you wish to prevent cannabis smells from traveling. Cannabis growers have found three ways to deal with this. These are:

- Ionizing
- Ozone generating
- Activated carbon air filtering

Ionizing

Ionizers are air purification systems that control odors, smoke, mold, bacteria, chemical gases, mildew, stale air, pollen, dust, and static electricity. Air ionization systems work by outputting negative ions into the area in which they are operated. These negative ions are used to neutralize odor molecules that are in the air. The ions will attract the odorous molecules to them and, when attached to the odorous molecule, will deactivate the odor molecule by neutralization. Some ions will cause the odorous molecules to fall to the ground so that they will not remain airborne. The problem with ionizing is that these deactivated particles and negative ions tend to stick to surfaces such as the floor, pots, plant leaves, walls, lights, reflectors, ballasts, and ducting. Some of the deactivated particles may be extracted by the outtake fan but your grow area will require cleaning every month if you use an ionizer.

Ionizers are cheap to buy but are only suitable for smaller growing operations where up to six medium sized plants are concerned. Large-scale growers still use them but there are better options of odor control available.

Ozone Generating

Ozone is also known as activated oxygen. Activated oxygen contains three atoms rather than two—the amount which we normally breathe. Ozone is a very vigorous sterilizer. Ozone can be found in nature but we can also buy units that generate ozone. Ozone has a lifespan of about 30 minutes. When ozone (O3) comes in contact with odorous molecules, one of the ozone atoms detaches itself from the ozone and attach-

Ozone generators are also another way of removing odors from the grow room.

es to the odorous molecules. This oxidizes the cell walls of the odorous molecules which eventually destroy the odorous molecules, leaving only oxygen behind.

Ozone does have some setbacks. Too much ozone is not good for plant or human health, although most ozone generators are specially adapted to render the health risks of ozone obsolete. The legal exposure limit for human beings is around 0.1 ppm (parts per million) for a maximum of eight hours. Ozone generators that are used for horticultural purposes tend to only generate 0.05 ppm and at a timed rate so that exposure is kept to a minimal amount.

Ozone generators are better at controlling cannabis odors than Ionizers.

Activated Carbon Air Filtering

Activating carbon is the safest, most effective way of dealing with cannabis odors and is part of any professional grow room. Charcoal is carbon. When we treat charcoal with oxygen it opens up millions of pores in the carbon atoms. This type of treated charcoal is known as activated charcoal and is the main ingredient of our activated carbon filter. The activated charcoal is usually broken down into pellets so that it can be used with air-filtering units.

Activated charcoal absorbs odorous molecules by chemical attraction. The activated charcoal is contained in a metal tube with filters screening the air that passes through.

The whole unit is called an activated carbon filter and is attached near your outtake vent. Not all activated carbon filters use charcoal. Some activated carbon is made from the husks of coconuts. Activated carbon filters need the carbon changed every couple of months. You will know when to change the carbon if it no longer filters out odorous molecules. Activated carbon can be found in most good filter supply stores. Make sure that you choose activated carbon pellets. There is another form of activated carbon called crushed activated carbon but this is not as effective as the version that comes in pellet form.

Ventilation

Ventilation is a very important aspect of indoor environment control. Most cannabis flowers are sticky. Dust sticks to bud. So your ventilation system must not be allowed to blow dust into or around your grow room. This is simply done by keeping the grow room clean and making sure that all air intakes are equipped with screens. You will have to clean the screens every so often to maintain a clean air flow into your grow room.

You will also need to ventilate your grow room if it gets too hot for your plants. This is the primary reason why most growers need a ventilation system. The other reason is to prevent the humidity from increasing in the grow room, which can cause mold and other plant problems. Fresh air also contains gases (oxygen, nitrogen, carbon dioxide, and traces of other gases) some of which are used up by the plants in the growing environment. This causes levels of these gases to fluctuate in the grow room. If a grow room does not have adequate ventilation then these gases will not be replaced and this causes problems with plant health. In order to provide optimal conditions for cultivating cannabis we must have a well ventilated grow space.

All good growers spend time getting their ventilation right before they start their grow. Here is a list of reasons to have a good ventilation system in your grow room.

1. To prevent mold.
2. To replenish various gases in the air.
3. To stabilize humidity.
4. To control air flow.
5. To boost yield using a slow release carbon dioxide system (covered at the end of this chapter).

Ventilation systems can be quite sophisticated.

There are two main components in a ventilation system: the passive intake (air in) and the vent (air out). The vent should be located high up in your grow room because hot air rises. The vent should come equipped with a fan to push air out through the vent. Odor control devices (activated carbon filters, charcoal filters) are usually attached to or located near the vent.

When the fan has sucked all the air out of the room through the vent, it will create a vacuum. Air will need to get back into your grow room again so it will find any way in that it can. Holes in the walls, frame, and roof are all vulnerable spots where air can be pulled in. Since we want our airflow to be under control we need to make sure that all false air intake spots are sealed first.

The passive intake (with a screen to prevent dust from getting in) should be installed low in the grow room so that, as air is brought in from outside, it passes through, around, and over the plants. This air will help to cool the plants and the space between the lighting and the plants' top colas before finally being extracted by the vent. Dust will also be forced out the vent. Passive intakes do not require a fan, but some growers do use them to regulate how much air enters the room.

Doing it right improves your dank. Colas are bending over from their weight.
These genetics are being pushed to the limit.

Nearly every cannabis grow room uses the above scenario for ventilation. Spend time designing your ventilation before you set up your grow room. The cost of setting a good system up is much lower than you think. Air-cooled hoods for HID lights need to be used in conjunction with a vent. Other ventilation methods are described in chapter 8.

Fans

Fans can be placed quite close to mature marijuana plants and a slight breeze helps them to develop stronger stems and branches. Fans also circulate the air around your plants, simulating an outdoor environment. A fan's ability to "move" air from one location to another is measured in cfm (cubic feet per minute). You should aim to replace the air in your grow room at least once a minute. If your room is hot then you may need to remove the air in your room as much as five times per minute. On average, growers use a fan with the capacity to circulate the room's air three times in one minute.

For example, if your grow room is 2x5x5, then it is 50 cubic feet in size. For this grow room you need a fan that ranges somewhere between 150 cfm (3x50 cfm) and 250 cfm (5x50 cfm). In this example, the 150 cfm fan can move all of the air out of the grow room 3 times per minute. The 250 cfm fan will do it five times a minute. The rate at which you want the air to be removed from your grow room depends on:

- How hot it gets inside the room.
- How cold the air outside is.
- If you are using CO_2.

You can find the cfm written on the side of the fan. Squirrel cage type fans are highly recommended.

Sometimes a very good air extraction system causes areas of the grow room to receive less of the new air than others. If you want to ensure that all areas of the grow room receive adequate amounts of fresh air then use a regular domestic oscillating fan. Oscillating fans also help to build up thick stems and branches. The speed at which you set your fan depends on how much the plants move. Plants like movement, but too much can make them uproot or fall over. Use common sense with these types of fans.

Humidity

Cannabis plants grow best under conditions between 40 and 80 percent relative humidity (rH). rH is the amount of water in the air. Introducing fresh air into the environment is the best way to control humidity. In short, if you have installed a good air circulation system then you should not have a problem with the humidity in your grow room. If your air has a high humidity level then you will need to purchase a dehumidifier. These expensive items are used to control rH in the room. They do this by simply cooling the air that travels through the unit, causing it to condense and lose some of its water vapor.

Cannabis grows well at levels of between 40 percent and 80 percent rH. If you have a rH measuring kit you can judge for yourself how much fresh air you need in order to achieve the optimum 60 percent level. These measuring kits are also expensive to buy and usually have to be ordered in by your local grow store. Good cannabis growers try to avoid the cost of dehumidifiers and rH monitors by simply installing a good air circulation system from day one.

Temperature

Cannabis likes the same temperature that people do, so the best meter for temperature control is you. If you find it's too cold in your grow room, so will your plants. Under normal circumstances, room temperature is easily controlled by thermostat, but in your grow space, lighting will impact on temperature. You should aim for 75 degrees Fahrenheit, but slightly warmer temperatures do help plants to grow a bit more quickly.

Hot air rises. Having extraction at the top or near the lights is the best way to get rid of the heat.

Monitor your room's temperature with one or more thermometers. Hot air rises so you can expect that the temperature of the air above the thermometer will be hotter than the air under it. Using more than one thermometer, you get an idea of the temperature ranges in your room (at root level and canopy or light level).

You do not want to go above 85 degrees Fahrenheit. If you do, you will only heat stress[2] your plants and stunt growth. Going above 125 degrees Fahrenheit can kill cannabis but this depends on the strain. Some equatorial strains can still grow at 125 degrees Fahrenheit as their genetic make-up can withstand it. In order to cool the room, you will need to ventilate it either by opening a window or installing a ventilation system, as described above.

During the flowering phase of the life cycle you will alter the photoperiod to what is called 12/12. (This procedure is explained in detail in chapter 7.) 12/12 means that for 12 hours your grow room lights will be on and for the next 12 hours they will be switched off. Since bulb heat contributes to the grow room's temperature, the temperature will drop when the lights are out. During the dark periods of the flowering phase the temperature is allowed to drop down as far as 55 degrees Fahrenheit. You should prevent temperatures going lower than 55 degrees at night because this stunts growth. Below 30 and you can expect serious plant damage. If the temperature does drop below 55 during the dark period then you need to heat the grow room. The best way to do this is using an electric heater. For an average-size grow room, a small, portable heater that plugs into a domestic socket will do.

The hand heat test. If your hand feels discomfort then so will your plants.

An analog display. Large and clear.

Digital display. More accurate with extra features but usually harder to read.

Analog dial timer. Cheap but harder to read.

Timers

Timers are important devices for controlling when lights, heaters, fans and any other electrical units in your grow should be switched on or off. Some lighting kits, ballasts, and fans come with built-in timers. If you do not have a built-in timer you can buy one from any good home electrical store or grow shop. Timers simply act as a regulator between your power source and the device that needs the electricity. You plug your device into the timer and then you plug the timer into your electrical output. Some timers have a digital display and others have an analog display. Simply set your timer to turn on when you want the device to turn on and to turn off at the time you want your device to turn off.

Timers should not be overloaded. Current must pass through the timer unit so you may need to use multiple timers in your grow room. To understand your timer's limits, consult the manual that comes with it.

CO$_2$ (Carbon Dioxide)

CO$_2$ is a gas that helps promote plant growth, especially floral growth. About 0.03 percent by volume of the Earth's atmosphere is made up of carbon dioxide. Carbon dioxide is natural and not harmful. Plants absorb carbon dioxide from the air and use it for photosynthesis. If the supply of carbon dioxide stops, so does the process of photosynthesis. Increasing the supply of carbon dioxide increases photosynthesis.

Millions of years ago there was much more carbon dioxide in the atmosphere. Somehow, plants have still not lost their ability to process high doses of carbon dioxide, which leads to lots of plant vigor at a faster speed of growth. The atmosphere on Earth today is different and has slowed down plant development—you could say that we have a planet full of underdeveloped plants!

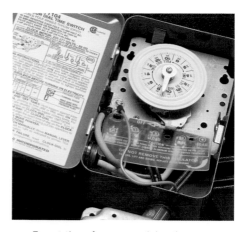

Expert timer for commercial scale grows.

Plants will use carbon dioxide in any growing environment. Using a simple air circulation system in your grow room will help replenish the carbon dioxide the plants have used. If you want to increase plant size, yield, and vigor and speed up growth, you need to look closely at increasing carbon dioxide levels.

Carbon dioxide can triple yields. A one-ounce plant can quickly become a three-ounce plant, depending on the plant's genetics. Every cannabis strain has a genetic threshold for bud production. It will not exceed that limit, even under optimal growing conditions. Introduction of supplementary carbon dioxide ensures that your plants will hit their optimal rate of growth. You do not need supplementary carbon dioxide to grow high-yielding plants, but the noticeable effects on the speed and quantity of bud production with supplementary CO_2 places the gas in the same category of importance for high yields as "plant genetics" and "light source."

Some serious bud enhanced by CO2 production.

CO2 Regulator.

Carbon dioxide generators are expensive industrial units that burn fuel to produce carbon dioxide. Although you can buy different types of generators that use a range of diverse fuel sources, they are really only suitable for very large indoor or green-house growing operations. Most growers who use carbon dioxide in their grow room choose a "timed release" system. This is simply a unit that releases a certain amount of compressed carbon dioxide from a tank at a timed rate of release.

Carbon dioxide tanks can be bought and refilled at any good welding supply store. It is best to use a welding supply store over any other type of store when you acquire carbon dioxide. If anyone asks, you are welding something. They are also the perfect place to refill your carbon dioxide canisters. Carbon dioxide can also be purchased from most fuel depots. The tanks come in different shapes and sizes but you should aim for multiple 20-pound tanks or the 50-pound type if you have a lot of grow space. We will calculate exactly how much carbon dioxide to intro-duce into your growing environment in the next section. Twenty-pound tanks are easier to lift, move, and fit into your grow room. Also, using multiple tanks allows you to refill on carbon dioxide while the other tank is releasing carbon dioxide into your grow room. Once you have a tank of carbon dioxide you need to purchase a tank regulator (an infrared sensor or combination flow meter will also do) and a timer. The tank regulator controls the quantity of carbon dioxide emitted and the timer controls when the gas is released.

Calculating How Much Carbon Dioxide You Need

How much carbon dioxide you need is straightforward, but requires a bit of infor-mation about your grow room and ventilation system. There are two steps:

1. Calculate the volume of your grow in cubic feet by multiplying the length x width x height of the room.

There is already carbon dioxide present in the room. It should be around 300 ppm. The optimal level for cannabis is 1,500 ppm. You will need to increase carbon dioxide levels by 1,200 ppm.

2. Multiply the cubic foot size of the grow room by 0.0012 to find out how much carbon dioxide you need to supplement your room in order to hit 1,500 ppm.

For example:
    1. A 10 x 10 x 10 room is 1,000 cubic feet in size.
    2. 1,000 x 0.0012 = 1.2 cubic feet.

An all in one plant Environmental Controller.

1.2 cubic feet of carbon dioxide will be needed to bring this room up to 1,500 ppm.

If you have an air-circulation system in your grow room you may wish to reduce the speed of your fan to prevent carbon dioxide from being vented too quickly (after all, you are paying for it and you don't want to waste too much of it). If you reach 1,500 ppm for carbon dioxide in your grow room you are allowed an increase of temperature to 95 degrees Fahrenheit because the increased carbon dioxide allows cannabis plants to grow in these temperatures without stressing them. If this does heat stress your plants then try to increase your ppm to 2,000, which should be better for your plants in temperatures of 95 degrees Fahrenheit. If you find that slowing down the vent fan to keep carbon dioxide in the room is still causing your plants heat stress then you simply need to regulate how many times carbon dioxide is released into your system with every air change. The more often air is vented out, the more carbon dioxide you need to release. A hose can be used in conjunction with the regulator to ensure that the carbon dioxide escapes at a point that is furthest away from your vent. This ensures that as many plants as possible get access to the CO_2 before it is finally vented out.

Remember that heat stress stunts growth, voiding the benefits of any carbon dioxide supplement. Get your air circulation right before you introduce high levels of carbon dioxide into the grow environment. A good air circulation system should be flexible enough to allow for a slow carbon dioxide release system to work. It is just a matter of controlling the timing of the release, the amount to be released, and how much air must be moved out of the grow room in order to keep it within a certain range of temperatures. During 12/12, carbon dioxide is turned off for the dark period, because without light there is little photosynthesis.

Climate Controllers

These devices serve multifarious tasks in the grow room. Much like a timer, they regulate the activity of the electrical device(s) they are connected too.

Climate controllers also go by the name of: environment controllers, climate monitors, and climate sensors. They come in both analog and digital formats. The more expensive the climate controller, the more functions it has and the more devices it can control. Climate controllers can be used to regulate the following systems in your grow room:

- Lights
- CO_2 disbursement
- Pumps
- Ventilation and extraction
- Humidity

The climate controller is usually fastened into your grow room wall. The devices that the unit is controlling plug into the separate slots of the climate controller. The controller itself is then plugged into your electrical mains and turned on.

Expensive climate controllers are self-regulated and come with built-in sensors that detect when the controller should be activated for a specific task or a set of tasks. You set how it controls those tasks.

By way of example, an advanced climate controller can be setup to do the following:

During the photoperiod the climate controller regulates the 12/12 photoperiod by turning the lights on for 12 hours and off for 12 hours. The controller monitors the heat in the room, which will vary when the lights are on and off. The heat sensors of the controller adjust the speed of the extraction fans to accommodate for the change in heat to meet your settings. If the temperature drops below your established temperature the controller turns on the heating device

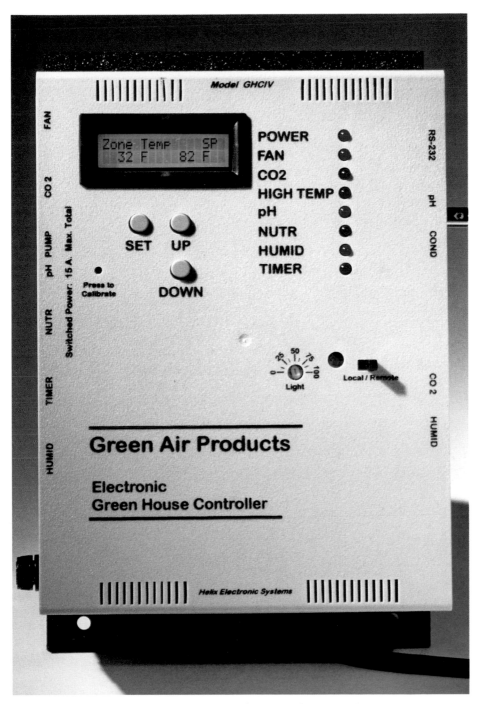

A sophisticated multipurpose digital green house controller.

Even connoisseur plants can improve their already gorgeous looks
with better environmental conditions in the grow room.

that you have attached to it to meet your fixed temperature or temperature range. At the same time, the controller can also regulate CO_2 systems and humidifiers in the grow room.

How much you want to spend on a controller depends on how many devices you want it to control and how much control you want over these devices. There are many controllers available to suit small to large tasks.

C.A.P. is a popular manufacturer of climate controllers and they have a product range varying from simply controllers for small grow rooms to full size greenhouse controllers. Consult your grow store for details on the type of the controller you are looking for. Basic controllers start at around $60.00 and expert controllers can cost up to $2,000.00

Soil Flushing

A soil flush is a last resort when all else has failed, as in the following scenario.

In this hypothetical situation, you are using a soil that holds a lot of water and you want to feed your plant. You take out the appropriate feeding bottle, add it straight to your plant, and pour the water in after. (This is never recommended. Always mix your plant food with water in a container, such as a jug or watering can, before administering it to your plant.) As you move to pour the correct dose over the soil, your hand shakes and the bottle spills. The next thing you know, half of your raw

While a soil flush may be considered a last resort, it can be a very effective one. The curative properties of water may keep your hard work from going down the drain.

feeding liquid has managed to find its way into the soil. You curse yourself for not following the instructions. What should you do? You pick up this book and turn to this page. You read about the soil flush and see that your plant still has a slim chance of survival. You know that all the raw chemicals could kill your plant and this is your last resort.

Here is How to Flush Your Soil
Step A
1. Take the potted plant to a sink.
2. Turn the plant on its side, making sure not to bend or break the stem.
3. If you think the stem will break, then find a long stick and place it in the soil, use thread to secure the plant to the stick at several points, and secure the stick to the pot.
4. Tilt the potted plant on its side so that the top of the pot with the soil is facing at an angle toward the sink.
5. Do this until all the liquid has poured out, noting the color of the liquid that runs out. Some nutrients will dye the water a pink, brown or yellow color. You may see this in the water coming out. When the water runs clear, you know that all the nutrients are flushed out. If the nutrient does not dye the water you can still continue the flush. Just pour everything out.

Step B
If your pot is perforated, continue. Otherwise, proceed to Step C.
1. Pull your plant back up and sit it in the sink.
2. Pour lots of water on top of the soil.
3. Wait until the water flows out of the bottom of the pot, observing the color of the flow as in step A.
4. Repeat this process until the color of the water becomes clearer. The soil will get very muddy when you do this and some of the mud will pass out with the water. (Try to keep hold of as much of it as you can.)
5. Once the water runs clear, tilt your plant on its side again and wait for all the water to drain out.
6. If your feeding solution doesn't have a color, then flush water through the plant a number of times to ensure that all the nutrients are flushed out. This usually takes about seven flushes with a three-gallon pot. Remember that if you see color change, then all your nutrients are flushed out and you do not need to flush anymore.
7. Quickly take your plant to a warm, dry area and wait for the soil to dry out.
8. Proceed to Step D.

Step C

1. You can use a screwdriver to make holes in your pot if it is made of light-weight plastic. You can always use thick masking tape later to patch the holes up. If you do this, then follow Step B. If you can't do this, then you need to perform an emergency transplant.

2. Prepare a new pot with soil, leaving a large gap in the middle where your plant will go.

3. Take your plant and use a knife to cut around the edge of the soil a close to the rim of the pot and as deep as you can.

4. Put your fingers in down around the inside of the rim and gently pull the plant and soil out of the pot. Try not to damage the roots.

5. Hold the soil over the sink and place it down near the drain, holding it together with your hands. If your root mass is big, you may need help.

6. Turn on the water and let it run slowly down over the soil.

7. Keep holding the plant for a number of minutes until you see a change in the color of the water that's coming from the soil. Do not crush the soil—just hold it. It will get muddy and will break up a bit, but this is to be expected.

8. When the water changes, place the plant into the new pot.

9. Fill up the spaces with new soil and use a stick to prop up your plant if needed.

10. Quickly take your plant to a warm, dry area and wait for the soil to dry out.

11. Proceed to Step D.

Step D

1. Every day, measure the pH of the soil. If you have flushed your plant properly, it should return to the near 7 mark (assuming that the water you use is a neutral pH of 7).

Sadly, few plants survive such an emergency soil flush. The soil flush is, in essence, overwatering your plant to the point of removing most of the minerals and nutrients in the soil. If your plant manages to pull through, you have done well. If your plant doesn't, then you know better next time. A soil flush causes the plant a great deal of shock[3] and should only be attempted as a last resort if your plant is dying and can't be cured by any other means. If your plant survives, it may have sustained some damage. If any of the leaves are burnt or look dead, you can remove them by clipping them away. These damaged plants usually take about two weeks to return to full health.

8 | Pre-flowering and Flowering

By now you've managed to set up the basic growing environment and experimented with modifying and controlling it to promote better, stronger plant growth. You will have observed your plants forming a number of nodes and a small leaf mass at the top, which you know is going to form the next set of leaves and branches. Your leaves should be flat and stretched out to receive as much light as possible across their surface area. If they are, then your plant is enjoying its environment. If not, then maybe you should consider turning to the Problem Solver in Chapter 13 to see what has gone wrong.

You should also note that almost everyone makes mistakes the first time growing. Very few first-time growers get to this stage without experiencing at least one problem, so don't feel bad if you didn't get it right the first time. The trick to growing healthier, more potent plants is to keep growing (and reading this book).

During the vegetative growth stage your plants will begin to grow quickly and produce more leaves and new branches. The stem will also grow thicker. This is the point when your plants really begin to look like marijuana.

Then, one day you will notice that your plants appear to be doing more than just growing vertically and producing leaves. You take a closer look and there appears to be new leaf growth at most of the node regions between the stem and the branches. Your plant is now developed enough to receive more light energy and convert this energy into more side branch growth. These new growths produce more leaves, branches, and, eventually, flowers. This type of new growth at the stem's node regions is called lateral branching or secondary branching. This is really where the extra node regions begin to take shape.

After a few more weeks of this secondary growth your plant will look bushier and certainly has more node regions. It is during this time that your plant has reached sexual maturity and is ready to show sex. How long this takes depends on the strain you are growing, but after the seedling stage has finished you are looking at a time period of 4 to 8 weeks of vegetative growth. With Sativa strains this can take much longer.

At a certain stage towards the end of vegetative growth, the plant enters its pre-flowering phase and, as a grower, you need to tailor your grow space and gardening approach to this new stage in your plants' life cycle. The next section explains how to identify the pre-flowering stage.

Pre-flowering and Early Sexing

Recall that during pre-flowering, plants start to exhibit their sex. As a grower, you should be hoping for as many females as possible. Pre-flowering occurs at the node regions. Towards the end of vegetative growth you need to check your plant nodes for what is called calyx development. A clone will carry the exact same genetic makeup as the plant it came from, so if you know your clone's history you will already be able to predict its sex.

This is a typical scene of a vegetative plant, with
lots of growth, which is nearing pre-flowering.

An overhead view of
the top cola node.

This vegetative plant has lots of healthy
node regions where flowers will grow.

This top cola node is properly called the
terminal bud or the apical bud.

This terminal bud is
bearing male flowers.

This terminal bud is bearing female flowers.   These other node regions are bearing female flowers.

Checking for Calyx Development

Choose a plant. First of all, examine the node regions of the plant where the branches meet the stem. You are looking for very small, pod-shaped organs here at these regions.[1] If you don't find any here then move outwards along each branch, checking each node region until you come to the tip. If you do not find calyx development then your plant has not reached its pre-flowering phase yet. You need to wait for it. Calyx development will come in time.[2]

There are three early indicators of plant sex, but they are not 100 percent accurate. So remember, these methods can fail, but are nonetheless often accurate predictors of your plants' sex.

First Early Sexing Method: Height

If you've been growing the same strain and all the seeds were started at the same time, then you may notice that some plants are taller than others: the smaller plants tend to be female and the taller ones tend to be male. You can separate these plants into two sections in order to see how good your guesswork was when you do definitively identify sex. The other thing to note is that male plants generally start to pre-flower before females. If you have taller plants that are producing new growths before the smaller ones, then the taller plants are probably male.

A terminal bud area a few weeks into flowering.

Second Early Sexing Method: Calyxes

A good way to identify plant sex at an early date is to examine the calyx[3] with the aid of a very fine magnifying glass. If the calyx is raised on a small, short stem, then it's probably a male. If the calyx isn't raised on a small, short stem, then it's probably a female.

Third Early Sexing Method: Force-Flowering

"Force-flowering" is probably the best early-sexing method. To force-flower a cannabis plant, simply take a cutting and place it in a cup of water or a cloning medium, such as rockwool. Expose the cutting to 12 hours of light followed by 12 hours of total darkness. The cutting should flower and display its sex—however, the plant must be mature enough to present its sex. An immature plant will not show sex because initial calyx development is not photoperiod-related. Plants normally mature around the fourth week of vegetative growth because sex is not genetically determined until the third week of growth. This also applies to "feminized seeds," which can, and often do, turn out to be male.[4] If your plants are exhibiting calyx development, then this is a suitable method of determining the plant's sex.

These methods are NOT 100 percent accurate. Later in this chapter we will explain how to definitively identify the sex of your marijuana plant.

PLANT TRAITS

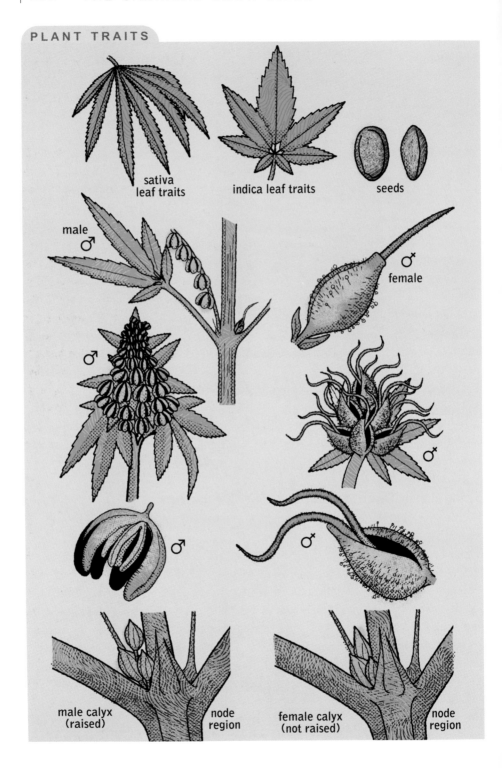

sativa
leaf traits

indica leaf traits

seeds

male ♂

female ♀

♂

♂

♀

♂

♂

male calyx
(raised)

node
region

female calyx
(not raised)

node
region

When to Flower?

Your plant will remain in the pre-flowering stage for between one and two weeks. During this period, the new growth regions begin to change shape depending on the plants' sexes. It is during this shape change that you can properly detect your plant's sex.

Pre-flowering is a sign that your plant is mature enough to start flowering. As a grower, you have a simple choice to make: do you want to flower now or do you want to continue vegetative growth? Here are a few issues to consider before you make a decision:

• Most cannabis plants can be kept alive for up to 12 years by simply keeping a light on the plant at all times. Even if the plant only receives light for a few hours a day it can still live for a long time. It all depends on how the plant is treated. These plants will grow to a certain height and then form into a bush. Eventually they will stop producing branches and will spend the rest of their lives growing new leaves to replace the old ones. By keeping the plant in vegetative growth longer, you allow it to reach its optimal size of vegetative growth and the plant will stop growing. Most growers flower before this, when they see calyx development, in order to speed up the growing process. For example, a

A very healthy flowering garden with the leaves pointing up and node regions filling in nicely.

plant that shows sex at the fourth week of vegetative growth can be kept in vegetative growth for a few more weeks to allow the plant to generate more node regions (leading to more branch and leaf growth). When the plant is flowered, this extra stage of growth should help the plant to achieve optimal results; however, the grow time is extended by a few more weeks to obtain this.

- Bud production does not increase at the same rate as plant growth. Bud production depends on your growing environment, your strain's genetic makeup, and the amount of nodes the plant has. All nodes are potential bud areas, but every strain has a genetic threshold for bud production.

- It is possible to get more bud with lots of plants that are flowered as soon as they're mature (which also keeps them shorter and smaller) versus extending vegetative growth with less plants until they reach their maximum height and size. The time frame for the shorter option also produces more bud turnover per year.

Keeping these things in mind, you can either choose to flower now or choose to keep your plant growing until it reaches its size threshold before you start flowering. If you take the longer route, prepare to have the space for it, because in the flowering stage, some cannabis strains can more than double in height and width.

If you want your pre-flowers to flower you only have to do one thing: introduce the 12/12 light schedule.

The All-Important 12/12!

If you've never heard of 12/12, listen up. 12/12 is the key to producing high quantities of bud from cannabis plants.

Cannabis plants grow outdoors naturally between the months of April and October/November. This means that toward September/November[5] the plants will be flowering. During this time the days get shorter and the nights get longer. When this occurs, the plants are subjected to 12 hours of light and 12 hours of darkness.

When this 12/12 photoperiod occurs, the plant is naturally stimulated to flower. As long as 12/12 continues the flowers will grow larger and more plentiful. This is part of the cannabis plant's natural cycle. Naturally, as a grower, you want a large quantity of flowers, and you achieve this by introducing the 12/12 light cycle.

Overhead view of several terminal buds a few weeks into flowering.

During pre-flowering you can manually turn on your lights for 12 hours and turn off your light for 12 hours every day or you can use a timer to automate the process. Throughout the 12 hours of darkness you should keep your grow area as dark as possible. Even something as seemingly harmless as a small desk light at the other side of your room will cause your plant not to react properly to 12/12, resulting in continued vegetative growth. In fact, any light that penetrates the darkness could stop your plants from flowering properly. That means your grow room must be sealed to the point where it is completely lightproof.

If you want to learn how to do completely lightproof your space then I suggest that you read up on photography dark rooms, either on the Internet or in your local library. Photographers use common items that can be bought in most hardware shops to make their film-processing rooms lightproof. If you borrow ideas from their tried-and-true methods (basically a thick black screening around the doorframes or any open light points) then you will have a great space for flowering plants. You should be a long way towards achieving this already if you followed the advice on covering your grow room with Mylar. If you have prevented any light from leaking out, then you should also have prevented light from leaking in.

A hermaphrodite bearing both male and female flowers on the top cola.

Problems with 12/12

If you switch to 12/12 before pre-flowers have shown, you may encounter the following problems:

1. Stress-related sex problems (hermaphrodites)
2. Abnormal bud growth

Stress-related Sex Problems (Hermaphrodites)

Stress-related sex problems can produce hermaphrodite plants, also known as "hermies". The stress of what's sometimes called early flowering triggers the plant into a situation where it thinks its chances of reproduction are slim to none. That situation induces a condition or act of self-pollination, in which the plant produces both male and female flowers on the same plant. The male flowers then pollinate the female flowers, which eventually produce seeds.

The reason for this is that the plant notices that the photoperiod is irregular[6] and should no longer be in the vegetative growth stage but in flowering. This shocks the plant into a last ditch effort to receive pollen because it feels that it's missed its chance to receive pollen already. In the wild, males release their pollen just around the time that females begin to flower.

HERMAPHRODITE

Hermies cause problems because they may carry the hermaphrodite trait with their offspring. Genetically, the hermie condition is near impossible to reverse once started. Sometimes even plants from the hermaphrodite's offspring that did not display the hermaphrodite condition can still carry the hermie trait to future offspring. If you ever see all-female seeds advertised by seed banks you have the right to know whether or not these seeds come from female plants that were stressed into producing male flowers. In general, growers try to avoid hermie plants because they spoil sinsemilla crops and breeding projects.

Abnormal Bud Growth
Abnormal bud growth is a side effect of the hermaphrodite condition. Because the plant produces male pollen sacks with female flowers you may notice that the bud looks different. Also, the quantity of female bud produced is decreased because of pollination.

Early-induced flowering[7] isn't the same thing as forcing your plants to flower. If you force flower a strain before it has pre-flowered it will flower at roughly the same time as a plant from the same strain that has been flowered after calyx development has occurred naturally. Force flowering simply acts by stressing the plant into a crisis condition.

You will get the best out of your plant by waiting until it starts pre-flowering before switching to 12/12.

Keep feeding and watering your plant as normal. Pay attention to the flowering areas as they begin to grow. At this stage you may want to switch to your flowering feeds. Soon you'll be able to see your plant's sex.

Pre-Flowering for the 24/0 and the 18/6 Photoperiods
Both under the 24/0 photoperiod and the 18/6 photoperiod cannabis plants will undergo calyx development when mature enough to do so. In the case of the 18/6 photoperiod, calyx development may appear more pronounced and even display its sex earlier than the 24/0 photoperiod.

It is easier to keep a plant in vegetative growth by using the 24/0 photoperiod because there are no dark periods. If you keep the plants under 18/6 the pre-flowering phase increase may cause a slow down in vegetative growth. Although pre-flowering under 18/6 does not cause flowering it certainly contributes to a decrease in vegetative activity. As soon as you go down to less than 14 hours of light the plant will normally start to flower. 12/12 is the best light regime for flowering and can be introduced as soon as calyx development appears.

The Male/Female Thing *or* How to Sex Your Plants

You now have nurtured your plants and watched them grow in the hope that you'll get some high-yield females in the end. If you end up without any female plants out of all of your seeds then send the seed bank a letter explaining how 15 out of 15 seeds were male. If you're lucky and sincere in your writing, the seed bank may send you some free seeds or give you a discount on your next order. Seed banks or breeders aren't responsible for male/female ratios. It simply isn't under their control. Some people get 100 percent females while others get 100 percent males, but it is rare that such a thing will happen. To get five or more females in a pack of 15[8] is a good ratio.

The two circles below indicate where the grower should look for initial calyx development.

In this illustration two new shoots can be seen emerging from the nodes. Most novice growers mistake these shoots in their initial stages of growth as calyx development. Initial calyx development occurs in the same region.

CALYX DEVELOPMENT

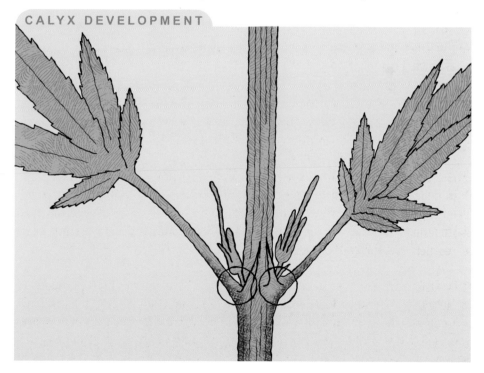

THE MALE FLOWER

These male flowers are very close to opening. They are hanging down in bunches.

Some of these male flowers have opened and others have yet to open.

Some males grow a terminal bud region devoid of leaves.

Male Flowering

Males do not need a photoperiod to spread pollen. As soon as calyx development shows, male flowers may appear within a few days under the 24/0, 18/6, or 12/12 photoperiods. Male flowers grow more vigorously and plentifully under the 12/12 photoperiod.

A male plant will continue to flower for the remainder of its flowering period, developing new calyx formations and male flowers. It can take anywhere between 12 hours and one week from calyx development for male flowers to appear and shed their pollen. It is very important to separate the males from the females as early as possible if you are growing a sinsemilla crop. In general males usually appear before females.

Pollen can easily be collected as described in Chapter 15. You can also gather falling pollen using a white sheet of paper placed in between the plant stem on the top of the pot. All fans must be turned off if you want to collect pollen this way. Fans will only blow pollen around your grow room.

Female plants can be pollinated at any time but are best pollinated between 15 and

These are some flowers under a HID. The color of the light from the bulb can cause the flowers to take on a different color.

There is quite an internode gap here but this should fill out with bud if the plant is growing optimally.

A few weeks into flowering and this cola is filling in to the point where the internodes are no longer seen.

30 days into their flowering period. Plants that are pollinated less than three weeks before harvest may result in immature seeds although plants pollinated two weeks before harvest have been known to produce seeds mature enough for germination.

Flowering

If all has gone well and you've cared for your plants, they will now enter the flowering stage of the life cycle. You will remove the males and should have a number of females to work with. This is going to be the most important time you'll spend taking care of your plants.

The male plant produces pollen sacks, which, when ripe, burst and scatter pollen to the female plants. The female plant produces white hairs at the internodes and top cola (head) of the plant during flowering. These hairs (pistils) begin to curl slightly and grow longer and thicker. The top cola should carry the most pistils. These pistils are sticky to touch (don't touch them too much as they also contain the sought-after THC) and become covered in resin during the flowering period. The reason for their stickiness is that the pistils are used by the female to catch falling pollen. If the female plant isn't pollinated she'll try to grow more sticky areas. Hence the results of a sinsemilla crop: bigger and better buds.

During the strict 12/12 cycle, a female plant will fill out more. More leaves, more branches, and more flowers develop until eventually, plants reach a peak period of flowering. Your plant will start to almost take the shape of a Christmas tree. The lower fan leaves will be stretched to the maximum in order to receive the most light. Running upward in a cone shape, the plant will exhibit strong floral and leaf development.

During the peak period of flowering, the female pistils on the flower's tips will swell. When the swelling occurs, the pistils will begin to change in color. They'll generally change from a white to an orange tint or from a red to a brown tint. All strains are different, but in general it's a white to red or a red to brown color change. It's best to use the breeder's recommended flowering times for harvest guidelines. When your plants do this you're ready to harvest and sample your favorite herb. Each strain has its own flowering times and each strain may also have a different color tint when they reach a flowering peak.

9 Advanced Indoor Soil-Based Grow Methods

New, advanced ways of improving your cannabis plants' yield have emerged over the past several years and some methods have become quite popular. The three most common types of advanced indoor growing are SOG (Sea of Green), ScrOG (Screen of Green), and cabinet growing. SOG and ScrOG are ways of growing serious amounts of top colas. Cabinet growing is a method of stealthily growing several plants in the corner of any room without drawing too much attention to your grow. Although these methods don't have to be soil-based (you can adapt a hydroponics setup to use these methods as well), soil is the most widely used medium in these setups, and so will be the focus of this chapter.

The idea behind these advanced indoor grow methods is that, in most cases, the cola is going to produce the most bud, so why not try to get that part of the plant to grow really big by creating an environment that concentrates on the top part of the plant? After all, the bottom branches of indoor cannabis plants don't catch much of the light cast from your HIDs. Enter SOG, ScrOG, and cabinet growing.

Preparing the "Special Clone Mother"

Before we discuss these popular advanced grow methods, we will touch on cloning because this is an important part of advanced cultivation. Before you select that special plant that you wish to replicate numerous times via cloning, you must first of all grow out a test crop from seed. During the third and fourth week of vegetative growth you take cuttings from all the test plants and label each one. How to take cuttings and grow them is discussed in Chapter 11.

You must not flower any of these cuttings. If any of cuttings get too big to manage then reproduce them by taking further cuttings from each one and labeling them. Continue to grow the test plants and flower them by manipulating the photoperiod. At this point you can remove the males and the corresponding male clones because we are only looking for a special female. At the end of the test plants' flowering periods you should be able to identify the special mother plant that has done better than all the others. The corresponding cutting that was taken from this plant is then allowed to grow to its full size. The other cuttings are simply discarded because you will not be using them. In order to ensure that you find a good special clone mother you should try and grow more than twenty plants. Good breeders will test grow as many as 100 or even 1,000 plants to find a truly exceptional specimen.

The reason for taking the cuttings before flowering is so that you will not have a bunch of flowering cuttings which need to be reverted to vegetative growth.[1] That would be too time-consuming. If the clone has flowers on it then it can be flowered right away by manipulating the photoperiod. The result is much like a piece of bud on a small stick.[2] Clones carry the same age as the parent plant they were taken from. Not only that, but they are sexually mature enough to flower if taken from a flowering plant. If they only had a week to go before flowering, then you will have to wait a week before you can flower them. You can flower two-inch clones if they were taken from a plant during the flowering cycle. They will finish when their flowering time is over but the quantity is reduced because the clone was not allowed to grow more node regions during vegetative growth. In short, clones are best if taken from the mother before flowering begins.

A cutting that is taken in the vegetative state allows the grower more control over the plant. That is why you should take lots of cuttings from different plants during the vegetative stage of growth and then later select the clone(s) that came from the special clone mother. You might want to allow the special clone mother to fully flower at the end of the test grow to confirm the plant's potency. The corresponding clone(s), on the other hand, will not have flowered yet because you will have kept the clone(s) in a constant state of vegetative growth under a 24-hour light cycle. It is your job, as the grower, to then take multiple cuttings and grow these multiple clones into a room full of highly potent, "special females"!

You should also keep at least one cutting from this original clone mother elsewhere and in the vegetative growth stage so that you can continue to take cuttings. This clone that is put aside becomes the new clone mother and is the source for all our future clones of this special plant.

Even with experience it can still be difficult to maintain an even canopy
height with clones. Still who doesn't want a garden like this?

The disadvantages of selecting for that special clone is that it takes time to grow the
test crop and you need two grow spaces to house your plants. Once you have finished
harvesting, you must grow the special clone for three weeks before you take multiple cuttings from her. How many cuttings you take depends on how many clones you
want to grow to full maturity next time around. Sometimes you might have to go
another round in order to generate enough clones. Clones also share the exact same
problems — be it pest resistance, nutrient requirements, or genetic disorders. If a
problem affects one clone then it will generally affect all the rest just as quickly. The
advantage of using clones is that you can have a room full of identical copies of that
special plant you really liked. You will not need to prune the plants to keep them in
formation. It is possible to produce twice the harvest size of the test grow based on
the selection of a clone that yielded more than others did.

For clarity we will list each process step by step.
1. Grow a large test crop.
2. Take cuttings from each plant and label everything.
3. Do not flower the cuttings.
4. Continue to grow the test crop.
5. Remove the males during flowering and their corresponding clones.
6. Select the best female at the end of flowering and her corresponding clone.
7. Grow the new clone mother but do not flower her.

This is a mother plant that has been pruned and is kept bushy by staking.

8. Take multiple cuttings from the new clone mother when she has developed lots of branches. You can use pruning techniques to increase branch numbers.

9. Use these clones as your next source of genetics for your following grow.

10. Keep at least one clone aside and do not flower it. It will be the next clone mother.

Growers like to sometimes swap or buy clones because it prevents them for having to grow a test crop and select a special female. Although this method is certainly less time-consuming it means that you will have to communicate with other growers and this is a security risk. Sometimes medical cannabis clubs offer clones for sale to medical users.

Although any of the advanced growing methods can be done from seed, you will not get all the benefits unless you use clones.

Sea of Green (SOG)

A SOG setup can be any size but must maintain the same basic shape and follow certain SOG rules. In SOG grows, you're looking at one plant per square foot or even one plant per 0.1 square feet. Very short Indica plants can be grown in as little space as 0.1 square feet. Most Indica varieties can be grown in less than 1.0 square feet, but in general most growers end up using 0.5 square feet per plant. Pure Sativa

You can use a screen with SOG if you wish. Although one is not necessary, it helps to train the plants.

This is the sort of density found in a SOG grow.

strains generally do not need to go much more than 1.5 square feet in SOG. This should give you a good idea of how many clones you will need for your grow area.

Next, you need to select pots for the setup. SOG calls for tube-shaped pots or pots of greater depth than width. You can make these yourself or buy these pots in a store. The objective here is to pack as many pots full of plants as you can into the SOG grow area so that it becomes a big cluster of pots with clones. This is the basic rule of any SOG grow: pack everything in as densely as you can. The clones are planted all at once, after which time no new plants are introduced into the SOG grow room. When they have reached the desired height (keep it small), they should be flowered. It usually takes about one to two weeks of vegetative growth before the clones are ready to be flowered.[3] Because the clones have been taken from a mother plant, they are effectively adult plants carrying the age of the mother plant with them and don't need to spend much time in the vegetative growth stage of the life cycle. Since you took them from a plant that was nearly flowering they'll start to flower shortly after you introduce the 12/12 light cycle.

The end result will be a full, dense canopy of bud, hence the name Sea Of Green. Because you're using clones, you only have to grow them for the remainder of their flowering times. You can expect to turn out a large quantity of bud every couple of months (a short period of vegetative growth with a full period of flowering).

Nebula from Paradise Seeds.
Photo Paradise Seeds

These Nebula plants were grown using SOG.
Photo Paradise Seeds

SOG essentially uses clone plantlets to increase the rate of bud production in a growing operation. It is especially useful where grow height is a problem because the plantlets will never reach their optimal size. SOG plants are always much shorter than plants grown from seedlings and they are flowered as quickly as possible in the SOG environment. You cannot do this with seedlings because young cannabis plants are not sexually mature enough to be flowered like this. In fact, sexual orientation is not even genetically determined until the third of fourth week of vegetative growth. This same rule applies to feminized seeds, which can become males under certain conditions.

ScrOG

ScrOG is like a SOG grow except that fewer plants are used in conjunction with a screen to fill the grow area with heavy top colas—hence its name, ScrOG or Screen of Green.

The screen is simply a large wire mesh placed between your light and the plants. Again, clones from a female plant are used, but we allow at least one square foot per flowering plant in the ScrOG method. The plants aren't flowered until they have covered the entire mesh with green. As the plants grow up through the wire mesh they're trained and worked around the netting to form a very even canopy. The top colas and side branches are all trained under the screen.

Like a SOG in concept the ScrOG uses fewer plants and requires a screen.

In this photo, we have a single Jack Herer plant grown using ScrOG.

There are many variations of the above two methods, yet they all utilize the same principles. SOGs and ScrOGs were originally developed to get the most out of poor quality fluorescent lights. The grower would line the roof of the shelf or box with fluorescent tubes to try and get the most out of their grow. Today's growers, using good HID bulbs, have taken these setups to a new level: pushing their buds to the limit. Some people even grow top colas that are the size of large corncobs or soda bottles!

ScrOG Growing by RealHigh

RealHigh is a ScrOG lover and has been growing ScrOG style for some years. He has added a bit to the ScrOG method through his experience with the process. This should help you understand more about the ScrOG method and what people have learned with this new technique.

My setup is like a SOG grow, but a screen is used to train the plant to grow horizontally, creating a canopy of buds beneath the light. The screen is simply made from chicken wire, nylon poultry fencing, or a construction of hooks and 20 lb. fishing line.

The screen is installed at a fixed height above the plant medium. For Indica varieties the screen does not need to be much more than 8 inches above the pots. Indica Sativa hybrids need about 12 inches, while Sativa plants tend to have

This plant is an Indica, so the screen is attached roughly 8 inches from the pot.

longer internodes, so you may have to use a screen that is about 18 inches above the pots. If your strain is a pure Sativa variety, like Haze or Thai, you may have to raise your screen to around 24 inches. This space allows the base of the plant a certain amount of vertical growth before branching occurs on the clone. The clone should start to branch just under the screen but if it does not, do not worry, because you are going to be training them anyway. The light should be suspended by adjustable chains so that it can be raised if necessary.

ScrOG growing doesn't require as many plants as SOG (allow at least one square foot per flowering plant), but takes anywhere from one to three weeks longer per grow because we will be in the vegetative growth stage longer than a SOG grow to allow the plants to fill out.

The plants are trained to grow horizontally under the screen until they're two weeks into the flowering cycle, at which point you let the tops grow vertically through the screen. You should always train the main growing tops from the outside of the screen moving inwards so that the colas are focused as closely as possible on the light dispersed from the bulb. You will not be able to get all of them centered under the light, but you should aim for this shape. As the tops grow vertically, push the large fan leaves down under the screen, allowing the light to get to all the developing bud sites.

If leaf growth is excessive, you can first cut fan leaves in half, making a shorter leaf and allowing light to get to the bud site. Leaving half the leaf on the plant still allows it to make energy for the plant to grow. Taking a whole fan leaf away in one go can stunt growth. In about a week, you can take off the rest of the leaf. Some people don't remove the leaf at all, but I do it to help with air movement, to reduce the chance of mold or fungus, and to allow more light to penetrate the bud sites. Just remember to remove a little at a time if you do remove leaf mass.

At this point, flowers are forming and growing vertically, creating a carpet of bud above the screen. Now we go below the screen and remove all the lateral branches and stray bud sites. The canopy has thickened enough that light is blocked from reaching this lower growth. It's only diverting your plants' energy away from the buds. You can remove all branches that haven't made it to the screen and the stray bud sites, but you may experience stunting. Although you want the plant to concentrate all of its grow energy on the developing flowers above the canopy, removing too much leaf mass and branching can prevent additional flowering.

This ScrOG set-up demonstrates how much bud one plant can produce.

There are two ways to deal with uneven canopies; use more uniform
clones or train them around the canopy using a screen.

The three main differences between a SOG and ScrOG grow are the number
of plants grown, the use of a screen, and the slightly longer grow cycle of the
ScrOG. Both methods can be done under the same light and in soil or with
hydroponics. There are many variations of the ScrOG grow—including V-
ScrOG, Stadium ScrOG, Flat ScrOG and Cylinder ScrOG—but they are all
based on the same principles. They work essentially the same way but use different shapes.

One of the best strains available for your ScrOG garden is C99. You will find that
a pure Indica or Indica-dominant cross will produce the best in a ScrOG grow. A
good ScrOG grow will average two ounces of bud per square foot of screen, but
you can't expect this the first few grows, because it takes proper timing and the
correct strain to accomplish this.

ScrOG was originally designed for grow areas limited in height and lit by fluorescents. Today's grower uses HID lights for growing ScrOG. He's taken it to the next level with these lights and is generating far greater results. Today's grower is always trying something new to improve the production of his favorite plant.

So there we have RealHigh explaining how he has worked with the ScrOG system. As you can see, he's added more to the basic ScrOG grow. With experience, practice and experimentation, you too can create your own customized grow.

Some Notes on SOG and ScrOG Growing

Even though MH and HPS lights can be used in conjunction with ScrOG and SOG grows, most ScrOG and SOG growers will use HPS because of the short vegetative period before flowering. Sometimes growers use smaller wattage HPS lights like the 250W and 400W series to keep the cost of electricity down and bud production within an acceptable range. In fact, ScrOG grows are so dense that smaller lights are sometimes more cost-effective than lights in the 600 to 1,000W range, but again this depends on your strain and level of experience. If you get it right you can effectively direct 95% of available light onto your bud. The end result is like a canopy of pure bud with the light belting down on top of it all for 12 hours a day.

Some ScrOG growers like to tie the center of the screen down to avoid it being pushed up by the center of the bud production, which should be the most vigorous since it is directly under the light. If the plants were to push the screen up it would affect the overall results because the light would not be able to reach all the bud areas. The pushing effect could also cause stems and branches to break.

You should not leave your plants growing in vegetative growth for too long because this causes more leaf matter to develop than bud, which will make our SOG or ScrOG grow less effective. Also watch out that you do not crush or pinch the stems as this will cause branches to develop at those areas or close to them. Branch development means that plant energy is being used in leaf and branch promotion rather than bud production.

You can experiment with different shapes of ScrOG to see how it affects your overall yield. Some ScrOG growers even advocate a dome shaped screen to match the curvature of light dispersal patterns—however, it must also be said that the differences between shapes in the final yields is not always significant and the overall effect is more exciting-looking than anything else.

Cabinet Growing

Although cabinet growing is not truly an advanced method of cannabis cultivation it certainly is a very popular one because of its ease of use, containment, stealth, and harvest results. A cabinet can be anything from a small closet, an old refrigerator, a box, or a simple cupboard. The grow area is usually small and can accommodate one to twelve plants at a time. The idea behind a cabinet grow is to keep a cycle of plants growing at all times. There are three things a cabinet grower needs to get started. They are:

1. Cabinet
2. Lighting
3. Air vent with fan

Most people simply set up their lights so they are adjustable by using versatile chains or a spring-type cord. A large hole is made in the cabinet to allow air to enter while another hole is made to allow air to escape. A fan is placed in one of the holes to extract the hot air being generated by the heat from the bulb. This vent and fan would be near the top of the cabinet, close to the light. Hot air rises and should be extracted from the top of the cabinet. The intake hole is on the opposite side of the grow area and can have a fan inside. This fan is generally moving quicker than the extractor fan to allow a fresh supply of air to circulate before leaving the grow room.

Your cabinet can be air-cooled in a few ways. The most common way is to mount a 4-inch dryer flange on the hood and link from the hood flange to the exhaust fan flange with a 4-inch dryer hose. A fan can be mounted on the hood, also.

The walls are painted flat white or Mylar is hung for reflective purposes. The plants are usually placed in separate pots and spend their entire life cycle within the cabinet environment. Clones are taken and placed on a shelf in the cabinet. Some people have made small compartments in their cabinets for clones and germination. Such a compartment can be any size, but is usually kept small enough to just keep the clones alive. This small compartment will probably have one or two fluorescent lights for the clones. It would be best to keep the compartment at the top of the grow chamber near the exhaust fan. You don't need an intake fan for these clones unless it is a big setup. A simple hole in the side will allow the plants to breathe.

After harvest, the clones are put into the grow cabinet and the process is repeated in a perpetual grow cycle; the legal term is a marijuana factory. In this kind of setup, you can harvest bud every 30 days with the right strains.

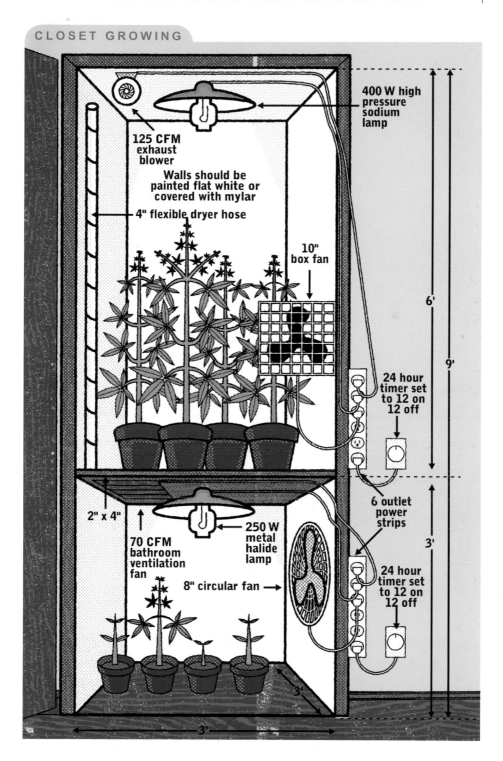

CLOSET GROWING

400 W high pressure sodium lamp

125 CFM exhaust blower

Walls should be painted flat white or covered with mylar

4" flexible dryer hose

10" box fan

6'

9'

24 hour timer set to 12 on 12 off

6 outlet power strips

2" x 4"

70 CFM bathroom ventilation fan

250 W metal halide lamp

8" circular fan →

3'

24 hour timer set to 12 on 12 off

3'

3'

Perpetual Grow Cycles

The objective of the perpetual grow cycle is to keep most of your plants flowering at all times. This means that you'll have an equal amount of plants in the vegetative growth and flowering stages at any given time. In essence, half of the grow is in its vegetative growth stage and the other half is in its flowering stage of the life cycle.[4]

Customizing Advanced Setups

As you can guess, all of the advanced grow methods mentioned in this chapter can be customized. Many cannabis cultivators have turned entire rooms into ScrOG or SOG grows. For those who are happy with four ounces of dried bud every month a small SOG or cabinet grow is the best choice. For those who want a bigger yield that lasts all year, a large ScrOG grow may be considered. When conditions are at their optimum potential, ScrOG growers can produce up to 30 or even 50 ounces of marijuana every two months in a medium sized room. For 30 ounces you would need roughly 30 square feet of space. That is a 5 x 6 foot room with one plant per square foot.

An expert's indoor grow room might also include the following advanced features:

- Several vertically suspended HID lights
- Roof, walls, and floor covered in reflective material (flat white paint or Mylar) and completely lightproof
- All lighting fixtures would meet at a junction box on the wall
- Ballasts would also be attached to the wall
- Plants placed in large containers
- Multiple air ducts and extraction fans would remove the hot air and replace it with fresh air.
- Activated Carbon Filters installed to minimize cannabis odor
- CO_2 generator to maximize yield
- Electrical generator to power equipment

If you are like the growers who contributed to this book, you will be continually experimenting to make the best use of your grow space. The room will become an intense hobby area and a most rewarding one too. In time you may even begin to learn more about plant genetics and start to develop some strains from your own breed and stock, perhaps even entering competitions or producing some of the finest seeds available on the market. For an in-depth look at breeding and genetics, turn to Chapter 15.

Mazaar, Jorge's Diamonds, Euforia and Power Plant are all good choices for a small, indoor grow. Each of these strains is easy to grow and bred to produce massive harvests. – Dutch Passion

DELTA-9 LABS

Strain:	FOG (Fruit of the Gods)
	Brainstorm Haze
	Canna Sutra
Lights:	600w HPS
	400w MH
Medium:	100% Organic Soil
Amendments:	Bat Guano

Keep it organic! Too many chemicals are taking away the true flavor of the strains.
Making and mixing your own soil through composting, even indoors, is
paramount for true success and continuity. – Ed of Delta-9 Labs

DELTA-9 LABS

Super Star is my recommendation for a Sea of Green set up. The plants grow with minimal branching which allows for many to be placed close together. The strain is easy to manicure since there is a high bud to leaf ratio. The top main buds grow large while creating a dense bud structure. – Ed of Delta-9 Labs

Strain:	LA Confidential
Lights:	600w HPS
Medium:	Soil and Coco
Amendments:	Worm Castings
	Bat Guano
	Seaweed

The LA Confidential loves lots of light. Whether it's a 600w HPS, 750w or 1000w, she will put out rock hard, medicinal buds. We like to use 600w HPS because we're able to spread more light using less energy. – Aaron of DNA Genetics

Headband, Sleestack, and X-18 Pakistani are the best DNA strains for the first time grower. All of these strains are capable of producing a high yield in a closet grow. These plants are very forgiving for someone whose situation isn't dialed in just yet. A little heavy-handed on the nutrients? Not a problem. These strains aren't as sensitive to disease and mold as most - even in a small space. — Don of DNA Genetics

GREEN HOUSE SEED CO.

Green House Seed Co. Breeding Facility circa 1996. These airtight tents were custom-built for Green House Seed Co. Each compartment houses a different strain, and is outfitted with a fan that creates negative pressure within the compartment to prevent cross contamination between the strains.

GREEN HOUSE SEED CO.

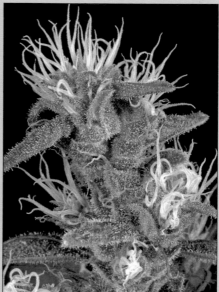

The best ScrOG-performing strains in the Green House Seed Company catalogue are Cheese, Trainwreck, White Rhino, Big Bang, K-Train, Bubba Kush and Chemdog. All these strains grow with a very branchy attitude, and perform extremely well in SCRoG systems, while each has it's own unique taste. The Cheese is a viney-growing plant, and a connoisseur strain with one of the most intense flavors in the cannabis spectrum. While Trainwreck is an iconic strain, White Rhino is ideal for the medicinal user. Big Bang, a.k.a SIMM18 is a government tested medicinal strain with long, bushy side branches. – Franco of Green House Seed Co.

HIGH BRED SEEDS

Strain:	Dieselryder
Lights:	1000w HPS
Medium:	Soil
Amendments:	Perlite
	Worm Castings

High pressure sodium lights tend to produce a shorter and stockier plant with
less stretch during the first few weeks of flowering.— the Joint Doctor of High Bred Seeds

Lowryder is good for an indoor grow because it flourishes under an 18 hour light cycle. The reason is due to the Lowryder's ability to flower under any light regime, so the more light the better. This is the same mentality behind leaving a vegetative room under 24 hours of light. – the Joint Doctor of High Bred Seeds

PARADISE SEEDS

Strain:	Nebula
	Jacky White
	Magic Bud
Lights:	600w HPS
Medium:	Soil and Coco
Amendments:	Blood Meal
	Bone Meal
	Bat Guano
	Worm Castings

The Paradise Seeds Mother Room has 1000 watt lights, both HPS and MH, but for flowering gardens we almost always use 600 watt HPS lights. The red light spectrum gives better results then the blue spectrum for flowering plants. – Luc of Paradise Seeds

PARADISE SEEDS

Two fine examples of varieties that do well in a Sea of Green are Nebula and
Ice cream. Nebula has an open structure that is excellent for indoor farming where the
plants give the best results in a sea of green set-up. Nebula stretches slightly and produces obese
buds twinkling with a coating of resin glands. Ice cream is good multi-branch plant that thrives in
a Sea of Green because of it's fantastic response tendencies. – Luc of Paradise Seeds

Strain:	Chronic
Lights:	600w HPS
Medium:	Soil
Amendments:	Perlite
	Worm Castings

Chronic after 7 weeks of 12 hours of light, then 12 hours of dark. – Simon of Serious Seeds

SAGARMATHA SEEDS

The best Sagarmatha strain for a closet grow is a Sativa, preferably Stonehedge, because they continue to grow during the Flowering stage. It takes a longer time to grow, but the yield is worth the wait. Start with a pH neutral, pre-mixed soil with perlite in it. Though square shaped pots allow you to pack more plants into a smaller space, I prefer to use round pots because the roots grow into a spiral, becoming more prolific than they would in a square space. Once the plant has become established, I may add more Nitrogen during the Vegetative stage and more Phosphorus and Potassium during the Flowering stage. At this point, I would trim the plant regularly, starting at the third node. Trimming the side branches encourages the plant to put more energy into the colas. When done properly, this method allows you to grow colas that can weigh 7-10 grams each.

—Tony of Sagarmatha

10 | A Look at Hydroponics

The Grower and the Growing Medium

You now know that plants need a base material, called the medium, that holds nutrients and minerals, drains well and allows air to get to the roots. As you begin to experiment with soil types and mixtures, you may want to investigate the use of alternative mediums to soil, such as rockwool, clay pebbles, and other artificial grow mediums.

In the early days of experimenting with artificial grow mediums, growers discovered that the roots didn't always respond well to the "soil-less" medium. Then, someone had the bright idea of creating a small unit to hold water and nutrients separate from the plant and medium. The roots then accessed the water after they grew down through the medium. Plants respond quite well to the use of a soilless medium in conjunction with this new design, which became the basic model for all hydroponic systems.

Hydroponics is a very successful way of growing marijuana if you're looking for large bud quantities or bud all year long. Hydroponics is the technique of growing plants without soil in beds of sand, gravel, or artificial mediums that are flooded with a nutrient solution.

Hydroponics is a highly popular cannabis cultivation technique, but new growers should note that it does require a certain degree of maintenance and expertise. If a hydroponic system is not well maintained, the whole unit can fail and kill your plants very quickly. This is the biggest problem that the hydroponic grower has to contend with. On the other hand, the results can be simply incredible!

Hydroponics, when done correctly, can produce a flowering plant in only 3/4 of the average time it would take with a soil grow. That's right! Hydroponics can grow bigger and better buds in 3/4 the time it takes to grow the same strain in soil.

Hydroponic Systems

A simple hydroponic system consists of a pot, a reservoir, a grow medium, a pump, and a complete set of nutrients. The system is set up in two layers: the top layer holds the grow medium and the bottom layer holds the water with added nutrients. The plant is grown in the medium where it will develop a stem and a set of roots. The roots will grow through the medium and down into the nutrient solution. Water and nutrients are pumped into the lower portion of the tank through a reservoir at timed intervals. The plants drink the solution and expose their roots to the air. If this is timed correctly, and the growing solution is maintained properly, the plants will flourish. This is because the plant can devote the energy it would normally spend using its roots to search for water, air, and nutrients towards upper growth. That said, hydroponic systems produce massive root clusters. One can easily pick up a three-gallon bucket full of root growth from a single plant. This is because roots thrive in hydroponic systems.

Nutrient Film Technique (NFT)

NFT systems are usually bought as all-in-one hydroponic tray systems. In other words, the reservoir that holds the pumps and nutrient solution is contained in the same system, although the grower can separate it if they wish. NTF systems are generally very flat and long, but some are sloping in their design to allow the nutrients to run towards

Two NFT trays. Notice how both trays are neatly slotted into an L-shape allowing for the grower to move left or right between modules.

and through the plant roots and medium. The unused nutrients are recycled to create a constant flow of nutrients to the roots and back into the reservoir.

In an NFT system, the plants sit on a rockwool slab that is cut to meet the NFT tray's length and width. Most NFT systems come with a lid that divides the space between the medium and solution to allow root growth for you. You should use this as a guide for how thick your rockwool slab should be.

Some NFT systems do not use a rockwool slab. Instead, the trays have holes in the lid where "net pots" should sit. A net pot is a plastic pot with lots of holes in the sides and a base that allows roots to grow out from the gaps and down into

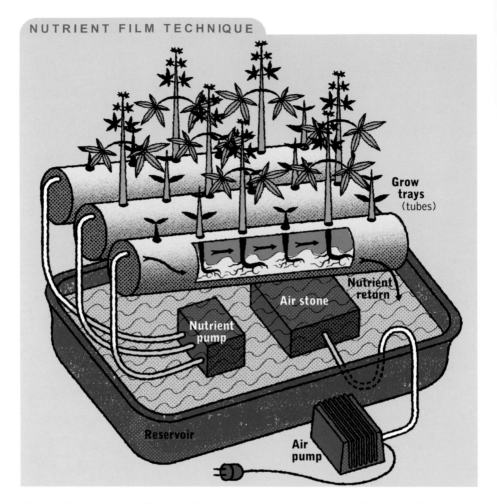

NUTRIENT FILM TECHNIQUE

Grow
trays
(tubes)

Nutrient
return

Air stone

Nutrient
pump

Reservoir

Air
pump

the nutrient solution. Clay pebbles are the most popular medium used by growers in conjunction with these pots because they are very good at supporting cannabis stems and tend not to escape through the net pots into the nutrient solution like vermiculite or perlite do.

Flood and Drain / Ebb and Flow

The flood & drain, also known as ebb & flow, system is another all-in-one system that is easily distinguished from other types of hydroponic systems by its greater depth. The grow medium is located above the reservoir, which delivers the nutrients and water to the roots at a set time and at a fixed rate. This means that throughout the day the plant will go through spells of dryness as the nutrients flow down through the roots and back into the reservoir again. The rate of flood and drain is measured so that the nutrient solution does not overflow the apparatus. An overflow hole in the system also helps to control flow by allowing the nutrients to spill back into the nutrient reservoir.

The nutrient solution is pumped into the medium and is slowly drained back into the reservoir again. The whole unit recycles the nutrient solution at timed intervals. These systems are generally flat to ensure that the nutrients find their way to all the plants. If it were sloped there would be an increased chance of some of the plants not receiving any nutrients at all.

Some systems have a separate reservoir, which sits under the system. A hose connects the reservoir to the system and a pump is used to push the nutrients from the reservoir and into the system, where it will flow back down into reservoir again. This setup requires less pumping than an NFT system, in some cases pumping nutrients to the plants only two or three times a day.

EBB AND FLOW SYSTEM

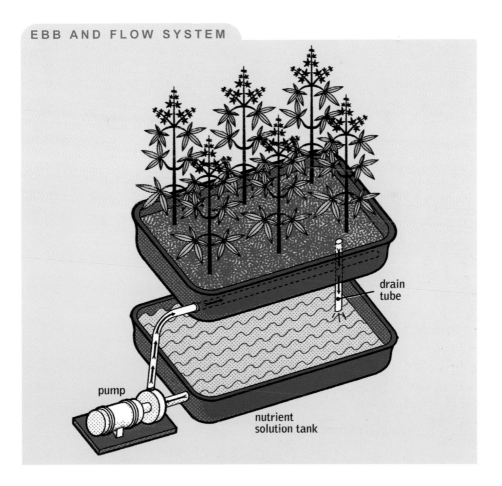

drain tube

pump

nutrient solution tank

This is a hi-tech Ebb & Flow system. There is plenty of space to handle recirculation of the water and like the most effective systems, it is well organized and clear of clutter.

Ebb & Flow units are so efficient that the distribution and control of nutrients work over long distances meaning one table can literally run the length of a large grow room.

Drip Irrigation

Drip irrigation works much like the ebb & flow method, except that the nutrients are moved to and from the plants much more slowly, via a dripper. In most setups, each plant is located in a separate chamber within the system. The nutrients are fed to the medium through a small dripper, which regulates the nutrient flow to and from the reservoir.

Most drip irrigation systems include separate compartments for plants to ensure that each plant receives nutrients. Some drip irrigation systems do not have separate chambers and, instead, plants are placed together in the same tray. In this kind of setup you must ensure that the nutrient solution reaches the base of the

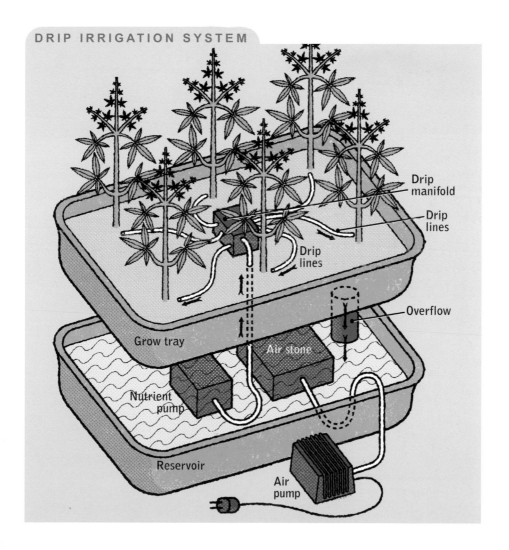

DRIP IRRIGATION SYSTEM

Drip manifold

Drip lines

Drip lines

Overflow

Grow tray

Air stone

Nutrient pump

Reservoir

Air pump

This hydroponic system uses drip irrigation. The young clones are growing in a medium of expanded clay pebbles.

The underside of a drip irrigation system reveals a healthy beginning to a root system that will eventually form a more complex mass to manage.

plants, where it can be distributed evenly to all of the plants in the tray. In drip irrigation systems, plants receive ample amounts of air and nutrients together, causing them to flourish in a well-maintained growing environment.

Aeroponics

Aeroponics is a branch of hydroponics that has steadily been developing into a field of its own. These systems are generally expensive and are used by professional growers. The unit itself is easily recognizable by its unique design, which uses tubes. The plants are grown in a medium that is placed into slots along a lengthy tube. The tubes can run anywhere from 1 to 60 feet in length. Inside the tube are nozzles that mist the roots of each plant with grow nutrients at regular intervals. The reservoir, which contains nutrients, is kept outside of the tube in a tank. The nutrients are pumped from the tank to the nozzles and then the remaining solution that drips from the plants is drained into another tank that is normally checked before being reused again.

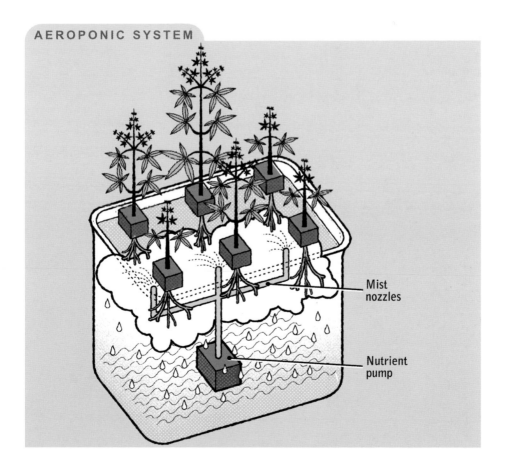

AEROPONIC SYSTEM

Mist nozzles

Nutrient pump

Wick

The wick system is one of the easiest hydroponic systems to make because it relies on a simple wick (or multiple wicks) to absorb nutrients from a reservoir and deliver them into the growing medium. In a wick system, the nutrient solution is held in a reservoir (a nutrient solution container) above which another container—the grow container—is placed. The grow container holds rockwool, or another type of soilless substrate, and the plants.

Building the system is simple. Before you add the substrate and plants, make several holes in the bottom of the grow container. Push the wicks down through the holes into the nutrient solution below. Something as simple as cotton strips from an old T-shirt can be used as wicks. The tops of the wicks are secured in place in the grow container to guarantee that the nutrients absorbed are evenly distributed

WICK SYSTEM

This clone nursery setup uses a wick system. At the back of the grow room you can see a large cluster of plants in a kiddy pool.

to all areas of the substrate. This ensures that your plants have access to adequate nutrients and water.

Less sophisticated than other hydroponic systems, the wick system does not offer growers much control over the rate of feeding. In a wick system, capillary action causes the nutrient solution to travel upwards along the wick. The problem with capillary action is that the amount of time it takes for the nutrients to travel up the wick and into your medium may be much less than the time it takes for your plants to use up those nutrients. To control nutrient delivery to your plants, you need to either add wicks to, or remove wicks from, your system. If you use too many wicks, you risk overwatering or overfeeding your plants. If you find that you need to add more nutrients and water quickly, then you should hand water the medium from above. Wick system growers often have to hand water to compensate for slow capillary action of the wicks.

Gravity

The gravity system is another hydroponic system that is easy to make. Aptly named, it relies on gravitational forces to deliver nutrient solution into your substrate and feed your plants. Gravity Systems are either sloped or horizontal.

GRAVITY SYSTEM

In a sloped system, the nutrients are held in a reservoir above the grow container and are allowed to flow from the reservoir to the grow container, where they will naturally flow downwards through the substrate to the plant roots. The solution is then delivered to another reservoir on the other end of the grow container. When the nutrients have completely run out of the original reservoir it is swapped around with one full of nutrient solution and the process is repeated again as needed.

The horizontal system works in much the same way, except that there is only one reservoir that is moved manually from an upward position (where nutrients drain out) to a downward position (where the nutrients are captured) after it is emptied into the grow container.

In both types of gravity system, the reservoirs and containers should each be equipped with a tap so that the nutrients are allowed a certain amount of time in the substrate before being released back into the reservoir again. Some advanced gravity systems use pumps to feed nutrients from the catching reservoir back into the original reservoir again.

Automatic Hydroponic Pots and Manual Hydroponic Pots

These are pots that are used for growing one plant at a time. In each pot, a pump delivers the nutrients into the bottom of the pot until the nutrients reach the roots (or they are manually fed by hand). The roots then drink as much as they can until they're dry. Once the roots are exposed, the pot is fed again with more nutrient solution. These units are good for the grower who wishes to grow one or more big, bushy cannabis plants in a simple stand-alone unit—note, however, they do require lots of supervision to ensure that they do not dry out for too long.

COMMERICAL POT

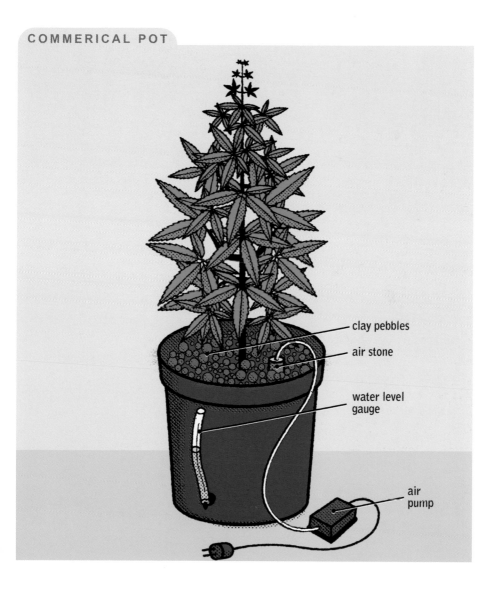

clay pebbles

air stone

water level gauge

air pump

EBB AND FLOW SYSTEM

Cleanliness is important at these early stages to prevent any disease-producing agents (pathogens) from infecting cuttings. Keeping them healthy is half the battle.

Healthy cuttings in rockwool show their vigor, as the roots are abundant and tightly packed with very few going out for a longer reach than others.

These healthy cuttings have even more densely and shorter packed root mass.

Propagation products like these rockwool blocks with hollow cores are reliable aids to successful cloning techniques.

The mini-version of the rockwool block can be inserted into the hollow blocks sometimes called delta blocks.

The proof is in the success rate. Experienced growers find that they can start hitting an optimal 90% or higher success rate.

These cuttings under lights have flat or upward pointing
leaves and there has been more growth.

A very important part of cutting propagation is to keep them from stretching and
creating long internode length. Less crowding and low lights helps deter this.

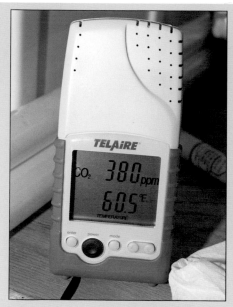

Digital measuring devices offer a higher degree of accuracy when maintaining control of nutrients, CO2, humidity and temperature.

Here the vent outtakes are well sealed to prevent light and smell leakage. The tight fit helps to keep airflow under your control.

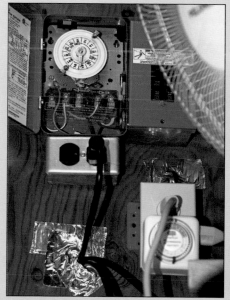

Sophisticated timing systems are worth investing in especially for safety. These electrical components are wall mounted to avoid contact with water.

This filter helps cut down on the smell. Skunk has a particularly strong odor and filters are essential.

If you have trouble visualizing any hydroponics design then visit YouTube.
All hydroponics are somewhat similar but vary in design.

Here the substrate is being prepared. In the background the trays are
waiting for a nutrient solution to be added.

The substrate is placed in the nutrient solution in the tray. Notice how they might float?
Adding plants will weigh them down.

The nutrient solution has diffused not only into the substrate but also into the rockwool cube.

Mesh is prepared above the canopy to make it easier to engage later. This view of this part of the garden shows an even spaced 16 plant layout.

With room enough to work in this hydroponics garden is going to produce 40 plants of high quality cannabis.

EBB AND FLOW SYSTEM

The canopy starts to break through the screen. Now it is time for the grower to begin directing where those colas should grow. The screen is mainly there for support.

The density of the canopy from hydroponics systems clearly suggests a yield that makes it worth all the effort. This harvest would make any grower proud.

Trichome-covered colas of end-goal glory with a magazine quality look. This can be achieved with a little growing experience and the right know-how, but don't underestimate the power of genetics.

Setting up the Hydroponic Environment
Hydroponic Nutrients

Nutrients are the most important part of your hydroponic setup. Nutrient solutions come in a number of different forms. It is vital to check that the solution you use is the best for your type of plant and setup. Some solutions should only be used with soil as they contain the wrong elements for hydroponic use. There are soil-based supplements/fertilizers and then there are hydroponic nutrients.

Most hydroponic nutrient solutions are complete nutrient solutions, meaning that they provide every element and compound needed for proper plant growth. Because of this, hydroponic nutrients can be pricey. Always spend your money on the correct nutrients because shortcuts can be expensive in more ways than one: they could lead to total devastation of your crop. In a hydroponic system especially, plants are entirely dependent on you, the grower, for nutrients and an imbalance in the system can quickly kill all of your plants.

Single Packs

If all the required nutrients are contained in a single pack, there is a chance that the elements will combine and precipitate in the pack. This can cause the solution to become unbalanced, making it useless to you and your plants. Keeping this in mind, get a complete nutrient solution that is contained in several bottles called twin or triple packs.

One brand, called Formulex, has managed to hold all the elements in a single pack using certain chemicals to prevent precipitation. This pack is very good for starting clones or seeds in a rockwool SBS tray and can be used in soil grows as well.

Specialized indoor twin nutrient pack that comes with indoor vegetative and indoor flowering formulas.

Twin/Triple Packs

For best results, the hydroponic grower should consider a twin or even a triple pack. Basically, in these multi-packs, the chemicals are separated in order to prevent precipitation. Optimum, Power Gro, Ionic, Earth Juice, and General Hydroponics (G.H.) Flora Series are the most common multi part nutrient solutions. The most popular one for cannabis cultivation is the G.H. Flora

Nutrients can also come in components A and B with mixing instructions on the label.

Series, a three-part system with Gro, Micro, and Bloom components. An experienced grower can adjust these nutrients to get optimum performance from their plants. These packs have instructions on the bottles as to how to mix the nutrients in water at different strengths, according to the grower's needs.

The Hydroponic Growing Medium

There are many hydroponic mediums to choose from. Rockwool is probably the most popular, is easy to work with, and comes in either slabs or cubes. The cubes vary in size from one to six inches cubed. The slabs can be cut to suit the shape of your pot or container.

Rockwool

Many growers like to use the cubes for seed germination and for rooting cuttings. This seems to be the easiest method. Many growers claim that rockwool should be pre-soaked for 24 hours in water with a pH level of 5.6 (7.0 for soil grows) in order to stabilize the pH level of the rockwool.

Expanded Clay Pellets

Expanded clay pellets are also called "grow rocks" and come in a variety of different sizes. They are an ecologically sustainable medium, usually manufactured into round shapes by baking clay in a rotary kiln at very high temperatures (at these temperatures clay will pop like popcorn, becoming porous). They are also

A three-part system usually consists of an additional micronutrient bottle, a great supplement for strains that suffer often from micronutrient deficiencies.

inert, pH-neutral, and contain no nutrients. They are good for use in hydroponic systems, as they add needed support to the cannabis plants' stems. Clay pellets are full of tiny air pockets, which make them light. Most clay pellets will float.

Clay pellets can also be reused. Just mix 10ml of hydrogen peroxide with 1 gallon of water and let them steep in the mix for a few minutes before drying them out. After a few hours they should be ready for reuse. Expanded clay pellets tend to be a bit more expensive than most other soilless substrates, but the fact that they can be reused makes this extra expense worthwhile. They can be used on their own as a growing medium in a hydroponic system, but since they are quick draining they should be mixed with another substrate when used with soil or soilless growing techniques.

Oasis Cubes

Oasis cubes also come in several formats, including Horticubes and Rootcubes. They are like rockwool cubes but are made from different materials. Prior to use, Oasis cubes should be completely saturated with water. If you use a tray to soak them, you can drain away the excess water by tilting the tray over on its side, leaving about an eighth of an inch of water in the tray. Feel the weight of the tray — it should feel heavy. Oasis holds a lot of water! Like rockwool, growers can expect a high success rate using Oasis cubes. Oasis should never be allowed to completely dry out.

A delta rockwool cube showing healthy
roots protruding from the base
in search of nutrients.

Note the thick base of the plant where the stem
meets the cube. It is important to have a medium
that can hold it firm.

Rockwool is a popular choice for many growers and comes in a large variety of forms.

Close up of clay pebbles.

Coconut Fiber

Coconut fiber provides added protection from root diseases and fungus infestation. It also contains natural rooting hormones. Coconut fiber comes dry and compressed, usually in block format. It must be re-hydrated to a texture similar to that of wet ground coffee. When re-hydrated, most of the compressed blocks expand to roughly nine times their original size. Coconut fiber can also be purchased in different thicknesses and lengths of mats (1/2-inch thick and 24 to 36 inches widths). These mats are very suitable for hydroponic systems as they can be placed directly into the tray without requiring much shaping. Coconut fiber also retains moisture, which helps to prevent the roots from drying out between watering cycles.

Soilless Mixes

Soilless mixes are pre-packaged bags of combinations of soilless substrates. The soilless substrates and ratios used are usually printed on the bag. They can include the following: vermiculite, screened peat, peat, perlite, composted bark, fine silica sand, quartz, construction grade sand and coconut fibers. Most growers prefer to prepare their own soilless mixes because it is cheaper and offers them more control.

Re-hydrated coconut fiber.

Perlite

Perlite is the name for a naturally occurring, silicon-based rock. Perlite is distinguished from other rocks by its ability to expand to up to twenty times its original size when heated. This increase is due to water present in the raw rock. When heated, the rock pops like popcorn into large pieces of nutrient- and water-retaining, puffy perlite. Perlite is a form of natural glass and is graded as chemically inert. It usually has a neutral pH of 7.

Vermiculite

Vermiculite is the name given to "hydrated laminar magnesium-aluminum-iron-silicate." When heated, vermiculite expands into worm-like pieces (the name vermiculite comes from the Latin *vermiculare*, which means to breed worms). These pieces can expand up to thirty times their own size. This makes vermiculite a good water and nutrient retaining material for horticultural use.

Preparing Nutrient Solutions

Always follow the instructions on the products and dilute to the strength that best suits your strain. All you need is a container in which to mix the nutrient solution and the nutrients themselves. Each of the packs should have A, B, and C written on them, and this method of tagging is used to calculate the mixture instruction

Analysis of Perlite*

Element	Percent
Aluminum	7.2%
Bound water	3.0
Calcium	0.6
Iron	0.6
Magnesium	0.2
Oxygen	47.5
Potassium	3.5
Silicon	33.8
Sodium	3.4
Trace elements	0.2
TOTAL	100.0

Analysis of Vermiculite*

Element	Percent
Silicon	30.6%
Aluminum	14.4
Magnesium	19.7
Calcium	4.3
Potassium	5.1
Iron	9.9
Titanium	3.2
Water	11.8
Trace elements	1.0
TOTAL	100.0

*Some elements subject to change

on the label. A usually represents the primary nutrients, B the secondary nutrients, and C the micronutrients. In some cases, A represents the vegetative food, B the flowering food, and C either the secondary nutrients or a secondary and micronutrient mixture. Check your pack for specific details.

In most cases the mixture is about 3.5 ml of each (A, B, and C) per liter of water. This is called a 100 percent strength mixture if you follow the instructions on the pack.

Hydroponic pH

After you have mixed your nutrient solution you'll want to take a pH reading of it. Just as in soil growing, you may need to adjust your pH level; however, you do not adjust pH to the same levels. For hydroponics, you will need a pH up and pH down adjusting solution. These are relatively inexpensive and can be added to your solution to balance the pH level. Cannabis plants in a soil system like a pH of 7, but in hydroponic systems they like a pH of 5.2 to 6.3. You'll discover it is easier to maintain a pH range than a set level. Check your hydroponic pH level as often as you can, as it can change very quickly in hydroponic systems.

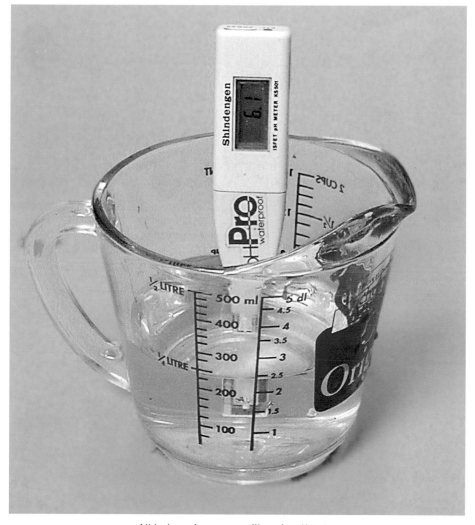

All hydroponic growers will need a pH tester.

Algae

Algae is part of a large group of non-vascular, mainly aquatic eukaryote capable of photosynthesis. Always keep your container away from exposure to direct light, as algae will grow if you do not. Most hydroponic kits are manufactured to be lightproof[1] to eliminate this problem. If you built your own system, like the bubbler described later in this chapter, then you will want to keep your solution sealed from the light using thick black tape to cover the lid and the entire reservoir. This will help prevent algae from growing in your system. A thick, black garbage bag also works well to keep the light out and algae from forming.

If you notice algae growth then you will need to clean your system. Wash the unit and replace the nutrient solution with a fresh mix. Throw out all old, algae-infested nutrients. Also try to find the source of the light leak and patch it up.

Grow and Bloom

Some of the double nutrient packs come in two different sets: grow and bloom. The grow solution is used during the plants' vegetative growth stage and the bloom is used during the flowering stage. The bloom formulas contain more phosphorus and potassium and less nitrogen. Other packs have a complete all-in-one function, but beware: they may lack important nutrients or minerals.

When your pH is off you can use commercial products to bring it either up or down.

With the root mass removed these recently harvested plants have just been taken from the hydroponics medium. Notice the thick nutrient fed colas.

A Word About Nutrient Strengths

When nutrients are mixed at full strength, cannabis has a tendency to suffer from chemical burn. It's suggested that when using any hydroponic formulations with cannabis you do so in moderation for your first grow. Many cannabis growers have bought these products anticipating the production of great big buds only to get great big plant burns.

In fact, even medium-strength formulas have the power to burn your plants. Consult the information on the packs, but in general 3.5 ml of A, B, and C per liter is called 100 percent strength. The same amount mixed with two liters or of water is 50 percent strength. Marijuana can grow very well with nutrient solutions of between 30 and 50 percent. It's best to start off with 30 percent strength and then increase as needed. You'll be surprised at how rich a bud content you'll produce with a nutrient strength of only 30 percent.

The most common problem associated with hydroponics is plant burns. I have rarely heard of anyone underfeeding plants in a hydro system. I have heard plenty of reports about overfeeding plants in hydro systems. Over time you'll get to know your strain and what it likes. The better you know your strain the better you'll be able to control the feeding amounts.

Trichome Technologies, voted Best Growroom in the 25 year history of High Times magazine.

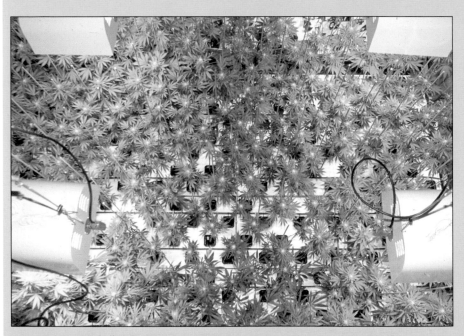

This custom built NFT setup is simply amazing in it's size, organization and efficiency.

Here, the plants are just a couple of weeks from full maturation and harvest.

This drying rack holds many different varieties of marijuana, separated by dividers.

Controlling the Hydroponic Environment
Monitoring Recycle Systems

Depending on the setup you're using, you may find it beneficial to recycle your water and nutrient solution. As the plants extract nutrients and minerals from the solution it will be depleted of its resources over time. For this reason we must understand how to monitor nutrients so that we know when to recycle and when to replace the solution. Monitoring systems are a bit expensive. If you have a ppm reader, also known as a total dissolved solids (TDS) meter, you can understand how much of your nutrients have been used and how much more you need to add to reach the optimal nutrient level. All reservoirs will become unbalanced and need replenishing. As a general rule, an initial amount is used to fill the reservoir. As the plants use up the solution, top up the reservoir to maintain a constant, appropriate level. If you start with 10 gallons of solution then you need to top up to that total of 10 gallons every few days.

If you don't have a ppm reader you can still grow a good crop using hydroponics, but it takes practice to get it right. If a hydroponic grower doesn't have a ppm reader, they tend to replace the reservoir more often instead of topping it up. That way the grower is certain that the new solution contains everything the plants need. If you have a ppm reader, you only need to top off the reservoir as needed. These readers can be expensive, but over time they'll help save money on the cost of pricey hydroponic nutrients.

Hard Water Problems

Hard water is the most common problem found in domestic water supplies. Water is classified as "hard" if it contains minerals other than H_2O in amounts above 1 GPG (grain per gallon). Soft water contains minerals other than H_2O in amounts below 1 GPG. Very hard water reaches levels above 7 GPG.

If you observe scales forming in your reservoir or what looks like kettle rust, then you haven't been maintaining your pH level in the correct range. Minerals will build up into grains in the solution, causing it to become hard. Your local water company can provide you with a readout on your water. You can also buy nutrient products to use with hard water. If scaling persists, just drain and clean your reservoir and mix a new batch of nutrients to the correct pH level. Some growers use a reverse osmosis water-filtering system to clean their tap water, producing distilled water that has a stable pH level of 7.0.

When to Add More Nutrients

Beginners should rely on a ppm meter, but a veteran grower learns to read the plant. The plant will reveal if it is has too much, too little, or just enough nutrients. It takes a few grows to learn to read the plant and this is part of growing experience. The plant may have siphoned all the nutrients or just some of them. Some nutrients are taken up by the plant and stored until it needs more. A top up can be done if you don't want to change the reservoir completely.

If you don't have a ppm meter to calculate nutrient levels accurately, simply record your nutrient mix ratio from day one. Let's say you used 3.5 ml of A, B, and C in a one-liter container. If the plant has used 1/2 a liter, all you need is to make another liter of 3.5-ml mix in another container and add 1/2 of that to the reservoir. This is a simple way of doing it, but you're left with 1/2 a liter of solution. By doing your math and making a mixing chart, you can mix different amounts as needed. Every now and again you will need to mix a fresh batch of nutrient because topping up becomes increasingly inaccurate over a period of time.

Affordable Hydroponics

Growing using hydroponics is not rocket science. It's a simple process that varies slightly depending on what kind of setup you choose. Most of the nutrient mixes are explained on the packs. If you follow the instructions and remember that cannabis only needs 30 to 50 percent strength nutrients, then you'll do just fine.

Over the years, many cannabis cultivators have experimented by building their own growing contraptions. There are more than 100 different types of systems that can be handmade at home. Out of these 100, about 15 are ideal for cannabis. One of the most famous and simplest systems is DWC (deep water culture), also known as the bubbler. This system is very cheap to assemble and yet still provides excellent growth rates. There's nothing like it for the price and it can be quite a rewarding way to grow.

The Bubbler

The bubbler is simply an all-in-one nutrient and plant holding container with a lid and a pump, but it produces extraordinary results! Using the bubbler method, you can produce optimal growing conditions for top yielding strains, as long as it is maintained and managed well, by you, the grower.

The pump will send air through the tube to the air stone and this releases air into the water. The air "bubbles" the solution causing it to splash at the surface, wetting the bottom of the net pot.

THE BUBBLE BUCKET

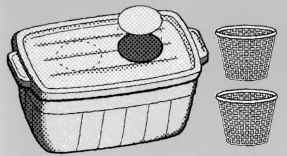

1. Get a container that can hold roughly 3 gallons of nutrients per plant. For a double bubbler use a container that can hold 6 gallons. For a single plant you can use a 3 gallon bucket. Make sure that the container comes with a lid.

2. Wrap the entire unit and lid with black gaffer tape. This will keep light out of the unit and prevent algae from forming in the nutrient solution.

3. Get some 6-inch net pots.

4. Cut circular holes in the lid, enough to allow the entire net pot to rest fully down into the lid. The rim of the net pot should be enough to keep it from slipping into the container totally.

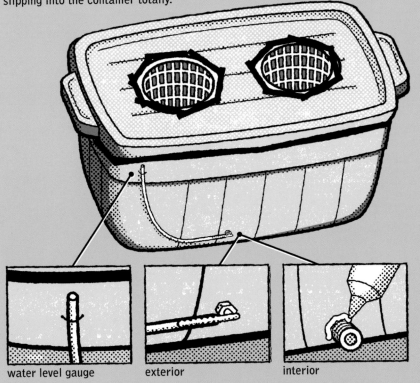

water level gauge   exterior   interior

5. Cut a hole in the bottom of the container. Insert a small valve in here and use some waterproof sealing around the sides. A good glue will work too. Make sure that the valve can accommodate the pump's air tube without leaking.

fish tank
air pump

air stone

hose

6. Insert the pump's
air tube into the valve.

7. Attach an air stone to the air
tube inside the container. Let it
rest on the bottom somewhere
around the middle of the
container.

8. Attach the air tube
to your pump.

9. Fill the container
with your nutrient
solution so that it
covers about an inch
of the bottom of the net pot.

10. Get your growing medium together - rockwool,
clay pebbles and place these into the net pots.

11. Transplant your rooted clone to the net pot.

12. Fill up the remaining area of the net pots
with more clay pebbles to support the clones.

13. Turn on your air pump 24-hours a day.

That's all there is to it!

Aerators add air to your nutrient solution reservoirs, keeping the solution full of oxygen and preventing stagnant water.

YouTube features hundreds of different home-made and commercial standalone hydroponics systems. Viewing them is a good idea.

A single standalone hydroponics system might just be what a novice or low-key grower is looking for.

NASA brings us one of the most important revolutions in hydroponics-type cultivation. This is called aeroponics and many hydro growers are turning to it for better results.

The clones will be able to live from the nutrients and water that is in the clay pebbles. As the roots grow down they will experience water bubbles coming into contact with them. They will gradually grow through the net pots and down into the nutrient solution, where they will drink until the unit is dry or the roots no longer touch the nutrient solution. Check the bubbler every day to see how much your plant has absorbed.

Let your roots get air periodically by letting a root zone form. To do this, simply let the solution level drop a few inches below the net pot. Do not constantly top up your reservoir; it is sometimes better to let the water level drop one gallon per 3 gallons and then just replace the missing gallons. Once a good root mass has developed, your plants will exhibit unprecedented growth!

You can also keep a spare container of the same size handy for when you want to completely change your nutrient mixture. Simply swap the lid over with the plants and root mass into the new bucket. You can do this by lifting the whole plant and root mass out by pulling on the lid with both hands. Just lift the plant and roots out by the lid and put it into the other container. Empty out the nutrients from the old one and replace it with new nutrients. This is a great and cheap hydroponics system that comes highly recommended.

11 | **Outdoor Growing**

Many of the elements that you need to complete your outdoor or guerrilla grow site are described in the indoor growing chapters of this book. If you skipped through Chapters 5 and 6, be sure to go back and scan through them—paying particular attention to information about germination, feeding, and cloning—as they will give you ideas about what your cannabis plants need to thrive.

Many cannabis enthusiasts claim that the best cannabis they ever smoked was grown outdoors. If you live in a climate that is warm enough for tomatoes to grow outdoors, then you have the perfect climate to grow good weed outdoors. If your climate is very warm and if you have a long summer, then you may be able to grow high-yielding Sativa varieties like the Australian bush, Haze, and skunk hybrid strains. Although these strains have long flowering periods, they also have the ability to yield more than two pounds of bud per plant when grown to full maturity outdoors.

As an outdoor grower, you may either choose your own backyard or a guerrilla grow in the woods or a field as the site for your patch. When you have found an area that suits your needs (refer to Chapter 4), you can start to prepare your plot. Be aware that seeds planted in untreated ground will have a low germination rate. To avoid this problem, most outdoor cannabis growers begin their plants indoors, germinating seedlings indoors and growing them in plastic pots. By cutting away the base of the pots and holding the soil in place using a piece of cardboard secured with strong tape, pots can be transported to the grow patch and planted. This method offers the advantage of cloning all females for transplanting to the outdoor patch—offering the ideal all-female, sinsemilla, high-yield, outdoor crop.

This field of outdoor plants runs all the way down to the background. Notice that these plants are bushier than a typical indoor strain.

This is a typical small outdoor patch that is somewhat concealed from public view and even has some turkey activity nearby.

The months of March and April are very good times to start your plants outdoors because they should mature and begin to flower by August or September—when the daylight hours start to decrease. So, you should plan to find your grow spot and start your garden by April. If you are using clones you will probably want to wait to transplant them until just before the flowering season, since clones only need to grow for a week or two before flowering. Pure Indica or Indica hybrid strains can be planted in May or June because they have shorter vegetative and flowering times than Sativa strains.

Try to remove as many weeds as possible while preparing your grow patch and don't leave heaps of earth around for people to notice. Carry the earth away in bags if you have to. You can then simply sow your seeds or plant your seedlings or cuttings.

If you must work with seeds outdoors, don't bury them too deep: 1/2-inch to 1-inch below the soil's surface is fine. If you are working with seedlings or cuttings, dig small holes and place the plants and "bottomless" pots described above directly into the holes, removing the piece of cardboard before doing so. Ensure that the pot is completely below ground and not visible to passersby. The roots will grow down through the hole in the bottom of the pot and into the surrounding soil.

PREPARING A PLOT

This could be a guerrilla grow or an outdoor area you want
to grow in. The area is covered in thickets and weeds.

Here the thickets and weeds have been cleared back.
The soil has not been touched or replaced though.

Here the transplants have been brought to the grow site. They
are spaced out to judge how they will eventually go in.

Replacing the soil is a good idea. You can either just turn the soil or bring in your own.

Combining soils gives growers more control over the medium in which their plants will grow.

This plot is semi-camouflaged. It is deep in the woods where people are less likely trek through but at the same time can be spotted if close enough.

Note the wide spacing between plants. Outdoor plants tend to get big and bushy and so need the space.

This is an outdoor balcony grow. Lots of people find this method a way to get something from a space that doesn't get used that much.

This whole backyard has been transformed into an outdoor cannabis garden.

You may choose to add prefab, store-bought soil to the patch. Look for a soil with a higher N than P and K value. Adding soil is a good idea because the store-bought kind does not contain living masses, such as weeds. Even though you may have weeded and treated your outdoor soil patch, it could still contain seeds or spores from weeds and other plants. You'll most certainly have to weed your outdoor area nearly every week during the initial growth stages.

After you have sown your seeds or planted your clones, simply sprinkle them with water. That's all you need to do. You don't need to adjust the soil pH yet or feed the soil. What you've done should be fine for starting seedlings or clones.

If nature does not provide water for your plants then you need to draw water and feed your plants when needed. There are a few irrigation techniques you can use to bring water to your plants, however, these may reveal your grow site to others. By simply digging a partial trench around your plants you can force the roots to grow in a certain direction. You can also channel running water from a stream to your plants by digging a water route. Water always runs downhill, so you need to

All the plants are together so walking through or around them is not possible.
However as we can see this lot will still generate some impressive results.

take this into consideration when investigating different schemes of irrigation. All of these irrigation methods may compromise your security and this is why watering by hand is still the single best way to water your outdoor plants.

Polymer crystals have water-retaining properties and can be used in conjunction with your soil mix so that the plant has some access to water during the dry spells. Simply fill a plastic bottle with water and the crystals and allow them to expand overnight so that they absorb as much water as possible before you mix them in with your soil. Polymer crystals will retain and then release the water at a very slow rate.

When growing outdoors you need to keep your plants healthy and free from unwanted predators that may find your top cola and leaves to be quite tasty. In the second week of vegetative growth, you may even want to spray the area with some pesticide. Pests and predators are discussed in detail in Chapter 12.

Outdoor Soil

If you have not yet read about soil in Chapter 5 you should do so now before reading on to understand exactly what kind of soil and nutrients your cannabis strain

These are seedlings that are growing under natural light. This mechanism is called phototropism.

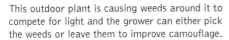

This outdoor plant is causing weeds around it to compete for light and the grower can either pick the weeds or leave them to improve camouflage.

Some outdoor plants are truly colossal. Here the weight of the bud is sending branches horizontal.

prefers and how to maintain the right balance throughout your grow. Frequently, an outdoor grow patch is selected because it looks like it is already sustaining some form of life such as weeds, grass, trees, and bushes. This usually indicates that the soil is probably a loam type, meaning that it has some sands, silts, clays, and humus in it. In some cases, the soil may be missing some of these components or have a very high percentage of one of them.

Check the soil in your outdoor patch. Sift through it to determine if it is primarily a sand, silt, clay, loam, or humus type. As you dig down you will find that the composition of the soil changes. Generally, the top few inches of surface soil will contain humus and some living matter. The next layer below this, the "topsoil," is the one that the roots will grow down into. Try to determine whether this topsoil needs more loam. If you need more you should consider adding more soil to your grow area. If you have chosen well, your grow patch will not need additional soil supplements and by simply turning the soil you should be able to achieve very effective results.

These are outdoor plants in pots. This is an alternative way to cultivate outdoors and allows the grower to move the plants as they please.

This particular plant has several branches that require tying up. This strain needs it or else the heavy buds will only fall to the sides.

If you want to dig your own patch, go down a minimum of 1.5 feet to a maximum of 3 feet. You should be able to remove a large amount of the ground's natural composition. Most growers would do this if there appeared to be too much clay in the topsoil. Clay on its own, as you know from reading Chapter 5, is not good for cannabis roots but is good when mixed with sand, silt and humus to form a loam. If you have sand, silt, and humus you can mix it with the soil you have dug up. Do this by using a shovel to break the clay in with the sand, silt, and humus.

The problem with digging up a patch is keeping it looking natural. If you are using vermiculite, perlite, or other colorful soilless substrates, be sure to keep them well below the surface. A good sprinkling of a coconut-based grow medium over the surface makes your patch look more like part of the surroundings. Coconut fibers also add nutrients to your soil. If you mix coconut fibers in with the soil you will also provide the roots with additional room to breathe and grow. Coconut substrates are very popular with outdoor growers and can be obtained from grow shops.

There is always the option of pruning back your plants to reduce crowding. However pruned branches tend to split into two or more branches.

Alternatively you may want to bring a branch down or out to the side more. One way of doing this is by using wires shaped as hooks.

The next section focuses on the specific challenges that outdoor growers face in caring for their plants from the beginning of the vegetative growth stage to the end of flowering.

Caring for Outdoor Plants
Weeding

The best way to weed is by hand. Don't attempt to add weed killer to your grow area unless you know a great deal about the weed killer you're using and how it reacts with cannabis. Some weed killers claim they'll protect your plant and only kill the surrounding weeds, yet are in fact not very agreeable to marijuana plants. If you want to test weed killers, then it's suggested that you create a small patch with one clone to see how the clone reacts to the weed killer. Also, remember that people could be ingesting or inhaling this cannabis so use a food-plant-friendly weed killer. To begin with, we recommend that you do your weeding by hand.

When you've weeded a grow area, your plant will grow much better without

Some strains have a high leaf to calyx ratio. These strains can be just as good in terms of potency and bud quantities as strains with low leaf to calyx ratios.

having to compete for nutrients and light. Generally, you'll have to weed the patch every week for the first 2 to 3 weeks and then once every month throughout the plants' grow cycle. Some grow areas may be weed-free in March but, come June, the area may seem like it hasn't been weeded at all because of the speed of weed growth. Whenever you visit your plants make sure you pull up a few weeds to keep them under control.

If you feel your area is very dense with weeds you may want to consider a ground cover. A ground cover is placed on the ground and cut to allow the marijuana plants to grow through it. Covers can be anything from plastic garbage bags to sheets of paper. Of course, this is not conducive to stealth growing, but it does keep the weeds from receiving light.

Most growers who wish to clear a large area for a bigger grow do so the year before. Around autumn growers can clear the area of any leaves, branches and dead matter with much more ease than in springtime or summer, when weeds and new plant growth can get in the way or hide potentially good growing areas.

There is absolutely no reason why anyone should ever fell a tree in order to grow an outdoor plot of cannabis plants, unless the tree is already dead.

Watering
This is nature's job, most of the time. If you find that your crop is experiencing a warm spell or drought during the summer you may wish to carry some water to your grow area. If you have to trek over long distances, then it's recommended you fill a backpack with plastic bottles of water. Some garden growers use sprinkler systems during dry spells. This is great but can attract unwanted attention to your patch.

How much water your plants need depends on the size of the plants. Larger plants can require a minimum of a gallon of water per day. Natural loam soil is able to hold water for anywhere from four to six weeks before becoming extremely dry under the sun. Deep pockets of water may be held underground. The best way to judge whether your plants need water or not is through a simple visual inspection. If they're wilting badly, they need water. If you want to ensure that your plants have a constant water source then factor this into your choice of outdoor location and use water-retaining polymer crystals.

If you want to check for an underground water source, simply dig a small hole about a foot deep next to your grow patch, taking care not to hit any major roots. Put your hand down inside the hole. Does it feel dry, or is it cool and moist? If it's cool and moist then the soil has stored some water below the surface that your plants can drink without any problems.

Nutrients can be added to the soil at any time during the plants' life cycle. Switching to a P feed during the flowering weeks will help promote bud growth. Outdoor soil treatment is much like indoor soil treatment, except for the weeding. For further information on feeding throughout the plants' life cycle refer to Chapters 5 and 6.

This plant has over 15 colas. It is as wide as it tall. By pruning and topping growers can manipulate their plants to form these bush shapes.

A generator pumps water up from the lake.   Irrigation tubes distribute water to the plants.

If you have good sunlight and enough water, then your plants will grow through-out the full cycle quite well. At the end of the flowering season you'll be ready to harvest your plant and reap your bounty.

The more you experiment, the more tricks you'll invent for yourself to get the most out of your yields. Some of the best cannabis growers use very exotic and original methods. A number of people have even tried outdoor hydroponics to get their plants to grow bigger and better.

Air Pruning

Depending on the soil's composition it should retain a certain amount of air between watering. The presence of too much air can necessitate "air pruning." If you dig a trench around an outdoor plant, the roots will not grow into the trench. Instead, they will sense that there is too much air and not enough nutrients or water to continue their development in this area of the medium. That is why roots do not grow above the surface of the soil, nor do they grow out of the bottom of

The plants receive a consistent supply of fresh water from the irrigation tubes.

your pots and onto the work surface or floor.[1] Air pruning by creating trenches around your plant will eventually cause the roots to grow in the direction of your choice and can be used by outdoor growers who wish to guide their plants towards a natural source of water or nutrients.

Outdoor Flowering and the Photoperiod

Towards the end of summer the photoperiod will naturally change outdoors. The cannabis plant automatically controls its own flowering by calculating the alteration in the number of hours of daylight and the uninterrupted darkness at night.

The plant hormone phytochrome is responsible for regulating when flowering should commence. In summer there is more daylight than darkness; as the year progresses, there is gradually less daylight and more darkness. Phytochrome reacts to this change and reaches a critical level, which triggers flowering in the plant. However, the plant must be mature enough for flowering to begin. If the plant is not mature enough, the photoperiod will have no effect on the plants flowering capabilities.

Our planet is green for a good reason. These growers
are keeping it very green. Photo Paradise Seeds

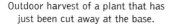

Outdoor harvest of a plant that has just been cut away at the base.

This outdoor harvest bunch can keep some growers going nicely throughout the better part of a year.

The photoperiod differs slightly from strain to strain because of the uneven amounts of light and darkness available at different latitudes around the world. Some plants only need eight hours of darkness to trigger flowering and others need more, but most mature plants will be begin flowering when the photoperiod changes to 12/12. Do not confuse the latitude you are growing in with the plant's own natural photoperiod. The plant's natural photoperiod regime is genetic and is part of its lineage. The seed bank you acquire your plants from should indicate if their strain requires special adjustments to the photoperiod, especially if it is an outdoor strain. All mature cannabis plants will eventually flower when the photoperiod changes.

The bottom line for outdoor growers it to estimate when the photoperiod naturally changes so that they do not miss the start of the flowering period due to late outdoor cultivation. It is far better to let a plant vegetate longer than to flower late. If you are behind schedule you may find that the weather is no longer suitable for cannabis cultivation. Early spring is always the time when growers should be thinking about planting their outdoor crop.

12 | Caring for Mature Marijuana Plants

Towards the end of the flowering stage, your cannabis plants will fill out and take on a Christmas tree shape. From vegetative growth to the end of flowering, the cannabis plant develops in three main sections: the top cola, mid-section, and base. The top cola will develop a large amount of bud. The mid-section contains stems along with old and new leaves and should fill with buds growing between the nodes. Although these buds will generally be smaller in size to those found at the main cola, they should be just as potent. Growers who find that bud taken from the mid-section is less potent have likely not developed their plants to full maturity. Towards the base of your plant, you will find large fan leaves and a small amount of bud. Growers should learn to treat each section differently to get the most out of their plants.

The bottom fan leaves are generally not smoked or ingested. If your plant is growing under an artificial light source and the fan leaves are not receiving much light, you may be tempted to cut them away. This is not a good idea. Fan leaves produce sugar that is used in bud production. Cutting away the fan leaves may cause bud growth to stunt, resulting in a smaller harvest. The only time to remove fan leaves is when a plant is either dying, badly burnt, or when the fan leaf is covering a large bud mass. Light is probably the most important factor in bud development and if the fan leaf is preventing light from reaching a bud you will want to remove or tie it back. Refer to the ScrOG section in Chapter 8 for information on clipping fan leaves.

You should always remove dead leaves from your plant and throw them away. Never leave dead matter on your soil as a fertilizer, as it tends to attract unwanted pests while it decomposes. Place dead matter in a compost heap where it will eventually turn to humus.

This chapter covers several important aspects of caring for mature plants, including: thinning, pruning, light bending, training, topping, bushing, increasing yield, and cloning. Using these plant care methods you can directly manipulate your plants to give them a better chance to achieve optimal growth.

Thinning

Thinning is the action of manipulating plant height and numbers either via cutting the plant at the stem or removing plants from the grow altogether. Plants naturally compete for light and plants that grow taller than the rest can easily prevent light from reaching other plants in the group. This is especially noticeable with unstable strains and new hybrids in which some of the population may grow more vigorously than others. The action of thinning your crop either by cutting or total removal creates a more even canopy and allows light to penetrate every top cola without some plants getting in the way of the other plants' light requirements.

Thinning generally applies to outdoor growers, but some indoor setups such as ScrOG and SOG may also need to be thinned.

As a cannabis grower, you should aim to produce plants of relatively uniform growth. When all of your plants are approximately the same height, you can more easily achieve optimal lighting conditions. If one plant grows more vigorously than the others, you risk ending up with light gaps. For instance:

- Distance from Plant A to light is 3 feet
- Distance from Plant B to light is 1.5 feet
- Distance from Plant C to light is 8 inches

Obviously, you will be wasting light, not to mention space, on this setup. The reason for uneven growth is simply that some plants tend to be more vigorous than others.[1] If this happens, the more vigorous plants will cause the smaller ones to receive less light. We use a process called thinning to control these vigorous plants.

Clones, taken from the same mother, should not need to be thinned because they will all possess the same genetic makeup. The only time that clones will not grow in a uniform manner is if light dispersal is uneven. Obviously the clones that receive more light have a better rate of photosynthesis and will grow more vigorously. If all the clones are treated in the same way, they should grow uniformly.

Longer internode development is the result of competition, but
there is still one massive bottle-sized cola on this plant.

If you discover a vigorous plant, either cut it down to the same level as the others or remove it from the grow altogether. Do not throw away the cuttings from thinning. You can clone these cuttings into new plants!

You may be tempted to thin the other way round, leaving the taller plants and removing the smaller ones. Recall that in cannabis growing, if you have started from seed, the taller plants are generally male and the smaller ones are female. For this reason do not give in to the temptation of removing plants before you actually identify their sex.

Thinning your grow makes it look nicer, tidier and helps to improve your overall yield by preventing potentially good plants from being covered by weaker ones that are growing much taller. Remember that height and size have nothing to do with potency. Some plants with very long internodes tend to grow very tall, covering other plants and diverting most of their energy into vertical growth rather than bud production. This kind of competitive growth will only lead to less than optimal results.

By the time you have finished your thinning you should have a uniform grow area with some clones that you can use to grow more bud.

Light Bending (Phototropism)

Light bending occurs when a plant grows at an angle toward the light. You may have noticed plants on the perimeter of your grow area bending toward the light to try and get their share. If your plants bend too much they will eventually grow toward or even into another plant and block other plants from the light. Also, during flowering the buds will become heavy and may cause plants to fall over.

A simple way to avoid light bending in an indoor grow environment is to simply switch your plants around. If a plant leans too much in one direction, then move it toward the middle of the grow space or turn the plant around. It only takes a day or two for the plant to straighten. If your plants can't be easily moved, as is the case with hydroponic setups and outdoor gardens, then you may have to tie your plants so they don't bend.

If you are growing outdoors and have a major problem with light bending you may have to cut away surrounding foliage to allow more light to reach your plants. If this is not possible, try using thread and small stakes, such as bamboo, to keep your plants upright. Remember: if your plants are bending they are trying to tell you that they need more direct light.

Pruning and staking your plants is an important part of maximizing use of space and overall yield.

Pruning for Yield

Pruning is the action of manipulating the number of node regions (potential bud sites) that your plant creates and has nothing to do with the thinning process. Cutting a plant at the stem will automatically result in "topping." For this reason, plants that are thinned via cutting will end up growing more than one top cola. Topping is discussed in the next section. This section covers pruning to increase yield.

Prune cuts are made using clippers held at a 45-degree angle to the shoot being cut. For every stem or branch that you prune, the cut area will develop two more branches. This process is natural: just look at any tree to see how the stem divides into branches which sub-divide into more branches which divide into new shoots and leaves. Marijuana plants grow branches out from the stem. Any filling out occurs when new leaves and branches develop at the node regions. Some of these branches may develop new shoots, but these are somewhat smaller and thinner and don't support as much bud growth. If you prune your plant you can make it more like the example of the tree.

Recall that Indica plants tend to be smaller than Sativas. If you learn to prune your plant properly you can produce small, bushy Sativa plants that grow in tiny spaces. Without pruning, a Sativa plant can stretch to five feet or more.

Keep in mind that there is a limit to how much you can prune a marijuana plant. If you prune the stem, it will split in two. You can prune both of these new stems and end up with four stems. You can try to prune each of these four stems to create eight stems, but results will depend on the strain and its genetically predetermined branching limit. You might be able to prune some of the lateral branches, but again, if the plant has reached its threshold it will not produce more branches. All strains are different in this respect.

Topping

Some marijuana growers will take a pair of clippers to the top of their plant just above the last branch formation during the third or fourth week of vegetative growth. The top is removed by shearing it away at the stem. What happens next is

Here a pruned plant frame is revealed after the leaves have been
stripped away so you can see the overall effect.

These two top colas are growing on the same plant as a result of topping.
As you can see both colas share the same volume of bud.

that the main stem splits off in two or more directions, creating a V-shape at the top of your plant. The end result after flowering is two or more top colas instead of one. Now, two top colas instead of one does sound appealing and some growers have even managed to force a plant to grow more than six top colas using this method. Unfortunately, this topping method of pruning doesn't always lead to better results.

Depending on the strain and the growing environment, the topped plant may produce two small top colas instead of one big one. Also, each strain has a threshold for bud production that cannot be improved upon because it is a genetically predetermined factor. On the other hand, some plants, when fully grown without topping, do not reach their threshold. The strain Blueberry is a good example of this. If you grow Blueberry without topping you won't achieve maximum bud production from that plant, but if you top the Blueberry, you will. Other strains aren't so flexible and the two top colas will simply share the same volume of bud that a single cola would have produced on the same strain.

It's advised that you keep in mind that pruning for yield using the topping method is strain-dependent and experiment carefully with this pruning method. Do this with 2 out of 10 plants in every grow. You'll find in time that during this vegetative prune

A pruned plant branch now shares a percentage of the yield. If this was divided into two then this cola would probably have half the bud you see here but good genetics can do more.

you will be able to shape your plant. Plants are generally pruned three to four weeks into their vegetative cycle, but can be pruned sooner or later or more than once.

Pruning during flowering is not advised as the plant will be forced to divert its energy from bud production into branch and leaf production. This results in a slower rate of bud growth. For optimal growth finish your pruning well before flowering.

FIM Technique

There is a topping method known as the FIM technique. If you push the leaves apart at the very top of the plant you should see a small bud (not a flowering bud but an actual leaf bud). Use a pair of nail clippers to pinch off about 3/4 of the bud. This should result in more than two top colas being developed. In a single FIM clipping you can produce up to eight new top colas.

The origins of this technique are humorous. As the story goes, FIM was discovered accidentally when a grower messed up a topping exercise. FIM stands for: "Fuck I Missed."

Super Cropping Technique

Another method of topping is called "Super Cropping." By taking a branch between your forefinger and thumb you can gently crush the branch, causing it to develop multiple branches above the crushed area. You must crush it on the

This plant has been clearly topped as you can see from the two virtually identical top colas.

correct side or risk breaking the branch. Just squeeze lightly until you feel the branch give, then let go. If it gives easily then you have crushed it on the correct side. If it is hard to crush and the branch splits then you have chosen the wrong side. Practice makes perfect with Super Cropping.

Super Cropping should be carried out during the second or third week of vegetative growth and it does stunt the plant. You should also note that plants that are Super Cropped can remain in the vegetative growth stage for twice as long as normal but the end result is a very bushy plant with multiple node regions that should all produce bud. Many growers have thrown Super Cropped plants away because they believed that the plants were not flowering in time. If you Super Crop your plants make sure that you have the patience to wait until the process is finished which is usually about four to six more weeks of vegetative growth.

By pruning what was a tall plant, a short bushy plant with multiple top colas can be created.

How to Make Cannabis Bushes

Some people prefer their plants small and wide. Fortunately for them, making cannabis bushes is a simple process. During the third week of vegetative growth, prune half the plant's branches. Cannabis plants need at least 50 percent of their leaves in order to continue growing without experiencing fatal stunting problems. If you prune off more than 50 percent of their leaves, you may end up killing your plants.[2] Do not prune only one side of the plant; prune both sides to achieve the 50 percent. You may also prune the main top cola if you want to split it into two or more parts.

If the prune cuts you previously made grow new branches and leaves, you may wait until the fourth or fifth week of vegetative growth and prune again, leaving 50 percent growth.

During the seventh week of vegetative growth you'll notice that your plant has started to grow outward more than upward. Let's say you have a plant with eight shoots. That means it is four nodes high. You prune the plant and end up with 16 shoots, but the plant is still only four nodes high. Now, this does not mean that you can keep doubling shoots forever. Pruning merely pushes the plant to grow all of its shoots early. If you keep pruning a plant that is four nodes high until the eighth week of vegetative growth, the greatest number of shoots you will get will be about 32. Most marijuana plants will not grow much beyond this factor, but again this is strain-dependent.

Now each new shoot has a junction point or a node that it grew from and each node should produce bud during the flowering stages. It is possible to create a marijuana plant that droops over the sides, completely concealing its own pot. With the right strain, it is also possible to have a single plant spread over an entire 6 x 6 foot space using this method. Creating cannabis bushes usually requires a few additional weeks of vegetative growth.

Here you can clearly see the difference between some plants that have not been topped or pruned and those that have been.

Training

Training was covered in Chapter 8 in our discussion about advanced SOG and ScrOG setups. Training simply means tying down your plant's main stem so that it grows in an S-shaped pattern. You can also train your plants to bend into other shapes, but the S-shape is the most common. Training is mainly used to prevent plants from reaching their natural vertical height without pruning, although you can also prune trained plants without a problem.

Training does not stop your plants from growing to their natural height, but instead promotes horizontal instead of vertical growth. You can also prune trained plants if you want, but most growers just rely on the training to achieve optimal results. Training is accomplished by bending the plant over, attaching a piece of thread to the stem and securing the thread to either another part of the stem or another plant or object. By tightening the thread bit-by-bit, day-by-day, you can successfully bend your plants without causing them undo stress.

Fishing line works very well in cannabis plant training. Some of the threading may be located very close to your lighting and heat can cause some threads to snap or even burn. Fishing line works best because it is one of the most durable and heat-resistant filaments you can buy. Make sure not to tie your line too tightly around the stem or you could end up cutting into it and causing plant stress, topping it or even killing it. People have managed to grow plants of all sorts of shapes using this method—from corkscrews to full circles. Some growers even like to grow their plants horizontally during the vegetative growth stage with just a single 90-degree bend at the base of the plant. When done correctly with the right strain, training can lead to excellent overall bud production.[3]

The roots at the base tell us that this is a clone, not a cutting.

If a stem breaks during training, simply hold it in place using a stake or stick and bind it with cheesecloth or a porous cloth bandage wrap. There are many types of plant waxes that you can buy from gardening stores to help close the wound. If you do not have a wax, applying honey to the wound also helps. Honey has healing properties that help rejuve-

These cuttings have been placed in a tray to develop roots in their medium.

nate plant wounds but must be carefully examined every day for fungi development on the honey-treated area. If you do find fungi development simply refer to Chapter 12 on how to solve this problem. Watch for any new growth at the break area and trim these away, because they will try to break away the upper part of the stem, effectively topping your plant. It is not uncommon to find roots trying to grow out from a damaged area, although the high percentage of air outside of the break zone will prevent the roots from growing much more.

Cloning

Cloning is a simple method of replicating your plants. In most cases, a clone is taken from a mother plant and grown into a new plant that contains the exact same genetic code as its mother plant.

In a selection of 30 seeds you may find a nice mother plant that you wish to keep. You can sustain and keep using her genetic profile indefinitely through cloning. Any cannabis plant can be cloned once it's been grown to a certain height and has developed a number of node regions.[4] The best place to take a cutting for cloning is above a node that has at least two nodes above it. The smallest cuttings on average are three inches in length. Once the cutting has been taken it is placed in the growing medium and should form new roots over the next one to three weeks.

MAKING CLONES

Check your mother plant and find the area you want to make the cutting on.

Use a pair of clean scissors or clean cutters to take a cutting below the area where you want to cut.

Do this quickly. Slice the base away a little bit above the cut zone to make a new cut zone with a clean blade.

Quickly dip the new cut zone into rooting gel or whatever propagation aid you are using.

Clipping the leaves helps to prevent necrosis from forming on the tips.

You can make your own incubation chamber with two plastic boxes, with one see-through like this.

These are mini rockwool cubes that you can use as your substrate.

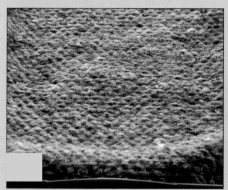

A cloth base helps to keep the rockwool damp and prevents the roots from making contact with the plastic below.

Your cubes can sit on the cloth like this. You can use seeds with this propagation method instead.

This is how your propagator should look with seedlings or clones growing inside.

You can use a seedling tray between the rockwool cubes and cloth. Here you can see the roots below.

Taking cuttings from healthy new shoots on the mother plant usually produces better results than areas that don't look as vigorous.

A tray of fresh and healthy cuttings for a new garden.

Cloning straight to soil can have a low success rate and is very dependent on the type of soil that you are using. Use the wrong soil and the clone will fail quickly. The best soil for cloning is a standard loam type with an even NPK ratio. Avoid using seedling or cutting soils as most of these have added hormones and nutrients that are not suitable for cannabis or cannabis cuttings.

Cloning in water also has a low success rate because the roots need air to breath once they have developed. If they remain submerged, the cuttings will eventually die. In water cloning, the cutting needs to be transferred to another medium, such as soil, rockwool, or a hydroponics system. This means that the clone will have to move through a number of mediums before finally being transplanted to the main growing environment. Multiple transplants can lead to stress and the overall success rate can decrease because of this.

Factory cloning done with multiple shelves and fluorescent lights.
Each of the labelled trays can easily be removed and replaced.

Factory clones can then be transplanted from the propagation tray to pots and sold at the market.

Some advanced growers like to use an aero cloning kit that acts like a miniature aeroponics systems for the propagation of clones. These systems can be expensive, however, and tend to require a lot of practice before getting cuttings to success- fully root in the system.

The best medium for cloning is rockwool cubes or Oasis foam bricks. In order to increase your success rate with cloning you may wish to purchase a rooting solu- tion, which can be bought from most grow shops.

Make sure you that use a clean instrument, or better yet a sterile instrument, when you make your cut. Try to take a piece of stem of no more than three inches between the cut zone and the next node level. The longer this section is, the more difficulty the cutting will have in the uptake of water and nutrients it needs to grow and produce roots. Take the cutting and dip the cut area into the rooting solution before placing it into the medium. Make sure that you close any holes where the cutting may have punctured the medium to prevent air from reaching

You can measure growth rates by using a ruler every few days to see how much your plant has developed.

the cut zone, which can stunt root growth. Do this by simply filling in any gaps with little pieces of the medium. Clones don't need much light to root. Try to avoid using the bigger grow bulbs for cloning as this can be a waste of electricity and bulb life. A simple window with some outdoor light is all you will need for the clone to root, although many people use fluorescent lights for clones.

When the clone takes root in the rockwool you will see the roots jut out from the sides of the cube. It is best to keep the cube size small so that you can observe the roots' progress. A two-inch square cube is ideal for rooting cuttings. Any bigger and it will take longer for the roots to grow outside of the cube. When they do, the clone should be transferred to its new grow medium: soil, hydroponics, or aeroponics. This is the most successful way of producing clones. The great thing about cloning is that you can create hundreds of female plants from a single mother. Clones also flower more quickly and you know what you are getting in the end because you have already seen, smoked and grown the plant that the clone was taken from. For information about how to obtain the best results with clones, turn to the section on SOG and ScrOG growing.

This connoisseur plant has been developed from a clone. Some strains are only available as clones.

Although you can take clones at any time during the plant's life, it is best to do so during the vegetative stage of growth. Clones carry the same age as the parent plant. Some clones used by seed-bank breeders are actually more than a decade old. They have been propagated for years and years by constantly taking cuttings from clones and then taking further cuttings from these cuttings. If you take a cutting a week before the plant is mature enough to display sex, then the cutting should only need a week after rooting before it is able to flower. If you take a cutting during flowering the clone should be able to flower right away after it has rooted. If you want to revert a cutting from flowering to vegetative growth, simply keep the cutting under 24 hours of light and clip away any calyx or flower formations that appear. After a short time under constant light, the cutting will revert to vegetative growth; however, any manipulation of the photoperiod will throw the plant back into flowering almost instantly.

Clones that are taken from a plant during vegetative growth are much easier to control than clones that are taken from a flowering plant. That is why we generally take clones during the third or fourth week of vegetative growth.

Growers can use cloning hormones or rooting hormones, which come in two main formats: powders and gels. Powder hormones are generally used for cloning in soil. The powder is tapped into a small hole in the soil and the cutting is placed into this hole. A small amount of the powder is then added to surface of the soil so that, with successive watering, the powder will seep down into the soil and promote root growth. Rooting gels are much better because they act as a seal, preventing air from reaching the cut zone. In addition, gels are not water soluble, whereas powders tend to be. This means that gels have a longer lifespan than powders.

A proper rooting hormone should contain the vitamin B1 (Thiamine). As an experiment, cut some roots from a test plant and place half of the "dead" roots into a solution of water and the other half into a solution of water and vitamin B1. The roots in water with added thiamine will continue to grow for quite some time, while the roots in the plain water solution will die.

The time it takes to root a clone depends on the strain and the cloning method used. Some strains, like Blueberry, are notoriously hard to clone. Others are much easier. On average, it takes about a week and half for a clone to develop a root mass suitable for transplantation. Do not be surprised if you find that it takes a set of clones more than three weeks to develop a root mass. The best way to tell whether or not your clones are rooting properly is to clone in batches from the same strain. If some of the clones do not develop a root mass after the others have, chances are that these clones have failed to root. Take one of the clones without any obvious root mass from the medium
and pull it up to check for roots. If none have developed, then the cutting has failed to root and should be discarded.

You should never let your cloning medium dry out. Keep it damp (not soaking wet) and check for fungi development regularly. Cloning environments containing damp mediums like rockwool are ideal breeding grounds for fungi. If you find that fungi is attacking your clones, consult Chapter 12 for details on how to eradicate it from your grow space.

Another method of cloning, called air layering, is described next by Strawdog.

The main difference between young clones and young seedlings can be seen in the cotyledons. Seedlings have these, clones don't.

How to Air Layer a Clone

Items Needed:

- Plant
- Match sticks or toothpicks
- Tape
- Razor blade (preferably sterile)
- Rooting hormone (Clonex)
- Tweezers
- Plastic wrap
- Scissors

1. Sterilize all your cutting tools before using them.
2. Find a branch that is at least 1/8 inch thick with a minimum of two nodes.
3. Use the razor blade to split the branch vertically/lengthwise. Cut at least 1/4 inch into the branch to meet the phloem.
4. Use tweezers to open the slit; do not break the branch completely.
5. Apply rooting hormone to the open wound. Tape a matchstick parallel to the stem for support.
6. Pack the open wound carefully with any grow medium, or use a rockwool cube to cover the area (just split the cube down one side and slide over the branch).
7. Wrap the area with the small plastic bag. The effect should be a funnel-shaped, plastic wrap enclosure
8. Pack the bag with grow medium before sealing with tape.
9. Use a pin to create holes around bag so that you can water the medium.
10. Use an eyedropper to keep the medium wet every day.

After two weeks, your cutting will have developed roots and you can cut away the branch below the roots. Now you have a clone with roots ready for growth. You can choose to remove the plastic bag if you feel that it is too tight to allow all the roots to pass through it and transplant the clone to its new growing environment.

This method is especially good for growers who wish to transplant a cutting with roots directly to a hydroponic or aeroponic system. It effectively allows you to skip at least one transplanting step, reducing the risk of shock to your clones. The fact that you can grow roots without using a medium (do not use rockwool if this is what you want to do) makes it an extremely effective cloning method for aeroponic systems.

A selection of vigorous clones to work with.

Bonsai Clones

Bonsai clones are easy to make. The objective is to produce a small bushy clone with multiple branches so that lots of cuttings can be taken from it.

Simply prepare a cutting using your preferred method and prune the clone using the "how to make cannabis bushes" technique. The end result is a clone with multiple branches and node regions that can give you a constant supply of cuttings.

Keep the bonsai short, about 1.5 feet in height, and you can store it in a very small place. Diminutive bonsai mother plants can be used to generate at least a hundred clones per year.

In countries where cannabis clones are legal, there is quite a market for them. Medical users especially like to buy clones from experienced growers because they know that the grower has worked on multiple strains to find a special mother that suits the medical users needs.

Sinsemilla Hermaphrodites

It is not uncommon for some strains to generate a few hermaphrodites in the final weeks of flowering. This is quite a familiar condition with sinsemilla crops as some plants, in a last ditch effort to continue their line via seeds, will generate a few male flowers to try to self-pollinate. In most cases, the pollen produced is not viable, but as

The pollen from this reversed female plant is guaranteed to produce many
seeds that will all be female plants. Photo Paradise Seeds

a precaution you should clip them away. Simply check your sinsemilla for small, yellow banana shapes in the bud during the final weeks of flowering and clip them away.

Increasing Yield

Yield, the amount of bud your plant will produce at the end of its grow, is what marijuana cultivation is all about. The more you grow, the more you'll learn about what your plants need. The two most fundamental factors in high-yield growth are strains (good genetics) and lighting. Optimal lighting along with good strains will lead to great yields and bud-rich plants. Of course, high yields may not mean highly potent bud. Remember, potency depends on both the strain and how well your plant is grown.

Many growers have found that some of the grow bloomers and advanced-feeding products actually produce greater amounts of bud, but reduce potency and produce a different taste. Learning which feeding products are best requires a degree of experimentation on your part, but experimentation is what growing is all about. To discover new methods of growing, the marijuana cultivator must experiment and, through failure, learn more.

I should caution you that, although marijuana has no physically additive properties, you may become addicted to growing! I know plenty of growers who gave up smoking pot and yet continue to actively develop new strains and discover new ways to increase yield. Cannabis cultivation is a very addictive hobby.

Reverting to Vegetative Growth

This is also called re-vegging, regeneration, or rejuvenation and can be done anywhere between the start of flowering and the end of the plant's peak bloom when it is ready for harvest. This does not work with strains that have autoflowering properties, like Ruderalis.

The first thing you need to do in order to revert a plant back to vegetative growth is to quit the flowering photoperiod of 12/12 and change it to a vegetative photoperiod of 24/0 or 18/6. The 24/0 photoperiod is certainly better because it reverts your plant to vegetative growth quicker.

The next thing you should do is to remove all of the plant's flowers and calyx development by clipping them away from the plant at their base. When your plant is bare of its flowers and calyx development you can then choose to reduce the height of your plant to a stage where it resembled its vegetative growth. After a few weeks, your plant will revert to vegetative growth and will no longer flower until the 12/12 photoperiod is initiated again.

When you are satisfied that your plant has reached a satisfactory level of node production, change the photoperiod to 12/12 and your plant will flower again.

Reverting to vegetative growth is a way to harvest more flowers from the same plant again, however, it does have the following disadvantages:

- Reverting to vegetative growth can take up to four weeks to occur properly. This time could have been spent by simply cloning the original plant and growing these clones out instead. Cloning is usually much quicker than rejuvenation.
- Plants that are rejuvenated tend to not produce the same quantities of bud that they did during their peak bloom, although it is not impossible for them to do so.
- The growing medium will contain higher levels of P than N and K. This needs

to be changed to higher or equal amounts of N to P and K. This can be hard to do without flushing your soil or performing a transplant. Both of these can cause stress, which may lead to sexual dysfunctions appearing in the flowering stage of a rejuvenated plant.

- Rejuvenated plants go through a certain amount of stress because of the photoperiod change and this can induce sexual dysfunction.
- Stress from cutting the plant during regeneration may also induce sexual dysfunction.

Some other grow books have suggested that rejuvenation compromises the genetic integrity of the plant. This is false.

A good example is found if you take an IBL strain (covered in Chapter 15), which is stable for all of its traits, and pollinate the females with a male from the same strain; you will produce a batch of offspring. Keep some of the male pollen used in this exercise and rejuvenate one of the females. After you rejuvenate her, use the male pollen again on her to create another batch of offspring.[5]

If rejuvenation compromises the genetic integrity of the plant, then these two sets of offspring will show variations. Do the normal offspring exhibit variations when evaluated against the rejuvenated female's offspring? No, they do not. Thus rejuvenation does not compromise the genetic integrity of the plant.[6]

Increasing Your Chances of Females

A well maintained grow room with plants growing in optimal conditions will naturally produce more females than males. There are some other things you can do to increase your odds of improving your male to female ratio. These are as follows:

- High nitrogen levels in vegetative growth have shown to produce more females than males. This might be a good to reason to use feeds with a higher N to P and K ratio rather than foods with an equal N to P and K ratio. Remember, though, that plant burn will only lead to stress and this will produce more males and hermaphrodites than females.
- High potassium levels in vegetative growth and flowering tends to produce more males than females. Keeping your potassium levels down is another good reason to choose a food with a higher N than P and K ratio where the P and K ratios are even, or where the K ration is kept lower than the P. Remember, though, that lack of K can cause plant stress due to this nutrient deficiency and this can cause more males and hermaphrodites to appear than females.

Taking care of your plants is what helps you to optimize
genetics to produce results with this frosty tasty look.

Some familiar stages of
the grow... a seedling.

Another familiar stage of
the grow... the male.

- Cannabis plants grow best under conditions of between 40 and 80 percent relative humidity (rH). In the higher rH range of between 70 and 80 your female to male ratio may increase.
- Cannabis plants grow best at 75 degrees Fahrenheit. If you do not allow the temperatures to increase beyond this you will improve your chances at getting more females than males. If the environment is supplemented with CO_2, the temperature may be allowed to increase as far as 95 degrees Fahrenheit.
- Using MH grow lights in vegetative growth will improve your female to male ratio.

End of the Grow

This concludes the propagation portion of this book. At this stage you should have a fair idea of the following:

- The history of cannabis
- How it is used
- The life cycle of cannabis

Harvest time is probably the most
enjoyable stage for most growers.

Good signs for the grower who is hoping
for females when these calyx show.

- THC and potency
- Different species and strains
- Security issues
- Types of seeds and where to get them
- How to germinate seeds
- Setting up your grow space
- Indoor/outdoor/guerilla growing
- Hydroponics and advanced grow techniques

With this amount of information you should feel ready to tackle and challenges with your grow. Right? Wrong. You still need to be able to answer the question, what do I do if something goes wrong? The next chapter focuses on how to solve problems with your grow. After that, we'll discuss what happens after the grow: from harvesting your bud to making hashish. We will also cover breeding.

13 | **Problem Solver**

Plant pests will always be a problem for cannabis growers and should never be ignored. An infestation or infection can kill all of your plants very quickly. Minor pest attacks can stunt plant development, which can prevent them from achieving optimal growth or even cause the hermaphrodite condition to appear in your sinsemilla crop.

Of course, some strains can cope with pest attack better than others and some experts will tell you that a little pest attack only serves to "harden" the plants up a bit. Although stress brought on by pest attack can cause the plant to produce its fruits and foliage more vigorously, there is a fine line between hardening a plant up and causing the hermaphrodite condition to appear along with impaired growth.

You should also keep in mind that, outdoors, pests have to contend with the forces of nature and predators, but they will thrive in clean, healthy indoor environments and spread quickly. As a result, you can expect pest attacks to be more frequent and damaging indoors than outdoors. Indoors, any pests must be dealt with immediately.

Domestic Pets

It must be said that, for an outdoor garden, a cat is the number one defense system against most small predators, but a cat can bring unwanted pests into an indoor grow room! Cats also like to play with indoor plants so be very careful with your plants and pets. Cats, especially kittens, like to use the base of cannabis plants as a litter box. Puppies and young dogs also like to play with cannabis plants (including biting their stems). Keep domestic pets out of your indoor grow room.

Pesticides, Herbicides, and Fungicides

Pesticides are substances for destroying pests. Herbicides are products that destroy weeds and plants. Fungicides are used to kill fungi. New growers should not attempt to use herbicide, as the risk of harming your plants is too great. Solutions to specific pest and fungi problems are covered below in detail.

ATTENTION! READ THIS:

Use only repellents and pesticides that are clearly marked for "Food Product Use" on the label. If a repellent or pesticide is not safe for food product use then do not use it on your plants! You could be smoking or cooking with your plants later and you don't want to end up in a hospital because of poisoned bud. If a pesticide is safe for food product use then it will be safe to use on your bud. Read the product instructions clearly and carefully. Do not take short cuts. Follow the instructions on the label with care.

Pesticides

Pesticides come in a variety of different formats. These include: pellets, sprays, powders and gases. Pellet-type pesticides usually come in boxes or tubs. The pellets usually range from 2 mm to 10 mm in length and are eaten by pests such as slugs, snails and larvae. Sprays come in liquid form or as a fine powder that you need to mix with water. Most liquid pest sprays come with a nozzle attached to the bottle so they can be used directly without mixing or transfer to another spray can. Powder pesticides that are not to be used as a spray are simply added to soil around the base of the plant, but not directly onto the plant itself. These powder pesticides are useful for removing low-level area pests like slugs and snails. Gas pesticides are also known as "pest bombs." These types of pesticides are used to fumigate indoor areas to eradicate pests. Dead pests can then be removed from the room.

Why Cannabis Resin and Soapy Pesticides Don't Mix

Soaking a flowering female with a soapy pesticide is not a good idea for several reasons.

Firstly, any liquid applied to the bud in large amounts will remove some of the trichomes simply because of the way in which it must be applied and not because of the solution coming into contact with the THC-containing resin glands. In fact, THC is not water-soluble, as we will explain in more detail when we cover hashish-making and resin extraction in Chapter 17. Repeated application of soapy pesticides as directed will only remove more trichomes.

Resorting to stronger measures to combat a bad pest infestation should
only been done in the vegetative growth stage.

While this activity looks pretty harmless, the resulting larvae can be very dangerous to your crop.

Secondly, soaps add additional water weight to the flowering plant, causing stems and branches to bend. This added weight and film of soapy water on the leaves and stems can stunt growth by slowing photosynthesis until the plant is dry again.

Thirdly, turning on indoor lights before plants are dry creates a risk of burning as the pesticide chemicals can change composition due to heat. The result is much like white powdery blotches on the leaves with indications of burning.

Try to avoid using soapy pesticides or any pesticides on a flowering cannabis plant by solving pest problems back in the vegetative stage of the cannabis life cycle, before any bud or resin is produced.

Pest Index

This index is by no means exhaustive. The pests described in this section were selected because they are the most common and are responsible for most cannabis-related pest attacks.

New growers should bear in mind that pest attack symptoms can look exactly like those caused by nutrient disorders, overwatering, underwatering, overfeeding, pH fluctuation or heat stress. In fact, the "bite mark" damage commonly associated with a pest attack does not always happen. This is because instead of eating the plant, some pests will suck on the plant leaves, flowers, branches and stems.

In some pest attack cases, the plants' leaves simply change color or curl. Leaf color changes or distortions like leaf curl are often associated with nutrient disorders or overfeeding, so before you make a nutrient disorder diagnosis you should examine your plants carefully for signs of pests. It is good practice to get in the habit of doing this every time you check your plants.

The main difference between a pest attack and a non-pest related disorder is the presence of the pests themselves. Since pest damage is highly variable you cannot rely on the damage alone to identify the pest. You need to find the pest, identify it and eradicate it. A magnifying aid is an extremely useful instrument for pest identification.[1]

In indoor spaces especially, acting quickly is critical. Try to commit the signs of infestation described in this section to memory, as this will help you to identify them quickly if you come across a pest attack in your grow. Remember, though, not all insects are bad for your garden. Some people make the mistake of killing pests that actually do not harm cannabis. Some of these insects instead prey on pests that you may want to eradicate. We will also list these "friendly" pests so that you can get to know them.

Ants

Ants are small insects from the family Formicidae. They are wingless, except during mating season. Ants are colony pests well known for their cooperativeness and industriousness; they can destroy cannabis plants quickly. Ants eat cannabis leaves and carry portions of the plant back to the colony for food storage and construction. Ants are easy to spot because of their size, speed of movement and numbers. Along with leaf discoloration, an ant-attacked plant may exhibit bite marks on the edges of the leaves. Ants also farm aphids, another type of pest that growers will want to eradicate. Ants can be removed using boric acid or any popular colony killer pesticide.

Aphids

Aphids are small, soft-bodied insects of the family Aphididae. Aphids are the single most common pest attackers experienced by cannabis growers both indoors and out. They mainly live on plant juices by sucking sap from stems, branches and leaves. They are about 1/8 of an inch long and can be any color, but yellow/green is most common. Some aphids have wings.

Aphids tend to secrete a frothy or foamy waste material called honeydew around their feeding areas they are most likely to be found attacking new growth or the underside of leaves near a node region, but they can be anywhere. Aphids are generally surrounded by their young, reproduce rapidly and spread quickly. In addition, some aphids transmit viral diseases. This pest must be obliterated from your grow as soon a possible.

Aphids are small and do not move very quickly so growers need to take extra care when checking their crops for aphids. An aphid attack looks a bit like underwatering, resulting in leaf wilt. You may also find that some plants stunt and exhibit signs of leaf curl.

Ants also farm aphids by gathering the honeydew they excrete, so you must remove any ants before you try to treat an aphid problem. Aphids can be removed from your grow using any pyrethrum-based insecticide. Spraying your plants with pyrethrum-based insecticide before flowering will help prevent future aphid attacks, but a full spraying tends to cause a certain amount of plant stress and may stunt growth. If you want to keep aphids out of your grow room, then you should spray down the grow room with the above mentioned insecticide before introducing the plants to the environment, making sure that you cover the corners and door frame.

To treat a mild aphid problem, try to spray only the infected areas of the plant. An aphid attack on flowering plants can be a problem because spraying can damage the bud and separate your trichome glands from the flowers. Try to solve aphid problems before flowering at all costs. Chances are that if you have prevented an aphid attack in the pre-flowering stage, then you should not get one during flowering period, unless aphid-contaminated items are brought into the grow room.

A soapy pesticide like Safer's Soap can also be used to deter aphids. A mixture of dishwashing detergent in hot water can be used to clean down the grow room and pots of any unwanted aphids by suffocating them. As stated in the introduction to this section, soap and detergents should not be used during the flowering period. Also, ladybugs are a natural predator of aphids and can be used to control them.

Cutworms, Caterpillars and Larvae

Insects that are in their early stages of development are problem pests because they are insatiable and will eat anything green that they can get their tiny mouths around. Their appetite is surreal when you actually discover how much a caterpillar can consume in a single day; one caterpillar can reduce a one-ounce cola to stem and stalk

A single caterpillar can cause havoc with your garden because of its ferocious appetite.

in less than four days. These pests pose a huge threat to your crop and must be stopped right away. Caterpillars especially like to eat young seedlings and new growth. They are also known to leave holes in leaves, but other pests can do this, too.

The only sure way to get rid of cutworms, caterpillars and larvae is to use a cutworm, caterpillar or larvae repellent. Usually, the same product will affect all three pests. Cutworms can also be hand picked from your grow. At night they sleep in a 'C' shape in the soil or under the cover of something like a piece of wood.

Deer
Deer are so curious that even electric fences won't stop them. Deer will eat leaves, stems, flowers and branches. Damaged areas are usually large, including complete topping of the main cola from the stem. There is a much kinder way to keep deer away from your crop; you need to get a hold of predator urine from a hunting shop. Find out which urine works best with deer to keep them away without attracting other plant-eating animals. Simply spray the urine on your patch and this will help keep the deer away. This method has a very high success rate at keeping deer from your grow.

Gnats

Gnats are insects with long, thin, fragile legs from the family Culicidae. Gnats can eat leaves but mostly suck sap from the phloem. The damage from a gnat attack is similar to that of an aphid attack and can be treated in the same way: using a pyrethrum-based insecticide. Gnats cause less damage than aphids but need to be treated quickly nonetheless.

Grasshoppers

Generally harmless to cannabis unless they are found in large numbers, grasshoppers are insects from the Acrididae family with legs designed for jumping long distances. The males make a high pitched clicking sound.

There is a particular species of grasshopper often called "locusts" that form in large migratory swarms and are highly destructive to nearly every kind of vegetation. Locust attacks are so severe that they can strip a plant down to its stem

A gnat problem can be solved by using fly tape. However, fly tape can catch good pest predators too, so use with care.

A grasshopper when alone is fairly harmless.

and branches within a few hours. During a locust attack, the grower can only take cuttings from his or her plant and continue the strain elsewhere. Locusts will even eat pesticide-laden plants when traveling in large numbers, so pesticides are rarely effective against these types of attacks.

Grasshoppers can be treated as tourists when they are in small numbers. They stay around only for a short period of time and move on. Grasshoppers are best hand-picked from your plants if you wish to control them. Also, birds eat grasshoppers, so attracting birds with bird feeders can help (although remove the feeders if you are planting seeds).

Groundhogs

Groundhogs are a burrowing, colonial rodent of the genus Marmota. They eat the shoots and leaves of the cannabis plant. Dry chlorine helps keep groundhogs away from your plants. If you find any groundhog holes near your grow area, apply dry chlorine around the hole.

Mealy Bugs

Mealy bugs are insects from the Pseudococcidae family. They are often described by growers as "hard aphids" because of a waxy powder that makes their backs look shell-like under a microscope. They attack plant tissue and suck sap from the phloem. Mealy bugs are treated in the same way as aphid attacks: using a pyrethrum-based insecticide.

Rabbits

Rabbits are burrowing, plant-eating mammals of the Leporidae family. They can be recognized by their long ears and short, fluffy tails. Rabbits are voracious eaters and can reduce a crop to nothing in a couple of days. They will continue to feed from the same patch until they're done or the patch is destroyed. The best way to keep rabbits from your grow is to use predator urine. Rabbits also shy away from cats and dogs.

Scale

Scale is closely related to the aphid and comes in several different forms. Scales are born mobile but will eventually solidify (at any plant location but mostly on the branch and stem) and insert a small hollow tube into the plant to tap into the juices. They also spread mold. Scale can be hand picked from your plants with ease because when they solidify, they stay on that area of the plant. Ants farm scale so ants need to be removed from your grow room before you treat a scale problem. Scale can also be scrubbed from the branches using a scouring pad. Dormant oil sprays, a form of organic pest control, also kill scale. You should be able to obtain dormant oil from any good grow store.

Slugs and Snails

These pests are molluscs of the class Gastropoda and characteristically have a flattened ventral bottom that they use for movement. They eat the leaves and stem and will kill cannabis seedlings. Slugs and snails are best hand picked from your grow area. Another way to remove them is to make a circle of table salt about four feet away from the base of your plants, then make another circle a foot in from that. Salt is deadly to snails and slugs and will keep them out. Slugs and snails can also be repelled or killed using slug and snail pest pellets.

Spider Mites

Always keep a bottle of pesticide that kills spider mites on hand because marijuana plants are extremely vulnerable to mite attacks. Spider mites can reduce your plants to garbage within a couple of days so you should never bring a plant inside if it has been outside.

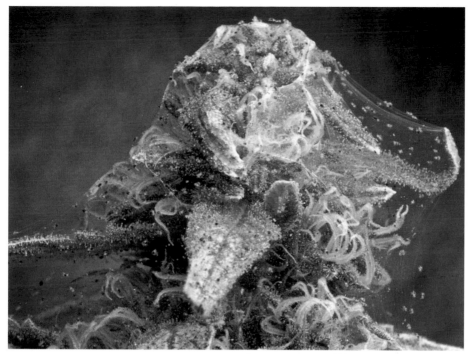

These spider mites have won. There is no coming back for this plant.
The key is to combat pest attacks as early as possible.

Spider mites are tiny; about half the size of the period at the end of this sentence. Spider mites cannot be seen without a magnifying aid but are normally spotted because they gather in large numbers to form clusters on areas of your plant. Spider mites feed off plant juices and so leaf wilt is a common symptom of a mite attack. If the attack continues the plant will eventually die. Spider mites also spin webbing on the affected areas of the plant.

Specialized spider mite pesticides like Avid will curb attacks. Sulfur also deters spider mites. During vegetative growth, spider mites can be exterminated using soaps. Sticky pest trap tape is not effective against them. After aphids, spider mites are the second most common pest attackers experienced by cannabis growers both indoors and out.

Termites

Termites are a type of Isoptera and live in colonies. Termites are very destructive, even in small numbers. They have the ability to chew through wood rapidly and can chop a plant at the base of its stem within a few days. Termites don't like water. If you overwater the soil around your plant, they will leave but you will be left with an overwatering problem.

There are commercial products available that kill termites, but most of these are not for plant use or human consumption. Termites can be killed by finding their nest and flushing it with water. Try to find the source of the termites rather than treating your plants.

Thrips

Thrips are a member of the Thysanoptera family and are minute, dark-colored insects with slim bodies that have wings in adult form. They usually attack the flowering parts of the cannabis plant and suck juices from the leaves. Thrip infestations usually cause the cannabis flowers to fall apart and look silvery in patches. Thrips are not typically around for long because their natural predators are beetles, ladybugs, lacewing and mites. Thrip infestations can be treated with any good thrip pesticide or pyrethrum. Also, thrips do not like garlic.

Whitefly

Whitefly are from the Aleyrodidae family and are usually about 4 mm in size, although there are more than 200 species of this insect that vary in shape, size and color. One particular species likes to spend its entire life within greenhouses, hence its name: "Greenhouse Whitefly."

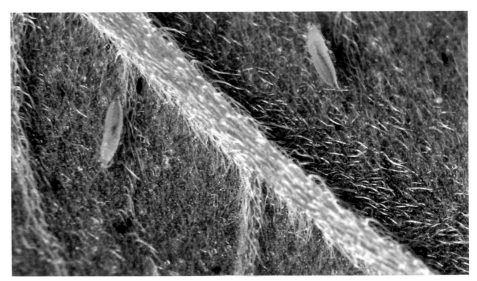

Thrips can be hard to identify as they change very quickly from grubs to flies, but as you can see here, they will leave evidence.

These tiny dots are bites where the juice of the plant has been sucked away by thrips. Clean the plant, pot and medium thoroughly, then introduce ladybugs for maintenance.

Whitefly normally have waxy white wings and use these to fly over short distances. If you shake your plant, you should be able to hear them before you see them. They make a buzzing sound when moving in small groups. The whitefly can be deadly to your crop and can reduce your plant to trash in days. They feed on plant juices and secrete a honeydew, which has the natural ability to develop a dark mold on the secreted areas. This mold will also affect your plants' health if left untreated.

Safer's Soap helps to kill whitefly and can be bought in most grow shops. Other soaps and sprays will also kill whitefly. The whitefly's natural predators are spiders, ladybugs and beetles. Pest tape can also be quite effective against whitefly. Whitefly are the third most common pest attackers experienced by cannabis growers both indoors and out.

Woodchucks and Other Small Rodents

Woodchucks will nibble your stems and collapse the plant. The way to solve this is by either using predator urine (see also deer and groundhogs) or building a very small mesh fence around the base of your outdoor plants. This will keep the woodchucks from eating your stems and branches. Use more than one layer of mesh and make sure that you keep it tight. Planting marigolds near your grow will also help keep the woodchucks away.

Pest Predators

There are many predators of pests that, at first glance, may appear to be plant pests but will not actually damage your crop. You should keep these "friendly" pests around, since they are nature's way of eliminating many of the pests listed above. Beneficial pests can even be bred or bought so that you have a constant supply of them. For instance, ladybugs will breed on their own if they have a constant supply of aphids and other insects to feed on. Many places now stock pest predators. Contact your local agricultural supply store to find out where predatory pests might be available. There are companies that provide this service and will even send some predator pests by mail order.

Beetles

Ground beetles are usually black, brown or have a bluish tint along with wings and solid covers that surround the wings on their backs. Beetles usually work best at ground level eradicating most types of snails, slugs, cutworms and other insect pests. They are usually found in soil or hiding under debris like rocks and wood.

Braconid Wasps

Braconid wasps are from the hymenopterous family of insects. Their eggs actually act as a parasite on unwanted pests like aphids, scale, cutworms and other kinds of larvae. In most instances this occurs shortly after the wasp has injected several of the pests with its own eggs. Injected cutworms will eventually develop several microscopic, cocoon-like pods on their back and sides. The braconid wasp larvae sucks the insect dry as it develops inside these cocoons.

Bugs

Certain types of what gardeners refer to as "true" bugs will curb unwanted pests. True bugs will actually suck all the bodily fluids out of their victims. The assassin bug (red underside), big-eyed bugs (has big eyes), pirate bugs (checkered black and white or gray and brown) and damsel bugs (long and large front legs and are gray, brown or tan in color) are the most common true bugs you will find although there are many more. Pirate bugs are especially effective against spider mites and thrips. Bugs are usually more than half and inch in size and will move relatively quickly around your plant.

Earthworms

It is worth mentioning earthworms here even though they are not pest predators. Earthworms help to aerate your soil along with depositing nitrogen, calcium, phosphorus and potassium in the soil. One organic type of feeding product is

A mantis will devour damaging pests in your garden but also friendly ones too.

Frogs are quite happy to sit amongst your grow and eat flies, which
are not a problem as adults but produce destructive offspring.

called worm casting and is mostly made from earthworm waste material. If you
farm earthworms you can create your very own organic fertilizer.

Lacewings

Lacewings will eat aphids and spider mites. They are usually green with large,
semi-transparent wings that extend well past the length of their bodies. The have
two long and thin protruding antenna from their heads, grow to about 2.5 cm and
can be approached and handled without much difficulty.

Ladybird Beetles

Ladybirds, or "ladybugs," are amazing predator pests because they eat a lot of
other insects that are damaging to cannabis. They eat aphids, mealy bugs, scales
and spider mites. Ladybugs must eat aphids and other insects in order to lay eggs.
The more they eat, the more eggs they lay. As a result, the amount of new ladybugs born is directly proportionate to the amount of pests they consume. One
female ladybug can consume up to 4,000 aphids in a lifetime and lay 2,000 eggs
as a result of this. Ladybugs are the cannabis grower's pest predator of choice.

Spiders

Unfortunately, a common garden-variety spider is not enough to prevent a pest
attack from occurring in your crop. You need them in large numbers to prevent

any damage and even then spiders are very slow in their work. They also tend to spin webs in places where you do not want them and are not very controllable; however, one type of spider is of enormous benefit to your grow and is easy to control. That spider is the common "daddy long legs" and will consume nearly any insect in your grow room. Because this spider flies, it is not restricted to building webs in awkward places, nor is it likely to cover your bud with spindle fibers like other spiders do. Also, those with arachnophobia don't seem to mind this type of spider as much because they are not very vicious looking and are easy to spot.

Recovering From a Pest Invasion

Sometimes the pests win. No matter how much you might spray to control or kill them, they keep coming back to your grow area. To solve this, you may have to create a clean room or simply find another patch, which means a total and complete cull of your harvest—you don't want to re-introduce any pests or diseases into your new crop.

If you are growing indoors, first set up another grow room of smaller size, just enough to support some cuttings and clones. Take cuttings from the plants you have and move the cuttings to that room. You'll use the cuttings again, eventually, in your clean grow room, if you want to continue those strains. Next, take all the grow equipment excluding the electrical equipment to the bathroom. Clean down all of

Natural born pest killers, these ladybugs will keep your garden organic and free of most pests.

the equipment with bleach. Fill a tub with water and bleach and allow the grow equipment to rest there for a day. Do not wash electrical equipment. Instead, clean it down with a cloth.

In the grow room, first start with the walls. Clean the walls down with bleach if possible. You may have to paint them afterwards. If you use Mylar, replace it afterwards. Do not reuse Mylar after a pest infestation as some pests can find ways to attach themselves to it. Don't neglect the corners, and clean out any holes, extraction holes, fittings, pipes, etc. Then, clean around the rim of the room. If your floor can be lifted up, you can also do this to get at the corners better.

After this cleaning has been done you can consider smoking the room. Various pest-killing smoke bombs can be bought in most grow stores. Follow the instructions carefully and smoke bomb the room. This will guarantee the demise of any bugs, or larvae, but remember that eggs can remain safe from these sprays. That is why the labels recommend a reapplication 7 to 10 days after the initial treatment. Once this is completed, clean the room as you did the first time. Repeat the process if needed. The more you clean it, the better it will be.

Now you should have a clean room, free of pests. Electrical items should be dusted before returning them to the grow room. Dry your other grow equipment, which was bleached, and return this to the grow room as well.

Next, your cuttings need to be checked for bugs. You will not move any plants back into the grow room until you have taken cuttings from these cuttings. Grow the cuttings out for a week or two and check them every day for bugs. If you find any then you may have to use a pesticide on the cuttings. When you're sure your cuttings are clean, take new cuttings and place them in a growing medium. Take these to your grow room and watch their progress, being wary of any signs of pests and bugs. If you've done this correctly, you should have eliminated all pests in your grow room.

Spider mites and other small pests can lay their eggs in cuttings and can be missed when you look for pests, because they aren't as obvious. The pesticides should have killed them but some pests, like powder bugs, lay their eggs inside the stem and seem to always come back. If you can't get rid of bugs like these then you may have to toss your plants away and get new ones. For breeders this can be a difficult task. A long-term project can be terminated by a few bugs wreaking havoc in the grow room. Breeders should pay strict attention to maintaining a clean grow room at all times. Remember: never take anything that has been outside into your grow room.

In some cases, parts of dying plants can be cut, cleaned, and saved.

A fresh start; cleaned cuttings from your old garden can be grown as clones.

Do not feed seedlings or newly planted clones. These are burnt.

No return. If your plant looks like this then death is inevitable.

You may not have to identify the exact fungi to know you have a fungi problem - take care of it quickly to save your grow.

Fungi

Fungi are types of bacteria, organisms, and disease which actually live by extracting nutrients from the plant. Fungi include molds, mushrooms, toadstools and rusts, and are usually made up of lichens, which lack chlorophyll and grow as they obtain more nutrients from the plant. Mold is a type of fungi that grows in high humidity. Most molds can be stopped by simply allowing fresh air into the grow room. Fungi can be eradicated using fungicides.

Fungus Botrytis

This is the most common variety of fungus found on cannabis plants. It is also called gray mold, gray blight or botrytis blight. It begins its life as a white powder-like growth, which eventually turns gray as it spreads.

Fungus forms spores that dislodge and are spread to neighboring plants. The spores can stay dormant for quite some time, so growers should treat all the plants in the surrounding area for botrytis. This is because the fungus has a tendency to spread itself without notice. These spores do not need living matter to stay alive. They can lay dormant almost anywhere.

Fungus Botrytis on some bud.

If you can solve a botrytis problem quickly then you may prevent spores from being produced—this is why growers need to keep a close eye on their plants. Fungi are very hard to clean by hand. Rotted areas must be clipped away.

Botrytis will grow wherever it comes in contact with plant nutrients. This means that the fungus is more likely to be found developing on necrotic plant tissue or other damaged areas of the plant where the nutrients are more readily accessible. From here, it spreads to other areas of the plant causing its feeding patches to rot. Cut areas after pruning and cloning are especially susceptible to botrytis.

High humidity will cause fungi to spread more rapidly, so lower humidity levels if needed. In some cases, lowering the humidity is all that is needed to prevent the fungi from spreading. Mold should also be treated the same way. If lowering the humidity does not solve fungi or mold problems, then you need to apply a fungicide to the infected areas. Fungicides can be used to remove the fungus, preventing further plant rot. Spores tend to fall downwards, so remove the top layer of soil from your infected plant and throw it away. After harvest, a previously infected grow area should be cleaned down to prevent further fungi growth during your next crop.

Root Rot

Root rot is a waterborne disease that attacks the plant roots. There are several varieties of root rot but all are treated the same way. Rot can cause a crop to fail rapidly. The symptoms are almost like those of a nutrient disorder, overwatering or underwatering. Wilting is a very common symptom of root rot.

Poor water drainage promotes root rot. Water and soil that is not suitably aerated (either by the growing method or by the soil's natural composition) promote root rot. Dead roots from a previous crop can also cause root rot. Root rot can easily be prevented by selecting suitable soil types and aerating water, if needed.

Root rot prevents the plant from accessing water and nutrients by attaching itself to the roots and smothering the plant. Root rot also causes pH to rise. In hydroponic systems, the root tips may look burnt, although some feeding products can dye the plant roots as well. In the advanced stages of root rot, the roots appear to be covered in a brown slime that looks like dead algae. Eventually, the base of the plant will rot away, causing the plant to topple. Once a root is dead it remains dead. The plant can grow new roots but not regenerate old ones. This causes plant stress and the effect is very similar to transplant shock.

This is a typical fungi/mold problem on bud. If you tear open
the bud it will appear necrotic. Don't smoke mold.

There are products on the market that can be used to eradicate root rot and are usually referred to as "root shields." In its advanced stages, root rot is very hard to stop. In severe cases, it cannot be stopped and the plant needs to be cloned to continue its line. In order to recover from root rot you should increase aeration of the medium if possible while applying the root rot fungicide. If you lower pH to below 6.0, you should prevent the rot from spreading. It is wiser to cull a number of plants then to allow the rot to spread to other areas of the soil, especially outdoors.

Overwatering promotes root rot. Better drainage systems, keeping your grow items clean and hydrogen peroxide will all help to prevent root rot. Vitamin B1 (thiamine) will help promote root growth.

Powdery Mildew

Powdery mildew is a common fungus that can rapidly infect a crop. Like botrytis and mold, it can be prevented using good ventilation and low humidity levels.

Powdery mildew starts its life, grows and produces spores much like botrytis, except that powdery mildew does not turn gray; it stays a fluffy white color.

The beginnings of a fungi related problem are here. Spot it early and
cut it away. You will probably need to keep cutting away throughout the grow.

Powdery mildew on a cannabis leaf.

Powdery mildew is easier to wipe off than botrytis, but tends to spread more quickly, causing the plant's leaves to be covered in a white film. This inhibits photosynthesis and leads to stunted growth. Powdery mildew also rots bud.

Powdery mildew can be curbed using the same techniques used in the treatment of botrytis.

Chemical Burns

Plants suffer from chemical burns due to overfeeding. A plant with a chemical burn can be likened to a half-smoked joint; at the tip of the joint you have a shriveled gray ash, in the middle you see the burn creeping towards new paper, leaving a burn pattern behind it and at the end, there is the part you have not smoked yet. A plant chemical burn looks similar, and the leaf will tend to curl down and inwards into a claw shape at the tips.

The plant has a vascular system that takes in water and food and distributes these elements first to the bottom fan leaves, then upwards to the rest of the plant. This process takes time, as you know from Chapter 5. You will notice that the damage from chemical burns also starts on the tips of the fan leaves, then slowly moves towards the center and up the plant, leaving behind crispy matter that flakes away between your fingers. This is a chemical burn.

The main cause of a chemical burn is overfeeding that can occur if you use soil that contains high ratios of nutrients, if you use strong feeding mixtures or if you feed your plants too often.

To rectify chemical burns consult Chapter 7. If you cannot find a solution to what appears to be a chemical burn, then check your medium's pH level. pH problems can sometimes resemble chemical burns or even nutrient deficiencies.

Nutrient Deficiencies

A nutrient deficiency looks like a cell collapse (the natural appearance of the firm leaves lose some or all of their stiffness), usually along with some form of discoloration and/or wilting. The affected part may wither and die, but it should not look like chemical burn. That is the major difference between a chemical burn and a nutrient problem. In time, you should be able to easily tell the difference yourself. If you suspect a nutrient deficiency be sure to check your pH. If your pH is not right, then solve the pH problem before you attempt anything else. If you feel that the problem is pH related, then consult Chapter 7 for solutions to this problem.

10 Steps to Saving Your Grow

Here is a quick, step-by-step approach to troubleshooting problems with your grow.

Step 1: Examine your plant, looking first for the presence of insects or disease. When you have completed this search, eliminate any pests or disease following advice from earlier in this chapter.

Also, note the type of attack to make sure that your bug problem isn't really a nutrient problem. The two can be confused. Are there any black dots on them, which would indicate bugs? Do your leaves look discolored, dry and limp, as if something has been sucking their fluids from them? This could be a nutrient disorder but pest attack can do this as well.

Nutrient problems damage the plant on a more consistent level than pest attacks, meaning that the damaged areas are not as sporadic. Nutrient disorders tend to be more linear, either affecting the bottom leaves moving upwards or the top leaves moving downwards. The disorder should be somewhat regular unless the pest

NUTRIENT DEFICIENCIES

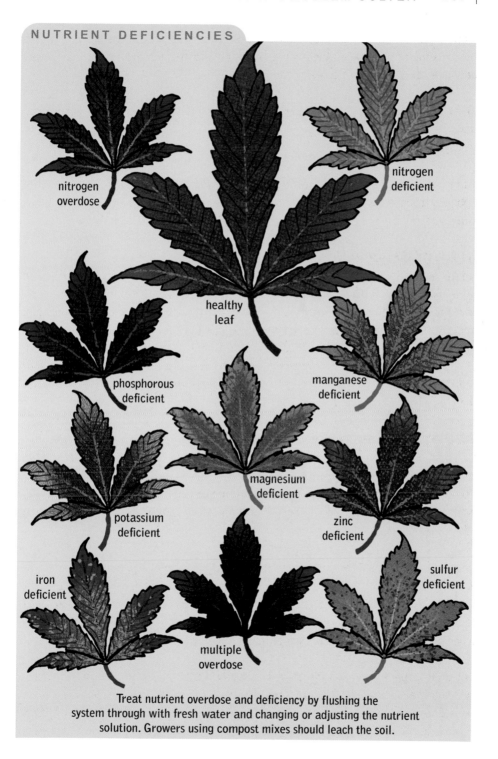

nitrogen
overdose

nitrogen
deficient

healthy
leaf

phosphorous
deficient

manganese
deficient

magnesium
deficient

potassium
deficient

zinc
deficient

iron
deficient

sulfur
deficient

multiple
overdose

Treat nutrient overdose and deficiency by flushing the
system through with fresh water and changing or adjusting the nutrient
solution. Growers using compost mixes should leach the soil.

Warped leaves are a sign that there is a deficiency problem, although
checking for pests or fungi is also mandatory.

attack has managed to occur over the entire plant. This is why it is important for you, the grower, to check on your plants regularly so that you can identify problems sooner rather than later. This is essential, because a problem left untreated is a problem that becomes increasingly more difficult to identify.

In short, pest damage is random and often concentrated on a single area of the plants before moving onto another. Nutrient disorders are more regular and affect the plant in a linear movement running either from bottom to top or top to bottom.

Step 2: If your plant is in the vegetative growth stage and the leaves are turning yellow at the base, and if this is moving slowly up the plant without upwards leaf curl, then you need more nitrogen (N). If your plant is in the flowering stage and shows signs of stunted or slow growth, or yellow leaves, and it looks to be dying, then you also need more N. This may also cause the stems to become soft and the leaves to become a pale green color. Normally, nitrogen problems occur with older leaf growth first. Severe problems result in stunted growth and eventually plant death.

If your plant is in the flowering stage and looks red or dark green/yellow, then you need to treat it with more phosphorus (P). This kind of deficiency results in stunted root development. Stems can become either very rigid or very weak, depending on the strain.

If these measures do not help, proceed to Step 3.

Step 3: If your plant's leaves are curling up, twisting and turning yellow, then check to see if your light is burning them or if the grow chamber has enough air circulation. This is usually the result of heat stress. Consult Chapter 7 for information on how to solve heat stress-related problems.

If these are not the cause of the problem, then consider adding more magnesium (Mg) to your medium. Epsom salts are good for this. Prepare a mixture of 1/4 to 1/3 tablespoon of Epsom salts to three gallons of water and water your plants with this mixture.

Magnesium problems generally start with old leaves first and show signs of yellowing between the veins of the leaf, moving outwards. The leaves curl upwards, hence the term "praying for magnesium." Necrosis is the eventual result of Mg problems. Although a plant can still grow to full maturity with Mg deficiency, it certainly results in below average results.

If you still experience problems, go to Step 4.

Step 4: If the tips of the leaves turn brown and curl slightly, then you have a potassium (K) problem. Solve this by adding more K to your plants.

Potassium problems result in red/purple stems, although this can be a genetic trait in the plant or due to a cold growing environment. To solve a cold growing environment problem, turn to Chapter 7 for advice.

Potassium problems normally affect new growth first, before moving on to the older leaves. A potassium deficiency will also eventually affect the stems causing them to become either soft or brittle, depending on the strain. In severe cases, the plant will eventually die.

If this does not solve your problem, move onto Step 5.

Step 5: Does your plant look wilted? Are the leaves drooping or curling down? This could be root rot or a watering problem, which sometimes can cause nutrient-like deficiencies to appear on the plant. Root Rot is covered earlier in this chapter.

If this doesn't work, check your soil. If your soil is very damp or very dry, then turn to Chapter 6 for information on soils and then to Chapter 7 for watering information, related watering problems and solutions to those problems.

If this does not solve you problem go to Step 6.

Step 6: If the veins are green but the leaves are yellow, this indicates an iron problem (Fe). Iron problems generally occur at new growth regions, which eventually turn necrotic and die. Add more iron to solve this problem. Although iron is not essential to plant growth, you will certainly end up with less than average results if it is lacking. Iron problems do not tend to cause leaf curl at the start, but as the necrosis spreads leaves may curl.

If this does not solve your problem then move on to Step 7.

Step 7: If the leaves are yellowing at the veins but the tips are fine and are not curling or twisting, you have a manganese (Mn) problem. Manganese problems can be solved by adding more Mn to your plants. If the problem persists,

Recovery is possible if you get to the problem early. The key is to inspect your plants regularly and most importantly, keep your plants and grow area clean.

necrosis will set in and the leaves may curl. Plants do not need manganese to grow to full maturity but a lack of Mn will result in less than average results.

Move on to Step 8 if your problem still persists.

Step 8:   If you still have not solved your problem, then add a secondary and micronutrient formula to your soil. This should help solve problems like Ca, S, Cu, B, Zn, and Mo deficiencies, which are hard to detect as their respective symptoms are often different from strain to strain. By mixing a secondary and micronutrient formula you should be able solve these problems.

If this still has not solved the problem then turn to Step 9.

Step 9:   Still haven't solved it? Then flush your soil using the information provided in Chapter 7 and find another type of plant food that has all of these: N, P, K, Ca, Mg, and S. Purchase Epsom salts and get a small canister of micronutrients, such as iron, boron, chlorine, manganese, copper, zinc, and molybdenum. Try using a nutrient mixture that we've already mentioned in Chapter 7.

If you don't want to flush your soil or transplant to another growing environment then proceed to Step 10.

Step 10: Your plant may be experiencing nutrient lockout. There are a number of factors that can cause this problem. If you followed Step 9 properly then you shouldn't have this problem, but we'll explain it anyway. Lockout occurs when the plant cannot access a nutrient or a group of nutrients. This could be caused by the absence of nutrients (a deficiency) or by a chemical reaction in the medium/solution, which either causes a toxic substance to block the roots or a chemical reaction to take place, creating a new substance that changes the chemical properties of the other nutrients. As you can see, this is a very broad subject matter. pH problems can lockout nutrients. The wrong soil type can also cause nutrient lockout. Under the right conditions, even water can lockout nutrients. However, these lockout causes occur rarely, and more than likely something other than what the cannabis plant needs has been added to the solution to cause this reaction.

When in doubt, transplant into fresh soil or a fresh hydroponic solution. Certain feeding products might contain active ingredients that do not work well with cannabis. Lockout can only be solved by flushing or a transplant. With hydropon-

These seedlings came from an unknown source. It will take months of time, effort and energy until they are mature enough to find out if the genetics are good or not.

ics, you will have to change your nutrients. Out of date liquid feeding products can precipitate, causing nutrient lockout. Salt is another compound that can cause nutrient lockout. Follow Step 9 to solve these problems.

Your plant may be pot-bound or root-bound, or may have simply outgrown its pot. When the entire root mass grows to its maximum capacity, this can cause the plant stress and a variety of other problems that may resemble a nutrient problem. The only cure for this is to transplant the plant to a bigger pot. Follow the transplant method described in Chapter 10.

No Cure for Bad Genetics

When all else fails, you may have to face the fact that you are dealing with "a bad seed." There is a lot of garbage in the market. Problems associated with bad genetics include mutations, warping, flowering problems and poor germination rates that will often cause nutrient symptoms to appear even though your nutrient problem doesn't exist. The only viable solution is to obtain new genetics — preferably from a different breeder. Make sure that you let the originator of the seeds know about your problem. Seed banks sometimes do pull a line from the market because of consistent problems like germination rates or weak, unpredictable genetics. The only way they can find out about such things is to get feedback from you, the client.

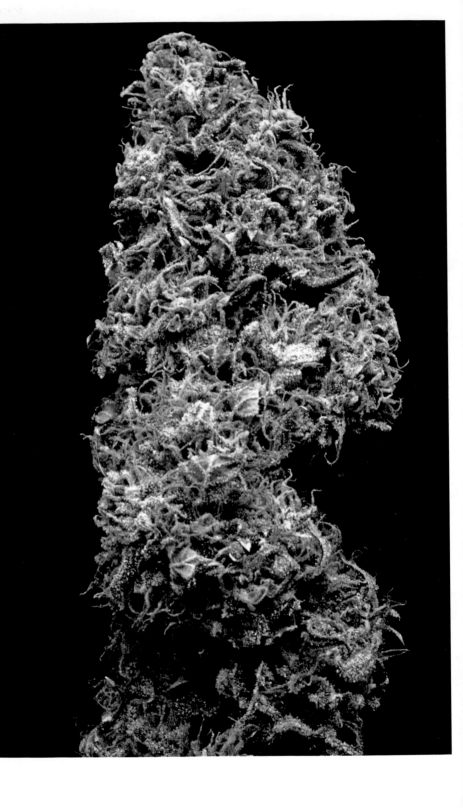

14 | Harvesting and Curing Your Bud

Harvesting is the act of reaping your rewards and is without doubt the most fun you'll have in your garden. Assuming that you have followed the guidelines for flowering times the breeder set forth and that your grow was successful, you should be in a position to harvest an extremely high yield from your crop.

First of all, you should know that harvesting is smelly and dirty work. It stinks up the place, so keep this in mind. Also, resin rubs off on nearly everything. Your fingers will be covered in a mass of resin and this will stain everything from metal to plastic, clothes, furniture, paper, books, equipment and other pieces of bud. Resin is sticky stuff that is very hard to wash off. It must be scrubbed off using a metal-type cleaning pad. Keep this in mind when you are harvesting your crop.

At the end of the flowering stage, examine your bud to see if it is ripe and ready for harvest. Here are some indicators to help you identify that it's harvest time; however, please note that not all of these indicators will appear on every strain.

- 50 percent to 70 percent of the pistils have changed color
- Plants have stopped producing crystals
- Plants have stopped producing resin
- The fan leaves and lower leaves have turned yellow and are starting to drop off
- The smell has reached a peak
- Bud mass has not increased in the past few days

Another good way to determine when to harvest is to create multiple tasters of the same bud. You can do this by harvesting plants from the same strain at different times. If you do not have enough plants to do this you can take selections of bud from a single plant. These samples can be tested to gauge the optimal harvest time for the strain. The next time you grow this strain, you will know exactly when to harvest. It must be said, however, that breeders' flowering times are generally pretty accurate. The experience of growing a strain more than once will also undoubtedly result in a more accurate timing of your harvest.

The Harvest

There is really only one way to harvest marijuana—anything else is just a variation on this theme. It should be noted that there are slight differences between harvesting an Indica and a Sativa plant.

If you are growing multiple strains, you should have a method of labeling which strains are which before you harvest. Otherwise, you will end up harvesting your bud into one big pile. This means that your entire labeling process from seedling stage to harvest will have been in vain. Keep your buds separate if you want to know your bud strain type when it is time to sample the results of your hard work.

A harvest of several different colorful strains conceal this grower in a shield of green.

Connoisseur bud is not all about yields but all about the quality and looks.
This Ultra Violet from Trichome Technologies looks great.

Quick Bud Samples

Some growers just can't resist a tester, but remember that these testers do not in any way reflect the final quality of well-cured bud. Just take a fresh bud sample and put it on a dish. Place the dish in a microwave on medium heat for about two minutes. Check the bud to see if it feels dry and brittle. If it doesn't, heat it a bit more. Once it feels dry and brittle it can be smoked. The smoke will be harsh and the microwave heat will destroy a good portion of the cannabinoids in the bud, but you should get something from your sample.

Another way of producing a quick bud sample is to take some fresh bud and put it into a sheet of paper. Fold the paper and press the bud down lightly. Place the paper on top of a working radiator and let the heat dry the bud. Check your bud later on in the day and it should be dry enough to smoke.

Expert Harvest Indication

There is a method that will allow you to determine precisely when to harvest. All you need is a magnifying aid and a little experience.

ne pistils grow out from the calyx they form resin glands (trichomes), which grad-
lly change in color before they shrink and wither. This withering of the trichomes
affects the look of the pistils, which in turn fade and tend to look burnt and dry. This
"unhealthy" appearance of the trichomes is perfectly natural. The plant has completed the blooming period and the trichomes are no longer needed to gather pollen. The
cannabinoid content of these trichomes is not lost, however. It is simply converted into
other psychoactive cannabinoid compounds. THC will also degrade as it is converted
into other psychoactive compounds. Eventually, exposure to light will further degrade
these cannabinoid compounds to next to nothing if the plant is not harvested.

The trichome withering process does not occur rapidly. It can take up to two
weeks before the plant has withered its trichomes and pistils entirely, but even
then new trichomes and pistils can be found growing among the faded pistils.
Eventually, the old pistils will die, to be replaced by the new pistils. The process
will continue until there is a change in the photoperiod or a cellular breakdown in
the plant and it dies.

Connoisseur bud may have a super amount of trichomes on the leaf. That frosted look
could cover the whole cola without there being a large number of pistils.

As the plant reaches its peak bloom, many of the pistils will change in color. Using a magnifying aid, you can observe this change in the trichomes themselves, which then affects the overall look of the pistils. By checking these trichomes daily you will be able to detect when the plant is nearing peak potency. The more trichomes change color, the more some will start to wither. The ones that wither first are usually in the minority because they were the first trichomes to form on the first pistils during the early days of flowering.

As some of these older pistils wither, the other pistils begin a visible transformation in color from white to orange, red or brown. At this point, you should be anticipating the "harvest marker" of 50 to 70 percent. When 50 to 70 percent of the pistils change color, the plant will have stopped producing new crystals (trichomes) and resin (cannabinoids secreted from the trichomes), the smell will have reached its peak and the bud mass will not have increased in a few days. At this stage, any of the major bud masses on the plant can, theoretically, be observed as follows:

It is important to keep harvests in mind when cultivating. Here you can see a grower has devoted adequate space for the plants to grow in. This comes with experience.

1. Less than 5 percent of the pistils are withering.
2. Approximately 90 percent of the pistils have reached maturity.
3. Less than 5 percent of the pistils appear to be in the early stages of growth.

The 90 percent group is the one that you should gauge your harvest with. Compare these to the ones that have gone past their peak bloom and harvest the plant just before they reach this stage. You should note that this usually corresponds with the breeders' flowering times. In the case of a plant with an unknown flowering time, you can use this expert method to predict when to harvest.

Timely harvesting is all about careful observation of the trichomes and their comparison to withered ones. Don't forget that trichomes can be harvested early or allowed to grow past their peak in order to affect the eventual high of the finished product.

a Harvest

one to four foot plant should be hacked at the base and picked up in its
irety. The weight of the Indica plant will probably amaze you if you have done
verything right. Try not to let it touch the ground, where the bud can gather up
unwanted dirt or dust. The plant should then be hung upside down in a cool room
with fresh air but no light.

When you hang the plants upside down the stems and branches automatically separate the buds, allowing space for air to flow around the freshly harvested flowers. The best temperature is between 60 and 75 degrees Fahrenheit. Relative
humidity is best kept at around 55 percent. Light degrades the overall THC quantity and quality. Light can also change the cannabinoid composition in your bud.
Your room doesn't have to be lightproof, but you should take care not to expose
your harvest to any direct light. Most growers use the bottom branches of the
plant as support when hanging them up. By tying some fishing line to the walls,
you can snag the bottom branch over the line to hang your buds upside down.

What is important here is that the grower is wearing gloves. These will
become thick with resin and so will the tips of these scissors.

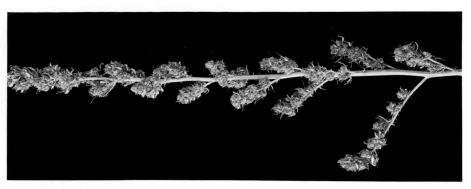

This plant has been fully trimmed of everything but the bud and stems.

Next, take a pair of clippers and remove as many of the fan leaves as possible. Then remove the secondary leaves and put these into a separate pile. Last but not least, gather some of the major trim leaf that can be removed easily from the bud. Trim refers to the small leaves that surround the bud and are usually covered in resin. This is a preliminary manicuring step only, designed to help ease the drying process. The real manicuring comes later. Leave the trim areas that are hard to remove for now; the trim you need to remove right after harvesting should pull away with ease. If there is no branch on the trim area that you are trying to remove, then leave it alone. Chances are that it will not pull free without taking some bud with it and you do not want to do this.

Leave the plant like this until a branch can break easily; it should literally snap between your fingers. This process takes about two to three weeks from start to finish, although some strains can take up to four weeks before the branches snap easily.

Now you have four different qualities of weed to choose from. The fan leaf will be an okay smoke, the middle leaves a little better and the trim will be very good. The bud is the prime stuff, though, and this will give you the best quality high.

Sativa Harvest

Outdoor growers like to grow Sativa plants, which can grow up to 12 feet, carrying more than 20 oz of bud each. It is not uncommon for some Sativa varieties to produce over 2lbs of bud per plant. However, these large plants are not harvested easily.

The process is similar to Indica except that the harvest itself can be quite labor-intensive. You need a canvas spread or another means of carrying the bud. The plant should be chopped at the base and spread out on the canvas. The canvas is

Do not underestimate the amount of work that goes on during harvesting.
Even a few plants could have you working the day through and then some.

then rolled up and tied tight for transport. Obviously, if you have more than one plant you might need more than one canvas sheet.

The plant should then be hung upside down in a cool room, with fresh air and no light. Because of the plant's size and bushiness, you may have to cut the branches and hang these up separately. Take a pair of clippers and remove the leaves and trim as suggested in the Indica harvest section.

Fan Leaves, Leaves, and Trim

These are cured by letting them dry on a flat surface, away from direct light and with plenty of fresh air. The leaves will dry after three weeks and are easily smoked at that stage. Test them out to see what you like and what you don't like. Another thing you could do with the trim is to make hash from it. We'll talk about this in Chapter 17. Don't try to speed up your drying process with ovens, microwaves or heat; let them dry out naturally and you'll have a much better smoke from the leaves. Cannabis connoisseurs will discard the leaves in favor of the more pleasing and potent bud that is also far less harsh to smoke. Remember, though, that even if you are a connoisseur, the leaves can be used to make hash.

HARVEST

A nice sized harvested branch awaiting manicuring.

Half the trim has been removed.

All the trim has been removed and the branch is ready for drying.

Manicuring

This is one of the most important parts of preparing your bud for the curing process. Manicuring is a type of aesthetic bud treatment that will also help you to separate the best from the rest. You will need a tray (or two, depending on how much bud you have) of some description, a black plastic bag, a sharp pair of small fine scissors and some rubbing alcohol. Rubbing alcohol can be used to remove resin strains from your scissors, which after a while will become sticky, dull, and even jammed with resin. The manicuring process can take a long time so some people like to set up their manicuring system in front of the television. Manicuring will get your fingers covered with resin, so prepare everything that you will need beforehand—food, drinks, joints, bongs, etc.

Take as much hanging bud as possible and place it down in a heap on top of a black plastic bag. Try to keep the strains separate and even label each heap so that you remember which strain is which. During the manicuring process it is easy to get buds mixed up. Place another black plastic bag over this lot to avoid light degrading THC levels.

Already the bud is starting to pile up. Remember that everything you see in this dish is prime bud with some stems. In the background the stripped parts can be seen.

Plants should be suspended upside down in
a cool dark room.

Once the plant is dried out, the
manicuring can begin.

It is important to use sharp scissors or
shears to cut away the excess leaves.

You are then left with a
mound of fresh bud.

Get your first plant out from the heap and use your fingers to remove as many of the branches and leaves as you can. This is your chance to remove trim matter that you may have missed during the preliminary manicure step. Chop the remaining branches into convenient workable sizes for hand-held manicuring. Repeat this process with all the other plants until you fill your tray with the first-round, hand-manicured plants.

Next you will start the more precise, second-round manicure. Pick up your first piece of bud and clip away as much of the branch or stem as possible. Now work your scissors in between the bud and leaf. In one quick pinch you should be able to separate the leaf from the bud by snipping the leaf at the base. Notice that the stem of the leaf is covered in trichomes; hang onto these leaves as they are very high quality trim. Repeat the process until you have removed as much leaf as possible. If you find that you cannot get at the leaf, then simply snip away as much of the leaf as you can by sheering them in half or as close to the bud as possible.

Rotate the plant by the stem to gain access to the other side of the manicured bud. This rotation movement is the quickest way to access all of the leaf sites on the plant.

When hanging up the bud a grower may decide to convert the grow area into a dark room to let their bud dry while others choose to keep growing. Whatever you decide, keep the bud in a dark place.

Take care when cutting not to remove pistils or calyx along with the leaf. To avoid pistil removal, try using the very tips of the scissors when you snip so that the blades do not go past the piece you want to cut. Repeat this process with the other first-round, hand-manicured pieces and you will eventually end up with very nice manicured pieces of bud that are ready for curing.

How much you remove depends on what quality of manicured bud you want to end up with. Undoubtedly the method above produces the best quality manicured bud from your harvest; however, the weight of the overall product will be reduced. Leaving on lots of trim leaves will allow them to actually dry in with the bud to create a medium quality manicured bud that weighs

Placing a fan leaf in a curing jar overnight will re-hydrate over-dried bud.

more than the best quality manicured bud. Ultimately, it is your choice: you can mani-cure your bud for maximum weight or for quality.

You will end up with several separate piles of leaf, both from the preliminary manicure step and the more intensive manicuring process. Some people dump this leaf. Others smoke it. Still others will make hash from it. Most of the leaf will be harsh to smoke but will contain some cannabinoids. The better leaf will have visible trichomes. You can easily locate the leaf that is high in trichome content using a microscope. A microscope is a useful aid for separating the better leaf from the rest for hash making, especially if you are planning to use the cold water extraction technique using bubble bags described in Chapter 17. Of course, what you do with your leaf is entirely up to you.

Curing

As soon as the branches are brittle, consider curing your bud using the canning method. Canning is a great way to get the most from your bud. Find a can with a removable lid. The more cans you have on hand, the better.

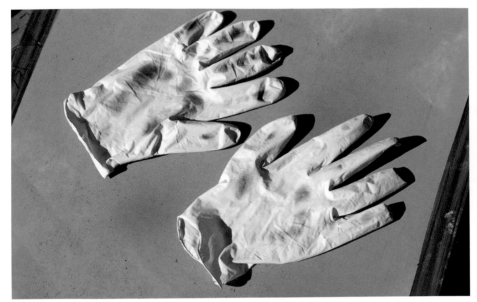

Wear harvesting gloves, fold them inside out after use, place them in the freezer and then after taking them out shake away the trim for some prime product.

Using a pair of scissors, clip your bud from the branch and place it into the can. The branches and stems are not much good to you. They do contain THC, but only in small quantities. Most stems and branches go on the compost heap.

Now take the can and place it in a cool, dark room or cupboard.[1] Every day, open the lid for a few hours (six hours is good) and then seal it again. Also, move the bud around a bit every couple of days. This is the most common curing technique, and it works best. Bud that is cured well smokes the best! Give the canning process between three and four weeks before sampling your goods. Eight-week old bud can smoke extremely well and year-old bud is vintage stuff but can lose potency.

Fresh bud (eight-weeks canned curing) is the pinnacle point of cured bud. After that the THC cannabinoids rapidly change composition and lose potency. Fresh bud is far better than aged bud. You may hear of other curing processes, but canning works wonders and is affordable too.

Canning sweats the bud, which causes it to retain its smell and flavor and allows the bud to burn more effectively. By opening and closing the can at different intervals you can control how damp or dry you want your buds to be. Try to use cans that have a large opening at the lid—enough to allow your whole hand to fit

TRICHOME TECH BUD

B1 is harvested after 50 days.   Kryptonite has over 16% THC.   NLx6 has over 22% THC.

Juicy Fruit has over 26% THC.   Ultra Violet has over 16% THC.   G-13 is harvested after 45 days.

A successful grow can keep a grower well supplied for months.

inside. This is because some of the trichomes will fall from the bud into the bottom of the can. Use your fingers to get at these trichomes. You can gather these into a small mass that can be smoked later on.

Drying your bud helps to relax THC particles by removing water from the bud. This makes THC easier to burn and thus more psychoactive than when it is damp. Applying heat will remove water and will affect the overall cannabinoid content of the bud. It is not a good idea to press bud or to pack tightly during the curing process, because bunching of THC particles makes them harder to burn.

Curing helps to break down chlorophyll, which has magnesium-containing green pigments. Magnesium is responsible for the sharp and harsh taste in the back of your throat when smoking fresh bud. This is another good reason to cure your bud.

If you over-dry your buds you may loose too much moisture, resulting in bud that has less taste and aroma than it should. The best way to add moisture back into your buds is to introduce new fresh bud to your cans. The new fresh buds will share their moisture with the dried bud, bringing them back to a more even level of moisture and restoring their aroma and taste. Some people uses fruit slices to bring back moisture, such as apple or orange slices. These fruit slices will also add their own aroma to the buds.

If you have dried your plants for three weeks hanging upside down you can subtract that time from the canning time. Although you can have good bud to smoke two weeks after your harvest, it is better to wait for four weeks or more.

- Chop your pants at the base.
- Cut them Into manageable amounts and hang them upside down in a cool, dry and dark place.
- Clip/pull the major leaf away.
- Allow to dry until the branches snap between your fingers.
- Clip the trim from the bud.
- Store in cans in a cool, dry place away from direct light.
- Check for mold.

15 | How to Breed Marijuana

If you want to continue growing a strain that you enjoy, cloning is your best option. You could also continue the strain by breeding two plants to produce seeds. You won't completely replicate the strain again using the seed method, however, unless the two parent plants are from the same IBL (inbred line). Even if the two plants are not IBLs, they should produce seeds that contain most of the parents' features. If you want to create a plant with characteristics from two different strains, breeding the marijuana from seed is your only option. That is the subject of this chapter, which begins with an introduction to simple breeding procedures and then goes on to cover advanced techniques like breeding a true strain and backcrossing.

Making Seeds

How easy is it to make seeds? It's easy if you have healthy plants and a stable growing environment. When your male plants burst their pollen sacks in your grow room, they'll pollinate the female flowers. You can also administer pollen directly to your females if you prefer.

Collecting and Storing Pollen

Pollen can be extracted from male flowers as soon as they open: you'll see the male flower open out from its calyx. It is best to gather pollen after it falls from the pod onto the leaves. You can shake the pollen onto the female flowers to pollinate them or grow your males separately and store their pollen for future use.

Film canisters are great for storing pollen. You can save pollen in a canister for the next harvest. Although it can be stored in the freezer for as long as 18 months,

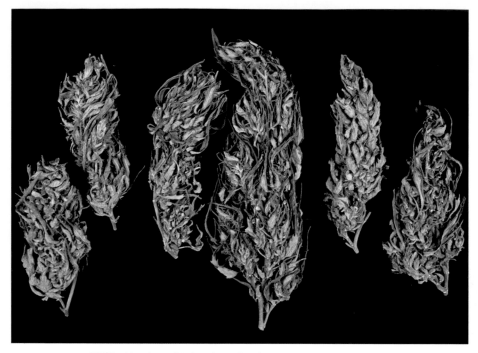

This bud has been dried and cured making it easier to extract seeds.

pollen is best used within six months of collection. Pollen has been known to keep for longer than 18 months, but is usually not viable past this time.

Collecting and Storing Seeds

If you have pollinated your plants, at the end of the flowering stage the bud will contain seeds. The seeds should be gray, tan or dark brown in color. They may also be striped, banded or lined with different colored markings. If they are pale cream or white in color, then they are probably not viable and you have harvested them too early. You should wait until the end of flowering to harvest your seeds.

Your seeds will be mixed in with the bud and it can take quite a bit of time to separate them from their sticky calyx pods. Do not squeeze the calyx directly because you can damage the seed inside. Just tease the seed out from the calyx with your fingers. If you do not want the bud, you can brush a seeded flowering branch against some fabric or a sieve to release the seeds from their respective calyx pods. It is easier to remove seeds from dry, cured bud than from freshly harvested plants.

If you plan to use the seeds in more than two years time, store them in an airtight container and place this in a freezer. If you plan to use the seeds within the next two years, storing them in a standard film canister or similar container will work well. Keep this canister away from heat and direct light and do not let it get damp or you risk spoiling your seeds. Containers placed in the freezer should not be opened until you are ready to use them. Allow the seeds to thaw at room temperature for at least 12 hours before use.

Simple Breeding

Your approach to breeding will depend on what you ultimately hope to achieve. Do you want to create a new strain, create seeds that are similar to the parents or cross two plants to create a simple hybrid strain?

Continuing a Strain Through Seeds

Say you purchased $120 worth of Silver Haze seeds and you want to make more seeds without any interference from another strain. That's easy; just make sure that the male and female plants you breed with are from the same strain batch. In this instance, the same strain batch would be Silver Haze from the same breeder. If you use Silver Haze from different breeders then the offspring may express a great deal of variation. This is because most breeders create their own versions of a popular strain. Their variety may have dissimilar characteristics from those of other breeders who have bred the same strain.

If you only have Silver Haze from the same breeder in your grow room, then all you need are a group of males and a group of females. Let the males pollinate the females and you will get more Silver Haze seeds, but you will loose some of the features of the original parent plants unless the strain you have is an IBL or from a very stable inbred pure line.

Making a Simple Hybrid

Again, making a simple hybrid is easy. Just take a male plant from one strain and a female plant from another; for example, Big Bud and Skunk. The result will be "Big Bud x Skunk," but there will be differences in the offspring. Some of the plants will exhibit more Big Bud traits and some will exhibit more Skunk traits. Genes not expressed by either parent may appear in the offspring.

If you want to breed for specific traits by eliminating variations, ultimately creating uniform plants or even an IBL, then you should start with a basic knowledge of plant genetics.

INTRODUCTION TO PLANT GENETICS

Genetics can be somewhat difficult to understand at first, so we'll start by explaining a few rudimentary concepts and the basic terminology.

Genes Genes are the units of heredity transmitted from parent to offspring, usually as part of a chromosome. Genes usually control or determine a single characteristic in the offspring. There are genes responsible for each feature of your plant to be inherited, including leaf color, stem structure, texture, smell, potency, etc.

Gene Pairs All life is made up of a pattern of genes. You can think of this pattern as being similar to the two sides of a zipper. One side is inherited from the mother and the other from the father. Each gene occupies a specific locus, or particular space on the chain, and controls information about the eventual characteristics of the plant. So, each gene locus contains two genes, one from the mother and one from the father. These gene pairs are usually denoted by a pair of letters, such as BB, Bb, Pp, pp, etc. Capital letters refer to dominant genes while lower case letters refer to recessive genes. By way of example, B can represent Big Bud while b can represent small bud. Any letter can be assigned to any trait or gene pair when you are working out your own breeding program.

Chromosome A threadlike structure of nucleic acids and proteins in the cell nuclei of higher organisms that carries a set of linked genes, usually paired.

Locus A position on a chromosome where a particular gene pair is located.

Allele Alleles are any of a number of alternative forms of one gene. For example, the gene for purple bud color may have two forms, or alleles, one for purple and one for dark red.

Homozygous Having identical alleles at one or more genetic loci, which is not a heterozygote (see below) and breeds true. Your plant is said to be homozygous for one feature when it carries the same gene twice in the responsible gene pair, which means both genes of the gene pair are identical.

Heterozygous Having different alleles at one or more genetic loci. Your plant is said to be heterozygous for one feature when the genes of the responsible gene pair are unequal, or dissimilar.

Phenotype The phenotype is the summary of all of the features you can detect or recognize on the outside of your plant, including color, smell and taste.

Genotype The genotype is the genetic constitution of your plant, as distinguished from the phenotype. The genotype characterizes how your plant looks from the inside. It is the summary of all the genetic information that your plant carries and passes on to its offspring.

Dominant "Dominant" is used to describe a gene or allele that is expressed even when inherited from only one parent. It is also used to describe a hereditary trait controlled by a gene and appearing in an individual to the exclusion of its counterpart, when alleles for both are present. Only one dominant allele in the gene pair must be present to become the expressed genotype and eventually the expressed phenotype of your plant.

Recessive "Recessive" describes a gene, allele or hereditary trait perceptibly expressed only in homozygotes, being masked in heterozygotes by a dominant allele or trait. A gene is called recessive when its effect cannot be seen in the phenotype of your plant when only one allele is present. The same allele must be present twice in the gene pair in order for you to see it expressed in the phenotype of your plant.

Dominant/Recessive and Genetic Notation Assume that the dominant 'B' allele carries the hereditary trait for Big Bud, while the recessive 'b' allele carries the hereditary trait for small bud. Since B is dominant, a plant with a Bb genotype will always produce Big Bud. The B is dominant over the b. In order for a recessive gene to be displayed in the phenotype, both genes in the gene pair must be recessive. So a plant with the BB or Bb gene will always produce Big Bud. Only a plant with the bb gene will produce small bud.

Now that we have explained the basic terminology of plant genetics, we can move on to the next step: rudimentary breeding concepts as laid out in the Hardy-Weinberg law of genetic equilibrium.

GREEN HOUSE SEED COMPANY: R&D LABORATORY

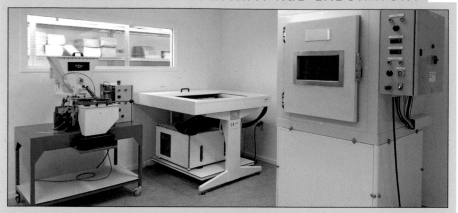

At the left is the Green House Seed Company seed coating machine. On the right, the seed dryer.

Green House Seed Company thermogradient table: used for germination testing of all strains.

Green House Seed Company seeds are coated with an anti-pathogen, root stimulator, fungicide and organic coloring for protection against negative environmental factors and ease of identification.

Arjan's Haze #2
Green House Seed Co.

Arjan's Haze #3
Green House Seed Co.

The Hardy-Weinberg Model of Genetic Equilibrium

An understanding of plant breeding requires a basic understanding of the Hardy-Weinberg law. To illustrate the value of the Hardy-Weinberg law, ask yourself a question, like "If purple bud color is a dominant trait, why do some of the offspring of my purple bud strain have green buds?" or "I have been selecting Indica mothers and cross-breeding them with mostly Indica male plants, but I have some Sativa leaves. Why?" These questions can be easily answered by developing an understanding of the Hardy-Weinberg law and the factors that can disrupt genetic equilibrium.

The first of these questions reflects a very common misconception: that the dominant allele of a trait will always have the highest frequency in a population and the recessive allele will always have the lowest frequency. This is not always the case. A dominant trait will not necessarily spread to a whole population, nor will a recessive trait always eventually die out.

Gene frequencies can occur in high or low ratios, regardless of how the allele is expressed. The allele can also change, depending on certain conditions. It is these changes in gene frequencies over time that result in different plant characteristics.

Arjan's Ultra Haze
Green House Seed Co.

Arjan's Strawberry Haze
Green House Seed Co.

A genetic population is basically a group of individuals of the same species (cannabis Indica or cannabis Sativa) or strain (Skunk #1 or Master Kush) in a given area whose members can breed with one another. This means that they must share a common group of genes. This common group of genes is locally known as the gene pool. The gene pool contains the alleles for all of the traits in the entire population. For a step in evolution—a new plant species, strain or trait—to occur, some of the gene frequencies must change. The gene frequency of an allele refers to the number of times an allele for a particular trait occurs compared to the total number of alleles for that trait in the population. Gene frequency is calculated by dividing the number of a specific type of allele by the total number of alleles in the gene pool.

Genetic Equilibrium Theory and Application

The Hardy-Weinberg model of genetic equilibrium describes a theoretical situation in which there is no change in the gene pool. At equilibrium there can be no change or evolution.

Let's consider a population whose gene pool contains the alleles B and b.

Assign the letter p to the frequency of the dominant allele B and the letter q to

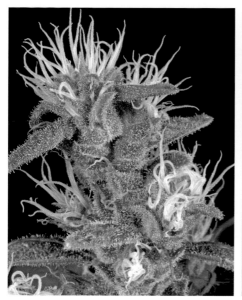

Big Bang
Green House Seed Co.

Blue Moonshine
Dutch Passion

the frequency of the recessive allele b. We know that the sum of all the alleles must equal 100 percent, so:

$$p + q = 100\%$$

This can also be expressed as:

$$p + q = 1$$

All of the random possible combinations of the members of a population would equal:

$$p2 + 2pq + q2$$

Where:

p = frequency of the dominant allele in a population
q = frequency of the recessive allele in a population
p2 = percentage of homozygous dominant individuals
q2 = percentage of heterozygous recessive individuals
2pq = percentage of heterozygous individuals

Blue Thunder
Sagarmatha

Brainstorm Haze
Delta-9 Labs

Imagine that, hypothetically, you have grown a population of 1,000 "Black Domina" cannabis plants from seeds obtained from a well-known seed bank. In that population, 360 plants emit a skunky smell, while the remaining 640 plants emit a fruity smell. You contact the seed bank and ask them which smell is dominant in this particular strain. They tell you that the breeder selected for a fruity smell and the skunk smell is a recessive genotype. You can call this recessive genotype 'vv' and use the formula above to answer the following questions.

Question: According to the Hardy-Weinberg law, what is the frequency of the 'vv' genotype?

Answer: Since 360 out of the 1,000 plants have the 'vv' genotype, then 36% is the frequency of 'vv' in this population of 'Black Domina.'

Question: According to the Hardy-Weinberg law, what is the frequency of the 'v' allele?

Answer: The frequency of the 'vv' allele is 36%. Since q2 is the percentage of homozygous recessive individuals, and q is the frequency of the recessive allele in a population, the following must also be true:

Bubbleberry
Sagarmatha

Canna Sutra
Delta-9 Labs

$$q2 = 0.36$$
$$(q \times q) = 0.36$$
$$q = 0.6$$

Thus, the frequency of the 'v' allele is 60%.

Question: According to the Hardy-Weinberg law, what is the frequency of the 'V' allele?

Answer: Since q = 0.6, we can solve for p.

$$p + q = 1$$
$$p + 0.6 = 1$$
$$p = 1 - 0.6$$
$$p = 0.4$$

The frequency of the 'V' allele is 40%.

Question: According to the Hardy-Weinberg law, what is the frequency of the genotypes 'VV' and 'Vv'?

Answer: Given what we know, the following must be true:

$$VV = p2$$
$$V = 0.4 = p$$
$$(p \times p) = p2$$
$$(0.4 \times 0.4) = p2$$
$$0.16 = p2$$
$$VV = 0.16$$

The frequency of the genotype 'VV' is 16%.

$$VV = 0.16$$
$$vv = 0.36$$
$$VV + Vv + vv = 1$$
$$0.16 + Vv + 0.36 = 1$$
$$0.52 + Vv = 1$$
$$Vv = 1 - 0.52$$
$$Vv = 0.48 \text{ or } 48\%$$

Or alternatively, 'Vv' is 2pq, therefore:

$$Vv = 2pq$$
$$2pq = 2 \times p \times q$$
$$2pq = 2 \times 0.4 \times 0.6$$
$$2pq = 0.48 \text{ or } 48\%$$

The frequencies of V and v (p and q) will remain unchanged, generation after generation, as long as the following five statements are true:

1. The population is large enough
2. There are no mutations
3. There are no preferences; for example, a VV male does not prefer a vv female by its nature
4. No other outside population exchanges genes with this population
5. Natural selection does not favor any specific gene

The equation p2 + 2pq + q2 can be used to calculate the different frequencies. Although this equation is important to know about, we make use of other, more basic calculations when breeding. The important thing to note here is the five conditions for equilibrium.

Church
Green House Seed Co.

The Doctor
Green House Seed Co.

Double Kush
Delta-9 Labs

El Nino
Green House Seed Co.

Euforia
Dutch Passion

First Lady
Sensi

Earlier we asked the question, "I have been selecting Indica mothers and cross-breeding them with mostly Indica male plants but I have some Sativa leaves. Why?" The Hardy-Weinberg equilibrium tells us that outside genetics may have been introduced into the breeding program. Since the mostly Indica male plants are only mostly Indica and not pure Indica, you can expect to discover some Sativa characteristics in the offspring, including the Sativa leaf trait.

The Test Cross

Some of you may be asking the question, "How do I know if a trait, such as bud color, is homozygous dominant (BB), heterozygous (Bb) or homozygous recessive (bb)?"

If you've been given seeds or a clone you may have been told that a trait, such as potency, is homozygous dominant, heterozygous or homozygous recessive. However, you will want to establish this yourself, especially if you intend to use those specific traits in a future breeding plan. To do this, you will have to perform what is called a test cross.

Determining the phenotype of a plant is fairly straightforward. You look at the plant and you see, smell, feel or taste its phenotype. Determining the genotype cannot be achieved through simple observation alone.

FOG (Fruit of the Gods)
Delta-9 Labs

Great White Shark
Green House Seed Co.

Generally speaking, there are three possible genotypes for each plant trait. For example, if Golden Bud is dominant and Silver Bud is recessive, the possible genotypes are:

Homozygous Dominant: BB   = Golden Bud
Heterozygous: Bb   = Golden Bud
Homozygous Recessive: bb   = Silver Bud

The Golden and Silver Bud colors are the phenotypes. BB, Bb and bb denote the genotypes. Because B is the dominant allele, Bb would appear Golden and not Silver. Most phenotypes are visual characteristics but some, like bud taste, are phenotypes that can't be observed by the naked eye and are experienced instead through the other senses.

For example, looking at a mostly Sativa species like a Skunk plant you will notice that the leaves are pale green. In a population of these Skunk plants you may notice that a few have dark green leaves. This suggests that this Skunk strain's leaf color is not true breeding, meaning that the leaf trait must be heterozygous because homozygous-dominant and homozygous-recessive traits are true breeding. Some of the Skunk's pale green leaf traits will probably be homozygous dominant in this population.

Hawaiian Snow
Green House Seed Co.

Jack Flash
Sensi

You may also be asking the question, "Could the pale green trait be the homozygous recessive trait and the dark green leaf the heterozygous trait?" Since a completely homozygous recessive population (bb) would not contain the allele (B) for heterozygous expression (Bb) or for homozygous dominant expression (BB), it is impossible for the traits for heterozygous (Bb) or homozygous dominant (BB) to exist in a population that is completely homozygous recessive (bb) for that trait. If a population is completely homozygous for that trait (bb or BB), then that specific trait can be considered stable, true breeding, or "will breed true." If a population is heterozygous for that trait (Bb) then that specific trait can be considered unstable, not true breeding, or "will not breed true."

If the trait for Bb or BB cannot exist in a bb population for that trait, then bb is the only trait that you will discover in that population. Hence, bb is true breeding. If there is a variation in the trait, and the Hardy-Weinberg law of equilibrium has not been broken, the trait must be heterozygous. In our Skunk example there were only a few dark green leaves. This means that the dark green leaves are homozygous-recessive and the pale green leaves are heterozygous and may possibly be homozygous-dominant too.

You may also notice that the bud is golden on most of the plants. This also sug-

Jack Herer
Sensi

Jack the Ripper
Subcool

gests that the Golden Bud color is a dominant trait. If buds on only a few of the plants are Silver, this suggests that the Silver trait is recessive. You know the only genotype that produces the recessive trait is homozygous recessive (bb). So if a plant displays a recessive trait in its phenotype, its genotype must be homozygous recessive. A plant that displays a recessive trait in its phenotype always has a homozygous recessive genotype. This leaves you with an additional question to answer as well: are the Golden Bud or pale green leaf color traits homozygous dominant (BB) or heterozygous (Bb)? You cannot be completely certain of any of your inferences until you have completed a test cross.

A test cross is performed by breeding a plant with an unknown dominant geno-type (BB or Bb) with a plant that is homozygous recessive (bb) for the same trait. For this test, you will need another cannabis plant of the opposite sex that is homozygous recessive (bb) for the same trait.

This brings us to an important rule: If any offspring from a test cross display the recessive trait, the genotype of the parent with the dominant trait must be het-erozygous and not homozygous.

In our example, our unknown genotype is either BB or Bb. The Silver Bud

Khola
Dutch Passion

La Lybella
Dutch Passion

Magic Bud
Paradise

Mongolian Indica
Sagarmatha

genotype is bb. We'll put this information into a mathematical series known as Punnett squares.

	b	b
B		
?		

We start by entering the known genotypes. We do these calculations for two parents that will breed. We know that our recessive trait is bb and the other is either BB or Bb, so we'll use B? for the time being. Our next step is to fill the box in with what we can calculate.

	b	b
B	Bb	Bb
?	?b	?b

The first row of offspring Bb and Bb will have the dominant trait of Golden Bud. The second row can either contain Bb or bb offspring. This will either lead to offspring that will produce more Golden Bud (Bb) or Silver Bud (bb). The first possible outcome (where ? = B) would give us Golden Bud (Bb) offspring. The second possible outcome (where ? = b) would give us Silver Bud (bb) offspring. We can also predict what the frequency will be.

Outcome 1, where ? = B:
Bb + Bb + Bb + Bb = 4Bb
100% Golden Bud

Outcome 2, where ? = b:
Bb + Bb + bb + bb = 2Bb + 2bb
50% Golden Bud and 50% Silver Bud

Recall:

Homozygous Dominant:
BB = Golden Bud
Heterozygous:
Bb = Golden Bud
Homozygous Recessive:
bb = Silver Bud

Mekong Haze
Delta-9 Labs

Mexican Sativa
Sensi

To determine the identity of B? we used another cannabis plant of the opposite sex that was homozygous recessive (bb) for the same trait.

Outcome 2 tells us that:
- Both parents must have at least one b trait each to exhibit Silver Bud in the phenotype of the offspring.
- If any Silver Bud is produced in the offspring then the mystery parent (B?) must be heterozygous (Bb). It cannot be homozygous-dominant (BB).

So, if a Golden Bud parent is crossed with a Silver Bud parent and produces only Golden Bud, then the Golden Bud parent must be homozygous-dominant for that trait. If any Silver Bud offspring is produced, then the Golden Bud parent must be heterozygous for that trait.

To summarize, the guidelines for performing a test cross to determine the genotype of a plant exhibiting a dominant trait are:

1. The plant with the dominant trait should always be crossed with a plant with the recessive trait.
2. If any offspring display the recessive trait, the unknown genotype is heterozygous.

Mr. Nice
Sensi

Nebula
Paradise

3. If all the offspring display the dominant trait, the unknown genotype is homozygous-dominant.

The main reasoning behind performing a test cross are:

1. When you breed plants you want to continue a trait, like height, taste, smell, etc.
2. When you want to continue that trait you must know if it is homozygous dominant, heterozygous or homozygous-recessive.
3. You can only determine this with certainty by performing a test cross.

We should mention that, as a breeder, you should be dealing with a large population in order to be certain of the results. The more plants you work with, the more reliable the results.

Hardy-Weinberg Law, Part 2

The question may arise, "How do I breed for several traits, like taste, smell, vigor and color?" To answer this question, you will need to learn more about the Hardy-Weinberg law of genetic equilibrium.

If you breed two plants that are heterozygous (Bb) for a trait, what will the offspring

NL5 Haze
Green House Seed Co.

Ortega Indicac
Dutch Passion

look like? The Punnett squares can help us determine the phenotypes, genotypes, and gene frequencies of the offspring.

	B	b
B	BB	Bb
b	Bb	bb*

*Take special note of this offspring and compare it with the parents.

In this group, the resulting offspring will be:

1 BB - 25% of the offspring will be homozygous for the dominant allele (BB)
2 Bb - 50% will be heterozygous, like their parents (Bb)
1 bb - 25% will be homozygous for the recessive allele (bb)

Unlike their parents (Bb and Bb), 25 percent of offspring will express the recessive phenotype bb. So two parents that display Golden Bud but are both heterozygous (Bb) for that trait will produce offspring that exhibit the recessive Silver Bud trait, despite the fact that neither of the parents displays the phenotype for Silver Bud.

Pamir Gold
Dutch Passion

Purple #1
Dutch Passion

Understanding how recessive and dominant traits are passed down through the phenotype and genotype so that you can predict the outcome of a cross and lock down traits in future generations is really what breeding is all about.

When you breed a strain, how do you know that the traits you want to keep will actually be retained in the breeding process? This is where the test cross comes in. If you create seeds from a strain that you bought from a seed bank, how can you be sure that the offspring will exhibit the characteristics that you like? If the trait you wish to continue is homozygous-dominant (BB) in both parent plants, then there's no way that you can produce a recessive genotype for that trait in the offspring, as illustrated in the Punnett square below.

	B	B
B	BB	BB
B	BB	BB

It is impossible for the recessive trait to appear. If both parents contain the recessive trait then they cannot produce the dominant trait.

Querkle
Subcool

Sensi Star
Paradise

	b	b
b	bb	bb
b	bb	bb

In order to breed a trait properly you must know if it is homozygous, heterozygous, or homozygous-recessive so that you can predict the results before they happen.

Mendel and the Pea Experiments

Gregor Mendel (1822–1884) was an Austrian monk who discovered the basic rules of inheritance by analyzing the results from his plant breeding research programs. He noticed that two types of pea plants gave very uniform results when bred within their own gene pools and not with one another. The traits he noticed were:

Pea Plant #1	Pea Plant #2
Solid seed shells	Wrinkled seed shells
Green seeds	Yellow seeds
White flowers	Purple flowers
Tall plants	Short plants

He noticed that the offspring all carried the same traits when they bred with the

Shaman
Delta-9 Labs

Sheherazade
Paradise

same population or gene pool. Since there were no variations within each strain he guessed that both strains were homozygous for these traits. Because the pea plants were from the same species, Mendel guessed that either the solid seed shells were recessive or the wrinkled seed shells were recessive. Using the genotype notations SS for solid seed shells and ss for wrinkled seed shells, he knew that they couldn't be Ss because one lot didn't exhibit any of the other strain's phenotypes when bred within its own gene pool.

Let's illustrate this using two basic Punnett squares, where SS is pea plant #1 with the trait for solid seed shells and ss is pea plant #2 with the trait for wrinkled seed shells.

	S	S
S	SS	SS
S	SS	SS

	s	s
s	ss	ss
s	ss	ss

The First Hybrid Cross (the F1 Generation)

Mendel made his first hybrid cross between the two strains and the results were all solid seeds as seen in the chart below.

F1 Cross	s	s
S	Ss	Ss
S	Ss	Ss

Up until this point, he didn't know which trait was recessive and which was dominant. Since all the seeds shells were solid, he now knows with certainty that pea plant #1 contained the dominant genotype for solid seed shells and pea plant #2 contained the recessive genotype for wrinkled seed shells. This meant that in future test crosses with other pea strains, he could determine if a particular seed shell trait was homozygous or heterozygous because he had identified the recessive trait (ss).

The Second Hybrid Cross (the F2 Generation)

The offspring in the F1 cross were all Ss. When Mendel crossed these offspring he got the following results:

F2 Cross	S	s
S	SS	Ss
s	Ss	ss*

*Take special note of this offspring and compare with parents.

Mendel had mated two pea plants that were heterozygous (e.g., Ss) for a seed shell trait. In this group, the resulting offspring were:

25% of the offspring were homozygous for the dominant allele (SS)
50% were heterozygous, like their parents (Ss)
25% were homozygous for the recessive allele (ss)

In his first cross to create the hybrid plant, Mendel ended up with no recessive traits for seed shape. But when he crossed the offspring, because they were heterozygous for that trait, he ended up with some having the homozygous-recessive trait, some having the homozygous-dominant trait, and some continuing the heterozygous-trait. In correct breeding terms, his first cross between the plants is called the F1 cross or F1 generation. The breeding out of those offspring is called the F2 cross or F2 generation.

Shiva Shanti
Sensi

Snowbud
Dutch Passion

Space Jill
Subcool

Stonehedge
Sagarmatha

Now since he has Ss, ss and SS to work with, you could use Punnett squares to determine what the next generations of offspring will look like. Compare your results with what you have learned about ratios and you'll be able to see how it all fits together.

More on Genetic Frequencies

Take a look at the cross below between two heterozygous parents. If two heterozygous parents are crossed, the frequency ratio of the alleles will be 50% each. Remember, the genotype can be Ss, SS or ss, but the allele is either 'S' or 's.'

	S	s
S	SS	Ss
s	Ss	ss

We can see S S S S (4 x S) and s s s s (4 x s). This means that the frequency of the allele 'S' is 50% and the frequency of the allele 's' is 50%. See if you can calculate the frequencies of the alleles 'S' and 's' in the following crosses for yourself.

	S	s
S		
S		

	s	s
S		
S		

Recall that the Hardy-Weinberg law states that the sum of all the alleles in a population should equal 100 percent, but that the individual alleles may appear in different ratios. There are five situations that can cause the law of equilibrium to fail. These are discussed next.

1. Mutation. A mutation is a change in genetic material, which can give rise to heritable variations in the offspring. Exposure to radiation can cause genetic mutation, for example. In this case, the result would be a mutation of the plant's genetic code that would be transferred to its offspring. The effect is equivalent to a migration of foreign genetic material being introduced into the population. There are other factors that can cause mutations. Essentially, a mutation is the result of DNA repair failure at the cellular level. Anything that causes DNA repair to fail can result in a mutation.

Strawberry Cough
Dutch Passion

Super Haze
Dutch Passion

2. Gene Migration. Over time, a population will reach equilibrium that will be maintained as long as no other genetic material migrates into the population. When new genetic material is introduced from another population, this is called introgression. During the process of introgression many new traits can arise in the original population, resulting in a shift in equilibrium.

3. Genetic Drift. If a population is small, equilibrium is more easily violated, because a slight change in the number of alleles results in a significant change in genetic frequency. Even by chance alone, certain traits can be eliminated from the population and the frequency of alleles can drift toward higher or lower values. Genetic drift is actually an evolutionary force that alters a population and demonstrates that the Hardy-Weinberg law of equilibrium cannot hold true over an indefinite period of time.

4. Non-Random Mating. External or internal factors may influence a population to a point at which mating is no longer random. For example, if some female flowers develop earlier than others they will be able to gather pollen earlier than the rest. If some of the males release pollen early and then stop producing pollen, the mating between these early males and females is not random, and could result in late-flowering females ending up as a sinsemilla crop. This means that these late-

flowering females won't be able to make their contribution to the gene pool in future generations. Equilibrium will not be maintained.

5. Natural Selection. With regards to natural selection, the environment and other factors can cause certain plants to produce a greater or smaller number of offspring. Some plants may have traits that make them less immune to disease, for example, meaning that when the population is exposed to disease, less of their offspring will survive to pass on genetic material, while others may produce more seeds or exhibit a greater degree of immunity, resulting in a greater number of offspring surviving to contribute genetic material to the population.

How to True Breed a Strain

Breeding cannabis strains is all about manipulating gene frequencies. Most strains sold by reputable breeders through seed banks are very uniform in growth. This means that the breeder has attempted to lock certain genes down so that the genotypes of those traits are homozygous.

Imagine that a breeder has two strains: Master Kush and Silver Haze. The breeder lists a few traits that they particularly like (denoted by *).

Master Kush	Silver Haze
Dark green leaf	Pale green leaf *
Hashy smell *	Fruity smell
White flowers	Silver flowers *
Short plants *	Tall plants

This means they want to create a plant that is homozygous for the following traits and call it something like Silver Kush.

Silver Kush
Pale green leaf
Hashy smell
Silver flowers
Short plants

All the genetics needed are contained in the gene pools for Master Kush and Silver Haze. The breeder could simply mix both populations and hope for the best or try to save time, space and money by calculating the genotype for each trait and using the results to create an IBL.

Super Lemon Haze
Green House Seed Co.

Super Silver Haze
Green House Seed Co.

The first thing the breeder must do is to understand the genotype of each trait that will be featured in the ideal "Silver Kush" strain. In order to do this, the genotype of each parent strain for that same trait must be understood. Since there are four traits that the breeder is trying to isolate, and 4 x 2 = 8, eight alleles make up the genotypes for these phenotype expressions and must be made known to the breeder.

Let's take the pale green leaf of the Silver Haze for starters. The breeder will grow out as many Silver Haze plants as possible, noting if any plants in the population display other leaf colors. If they do not, the breeder can assume that the trait is either homozygous dominant (SS) or recessive (ss). If other leaf colors appear within the population, the breeder must assume that the trait is heterozygous (Ss) and must be locked down through selective breeding. Let's look closely at the parents for a moment.

	S	S
S	SS	SS
S	SS	SS

If both parents were SS, there wouldn't be any variation in the population for this trait. It would already be locked-down and would always breed true without any variations.

	S	s
S	SS	Ss
S	SS	Ss

With one SS parent and one Ss parent, the breeder would produce a 50:50 population — one group being homozygous (SS) and the other heterozygous (Ss).

	S	s
S	SS	Ss
s	Ss	ss

If both parents were Ss, the breeder would have 25 percent SS, 50 percent Ss and 25 percent ss. Even though gene frequencies can be predicted, the breeder will not know with certainty whether the pale green leaf trait is dominant or recessive until they perform a test cross. By running several test crosses, the breeder can isolate the plant that is either SS or ss, and eliminate any Ss from the group. Once the genotype has been isolated and the population reduced to contain only plants with the same genotype, the breeding program can begin in earnest. Remember that the success of any cannabis breeding program hinges on the breeder maintaining accurate records about parent plants and their descendants so that they can control gene frequencies.

Let's say that you run a seed bank company called PALE GREEN LEAF ONLY BUT EVERYTHING ELSE IS NOT UNIFORM LTD. The seeds that you create will all breed pale green leaves and the customer will be happy. In reality, customers want the exact same plant that won the cannabis cup last year or at least something very close. So in reality, you will have to isolate all the "winning" traits before customers will be satisfied with what they're buying.

The number of tests it takes to know any given genotype isn't certain. You may have to use a wide selection of plants to achieve the goal, but nevertheless it is still achievable. The next step in a breeding program is to lock down other traits in that same population. This is the hard part.

When you are working on locking down a trait you must not eliminate other desirable traits from the population. It is also possible to accidentally lock down an

Third Dimension
Subcool

Vortex
Subcool

unwanted trait or eliminate desired traits if you are not careful. If this happens then you'll have to work harder to explore genotypes through multiple cross tests and lock down the desired traits. Eventually, through careful selection and record keeping, you'll end up with a plant that breeds true for all of the features that you want. In essence, you will have your own genetic map of your cannabis plants.

Successful breeders don't try to map everything at once. Instead, they concentrate on the main phenotypes that will make their plant unique and of a high quality. Once they have locked down four or five traits they can move on. True breeding strains are created slowly, in stages. Well known, true breeding strains like Skunk #1 and Afghani #1 took as long as 20 years to develop. If anyone states that they developed a true breeding strain in one or two years you can be sure that the genetics they started with were true breeding, homozygous, in the first place.

Eventually you will have your Silver Kush strain, but only with the four genotypes that you wanted to keep. You may still have a variety of non-uniform plants in the group. Some may have purple stems, while others may have green stems. Some may be very potent and others not so potent. By constantly selecting for desired traits you could theoretically manipulate the strain into a true breeding strain for every phenotype. However, it is extremely unlikely that anyone will ever create a

100 percent true breeding strain for every single phenotype. Such a strain would be called a perfect IBL. If you're able to lock down 90 percent of the plant's phenotypes in a population, then you can claim that your plant is an IBL.

The core idea behind the true breeding technique is to find what is known as a donor plant. A donor plant is one that contains a true breeding trait (homozygous, preferably dominant for that trait). The more locked down traits are homozygous-dominant, the better your chances of developing an IBL, which does not mean that the line of genetics will be true breeding for every trait, but rather that the strain is very uniform in growth for a high percentage of phenotypes.

Some additional advanced breeding techniques that will help you to reduce or promote a trait in a population are discussed below. Using these techniques may not create a plant that is true breeding for the selected traits, but will certainly help to make the population more uniform for that trait.

Advanced Breeding Techniques
Simple Backcrossing
Our first cross between the Master Kush plant and the Silver Haze is known as the F1 hybrid cross. Let's pretend that both traits are homozygous for leaf color: the Silver Haze is pale green and the Master Kush is dark green. Which is SS or ss? We won't know until we see the offspring.

F1 Hybrid Cross	s	s
S	Ss	Ss
S	Ss	Ss

This F1 cross will result in hybrid seeds. Since S is dominant over s, we'll know which color is more dominant and from which parent it came from. In this example, the overall results are pale green. Thus, the pale green allele is dominant over the dark green.

S = Silver Haze pale green leaf trait is dominant
s = Master Kush dark green leaf trait is recessive

We also know that because no variations occurred in the population, both parents were homozygous for that trait. However, all the offspring are heterozygous. Here is where we can take a shortcut in manipulating the gene pool for that population. By cloning the parent plant SS, we can use this clone in our cross with the Ss offspring. This is known as a backcross. Obviously, if our parent is female then we'll have to use males from the Ss selection in our backcross, and vice versa.

F2 Backcross	S	s
S	SS	Ss
S	SS	Ss

Now our first backcross will result in 50 percent homozygous (SS) offspring and 50 percent heterozygous offspring (Ss) for that trait. Here all the offspring will exhibit the pale green leaf trait. If we didn't backcross but just used the heterozygous offspring for the breeding program, we would have ended up with 25 percent homozygous-dominant (SS), 50 percent heterozygous (Ss) and 25 percent homozygous-recessive (ss), as shown below.

F2 Hybrid Cross (without backcrossing)	S	s
S	SS	Ss
s	Ss	ss

Backcrossing seriously helps to control the frequencies of a specific trait in the offspring. The F2 Hybrid Cross produced some plants with the dark green leaf trait. The F2 Backcross did not.

The F2 backcross is an example of simple backcrossing. Let's see what happens when we do our second backcross (F3) using the same original parent kept alive through cloning. Our second backcross is referred to as squaring. Since we're dealing with only two types of offspring, Ss and SS, we'll either repeat the results of the F2 backcross...

F3 Backcross with heterozygote	S	s
S	SS	Ss
S	SS	Ss

...or we will successfully lock down the desired trait as follows:

F3 Backcross with homozygote	S	S
S	SS	SS
S	SS	SS

In the F3 Backcross with the homozygote, all of the offspring are homozygous-dominant

This clone mother is kept in circulation for up to 6 months. Bending of the branches allows for more shoots to grow out which enables many cuttings each week to be possible.

(SS) and thus true breeding for that trait. These offspring are the result of squaring and can never produce the ss traits because the SS trait is now true breeding and stable. The F3 Backcross with the heterozygote has some Ss offspring. If we breed the Ss and Ss offspring, we can produce the ss trait. This line would not be stable.

How to Generate a Clone Mother

The best way to generate a clone mother is to grow a large population of plants from the same strain. If the strain is an IBL, then you should find that the plants do not exhibit much variation. It can be difficult to find a clone mother from an IBL strain, though, because IBLs are created to provide a population of plants from seed, which all resemble the clone mother that the breeder enjoyed and wanted to share with you.

The best way to generate a clone mother is to select her from a large population of F1 hybrids. If you do not find a clone mother in the F1 population, then allow random mating to occur and see if you can generate a good clone mother in the F2 population. If you do not find the clone mother in the F2 population, then either grow a larger population or select different parents to create a new F1 population.

A clone mother is only as good as the environment she is grown in. The environment influences how the genotype is displayed in the phenotype.[1] Although indoor plants can grow outdoors and outdoor plants can grow indoors, the expressed phenotype of the genotype may change because of the diversity in growing conditions. This is why breeders urge that you grow their strains in the recommended environment.

Selfing

Selfing is the ability of a plant to produce seeds without the aid of another plant and refers to hermaphrodite plants that are able to self-pollinate. Hermaphrodite plants have both male and female flowers. This usually means that the hermaphrodite plant is monoecious. Most plants are dioecious and have male and female flowers on separate plants.

Monoecious cannabis strains will always display both sexes regardless of the growing conditions. Under optimal growing conditions, a monoecious cannabis strain will still produce both male and female flowers on the same plant. Under optimal growing conditions, a dioecious cannabis strain will produce male and female flowers on separate plants.

Stressful growing conditions can cause some dioecious cannabis strains to produce both male and female flowers on the same plant. Manipulating an irregular photoperiod during the flowering stage is an easy way to encourage the dioecious hermaphrodite condition. Not all dioecious cannabis strains can become hermaphrodites. The dioecious cannabis strain must have a preexisting genetic disposition to become hermaphrodite under stressful conditions in order for male and female flowers to appear on the same plant.

If you find a dioecious cannabis strain that has the hermaphrodite condition, you can separate this plant from the rest and allow selfing to occur. If the male pollen is viable on this plant then the hermaphrodite will produce seeds. Selfed plants that produce seeds will eventually generate offspring that:

1. Are all female
2. Are all hermaphrodite
3. Produce male, female and hermaphrodite plants because the environment also influences the final sexual expression of the selfed plant
4. Express limited variation from the original selfed plant

Breeders should note that it is nearly impossible for a hermaphrodite to create male plants, although the environment can influence males to appear. Hermaphrodites usually create female-only and hermaphrodite seeds. The female-only seeds often carry the hermaphrodite trait. Selfing has become popular among those who wish to breed all-female or feminized seeds. Unfortunately, feminized seeds do very little for the cannabis gene pool as the hermaphrodite condition prevents growers from generating a sinsemilla crop.

Well-informed breeders tend to shy away from producing feminized seeds. Feminized seeds should only be used for bud production and not for breeding. Generating seeds from feminized plants is only advised for personal use and not for distribution.

Notes on Selfing by Vic High
These notes were drawn and edited from an online description. Notes provided by Vic High, BCGA breeder.

100% Female Seeds
[Vic] has stressed literally hundreds of plants with irregular photoperiods. What he does is put the lights on 12/12 for 10 days. Then he turns the lights on 24 hours, then 12/12 again for a few days, then back to 24 hours for a day, then

This is a male in full flowering. In fact, the pollen has already been released, as evident from the powder on the leaves. This one plant alone would invalidate a sinsemilla project.

12/12 again for a few weeks. If he does this and no hermaphrodites come up, he has found a 100% XX female that can't turn hermaphrodite naturally. He claims that your chances of finding a 100% XX female are vastly increased when using Indica genetics. He also suggests that the more Afghani or Nepalese genetics the plant has, the better the chances of finding a natural XX female. In his own words, "Where did nature give weed a home originally?"

[Vic] then uses gibberellic acid, mixing 2/3 pint of water with 0.007 grams of gibberellic acid and 2 drops of natrium hydroxide to liquefy the gibberellic. He then applies as normal and creates male flowers. He has gotten down to the 4th generation without loss of vigor, and with no genetic deficiencies or hermaphrodites. He claims that the plants are exact genetic clones of one another, complete sisters. Basically, it's cloned from seed instead of from normal cloning methods.

It has also been said that it's easy for the home grower to find an XX female. It's a very time-consuming process but a straightforward one. Mr. XX, an anonymous grower, advises home growers to confine themselves to a single strain. Mr. XX used a Skunk #1 x Haze x Hawaiin Indica. He says to separate those plants from your main grow and stress them severely. Do this repeatedly with every new crop of seeds you get of that strain until you find the XX female. While this is time consuming, it is by no means impossible.

Southern Lights, bred for the aroma New York City Diesel and the
high of the Sensi Star, changes color with the seasons.

Professional breeders, like Serious Seeds, keep their facilities clean and well organized so that problems can be quickly identified and resolved.

Concluding Thoughts on Breeding

Experimentation results in new hybrids. Stabilized hybrids result in new strains. It is far better to generate one excellent strain that to generate several unstable average ones. Breeding is a long-term commitment. Many breeders stop breeding after only a few years because of lack of time, space and money. Although they may have learned something about breeding in that short time, they will not have had the opportunity to put it into practice. If you want to breed cannabis then be prepared to spend a few grows getting the basics right first.

Breeding is all about recognizing which traits are worth continuing. Do not be afraid to admit that you do not have anything worth breeding. Some of the best breeders have gone through dozens of different populations before finding a plant that stands out from the rest.

There are many reasons to breed your own strain of cannabis. Try to find an original idea for breeding your own cannabis strain; original ideas always seem to work out best.

16 | **Top Ten**

This section contains a list of cannabis strains that you will more than likely come across if you shop around. These strains are very popular with growers who like to post pictures of their crops on the internet. The majority of these strains are also featured in various cannabis plant competitions around the world and most of them have won awards.

We have compiled a top 10 list of these favorite strains arranged in alphabetical order, per species type, with a key denoting whether the plants are suitable for new growers, are true breeding and can be grown indoors or out, along with a potency/high type rating and the format in which the strain is available.

Key

★	= A very good strain.
★	= Suitable for new growers.
★	= Better for experienced growers.
TB	= Indicates an IBL strain or a strain that is stable with a lot of breeding properties.
OUT	= Not suitable for indoors.
IN/OUT	= Suitable for both indoors and outdoors.
H	= High potency.
M	= Medium potency.

Sensi Seeds' Hash Plant is an amazing strain that is descended from one of
the finest hash-making cultivars from the Hindu Kush. Photo Sensi Seeds.

Paradise Seed's Durga Mata is a reliable, homo-
geneous variety and is a perfect choice for a sea
of green garden. Photo Paradise Seeds

Dutch Passion's Twilight is a beautiful purple
variety with high yields and Afghan taste.
Photo Dutch Passion

Top Ten Indica

Name	Rating	IBL	Indoor/Outdoor	Potency	Seeds/Clone
Afghani	★	TB	IN/OUT	M	Seeds
Afghani #1	★ ★	TB	IN	H	Seeds
BC Hash Plant	★ ★		IN	M	Clone
Black Domina	★		IN	H	Seeds
Champagne	★ ★		IN	H	Clone
G-13	★ ★		IN	H	Clone
Hindu Kush	★	TB	IN	M	Seeds
Masterkush	★	TB	IN	M	Seeds
Northern Lights	★ ★	TB	IN	H	Seeds
Shiva	★	TB	IN	M	Seeds

Here are some other Indica strains that you might want to try out: Bazooka,
Cream Sodica, Domino, Durga Mata, KC36, Kong, Kush, M-9, Mango, Mangolian
Indica, Mazar, Pluton 2, Purple Star, Romberry, Shishkeberry, Slyder, Twilight,
Williams Wonder.

Sagarmatha's Matanuska Tundra is an Indica that can be
grown indoors and outdoors. Photo Sagarmatha.

Dutch Passion's Blueberry is 80% Indica and 20% Sativa; when smoked, it has a taste of blueberry. Photo Dutch Passion.

Sagarmatha's Yumbolt is an Indica–Sativa mix that has a sweet taste and a comfortable, stoney high. Photo Sagarmatha.

Top Ten Mostly Indica

Name	Rating	IBL	Indoor/Outdoor	Potency	Seeds/Clone
Big Bud	★	TB	IN	M	Seeds
Blueberry	★ ★	TB	IN	M	Seeds
Chemo	★ ★		IN	H	Clone
Chronic	★		IN	H	Seeds
Early Girl	★ ★		OUT	M	Seeds
Great White Shark	★ ★		IN	H	Seeds
Matanuska Valley ThunderFuck	★ ★		IN/OUT	H	Clone
Northern Lights #5	★ ★	TB	IN	H	Seeds
Sweet Tooth	★ ★		IN	H	Seeds
Top 44	★ ★		IN	M	Seeds

Here are some other mostly Indica strains that you might want to try out: Aurora Borealis, Big Treat, Buddha, Chitral, Early Bud, Eclipse, El Nino, Hawaiian Indica x Skunk #1, Hawaiian/Skunk, Himalayan Gold, Inca Spirit, K2, M39, MCW (Mighty Mite x Chemo x Widow), Mister Nice, Misty, Northern Lights #1, Northern Lights #2 (Oasis), Peak 19, Romulan, Sensi Star, Shiva Shanti, Texada Timewarp, Yumbolt.

Green House Seed Co.'s Neville's Haze is almost pure Haze with a strong psychoactive and stimulating high. Photo Green House Seed Co.

Dutch Passion's Durban Poison is an exclusively inbred, 100% Sativa that produces large buds with lots of resin. Photo Dutch Passion.

Sensi Seed's Mother's Finest is a Hazey offshoot of the Herer line and won first place for Sativa at the 2002 Cannabis Cup. Photo Sensi Seeds.

Top Ten Sativa

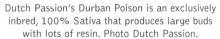

Name	Rating	IBL	Indoor/Outdoor	Potency	Seeds/Clone
Australian Bushweed	★ ★		OUT	H	Seeds
Cambodian	★		OUT	H	Seeds
Durban Thai	★		OUT	H	Seeds
Haze Strains	★ ★		OUT	H	Seeds
Malawi	★		OUT	H	Seeds
Mullimbimby Madness	★ ★		OUT	H	Seeds
Neville's Haze	★ ★		OUT	H	Seeds
Purple Haze	★ ★		OUT	H	Seeds
Swazi	★		OUT	H	Seeds
Thai	★		OUT	H	Seeds

Green House Seed Co.'s Arjan's Haze #1 has an extremely psychoactive high, strong and long lasting with a spicy sativa taste. Photo Green House Seed Co.

Trichome Tech's Washington is an Indica–Sativa hybrid that matures in 45 days and has a THC content of 22.6%.

Dr Greenthumb's Jazz is a Sativa-dominant strain that can be grown indoor and outdoor. Photo Dr Greenthumb.

Top Ten Mostly Sativa

Name	Rating	IBL	Indoor/Outdoor	Potency	Seeds/Clone
Cinderella 88/99	★ ★		IN	H	Seeds
Durban Poison	★ ★	TB	IN/OUT	H	Seed
Early Pearl	★ ★	TB	OUT	M	Seeds
Haze #1	★		OUT	H	Seeds
Kali Mist	★ ★	TB	IN	H	Seeds
Lambs bread Skunk	★ ★		IN/OUT	H	Seeds
Power Plant	★ ★		IN	H	Seeds
Skunk #1	★ ★	TB	IN/OUT	M	Seeds
Super Silver Haze	★ ★		IN/OUT	H	Seeds
Voodoo	★		IN/OUT	M	Seeds

Here are some other mostly Sativa strains that you might want to try out: B-52, Beatrix Choice, Durban, Durban x Skunk, Durban/Thai, Early Skunk, Haze #19, Haze Skunk, Mexican Sativa, Original Haze, Purple Skunk, Sensi Skunk, Shaman, Silver Haze, Skunk Passion, Skunk Red Hair, Super Haze, Swazi x Skunk.

Green House Seed Co.'s White Widow is based on Brazilian and South Indian genetics and gives a relaxing high. Photo Green House Seed Co.

Sensi Seed's Jack Herer is a delicate balance of Sativa and Indica; it has won nine cannabis awards. Photo Sensi Seeds.

Paradise Seeds' Dutch Dragon is a Sativa–Indica mix that tastes sweet and produces a nice, clear high. Photo Paradise Seeds.

Top Ten Indica/Sativa Mix

Name	Rating	IBL	Indoor/Outdoor	Potency	Seeds/Clone
AK-47	★ ★	TB	IN	H	Seeds
BubbleGum	★ ★	TB	IN	M	Seeds
California Orange	★ ★	TB	IN	H	Seeds
Jack Herer	★ ★		IN	H	Seeds
Pole Cat	★ ★		IN	M	Seeds
Purple Power	★ ★		IN	M	Seeds
Schnazzleberry	★ ★		IN	H	Seeds
Super Skunk	★ ★	TB	IN	H	Seeds
White Russian	★ ★		IN	H	Seeds
White Widow	★		IN	M	Seeds/Silver

Here are some other Indica/Sativa mix strains that you might want to try out: Apollo 11, Aurora, Blue Heaven, California Indica, C4, Dutch Dragon, Early Riser, Euphoria, Flo, Frost Bite, Fruit Loop, Green Spirit, Hawaiian Indica, Holland's Hope, Jack Flash, Juicy Fruit, KC 33, Killer Queen, Leda Uno, Malibu Blue, Mighty Dutch, Nebula, Night Queen, Orange Crush, Orange Strains, Plum Bud, Purple #1, Rosetta Stone, Shiva Skunk, Silver Pearl, Skunk Indica, Space Queen, Special K, Trance, White Rhino.

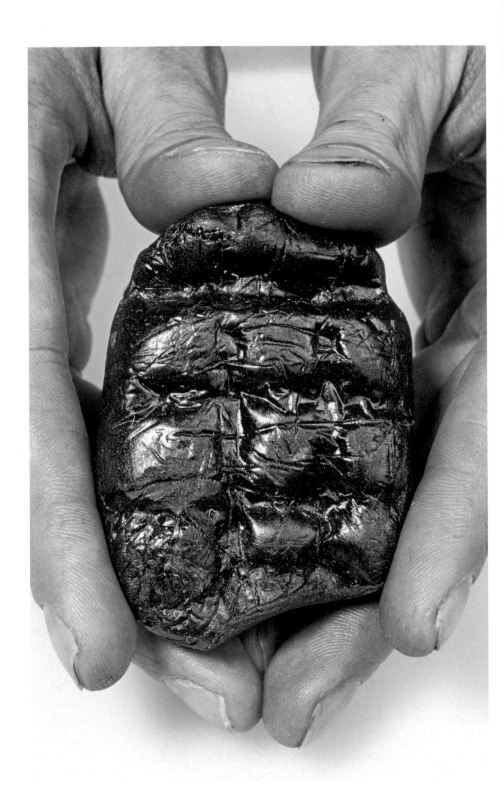

17 | **How to Make Hash**

Hash is a compressed form of cannabis, but it isn't just compressed bud. In fact, contrary to what some people think, compressed bud has nothing to do with hashish.

Earlier in this book, we discussed capitate trichomes and how these tiny stalked resin glands contain cannabinoids—the major compounds produced by the cannabis plant, which include THC. THC is found in the male leaf, but the female produces THC in her leaves, trichomes and calyx. THC is rarely extracted from the male leaf because it is contained inside the leaf, but since the resin glands can be wiped from the female plant it is much easier to perform THC extraction from a female. The gland heads, or rounded tips of the trichomes, secrete the major cannabinoids in an oil-like substance, often referred to as resin, in order to gather fallen pollen from the male plant. This resin can be removed by rubbing your fingers over the bud.

The stalks that support the gland heads are second to the gland heads in the amount of cannabinoids produced. Under certain conditions, the glands and stalks can burst. In the case of a strain like Afghani #1 that is thick with resin, this explosive action of the gland is automatic. Strains that are prone to bursting their trichomes form ball-shaped pistil clusters rather than the usual straight or curled pistil shapes. These ball-shaped clusters are a good indication that a strain is a suitable candidate for resin extraction.

Gathering the Stalked Capitate Trichomes

Hash is made primarily from the collection of the stalked capitate trichomes. When the collected trichomes are compressed, they form the blocky mass that is referred to as hashish. There are many ways to do this, ranging from bulk hash production to

Skuff that has been recently screened. You might like to compare this with the picture on p. 11 to see the variation in colour and texture.

rolling small, finger-size quantities. Each method produces a different quality or grade of hashish. Some methods gather only the trichomes, while other methods gather trichomes and other subsidiary elements like leaf particles and branch shavings.

Water extraction is the best way to achieve trichome-only extraction. We won't discuss older methods used for mass production, as these are somewhat substandard to the home methods mentioned below. The quality of your hashish is determined to a large degree by the genetics you started with in the first place. If you used plants that weren't very potent, don't expect to produce very potent hash.

Skuff

When you harvest your bud you will have trimmed the leaves away from the bud. This trim is referred to as skuff. Skuff should be sticky, so whether it's on the stem, branch, leaf or bud, if it feels sticky, then you can use it to extract the resin. If you really want to be a connoisseur, then you should examine your skuff for trichomes with a microscope. If none of the skuff parts have trichomes, discard them. Take the remaining skuff and store this for 3 to 6 weeks, in much the same way as you would canned bud, before using the basic and advanced extraction methods detailed below.

Screening Basic Methods
Flat Silk Screening

Screening is a process much like grating cheese, but on a far finer level. A silk screen is stretched across a square wooden frame and nailed tightly to it. The screen typically has a pore size of between 120 and 180 microns. The smaller the microns, the higher the quality, but the less you will produce. Larger micron pores will result in larger sieved amounts but will allow some leaf matter and branch trim to drop through, degrading the quality of hash you smoke.

Here's how it's done: the bud is placed over the screen and can either be dragged across the screen manually or by using a roller. Manual screening is much easier if you're using smaller quantities of bud, but for large quantities you should consider another method, like automatic tumbling in a drum machine. A sheet of glass placed under the screen is the best way to catch the matter that falls through. After the screening process is complete, the screen can be patted down to shake off any powder that sticks in the pores.

The leaf flowers on the right are trimmed down and manicured on the left.
This manicured bud is then used for screening.

A nice selection of hash making product sliced to see the compressed trichomes contained in the blocks.

Flat Metal Screening

This is done much like the flat silk screening method, but before the flat silk is used the bud is subjected to a grating process. The grate is usually made from tough nylon or stainless steel and is of equal proportion in pore size to the silk screen. By first using the metal grate, you can remove more matter from the bud than the single silk screen would. The bud matter that passes through the metal screen can then be sieved through the silk screen by shaking the screen back and forth over a glass surface. This way you end up with two grades of sieved bud residue.

Multiple Screening Method

This is a refined version of the above two methods. Any number of screens can be used in this method, but the average is four or five. Each screen, running from start to finish, should have a different micron measurement, starting from the largest and running down to the smallest silk screen. The bud matter is sieved through the first screen, then down onto the second screen. The process is repeated with each new screen until most of the matter has passed through. You should end up with several screens that contain bud matter running down to the finer trichomes on the last screen. This is an excellent way to achieve the best results. You end up with several screens, each containing different qualities of cannabis residue.

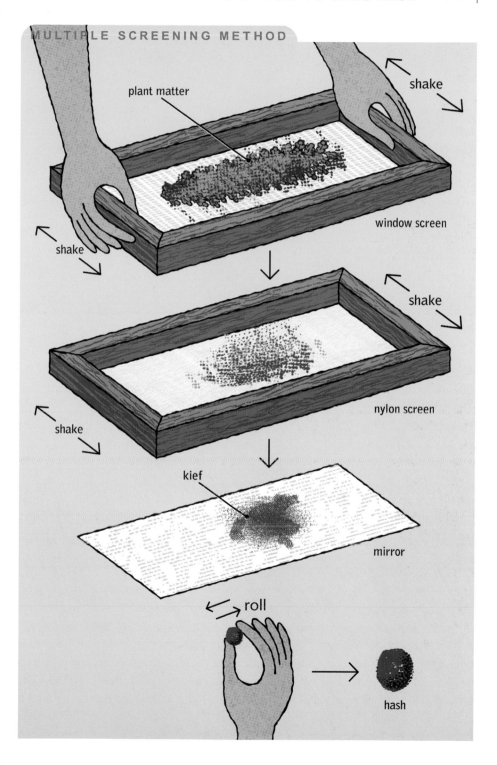

MULTIPLE SCREENING METHOD

plant matter

shake

shake

window screen

shake

shake

nylon screen

kief

mirror

roll

hash

Personal stash collection of a variety of bud and hash. Hash in grass
can turn a session into a very profound group experience.

Advanced Screening

Now that you have an idea of what screening is about, we can look at it in closer
detail. The following advanced technique can be applied to all of the above screening methods.

We stated that a metal or nylon screen could be used first, followed by a silk
screen. Nowadays, steel fabrics can be bought in sizes that have much smaller
pores than even the finest silk screen. You should typically look for a metal or nylon
screen that ranges somewhere between 100 to 140 lines per inch. The screen most
commonly used by home hash makers has 120 lines per inch. A wooden frame is
constructed to hold the screen in place and can be glued or nailed into position.

Take four small wooden blocks and place them over a sheet of glass or a mirror.
Place the screen over the blocks, leaving a gap of an inch between the mirror and
the screen. Place a small amount of skuff on the screen and gently roll it back
and forth across the screen using a credit card or similar object. Do this very gently, over and back, over and back, and over and back with very little pressure. You
may have to push the skuff as many as a hundred times before you can see the
tiny resin glands gather on the mirror below.

Once you have collected as many resin glands as possible, use the card to sweep them off the mirror and onto another surface. Take the used skuff and, this time, apply a little more pressure as you roll it back and forth across the screen. With this extra force you'll be able to remove any resin glands that didn't fall through the first time, but you may also push through some less valuable material such as branch shavings and leaf particles. This second round of pressing will result in a lower quality grade of skuff.

Skuff is skuff; from the time you cure your trim to the point where you sieve it through, it is still skuff. Your objective is to try and collect as much resin from the skuff as possible. You won't end up with hash, but you will end up with different grades of skuff that can be used to make hash later.

You can smoke the different grades of skuff there and then, but you may notice that it's hard to do so. Since this powder is so fine, it will easily fall from a joint or pass through the pores of a pipe screen. In order to solve this problem you must compress the skuff into hashish. This is covered later in the chapter, after we've outlined three other advanced extraction techniques.

Contrasting different hash. There is no way to know which is more potent or tasteful by coloring or texture. You need to sample before you know for sure.

Hashish comes in different shapes, from round balls to small chips to larger blocks. Many people who make their own hash like to try out new forms.

Drum Machines

A drum machine is an automatic screening device. You will probably have to build one yourself, but this is easy enough to do with the right materials. The size of the unit depends on how much cannabis you wish to sieve at a time. Most drum machines have a 1.5- to 2-foot diameter.

The screen is placed in-between the two wooden cylinders and the cannabis trim is placed inside this screen. A small motor attached to the side rotates the drum. As it slowly rotates (at a rate of about two rotations per minute), the trichomes drop through the sieve onto the surface stand between the legs of the drum. A simple mirror or sheet of glass is used to catch the skuff. You can keep the tumbler rotating for up to one hour to get the most from your skuff without applying any pressure.

If you want to apply more pressure, simply place a small wooden ball (or anything that is slightly heavy with a smooth, rounded surface) inside the barrel of the drum. As the drum rotates, the object inside will add a little more pressure to the skuff as it comes in contact with the screen. Different sized screens can be used to extract different qualities of skuff.

Basic Water Extraction

Resin glands can be removed from the cannabis plant by agitating the trim in cold water—typically ice cold water or water that has been chilled in a fridge overnight. The trim is placed in a bucket, which is then filled with cold water. The water and trim are swirled and mixed with a wooden spoon or an electric whisk. Let the mixture sit for a few minutes before scooping out the skuff floating on the surface. The remaining liquid is strained through a coffee sieve to collect most of the trichomes, as they won't pass through with the water. Let the coffee sieve dry and you'll have excellent grade trichome extract to use to make hash. The basic idea behind this is that cold water breaks the glands away from the leaf matter. The glands eventually sink to the bottom of the bucket because they are heavier than water. The bulk leaf matter should stay afloat and can be easily scooped away.

Advanced Water Extraction

Developed by Bubble Bag (bubblebag.com) in Vancouver, this is an excellent kit that results in some of the best quality hash. The kits come in four types: one gallon, seven bags; five gallon, seven bags; twenty gallon, seven bags; and five gallon, three bags. Whichever one you buy, it will certainly be one of your best investments.

Taking a block of hash, melting it down and rubbing it will eventually break it into more manageable pieces that can be prepared more easily for use.

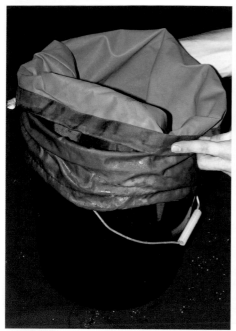

Bubblehash is made by starting out with bubblebags and a bucket.

Trim is added to the first bag and it is from this that the trichomes will be removed.

Ice is added and the mixture is well stirred. This is to breakup the trichomes from the plant material.

The mixture is then strained through the bubblebags and their decreasing screen sizes to extract the trichomes.

Freshly made bubblehash. This is some prime hash from what would
have been otherwise been trim that would have gone in the bin.

Supercritical Fluid Extraction

This is the ultimate way of making high quality hash oil with butane.

Solvents can also be used to extract raw cannabis oil from harvested cannabis flowers. Raw cannabis oil contains:

- Psychoactive cannabinoids in high percentages
- Plant tissue in low percentages
- Chlorophyll in low percentages
- Trace elements in low percentages (non-psychoactive water soluble matter)

Raw cannabis oil is best extracted from highly resinous strains like the Afghani cannabis plant. Strains that have a semi-dry or dry floral trait should not be considered candidates for cannabis oil extraction because the amount of oil extracted does not necessarily justify the procedure, although the end material is a very high-grade form of hash oil. With these dry strains you may have to perform the extraction process several times before a substantial amount of psychoactive oil is produced. Like any other cannabinoid extraction process, you are better off using a resinous strain to rationalize the end results.

Isopropyl, ethanol and acetone used to be popular solvents for hash oil extraction but the process for each one is time consuming, costly and material-intensive. They often result in smaller amounts of a lower grade than you hoped for. There is a much easier and more affordable way to enjoy a purer form of cannabis oil; the process known as butane extraction produces better results in a much shorter time frame.

Butane extraction is the most popular form of raw hash oil extraction because it is based on an industrial process known as SFE (supercritical fluid extraction) and is very easy to perform. You should only use butane fuels that are recommended for flameless lighters (jet torch will also do). These types of butane are much cleaner and extract raw hash oil better than other butane fuel types that you commonly find at the drugstore or fuel depot. A good tobacconist shop should stock flameless lighter butane.

Butane is a very good solvent for hash oil extraction because it separates cannabis oils from most other useless plant/bud matter. This type of filtered oil is sometimes nicknamed "Hash Honey Oil" because the results are like an amber honey. SFE can produce very fine and pure cannabis oil from resinous strains. It simply separates cannabis oils from plant tissue, chlorophyll and the other trace elements

Hash plant can be used either for just bud or hash, but is promoted mainly as a hash-making strain. There are many good hash making strains out there.

that we find in most raw hash oils. You can imagine the final weight of the butane extracted oil to be the equivalent of the total weight of anything sticky or oily on the plant, separated from the rest of it.

Once you have obtained the butane, you need a pipe that measures 1.5 to 2.0 inches in diameter, is 16 to 24 inch long and is made from either polypropylene (PP) or polyethylene (PE). Basically, the bigger the pipe, the more bud it can hold. Do not use PVC piping because it can be a health hazard. Either PP or PE piping works best and can be found in any good DIY store. Each end of the pipe will need a cap. You should be able to get some PP or PE caps at a home improvement store, or someone can make them for you. If you cannot find any suitable caps, you can try using large bottle caps and "blue tack" to hold them in place.

You need a stand to hold this pipe. A lab stand is perfect for the job but anything that will hold the pipe up off the ground is fine. You also need a filter. An extremely fine cloth filter, like a bandage wrap with pores or fine pipe gauze, will work well. Any filter that will allow oil to drop through but leave the plant matter in the pipe is ideal. Coffee filters will not work very well unless they have a large pore size. You also need a clear plastic measuring cup, a clean wooden stick (like a medical tongue depressor) and some nicely manicured bud. You should be able to use 1 oz or more of bud in the above pipe design.

In the diagram below you can see the parts in alignment without the stand. The parts are as follows: 1) butane canister, 2) top cap with hole for canister, 3) tube for holding the bud, 4) filter, 5) bottom cap with perforations, 6) cup to catch the oil and butane.

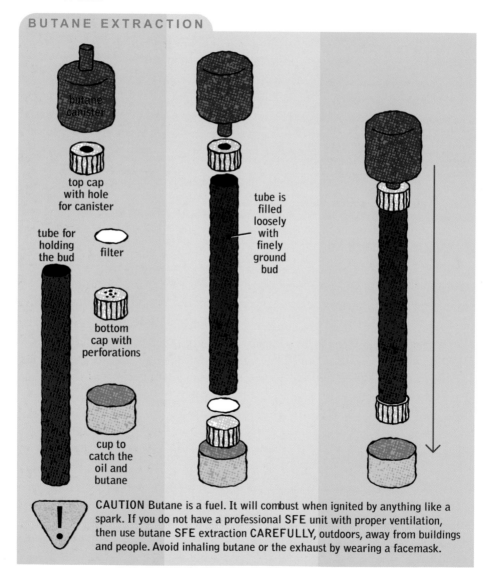

BUTANE EXTRACTION

butane canister

top cap with hole for canister

tube for holding the bud

filter

bottom cap with perforations

cup to catch the oil and butane

tube is filled loosely with finely ground bud

CAUTION Butane is a fuel. It will combust when ignited by anything like a spark. If you do not have a professional **SFE** unit with proper ventilation, then use butane SFE extraction **CAREFULLY**, outdoors, away from buildings and people. Avoid inhaling butane or the exhaust by wearing a facemask.

The whole unit should snap into place as follows.

Note: Butane is a fuel and will combust when ignited by anything like a spark. If you do not have a professional SFE unit with the proper ventilation, then use butane SFE extraction carefully, outdoors, away from any buildings and other people. Avoid inhaling butane or the exhaust from butane extraction by wearing a facemask.

Procedure:
1. Drill a hole in the end of the first cap that allows the nozzle of the butane canister to fit neatly into it.
2. Drill six small holes near the center of the second cap.
3. Place the filter in this second cap.
4. Attach the second cap to the pipe.
5. Fill up the pipe extremely loosely (never cram it in) with finely ground bud.
6. Attach the first, or top cap to the pipe.
7. Mount your pipe on your stand and place it over your clean measuring cup.
8. Open the butane can and turn it upside down, placing the nozzle in the top cap. Fill the pipe up slowly, allowing the butane to draw the oils down through the tube.
9. Remove the butane canister when its weight stops decreasing (meaning it is empty) and move a safe distance away.
10. Wait fifteen to twenty minutes before approaching the apparatus even if the top cap has given up any viable signs of fume release. The butane should have evaporated away, leaving an oil/butane mixture in the cup.
11. Open the top cap to allow all fumes to escape. Butane will still be active in the cup and bud in the pipe so leave these two alone for another twenty minutes. The remaining oil in the cup is raw hash oil with some butane.
12. Any remaining butane can be evaporated by placing the cup into a dish of hot water.
13. You now have raw hash oil. It should be ready to smoke in a few hours.

Tips for Butane Extraction

I have heard of numerous SFE accidents caused with butane. All of them happened the same way. Most SFE butane extraction accidents occur when the pipe is full of bud and butane is dripping down into the cup below. Any flame, spark or ignition will cause that butane to become unstable. Almost all of the accidents I have heard about occurred because a flame or spark ignited the butane. In most cases it was a smoker who caused this. Do not smoke when you are performing SFE with butane, period. If you can do that then butane extraction is actually one of safest methods of hash oil extraction available to the home grower.

During the SFE process the butane must be left alone to drain down into the plastic cup along with the raw hash oils that it collects on the way down. Vapor and fumes will come out through the top of the cap and the cup.

After about fifteen minutes, most of the butane will have passed through. There may be some remaining butane/oil extract near the filter and end cap, but forcing this through (by either blowing, tapping or pushing) into the tube may add unwanted matter to your extract. A brief shake is all that is needed to help the remainder into the cup. Use the wooden stick to wipe away any oil/butane mixture from the base of the filter. This butane/oil extract in the pipe and cup is still part of the SFE process and the butane will continue to evaporate.

Butane has a low boiling point (it even evaporates at room temperature) and if you need to boil off any excess butane in the cup simply place the cup into a bowl of hot water (not boiling!) and watch the butane evaporate. This is why butane extraction is best done outdoors. Butane will eventually evaporate into the atmosphere instead of into your home where it can become a fire hazard. You should eventually be left with an amber-colored substance in the cup. This is your high-grade hash oil!

The butane should be completely evaporated by heating the cup of raw hash oil/butane in hot water. Your high-grade hash oil is sticky to touch and best smoked in small quantities because of its quality. Oil is best enjoyed by placing a small glob of oil on some foil and heating the foil lightly from beneath, causing the oil to boil and vaporize. This vapor should be then consumed using a Pyrex straw (plastic straws burn and inhaling burning plastic is not good). As a note: cannabis oil is an excellent format for medicinal use because it is very pure. By vaporizing cannabis oil, the user can enjoy a pure form of cannabis without carbon monoxide.

Here are some other tips for butane extraction:

- After you remove the hash oil from the cup you can use some isopropyl (90 percent minimum content) to collect any residual oil that may by still in the cup. Add a small amount of isopropyl to your cup and swirl it around. Heat the cup at a very low heat (less than 200 degrees Fahrenheit to avoid THC evaporation) to evaporate the isopropyl, leaving the remaining hash oil collected from the rim of the cup.
- You can perform a second extraction using the same procedure with the used bud to remove any excess oil that is still left in the bud. The bud will then be

Pressing hash usually results in some rough edges. Just leaving a wet
mass of trichomes to dry can produce the same effect as here.

mostly devoid of any cannabinoid compounds and should be disposed of.

- A slow release of butane into the pipe allows sufficient time for the SFE to take place, improving the quality of the process and the final amount. Try not to force all your butane in too quickly.
- The butane you use must be as pure as possible. Bottled butane is usually mixed with chemicals so that when it leaks you smell it. These chemicals can interfere with the butane/cannabis SFE process.
- Use a bud grinder to make sure that your bud is powdered down as much as possible. The finer the mix, the better the extraction results.
- You should be able to get between 5 and 10 grams of hash oil for every 1 oz of good quality, resinous bud that you use.
- You can also process leaf or trim using butane SFE. You can expect about 0.5 to 2 grams of hash oil for every 1 oz of trim used. This depends on the quality of the trim.

Pressing Resin into Hash

Again, the quality of the resin glands will determine the quality of hash that you will smoke. In the first chapter we talked about Zero Zero. Recall that hashish can be

Here we see very tightly pressed hashish on the right, lesser compact
ones on the left and loose particles in the foreground.

graded, based on quality, from high (00) to low (3). This is calculated based on a simple ratio of cannabinoids to vegetable material. Good quality hashish has a high ratio
of cannabinoids to vegetable material. In Morocco, 00 is used to describe hash that
has the highest level of cannabinoids to vegetable material achieved by the extraction process. You can imagine that this is the finest resin available, compressed into
hashish; you may also be pleased to know that compressing hashish is simple.

Take your extracted resin glands and put them into a cellophane bag. Fold the
material into a flat block shape and tape the ends of the cellophane to create the
package. Try to create the best flat block you can by pressing it with your hands
to make it more even. Using a pin, make a few holes on both sides of the bag; one
hole per square inch is a good measurement to go by.

Get two or three newspaper pages and dampen them down with a clean cloth that
has just been rinsed. Don't saturate or break the paper, just dampen it. Set an iron
to low heat and place the newspaper over the cellophane bag. Hold the iron over
the paper and press it down with medium pressure for about fifteen seconds. Turn
the bag over and place the newspaper on top again. Dampen the paper again, as
needed. Repeat the pressure for the same amount of time. You should only have
to do this once or twice per side.

This joint is being topped up with a sweet coating
of honey oil for a truly strong smoke.

Let the bag cool for five minutes and remove the cellophane. You should have a nice
block of hash. In addition, your hash will be of a much better quality than the street
hash you find on the market. Street hash tends to be made from the less fine skuff
material in order to make more blocks of hash. If you smoke homemade hash then
you'll probably understand why 90 percent of street hash is sold at rip-off prices. Those
big ounce chunks probably only contain 10 percent of the good stuff, if any at all!

This technique of screening and pressing is used to make hash in many countries.
As you can imagine, in order to produce bulk amounts you would need to use a lot
of skuff in conjunction with numerous drum machines working around the clock.
If you harvest more than ten plants then it is worth using one or two to make a
nice chunk of hash or some oil for yourself. Since good homemade hash is devoid
of leaf matter and other foreign elements, it is a very pure smoke which guaran-
tees a hit every time. Cannabis connoisseurs regard homemade hash as one of the
best ways of getting the "best" from the plant. Treat yourself to a little homemade
hash at harvest time if you can. It is well worth the experience and who knows,
you may just decide to produce a load of homemade hash instead of bud! Give it
a whirl—you should be pleased with the results.

18 | Important Cannabis Issues

This chapter deals with some important questions surrounding the health risks and social issues associated with cannabis use. It should be the endeavor of every cannabis user to learn as much as they can about the plant, its immediate effects, and the long-term consequences of use. If you encourage yourself to learn more about these aspects of cannabis, you may eventually encourage other users to do the same. Try to stay up to date with the latest information and be sure to remain unbiased by checking alternative sources. Over the course of many years there have been numerous studies. Some of these studies were conducted with agendas. These same agendas (on both sides) continue today. However there has been much improvement in our understanding of how cannabis works.

There are a few pseudo-scientific claims that are commonly used to support the argument for cannabis prohibition due to the presence of stronger, more potent cannabis on the market:

- Cannabis is getting stronger
- The stronger the cannabis, the greater the health risks
- Hydroponics makes cannabis stronger
- New lighting technology means stronger cannabis
- Feeding products and growth hormones make cannabis stronger
- New extraction techniques make hashish stronger
- More crystals means more THC and stronger cannabis

In the pages that follow, we examine each of these claims, or myths. Growers will also learn something from this discussion.

Myth #1: Cannabis is Getting Stronger

The concept that "Today's cannabis is stronger than the cannabis of the 60s or 70s" is unsubstantiated by fact. Open any seed bank catalogue that has strains from the 60s and 70s in stock. Order them, grow them, sample your results and you will learn why they are still some of the most expensive seed lines on the market. Strains developed in the 60s and 70s are arguably still the most potent cannabis strains around.

Not only are people more informed as to what constitutes bad cannabis nowadays, low potency plants are also less likely to be available and/or purchased. This does NOT imply a potency increase. What it does suggest is that people might need to USE LESS cannabis to get the SAME EFFECT as using a lot of bad cannabis. When you think about use in terms of smoking and its affects, it is easy to see that smoking less is far better than smoking more.

Consider this: If the cannabis of the 60s was weaker than the cannabis of the 21st Century, why would internationally known seed banks still advertise some of the oldest stabilized cannabis plants of the 60s and 70s as their most potent?

Haze strains, Thai and other Sativa (species of cannabis) strains of the 60s (imported largely from Asia) are landrace strains that were cultivated by locals for their high cannabinoid content and hemp material. They were bred for hundreds, maybe even thousands, of years.

The suggestion that hybridizing these plants in conjunction with breeding techniques has somehow made cannabis stronger is a false notion. What has happened is that a new species of cannabis has emerged on the market that was not previously widely available. This species is called Cannabis Indica and it is the reason why cannabis may seem different, but is not necessarily stronger or more potent.

Cannabis Indica and Cannabis Ruderalis were not common in 60s America and Europe, which was then mostly a Sativa market. Cannabis Sativa by its nature gives a head high effect. Cannabis Indica gives a body down effect. This has to do with the plants' flowering times and cannabinoid contents. Cannabis Sativa and Cannabis Indica can be bred together to produce a hybrid plant that is a 50/50 mix, mostly Sativa or mostly Indica. However, this does not increase potency. Potency is genetically determined—you cannot GENERATE new genes that were NOT THERE in the first place.

G13 is a strain reputed to have been developed by the US Government in the mid-seventies.

Traditional Skunk#1.

New breeding techniques give growers and breeders more control over plant characteristics, but this does not lead to a potency increase. If seed banks could breed plants that were even double the potency of the strains of the 60s, they would be selling them. What we have gained over the years are strains that produce more flowers, and therefore higher yields, but this has nothing to do with the intoxicating properties of the plant.

Fact: Big plants do not equal more potent plants, quite simply because the traits for yield and potency are governed by different genes.

Myth # 2: The Stronger the Cannabis, the Greater the Health Risks

Long-term users experience something called tolerance. If you smoke cannabis every day, your tolerance level will increase within a few days. You will notice that you will need to take slightly more to get the same effect that you experienced when your tolerance level was at its lowest—when you first started using cannabis. This does not mean that you will have to keep increasing the amounts that you take in order to experience an effect. Your tolerance levels will eventually peak and the amount that you need to take in order to experience the effect will remain at this fixed level. Increasing the amounts that you take will no longer

Skunk hybrids are popular. This is Shiva Skunk.

heighten the effects, but merely sustain them for longer. Usually, cessation of use for a week or two is enough to bring your tolerance back down to its initial level. When a user experiences a peak in tolerance this usually means that they are using the drug too much. Through experience you learn to respect your limits for cannabis. Other recreational drugs, like alcohol, can be pushed past your peak tolerance by consuming more. The effect of alcohol consumption increases vigorously with the amount taken and it is possible to exceed tolerance levels to the point at which users can even develop "alcohol poisoning."

A health-related misconception is that "high THC levels mean higher volumes of smoke being held in the lungs for longer, which is equivalent to smoking lots of cigarettes." THC levels, percentages and concentrations do not equate to more smoke. In any given volume of smoke there is a ratio of THC-related compounds to other gases, such as carbon monoxide, that are released during the burning process. One ounce of poor quality cannabis will give off the same volume of smoke as one ounce of high-quality cannabis. Also, many people do not smoke cannabis in joints, but take the healthier, carbon-monoxide-and-tar-free route by using vaporization techniques. Smoke-free vaporization is discussed in detail later in this chapter.

Sensi Star. Photo Paradise Seeds

Myth #3: Hydroponics Makes Cannabis Stronger

Hydroponics is a method of cultivation whereby soil is replaced by a soilless substrate, such as rockwool, Oasis, perlite or vermiculite. The plant is placed in this soilless substrate and fed an aerated nutrient solution. This method allows the plant to receive the optimal levels of water, air and nutrients it needs in order to survive and thrive.

The very nature of hydroponics allows the plant to expend less energy in the pursuit of nutrients, air and water, and to divert more energy towards plant growth. This results in increased plant size, better health and bushiness (plants grown in hydroponics tend to produce more nodes because of the optimum growing conditions involved). This does not result in increased potency.

Why? Because potency is determined at a genetic level. The environment may influence the final expression of the gene but it certainly does not allow the gene to increase potency. Potency cannot increase past the gene's threshold with any known type of growing method, growth hormone or stimulant.

A plant's genotype (what is encoded as the plant's DNA) is expressed in the plant's phenotype (what you can see, smell, taste, etc.) when the plant is growing.

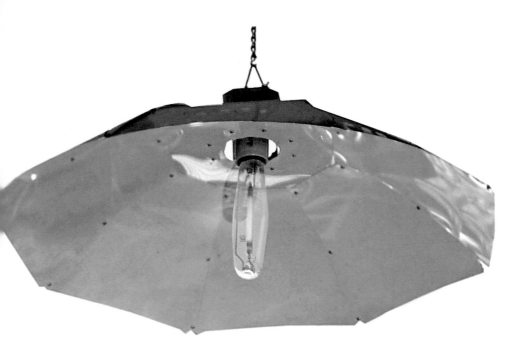

New light technology increases quantity, not potency.

Phenotypes are genetically governed but are also influenced by the environment. Even in optimum growing conditions the plant will never increase past the threshold for potency levels or size contained in its genotype.

It is also worth noting that hydroponic growing does not guarantee that you will automatically increase your overall yields. Many new soil-based methods can achieve the same or better results. The notion that hydroponics somehow increases cannabis potency is flawed.

Myth #4: New Lighting Technology Means Stronger Cannabis

HID lighting has indeed changed the world of indoor growing over the past twenty years. HID lighting like MH (Metal Halide) lights and HPS (High Pressure Sodium) are the choice of professional indoor cannabis growers the world over. However, all these lights do is provide the optimal lighting conditions plants require in order to live up to their full genetic potential. It does NOT improve potency, which, again, is genetically determined.

Also, HID lights may be a good replacement for natural light, but natural light is still the best light you can use for cannabis cultivation. Geographical and environmental conditions prevent growers from having complete access to this light for at least six months of the year. Some Sativa plants require up to six months flowering before they reach their full potential—which, after three months of vegetative growth, adds up to nine months growing time! Lighting is clearly important to achieving optimal growth, but the notion that new lighting technology led to stronger cannabis is flawed.

Myth #5: Feeding Products and Growth Hormones Make Cannabis Stronger

Most feeding products contain primary nutrients, secondary nutrients and micronutrients. None of these nutrients, in any combination, will increase a plant's potency. They are simply elements that the plant needs in order to grow and thrive.

The only way in which a growth hormone can affect cannabis potency is if the hormone causes DNA repair malfunction, which can lead to a mutation of the plant's DNA. However, this type of mutation is not controllable and the chances of it happening and resulting in increased potency are very slim. In addition, the plant may exhibit other side effects that could be negative. So, even if you did succeed in increasing the potency via a growth hormone or a DNA repair mutation, you could end up with a sickly or inferior plant that is hard to grow or reproduce. The notion that feeding products and growth hormones make cannabis stronger is flawed.

Potency is related to genes, not growth hormones or nutrients.

Myth #6: New Extraction Techniques Make Hashish Stronger

This myth may contain an element of truth but it is worth discussing anyway. The reason why hash may seem stronger is because it is not always pure on the black market. In fact, most mass-produced hash contains traces of adulterates like tranquillizers, opium, heroin and even commonly-purchased medicines to help add spice to the product. This is very common with imported cannabis products, but does not mean that cannabis produced in your home country is not adulterated too.

The black-market creates an incentive to produce and sell adulterated cannabis products. Remember that there are absolutely no content restrictions on illegal cannabis and most people have no way of knowing what it is they are taking. Hashish can be cut just like other drugs during production so that the drug manufacturer can sell their product for more money. Cannabis prohibition fuels that!

The only way to create stronger cannabis outside of breeding for potency is to prepare high quality extraction.

New hashish extraction methods, like cold water bubble hash extraction (the best of methods), do not increase potency; they simply reduce the amount of foreign bodies (leaf, stem, dirt) in the hash. The objective of the extraction method is to produce almost pure THC. This does not make the product stronger, or more potent, per se. It makes it more concentrated and pure, so that smaller doses are needed to achieve an effect. At the same time, consuming more of a purer substance does make the effects stronger.

Myth #7: More Crystals Means More THC and Stronger Cannabis

Crystals are simply indicators of trichome development on the flowering

Lots of trichomes does not mean lots of potency. This plant with minimal trichomes could be more potent than strains with lots of trichomes.

Trichomes containing cannabinoids in quantities and levels that relate to potency.
The potency of the trichome is genetically inherited. Photo Paradise Seeds.

pistils and the surrounding leaves and stems of the female cannabis plant. Under close observation, these crystals look like mushroom heads on a long stalk. That is why they are also known as stalked capitate resin glands. The head of the trichome and stalk contain the highly prized cannabinoids.

Trichome growth and potency levels are two very different traits. You could have an extremely frosty plant with low cannabinoid content in the trichomes or you could have a plant with hardly any trichomes that are extremely high in cannabinoid content.

Although high trichome numbers do not mean high potency levels, breeders generally try to stabilize high trichome numbers with high cannabinoid levels for aesthetic and manicuring purposes intended for the final product's presentation. The notion that more crystals mean more THC and therefore stronger cannabis is also flawed.

The Truth About Hyper-Potent Cannabis

Random mating of plants may eventually lead to the emergence of a plant with the right genetics to contribute to a breeding program for hyper-increased potency.

• Most new traits are discovered accidentally, and not always by people with breeding knowledge who can harness the trait and continue it.

• If you did discover this trait, you would have to grow extremely large selections of test offspring to breed such a plant. You would have to test each and every plant to find the trait and stabilize it, so that all of its offspring would produce the same hyper-potent trait. This could take a matter of months or a number of lifetimes to achieve.

• Sometimes the authorities get to it first, bringing your hyper-cannabinoid breeding program to an abrupt halt.

• The strains of the 60s and 70s still have not been beaten for cannabinoid levels because these old strains have been selected by generations of local growers; this is compared to our mere 40 years of cannabis cultivation and breeding agendas.

• It is less common to find poor strains being produced by breeders these days. This means that nearly all commercial cannabis is potent in some way.

• Only a handful of cuttings (clones) in the world exist which have proven to be hyper-potent—Cali O, MTF, Champagne, Chemo and G13, to name a few.

• Clones are not sold by internationally known seed banks, perhaps because clones are difficult to ship around the world.

• Only good (not to mention lucky) breeding techniques or GM (genetically modified) crops can make cannabis genetically stronger, or more potent.

• The only group that claims to have truly hyper-potent cannabis plants is the U.S. government, which conducts experiments into genetically modifying cannabis. They have never released them to the public.

So, What Has Actually Changed?

Maybe now would be a good time to list some actual changes that have taken place over the years.

Original Cheese — named for it's deep pungent odor. Photo Dr. Greenthumb

1. The introduction of Cannabis Indica species has led to the development of hybrid plants that combine the head high effect with the body down effect.

2. Good cannabis breeders have eradicated poorer forms of cannabis from the gene pool in their breeding programs. This includes hermaphrodite plants that can never produce sinsemilla crops. The net effect is that there are less poor cannabis plants on the market so nearly every type of home grown cannabis is good to some degree, as long as it has been grown, flowered, harvested and cured correctly.

3. Sinsemilla crops are flowering female plants that do not bear seeds because the males have been removed before pollination occurs. This does not increase potency. It does however increase yield, because the plants can divert energy from seed production towards flower production.

4. There are many variations of cannabis on the market with different tastes, smells and high types. The Sativas of the 60s and 70s are very strong and are not really suitable for the novice smoker.

5. Imported hashish usually contains adulterates. It is rarely, if ever, just cannabis.

Most strains are bred for higher yields rather than higher potency levels.

The bottom line is that since the cannabis plant first started being used by humans, the gene pool has not undergone any form of a major potency increase. What has changed is our ability to stabilize traits in a plant population and to ensure that traits are continued in the offspring.

How to Avoid Taking Cancer-Causing Agents

Is cannabis a carcinogen? The answer is yes, if you smoke it using a flame directly in contact with the cannabis, which causes a process called combustion. This is because carbon monoxide is released during combustion and carbon monoxide can be deadly to humans.

Whatever way you look at it, regular inhalation of carbon monoxide will eventually destroy your lungs. If there is a history of cancer in your family, then chances are that constant, prolonged inhalation of carbon monoxide will cause cancer to develop in you. The risks are staggering if you think about it. Most people who breathe in a lot of carbon monoxide die from carbon monoxide-related diseases. Of course, pollution from modern society (cars, industry, etc.) has produced much more carbon monoxide than cannabis smokers ever have or will.

Nicotine was also recently discovered to be a carcinogen. It was thought for a long time that it was just the tar and carbon monoxide that were carcinogens, but the more we look at less suspicious substances, the more we find that they are indeed carcinogens as well.

At the moment, it is not known if cannabis is a carcinogen because cannabis is made up of so many different types of materials, including cannabinoids and their thousands of related gases that are released during combustion. The number of compounds we need to analyze to be able to say for sure probably runs in to the ten of thousands.

Before anyone discovers carcinogens in these compounds, we might as well assume that some of them are bad, and are actually the result of the combustion process. It makes good sense to remove the risk of contact with carbon monoxide from the equation. This is easy to do: you can either cook with cannabis or use a process known as vaporization.

Cooking with Cannabis

Non-smokers can enjoy marijuana without the effects of carbon monoxide. The Marijuana Chef Cookbook, by S. T. Oner, is a great cannabis cooking guide for all marijuana lovers. It covers the basics of cooking, cannabis drinks, desserts, vegetarian marijuana meals, main marijuana courses, starters and soups. It contains quite a number of recipes for you to choose from.

Cooking with cannabis is a healthy way to enjoy cannabis. Many cannabis users have found that cannabis foods are just as delightful as smoking a joint or using a vaporizer. If you like cannabis you should give cooking a try.

Save the cows. Go with the green or just have fun.

Hash butter a.k.a cannabutter.

Vaporization

Vaporization is the key to the future of smoking cannabis. The vaporization technique simply uses heat instead of a flame to convert your cannabis matter into a fume rather than smoke that contains carbon monoxide.

Imagine placing a small amount cannabis on a knife and gradually heating the knife over a stove. As the knife heats up, the cannabis begins to heat up as well, but it does not burn or catch fire right away. As the knife heats up, a vapor drifts out from the bud. After a while, the knife will become very hot and the cannabis will catch fire (if there is still some matter left) and give off a plume of gray and blue smoke.

There is a point at which the cannabis is converted into fumes without releasing carbon monoxide. It will only start to release the cancer-causing agent when the temperature of the knife increases to the point at which cannabis reaches its combustion threshold and starts to burn. In other words, you do not need to burn cannabis in order to smoke it. All you need to do is heat the knife to the point at which THC vaporizes. This is what a vaporizer does.

Like a bong, hookah or any glass pipe, the vaporizer holds the vapor or fumes in an enclosure before you inhale. Most vaporizers are electric and require charging before the heating element is ready for the application of cannabis. Since the temperature

You don't need to
burn this to enjoy it.

This is a commercial vaporizer. You can get a very
enjoyable experience from this.

of the heating element never rises above the threshold of THC combustion, you do
not release carbon monoxide. The boiling point of THC is 200°C (392°F). Between
200°C and 300°C will release THC more quickly. Between 300°C and 400°C carbon monoxide may be released along with THC. Between 400°C and 500°C carbon monoxide will be released along with THC. Temperatures of 500°C and above
result in complete combustion with maximum carbon monoxide emissions; everything burns up, leaving very little ash. Vaporizer users stick with 200°C (392°F)
to achieve the desired effect of keeping carbon monoxide levels either at zero or
to natural levels present in air.

Vaporizers can be bought in all sizes, shapes and forms. Pharmaceutical companies
spend hundreds of thousands on industrial vaporizers in order to reduce carbon
monoxide emissions from their factories. Make sure that your vaporizer has an
adjustable temperature function so that you can choose how hot you want the element to get.

Before you buy a vaporizer you may want to check out the low-cost, do-it-your-
self method described below. Remember, though, that you are much better off buying a professional vaporizer to ensure that no carbon monoxide is released.

Cannabis Legalization and Social Issues
Cannabis and Young Adults

Many parents and teachers are opposed to cannabis decriminalization and legalization because of concerns about risks to the health, wellbeing and future of children. This is very understandable.

All parents agree that children should not use drugs. Never promote cannabis among children.

If you have seen the Academy Award-winning film *Traffic*, then you will probably understand that there is also a need for closer parent/child communication with regards to drug education. The concept that cannabis decriminalization or legalization will lead to more (or less) children using cannabis is flawed. But then, the illegality of cannabis doesn't seem to stop them from using it either. Cannabis is a very popular recreational drug.

Ask yourself this basic question: if my child is determined to get hold of cannabis, would he or she be better off procuring it from the black market or from a controlled, regulated manufacturer or retailer where other drugs, such as alcohol, are purchased from?

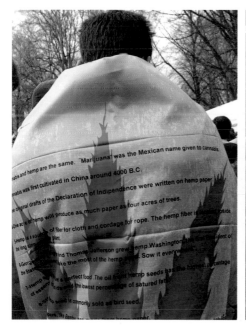

A cannabis activist is the new caped crusader.

A cannabis enthusiast in his native habitat.

Some people suggest that cannabis is only taken for euphoria. However, there are many other reasons why people take cannabis. Some take it for medical use. Others take it to feel more relaxed and not for its euphoric properties. Cannabis is a substance that has many more uses than getting you high.

The Alcohol vs. Cannabis Debate

Even though alcohol is water-soluble and is cleared from the body at the rate of one unit per hour (the amount in half a pint of beer, a single whisky or a glass of wine) it can still kill you. A drop of pure alcohol is enough to send any grown man to the local ER ward; some will even die if the problem is not treated quickly enough. That is why there is a legal limit on how much percentage of alcohol is allowed per bottle. Go above this limit and you can seriously hurt people, if not kill them outright.

Alcohol poisoning is common. Upwards of 5,000 people die from alcohol overdoses every year in the United States alone.

50 percent of THC is still present in the body five days after use, and 10 percent after a month. Traces can be detected in hair and urine for months after that. However, this does not mean that the psychoactive effects of cannabis are still active in the brain. It simply means that the body is disposing of THC in its own way, over time.

Cannabis does not directly kill people. Unlike alcohol, pure, concentrated THC will not kill you unless you have some rare allergy to it. There are more deaths associated directly with alcohol than there are indirectly with cannabis. The only deaths associated with cannabis are either indirect (cancer from smoking) or avoidable (car crashes or other accidents).

Animal testing has shown that extremely high doses of cannabinoids are needed to have a lethal effect on the animals. At this moment, the hypothetical toxicity amount needed to cause death derived from these studies is 1:40,000 for cannabis. That means that you would have to consume 40,000 times as much cannabis as you normally would in order to reach the hypothetical toxicity amount that causes death.

In the annals of medical history no one is ever reported to have died from a cannabis overdose, while hundreds of thousands have died from alcohol overdose or alcohol poisoning. Alcohol abuse will also damage more vital organs in the body than cannabis use. In most cases, cannabis-related damage (mainly lung disease) can be reversed by discontinuing the use of the drug or taking it in another form (unless cancer is contracted, in which chemotherapy is usually the treatment option).[1] With

Cannabis is natural. It is not synthetic.

alcohol, most damage cannot be reversed and damaged organs can only be replaced via a transplant operation (if you can afford one or can afford to wait for one).

Deaths recorded in the United States in any typical year are as follows:[2]

Tobacco deaths	400,000
Alcohol deaths	80,000
Workplace accidents that result in death	60,000
Automobile accidents that result in death	40,000
Cocaine deaths	2,200
Heroin deaths	2,000
Aspirin deaths	2,000
Cannabis deaths	0

The Califano Report from The National Center on Addiction and Substance Abuse (CASA) at Columbia University is also worth noting.

Far more people are hospitalized for alcohol-related illness than cannabis-related illness even though cannabis is the third most commonly used drug in the Western world. Also, there are more types of alcohol-related illness than cannabis-related illness to deal with. The burden on taxpayers to solve alcohol-related illness is significantly higher than cannabis-related abuses, even in countries that have decriminalized or tolerate cannabis use.

Tobacco legalization in light of cannabis criminalization is irrational.

For goodness sake, it's just a plant!

Any type of drug abuse can cause a different personality to emerge. Abusers cannot manage themselves properly and can become stubborn, find it hard to deal with disapproval and feel misinterpreted. This is common to all types of drug abuses and should not be singled out with cannabis alone. Mobile phone addiction, internet addiction, computer game addiction and television addiction can also cause these types of personality disorders to emerge and yet mobile phones, computer games, the internet and television are not illegal. All these things have suspected or proven health risks associated with them, too—that is why there are warnings included with the instructions!

Driving While Under the Influence

Cannabis has been brought into the intoxicating driving debate. The bottom line to any debate is that you should not do drugs and drive, period. Even though some people have suggested that cannabis causes more road accidents than alcohol there does not appear to be any data to support this.

The Federal Bureau of Prisons estimates that they have roughly 170,000 inmates for any given month. Out of these, roughly 84,000 (55 percent) are in on drug-related offenses. These figures indicate more drug-related incarceration per capita

The church. Photo Greenhouse Seed Co.

than any other nation in the world. Since 1965, America has arrested more than ten million people for marijuana-related offences.[3]

In 2002, the annual report on the state of the drug problem in the European Union and Norway concluded that "Use of illegal substances is concentrated among young adults and particularly males in urban areas, although some spreading to smaller towns and rural areas may be taking place."[4]

Recent cannabis use (last 12 months) was reported by 5 to 15 percent of young adults in most countries. Recent amphetamine use was reported by 0.5 to 6 percent, cocaine use by 0.5 to 3.5 percent and ecstasy use by 0.5 to 5 percent.

Lifetime experience of cannabis is reported by 10 to 30 percent of European adults, while amphetamines, cocaine and ecstasy have been tried by about 1 to 5 percent.

Cannabis use increased markedly during the 1990s in most EU countries, particularly among young people, although in recent years its use seems to be leveling off in some countries. Cocaine use may have increased in recent years in some countries, although this trend is less clear.

If you have not read George Orwell's 1984 or Animal Farm, then do.

There is an incentive for individuals who are subjected to drug tests to choose harder drugs as their form of recreational drug because these substances disappear from the system more quickly. This is another indication that drug testing does not help the cannabis problem in any way.

Cannabis remains one of the most confiscated drugs in the world and makes up almost a whopping 80 percent of all illegal confiscations, even though it is considered a less problematic drug than alcohol or harder drugs. If cannabis were legalized tomorrow, drug enforcement agencies would automatically lose 80 percent of their figures, which are used as a basis for government budgeting on drug enforcement programs. On many levels, cannabis prohibition could be more about money than most government officials would care to admit.[5]

Cannabis and Brain Damage

There is no scientific evidence to suggest that THC damages the brain in any way. Animal asphyxiation experiments, using monkeys, were conducted in the 70s and subsequently used to prove that cannabis kills brain cells. Monkeys were gassed to death with cannabis smoke over a long period of time. The monkeys had electrodes implanted in their brains to monitor the effects of the exposure to cannabis smoke. The animals

It has never been demonstrated that cannabis can kill.

died and the brain cells were counted. A healthy monkey was also killed as a control experiment and its brain cells were counted. The U.S. government was brought to court on this issue to reveal the experiment under the "Freedom of Information" act. When the hoax was exposed (along with the unnecessary animal deaths), the U.S. government never used these findings again. The study was harshly condemned for its inadequate sample size of only four monkeys, its complete failure to manage experimental prejudice and the misidentification of the monkeys' brains as "damaged."

Cannabis and the Immune System

Cannabis use may affect the immune system. For some illnesses, it is advised that you discontinue cannabis use until the illness has passed. Consult your doctor for further information. This is because cannabis may cause fewer white blood cells to be produced, which are used in the fight against some diseases. Discontinuing cannabis use will restore the immune system to its previous condition.

Cannabis and Sexual Dysfunction

Sperm production may be decreased with cannabis use; discontinue cannabis use and sperm production should return to normal levels again. There is no scientific evidence to suggest that young men will develop breasts if they use cannabis. This is a red herring associated with a testosterone decrease in some individuals who use cannabis. There is absolutely no evidence to support a case that this decrease is permanent. Cannabis tolerance can also occur, bringing testosterone levels back to normal again, even though cannabis use has not been discontinued. If you want to reproduce, stop using cannabis.

Cannabis and Pregnancy

The bottom line here is the same advice that has always been administered to pregnant women: when pregnant, only take drugs that your doctor recommends. It is your duty to discontinue cannabis use if you are pregnant.

Cannabis and Human DNA Repair Malfunction

There is no scientific evidence to support the claim that cannabis directly causes DNA repair malfunction in human beings. DNA repair malfunction results in a mutation at the cellular reproduction level. A DNA repair malfunction is usually random and can result in anything. There are no specific conclusions to random D.N.A repair malfunction, although scientists can cause certain types of malfunctions to appear using specific techniques. However, these techniques may result in other types of uncontrollable mutations occurring alongside the controllable one. The notion that cannabis can cause a certain type of, or any type of, DNA repair malfunction in human beings is not scientifically proven.

These political and legal problems over an herb do not make sense.

Even medical users find themselves persecuted for reasons
that have never been established scientifically.

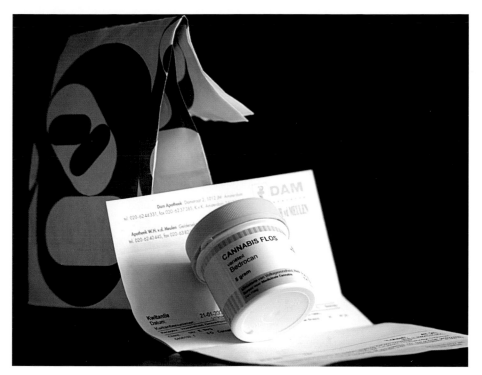

Some sanity has been recovered in places where it is now recognized that cannabis is medicine.

Medicinal Use

In March 1999, the U.S. government-sponsored Institute of Medicine (IOM) Report concluded that:

> Until a nonsmoked rapid-onset cannabinoid drug delivery system becomes available, we acknowledge that there is no clear alternative for people suffering from chronic conditions that might be relieved by smoking marijuana, such as pain or AIDS wasting.

The U.S. DEA ignored this and has said:

> Any determination of a drug's valid medical use must be based on the best available science undertaken by medical professionals. The Institute of Medicine (under the National Academy of Sciences) conducted a comprehensive study in 1999 to assess the potential health benefits of marijuana and its constituent cannabinoids. The study concluded that smoking marijuana is not recommended for the treatment of any disease condition.

Becoming a part of the cannabis community can be rewarding...

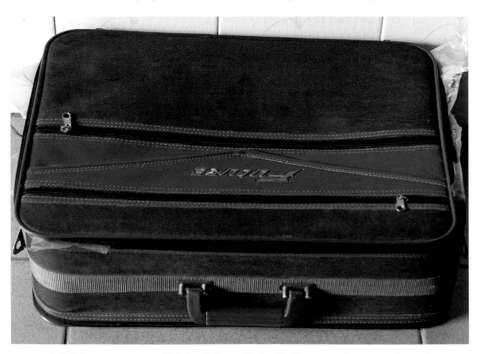

... but if for any reason you feel that it is negatively affecting your life, you can always stop.

Cannabis and Harder Drugs: The Gateway Theory

The suggestion that marijuana use leads to the use of hard drugs is based on the belief that once the person breaks the law they will be susceptible to breaking the law again. Most hard drug users have taken cannabis; however, out of the hundreds of millions of people worldwide who have tried cannabis, we do not find hundreds of millions of hard drug users. In fact, one in 100 cannabis users will likely try a harder drug, but this is not because of cannabis use. How many bicycle riders grow up to become motorcycle drivers?

That said, if a cannabis user cannot get cannabis, then they may take a harder drug that is more readably available from a dealer. This is why drug dealers are also called drug pushers. The cannabis user may be pushed to buy something else because the dealer does not have cannabis available. This is very important, and we find that most cannabis users come in contact with hard drugs as a result of contact with the same source who does not have any cannabis available. Drug dealers can also use this tactic to sell the user stronger and more expensive drugs. This is a major reason why cannabis should be disassociated with other forms of harder drugs. It is a problem that springs from prohibition.

Cannabis and Memory

Cannabis does affect short-term memory until you terminate its use. There is no evidence that cannabis can affect the memory permanently.

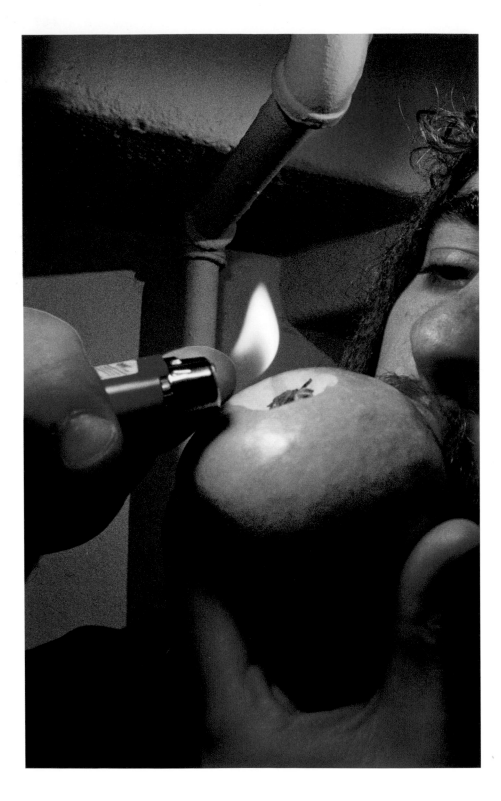

19 | How to Enjoy Your Bud

The following chapter contains instructions for making various tools to ingest cannabis smoke. While this may be a very effective way of ingesting cannabis, please know that there are many other methods that will allow you to experience the high of THC without smoking. However, ingesting cannabinoids via a nice piece of chocolate cake may sound lovely, and usually is, but it is much more difficult to regulate your dosage. Start small and try to remember that practicing moderation is key to an enjoyable experience.

Variations in strain, growing conditions, and how it's been taken will all effect how you experience the high. The people you are with, your environment, and your general mental state will also greatly effect how you feel once you've taken cannabis. Remember to relax and enjoy yourself. "Bad trips" or negative experiences with cannabis are often associated with taking it in an unfamiliar environment with unfamiliar people. The important thing to remember when having a bad trip (also known as the Horrors or the Frights) is that cannabis is a plant, the effects are not permanent, and you will likely survive this attack of the Frights after a little nap. If a nap is not in the cards, the best thing to do is find a safe, quiet spot away from lights, noise, seemingly terrible people, actually terrible people and anything else that may be causing mental disquiet.

Alcohol will also change the nature of your experience with cannabis. When taken to excess, the combination of the two substances can induce nausea and/or temporary loss of consciousness, often referred to as a "Whitey". This is not a state of being to strive towards. In fact, you'd be much safer and happier in a general way if you were to avoid having a Whitey at all. The best way to avoid a Whitey and to have a good time is to, once again, practice moderation. Take care of yourself, take care of your plants and enjoy!

HOW TO ROLL A JOINT

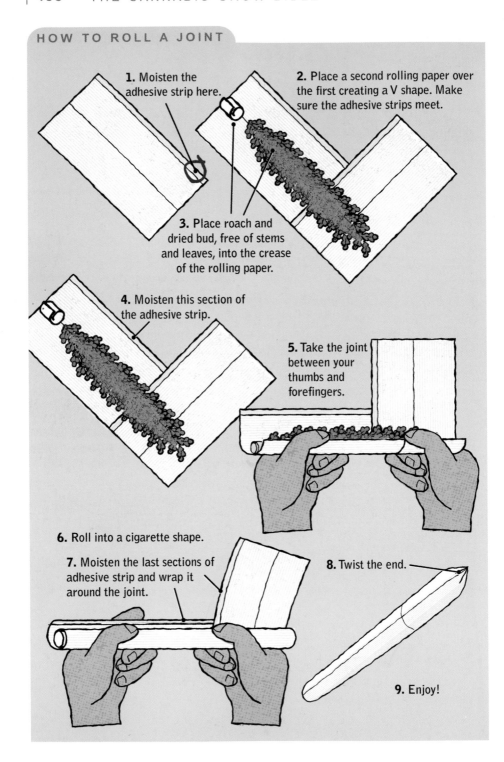

1. Moisten the adhesive strip here.

2. Place a second rolling paper over the first creating a V shape. Make sure the adhesive strips meet.

3. Place roach and dried bud, free of stems and leaves, into the crease of the rolling paper.

4. Moisten this section of the adhesive strip.

5. Take the joint between your thumbs and forefingers.

6. Roll into a cigarette shape.

7. Moisten the last sections of adhesive strip and wrap it around the joint.

8. Twist the end.

9. Enjoy!

HOW TO MAKE AN APPLE PIPE

What you need:
- Ballpoint pen
- Knife
- Apple
- Bud

1. Remove stem and cut a bowl shaped impression into the apple. The bottom of the bowl should reach the top of the apple's core.

2. Pierce the apple to the core with a ballpoint pen. Turn the apple 1/4 way and pierce it again, making sure you reach the core.

3. Place dried bud in your new apple pipe

Carb – use your finger or thumb to regulate

Put your mouth here to inhale

HOW TO MAKE A TINFOIL PIPE

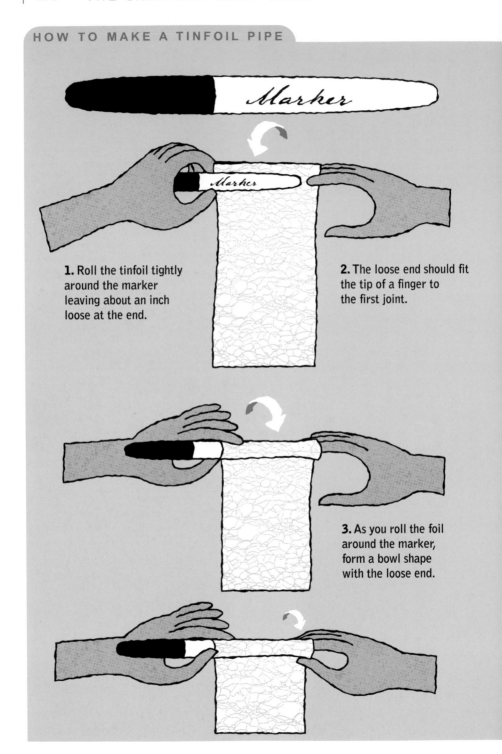

1. Roll the tinfoil tightly around the marker leaving about an inch loose at the end.

2. The loose end should fit the tip of a finger to the first joint.

3. As you roll the foil around the marker, form a bowl shape with the loose end.

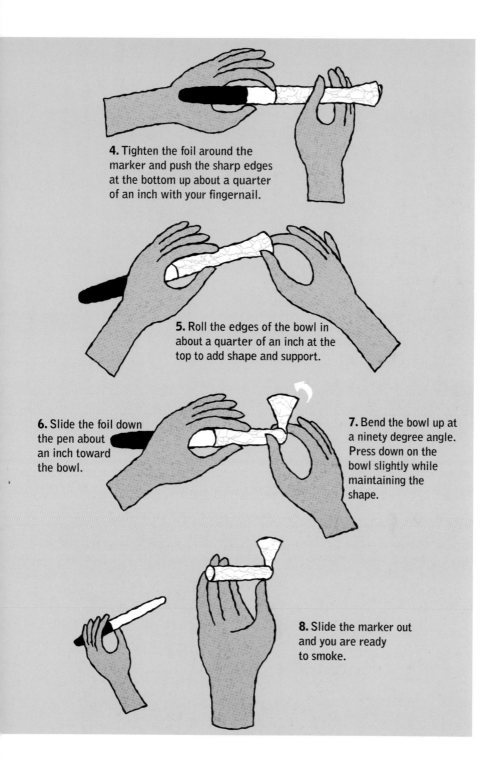

4. Tighten the foil around the marker and push the sharp edges at the bottom up about a quarter of an inch with your fingernail.

5. Roll the edges of the bowl in about a quarter of an inch at the top to add shape and support.

6. Slide the foil down the pen about an inch toward the bowl.

7. Bend the bowl up at a ninety degree angle. Press down on the bowl slightly while maintaining the shape.

8. Slide the marker out and you are ready to smoke.

HOW TO MAKE A BUCKET BONG

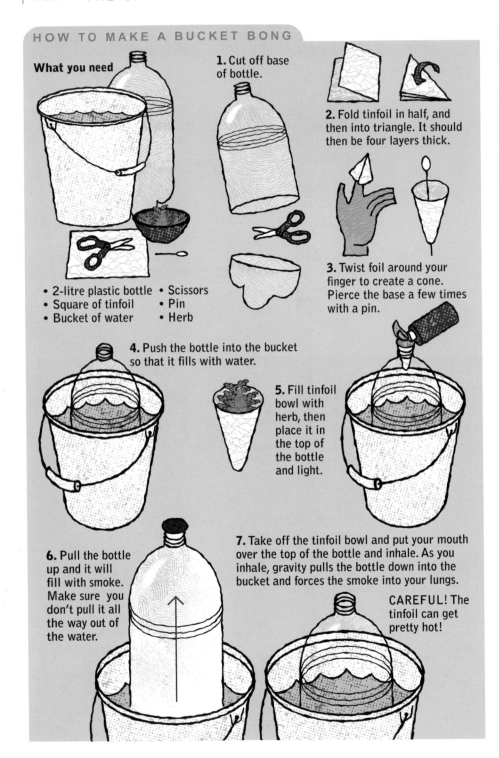

What you need

1. Cut off base of bottle.

2. Fold tinfoil in half, and then into triangle. It should then be four layers thick.

3. Twist foil around your finger to create a cone. Pierce the base a few times with a pin.

- 2-litre plastic bottle
- Square of tinfoil
- Bucket of water
- Scissors
- Pin
- Herb

4. Push the bottle into the bucket so that it fills with water.

5. Fill tinfoil bowl with herb, then place it in the top of the bottle and light.

6. Pull the bottle up and it will fill with smoke. Make sure you don't pull it all the way out of the water.

7. Take off the tinfoil bowl and put your mouth over the top of the bottle and inhale. As you inhale, gravity pulls the bottle down into the bucket and forces the smoke into your lungs.

CAREFUL! The tinfoil can get pretty hot!

HOW TO MAKE A LIGHT BULB VAPORIZER

ITEMS NEEDED: A screw-type domestic light bulb, plastic screw-type bottle top, two straws or a 10cm and 3cm glass tube, a multi-purpose pocket knife and water.

1. Use the knife to cut the base of the bulb at the last screw-threading groove. The knife should sink in easily because the metal is very light.

2. After cutting, the base should come off easily.

3. If you look into the bulb you will notice some glass in the way of the element.

4. Push down on this area very gently with the knife, turning the knife as you do so.

5. With very little pressure, the glass inside will crack and the element will become dislodged. The knife will pass all the way through.

6. Empty the bulb. There will be broken glass, so be careful. Tip the bulb back and forth until a wire protrudes. Pull this wire to get the element out.

7. Using the knife, churn out any remaining glass still present on the rim of the opening.

8. Look inside and make sure that all the glass has been tipped out. Rince the bulb out with water to remove all of the remaining dust. Let dry.

9. Make two holes in the top of the plastic bottle cap.

10. Insert your straws or glass tubes into the holes in the bottle cap.

11. Place some bud in the bulb before sealing. Screw the bottle cap to the bulb. The cap should easily screw onto the bulb's grooves.

12. If you used straws, cut thm down to match the example here. The smaller straw is an air-flow straw. It allows air to enter the bulb as you inhale cannabis fumes through the longer straw.

20 | *The Cannabis Grow Bible* Checklist

Through practical application of the information contained in this book, the journey from novice grower to guru is attainable. This final chapter is designed to serve as a checklist summarizing the most important factors in achieving superior cannabis growth results. These factors are listed and discussed briefly below:

- Good Genetics
- Proper Lighting
- An Ounce of Prevention
- Air Circulation and Ventilation
- The Right Medium
- Optimal Pot/Container Size

- Safe Fertilizers
- 12/12
- Avoiding Plant Stress
- Carbon Dioxide (CO_2)
- Labeling

✓ Good Genetics

It goes without saying that a plant with genetic traits for low bud production and potency will not produce an outstanding crop. If you start with bad genetics you'll only end up with poor results, no matter what you do or how skilled a grower you may be. To obtain good genetics, you should get your seeds from a seed bank that advertises strains from reputable breeders. A number of quality breeders enter competitions, such as the Cannabis Cup in Amsterdam. You should pay a visit to Amsterdam and sample what the breeders have to offer in the coffee shops. The coffee shop owners may tell you where you can purchase seeds from bud that you enjoy smoking. Most of the cannabis pictures in this book are of well-known strains that breeders have produced and can be bought through seed banks.

Selecting good clone mothers is also important. By selecting a good mother plant you can create a population of clone mothers that increases your overall yield. Obtaining good genetics is crucial for good growing results.

✓ Proper Lighting

Light is a very important factor in plant growth and bud production. If you aren't getting the bud sizes that this book highlights, you should consider upgrading your lighting system.

Although results can be achieved using a 250-watt HID or fluorescent tubes, a 400-watt HID is better. A 600-watt HID will produce a much better crop than a 400-watt HID, and a 1,000-watt HID is the absolute best light available on the market. Of course, not everyone wants to grow large amounts of bud and a 1,000-watt HID can be expensive to run. Nonetheless, a 1000-watt HID light will improve your results.

Conserving light is also important. Use reflectors, white walls, and Mylar to keep the spread of light even and contained in your grow room. Any light leaks mean that usable light is being lost and you are paying for it, so try and use as much of it as possible. Your plants will love you for it.

Try to keep lights as close to the plants as possible without burning them. Keeping the distance from bulb to plant at a minimum is very important. Proximity increases overall yield and reduces internode length development. Keep those internode lengths down and you will get much better results.

✓ An Ounce of Prevention

Prevention is better than cure. Any problem will stunt plant growth to some degree. Anticipating and preventing the problem before it happens entails knowing what problems to expect and being adequately prepared through advance planning. This book has explained some of the problems common to cannabis. Healthy plants are rewarding plants, so take good care of your plants' health and you will reap the rewards for doing so.

Check on your plants regularly. Spend time checking them for fungi and pests. This is what cannabis gardening is all about and can quickly turn into a routine that you enjoy as you watch your plants grow strong and healthy.

✓ Air Circulation and Ventilation

Air circulation is very important. Outdoor plants don't have this problem, but the growth of indoor plants can sometimes be stunted or slowed if they don't receive enough fresh air. Fresh air is important to replace any impurities that build up in your grow room. The percentage of different compounds that make up air can change or fluctuate if new air isn't introduced into the grow room and can cause problems with your grow. Heat can also build up in spaces that don't have good air ventilation, and a rise in temperature can cause stunted plant growth. Try to keep fresh air moving around your grow room at all times for the best results.

Air circulation brings a mild wind to your grow and this is very important for stem and branch growth. By stressing it slightly, the wind will cause the plant to react with thicker stem and branch growth. This is important for bud production, and the plant will be thicker, stronger and healthier overall. I've witnessed growers use fans in their grow rooms that can triple the width of a stem. On more than one occasion I've seen indoor stems that are two inches thick on a plant that is only four feet tall. These plants tended to produce the most bud in the same strain population, too. The reason for this was because they were located very near to the main fan and placed directly under the light. In other words, those growing conditions were optimal for that plant.

Dust is also a problem for indoor growers. In a grow room, you need to use ventilation to keep dust from settling on your sticky bud. Those tiny pistils are producing the resin that you want. A big blob of dust on a pistil will stunt its growth and reduce the overall effect the bud has when sampled.

✓ The Right Medium

Soil is the most popular choice of medium. If the soil isn't suitable for growing cannabis, no matter how skilled a grower you are, your plants will not reach their optimum potential. You may have to experiment with soils before you find one that suits your cannabis plants. Never underestimate the importance of soil. Make sure the pH is right and the nutrients that your plant requires are present in the soil. Soils should hold a bit of water, but should also drain well—you don't want muddy or fast-draining soils. Aim for the middle ground and choose a soil that does both well.

Hydroponics is an important development in plant horticulture but requires more maintenance than soil growing. Growing in hydroponic systems can improve yields and speed up the growing time considerably. If you have the time and money give hydroponics a shot. It can be a wonderful way to improve your yields.

✓ Optimal Pot/Container Size

A four-inch-square pot may be suitable for clones or SOG-type growing situations; however, anything less than this can stunt growth because the plant roots will not be able to develop fully. "Pot bound" or "root bound" plants can experience nutrient deficiencies as well. For these reasons most growers prefer to use three-gallon buckets, which are also commonly called three-gallon nursery pots. Three-gallon pots tend to permit enough root growth to allow the plant to flourish. To achieve even more effective results you should try using five-gallon nursery pots. Five-gallon nursery pots will help to produce very sturdy and strong plants with thick stems and plentiful node development. The problem with five-gallon pots is that they take up quite a bit of space, so less plants will fit into the grow room.

I once saw a plant in a five-gallon pot that was left in the vegetative growth stage for an additional three weeks after calyx development to encourage increased branch and node development. When flowered, the plant became a monster bud manufacturer and produced a much larger yield than any other plant in that particular crop. If you have the right genetics and the time to veg your plants a little longer, a five-gallon pot can make all the difference in the final yield.

Cannabis also tends to do most of its rooting during the vegetative stage of growth. As soon as flowering begins, root development slows down considerably. Try to allow for good root development in the initial stages of growth by giving the roots plenty of room to grow. It is possible to produce colossal, two-pound yielding plants in five-gallon pots with the right genetics, light and grow time.

For hydroponic set-ups you can buy net pots that usually range from between two and eight inches square. The most common net pot is the five- or six-inch type. This size net pot is suitable for simple hydroponics systems like "The Bubbler." For large Sativa plants, an eight-inch net pot is more suitable. Make sure that if you plan to grow a plant to yield more than one ounce, you should choose at least the five-inch type net pot to ensure adequate support for the stem and root mass.

✓ Safe Fertilizers

If you provide the food that your plants require they will provide you with good results. Cannabis plants like food but not too much food. You should also note that some fertilizers could change the taste of your bud. Many people claim that this is a myth, but if you smoke enough varieties from different grow techniques, you'll be able to taste the difference between natural outdoor bud and indoor bud that has been chemically treated. Some people have complained about headaches from smoking indoor cannabis that has been burnt through overfeeding. There are many potential reasons for this, but the main reason is that instead of using a feeding solution for food plants, the grower used one for plant appearance, like the kind used for roses. Some of these non-food plant fertilizers contain ingredients beyond the standard primary, secondary, and micronutrients. These extra ingredients can often be toxic and a warning label on the side of the fertilizer container should indicate this. The same goes for pest sprays—another good reason to grow your own bud.

However, if you have read this book then you will know to stick to food fertilizers and sprays that can be used on food plants. If you get your feeding mixtures right you'll boost the overall performance of your plants and keep them healthier too.

Hormones can also increase the overall yield and vigor of your plants, but they can be expensive. In some countries hormones are banned because of the risk that they might interfere with a plant's genetics as well as yours. Research hormones thoroughly before using them, but note also that many growers have used reputable, brand-name hormones and achieved larger bud quantities.

Keep notes of feeding times and amounts to help you gauge your feeding routines. It is sometimes easy to forget when you last fed your plants and what mixtures you used. Keep these notes safely hidden from prying eyes.

✓ 12/12

If you use 12/12 and keep your flowering room completely lightproof, you will improve your overall yield. A 100 percent lightproof room will increase yields by as much as 30 percent more than a room that is only 99 percent lightproof; that is how important total darkness is to your plants during the flowering stage of the life cycle.

✓ Avoiding Plant Stress

Multiple transplants should be avoided in order to minimize plant stress. By solving problems quickly and taking good care of your plants you will achieve much more effective results. Stress-related disorders are often responsible for lowering yields.

This book has covered many aspects of plant stress that can be avoided by simply implementing the good growing practices covered within these very chapters.

✓ Carbon Dioxide (CO$_2$)

CO$_2$ supplements boost yields and should be employed if you have the resources. My experience has shown that CO$_2$ can naturally enhance yields to almost double that of a similar grow that does not include a CO$_2$ supplement.

Although you can produce great results without using CO$_2$, it does make all the difference. Growers who use CO$_2$ rarely ever turn away from it. It is a wonderful way of achieving very high yields with the right genetics.

✓ Labeling

Never underestimate labeling. Label everything you can. This includes labeling seeds, seedlings, vegetative plants, flowering plants, clones, your harvest, your manicured bud and your stored end products.

Labeling prevents mix-ups from occurring. If you mix up your plants, you are left with the problem of trying to guess correct flowering times and strain type. Labels can be bought in most good grow stores. Plastic labels should be used in conjunction with a non-permanent pen so that they can be reused.

My experience as a grower has taught me that the cannabis plant is so diverse that no one country, seed bank, or breeder can claim to have all the best genetics. In fact, the majority of high-quality genetics are available to *any* grower through the right seed bank. Not all seed banks send their seeds everywhere in the world, but you will be able to find a few that do. There is nothing preventing good growers from obtaining what they need by checking a few things out.

If you understand and control the above points, then you will achieve the goal of growing superior bud. We hope that this book has helped in some way and that you will continue to refer to it in the future.

If you know people that have an interest in cannabis then tell them about this book. This is the kind of information that they need to make their own high quality bud. The results are cheaper and better, as you will see!

Remember: Do not break the law. Before you get seeds or clones, or grow cannabis, check your country's laws to ensure that your actions are not illegal. We would like you to grow cannabis but we do not want you to get into legal trouble.

Have fun and thanks for reading this book.

Greg Green

++ | Resources

CANNABIS WEBSITES

cannabis.com — General Cannabis Information Website
cannabisculture.com — Cannabis Culture News and Forums
cannabishealth.com — Cannabis Health Website
canamo.net — Spanish Cannabis Magazine
drugwarfacts.org — Information on the Drug War
erowid.org — Drug Information Website
fsbookco.com — Online Bookstore
grow.de — German Cannabis Magazine
growadvice.com — Cannabis Growing Website
highlife.nl — Dutch Cannabis Magazine
hightimes.com — High Times Magazine
marijuananews.com — Marijuana News and Legal Information
norml.org — National Organization for the Reform of Marijuana Laws
safeaccessnow.org — Americans For Safe Access
skunkmagazine.com — Skunk Magazine
tokeup.com — Online Cannabis Community
weedworld.co.uk — British Cannabis Magazine
yahooka.com — General Cannabis Information Website
420magazine.com/forums — Cannabis Growing Website

FURTHER READING

The Cannabible 3 by Jason King, Ten Speed Press, October 2006
The Cannabis Breeder's Bible by Greg Green, Green Candy Press, April 2005
Dank by Subcool, Quick American Archives, October 2008

Hashish by Robert Connell Clarke, Red Eye Press, 1998

Hemp Diseases and Pests by J. M. McPartland, R. C. Clarke, D. P. Watson, Cabi Publishing, September 2000

Marijuana Cooking by Bliss Cameron and Veronica Green, Green Candy Press, March 2005

Marijuana Gold: Trash to Stash by Ed Rosenthal, Quick American Archives, December 2002

Marijuana Home Grower's Manual by Billy McCann, Green Candy Press, March 2009

Marijuana Horticulture by Jorge Cervantes, Van Patten Publishing, February 2006

Marijuana New School Outdoor Cultivation by Jeff Mowta, Green Candy Press, December 2006

HASH AND PROCESSING

bubblebag.com — Bubble Bags

greenharvest.ca — North American Seller of Pollinator

mixnball.com — Designer Herb Grinders

pollinator.nl — The Original Pollinator

HYDROPONICS AND LIGHTING

4hydro.com — Sunburst Hydroponics, USA

bchydroponics.com — BC Canada

dicounthydro.com — Online Hydroponics, USA

hydrofarm.com/wheretobuy.php — Store Locator for Hydrofarm Products

hydrogarden.com — European Hydroponic Supplies

hydromall.com — Worldwide Store Search

hydroponics.com — North American Hydroponic Supplies

somhydro.co.uk — Summerset Hydroponics, UK

MEDICAL CANNABIS INFORMATION

Now that you are able to grow your own medicine why not join up with the International Association for Cannabis as Medicine (IACM). They can be contacted at the following address below.

Arnimstrasse 1A

50825 Cologne

Germany

Phone: +49-221-9543-9229

Email: mailto:info@cannabis-med.org info@cannabis-med.org

Website: cannabis-med.org

The members of the Board of Directors are composed of eight medical doctors. Ask them to send you information on medical cannabis and they will invite you to become a member of IACM. This is an excellent resource for updates on medical cannabis information, which includes a publication called the Journal of Cannabis Therapeutics.

SEEDBANKS

bigbuddhaseeds.com — Big Buddha Seeds (Breeders)
delta9labs.com — Delta-9 Labs (Breeders)
dnagenetics.com — DNA Genetics (Breeders)
drgreenthumb.com — Dr. Greenthumb (Breeders)
dutch-passion.nl — Dutch Passion Seeds (Breeders)
flyingdutchmen.com — The Flying Dutchman Seeds (Breeders)
greatcanadianseeds.com — The Great Canadian Seed Company
greenhouseseeds.nl — Green House Seed Co. (Breeders)
hemodepot.ca — Hemp Depot Canada
high-land.co.uk — The Highland Company
highestdseeds.com — Sagarmatha Seeds (Breeders)
kcbrains.com — KC Brains (Breeders)
legendseeds.com — Legends Canada
lowryder.co.uk — The Joint Doctor's Lowryder
paradise-seeds.com — Paradise Seeds (Breeders)
seedboutique.com — Gypsy Nirvana's Seed Boutique
sensiseeds.com — Sensi Seeds (Breeders)
seriousseeds.com — Serious Seeds (Breeders)
vancouverseed.com — Vancouver Island Seed Company (Breeders)
vancouverseedbank.ca — Vancouver Seed Bank

VAPORIZERS

americansmokeless.com — Portable Vaporizer
inavap.com — INAVAP Vaporizers
vaporizergiant.com — Vaporizer Giant
vaportechco.com — Vapor Tech Vaporizer

++ | Glossary of Terms

A

acidity: The state, quality or degree of being acid, indicated by a pH value below 7.

aerate: To loosen or puncture the soil in order to increase water penetration.

aeration: A term used in horticulture to mean exposure to air, in particular to the gas oxygen.

Afghani strain: A short, highly resinous strain of Indica from Afghanistan.

agriculture: The process of raising a crop that includes growing, sustaining and breeding. In short, farming plants.

air layering: A specialized method of cloning a plant; growing new roots from a branch while the branch remains connected to the parent plant.

alkalinity: The alkali concentration or alkaline quality of an alkali-containing substance; having a pH value above 7.

allozyme: Different types of enzymes influenced by a single gene on a single locus.

anaerobic: Respiration that occurs without oxygen.

androecious: Plants that have only male flowers.

autoflowering: Plants that flower, not in response to changes in the photoperiod, but due to internal influences, usually related to age / maturity.

B

bacteria: Microscopic single-celled organisms that undergo chemical reactions such as fermentation; can also mean diseases.

bactericide: A chemical compound that kills or inhibits bacteria.

ballast: A transformer used mainly with HID lighting equipment.

biodegradable: Undergo natural decay usually aided be microorganisms.

biodynamic: A field in biology that deals with energy systems in living things.

blight: Any of a number of plant diseases resulting in the sudden, conspicuous wilting and dying of affected parts, especially young, growing tissues.

Blotch/blotching: Any of several plant diseases caused by fungi and resulting in brown or black dead areas on leaves or fruit.

bract: A small leaf or scale-like structure

associated with and surrounded by an inflorescence or cone.

C

calyx: Outer whorl of flowering parts; collective term for all the sepals of a flower.

cannabinoids: The psychoactive compound
found in cannabis.

cellular necrosis: The death or collapse of
cells in living things.

cerebral: Part of the brain.

chillum: A small fat pipe made of clay.

chlorophyll: The green pigment in leaves.
When present and healthy, it usually domi-
nates all other pigments. Also important in
the conversion of $CO2$ and $H2O$ into glucose,
which plants feed on.

chlorosis: The yellowing of normally green
plant tissues due to the destruction of the
chlorophyll or the partial failure of the
chlorophyll to develop.

clone: To reproduce or propagate asexually;
rooted cuttings, normally considered female
in the context of this book.

CO₂: The chemical formula for carbon dioxide.

cola: Refers to the main branch of cannabis
flowers located at the top of the stem.

compost: An organic soil amendment resulting from the decomposition of organic matter.

corolla: Inner whorl of floral parts; collective
name for petals.

cotyledon: Leaf of the embryo of a seed
plant, which upon germination either remains
in the seed or emerges, enlarges, and becomes
green.

crop rotation: To grow a different type of
crop in the same area after harvesting the old
one.

D

decomposition: The process of decaying.

dioecious: Male and female organs appear on
separate individuals in the population.

dissemination: To spread around, as in scat-
tering.

E

evolution: The gradual changes in an organism from generation to generation.

F

fan leaves: The largest leaves of the cannabis
plant; they gather the most available light.

fertilizer: A plant food, which, when complete, should contain all three of the primary
elements: NPK.

flowering stage: The peak period of development of a plant, when the cannabis plant displays its sex and produces flowers and bud.

foliage: A cluster of leaves.

fossil fuel: A fuel derived from natural
resources.

fungicide: A compound toxic to fungi.

G

genotype: The genetic constitution of an individual, especially as distinguished from the
phenotype; the whole of the genes in an individual or group.

gene pool: The amount and types of genes
present in any one species.

germination: The process of the sprouting of
a seed.

glands: Refers to resin-producing part of the
cannabis plant.

global warming: A rise in the global mean
surface temperature.

growth stimulators: Hormones used to promote growth in living organisms.

gynoecious: Plants that only bare female flowers.

H

hash/hashish: Compressed cannabis resin.

hash oil: Refers to cannabis resin when it is in a liquid state.

hemp: The stalk and stems produced from the cannabis plant, often used to make fabrics.

hermaphrodite: A plant producing both the male and female flowers.

heterogeneous: Showing variations in structure and parts.

HID: High intensity discharge.

hormonal regulators: Enzymes that regulate biochemical operations.

HPS: High pressure sodium.

humus: The brown or black organic part of soil resulting from the partial decay of leaves and other matter.

hybrid: The offspring of two plants of different species or varieties of species.

hydroponics: The science of growing plants in mineral solutions or liquid, instead of in soil.

I

IBL: Abbreviation for inbred line. An inbred line is a nearly homozygous line produced by continued inbreeding, usually through self-fertilization.

Indica: A species of cannabis plant.

infectious disease: A disease that is caused by a pathogen which can spread from a diseased to a healthy plant.

inflorescence: The flower cluster of a plant.

internode: The distance between branches along the stem of a plant.

interplanting: To grow in between rows.

L

landrace: An ancient or primitive cultivated variety of a crop plant.

leachate: The products of leaching through a substrate.

loam: A rich soil composed of clay, sand and organic matter.

lumen: A scientific measurement for luminosity from a light source.

M

manure: Animal excrement used as a fertilizer.

marijuana: Another term for cannabis.

MH: Metal halide.

macronutrients: Elements, such as carbon, hydrogen, oxygen, or nitrogen, required in large proportion for the normal growth and development of a plant.

microbes: Microscopic organisms.

micronutrients: Mineral elements that are needed by some plants in very small quantities.

microorganisms: Microscopic organisms.

mildew: A powdery growth on the plant's surface.

monoecious: Hermaphrodite; having both sexes on the same individual plant.

mother plant: A plant kept by the grower for its vigor or likable characteristics, to be used for cloning and breeding.

mulch: A substrate covering made from organic material like wood or straw,

mutation: A change in genetic material brought about by an abnormal influence such as radiation.

N

necrotic: From necrosis, meaning death of cells or tissues through injury or disease, especially in a localized area of the body.

node: Position on a stem from which one or more structures (especially branches) grow.

NPK: Abbreviation for nitrogen (N), phosphate (P), and potassium (K), the three primary nutrients for plants.

O

organic: This refers to a method of gardening using only materials derived from living things and not from synthetic material.

osmosis: The process by which a solvent passes through a semi-permeable membrane into a region of greater solute concentration, so as to make the concentrations on the two sides almost equal.

P

parasite: An organism living on or in another living organism (host) and obtaining its food from the latter.

pathogen: An entity that can incite disease.

perlite: A form of obsidian consisting of vitreous globules expandable by heating and used for insulation and as a plant-growing medium.

pH: A measure of the acidity or alkalinity of a solution, numerically equal to 7 for neutral solutions, increasing with greater alkalinity and decreasing with greater acidity. The pH scale commonly in use ranges from 0 to 14.

phenotype: The observable physical or biochemical characteristics of an organism, as determined by both genetic makeup and environmental influences.

phloem: The food-conducting tissue of vascular plants.

photoperiod: The duration of an organism's daily exposure to light, considered especially with regard to the effect of the exposure on growth and development.

photosynthesis: The chemical process in plants in which carbon dioxide and water are converted into glucose by the influence of light energy.

phototropism: The inclination, which plants have, to grow towards light.

pistil: The ovule-bearing organ of a flower.

plumule: In the embryo this is the main bud of the ascending axis of a plant.

pollen: The male gametes or microspores of a seed plant, produced as a fine granular or powdery substance in the anthers of a flower or the male cone of a gymnosperm and usually transported by wind or insects.

pollinate: To convey pollen to, or deposit pollen on, a stigma, ovule, flower, or plant and so allow fertilization.

polytypic: Having several types or variations.

pot bound: See root bound.

potency: The strength of the cannabis drug, usually measured by the THC levels in a plant.

propagation: To get a plant started for the main grow room; may also imply the total cultivations of a plant from seed to harvest, including breeding).

protein: Macromolecules made from amino acids.

pruning: The cutting and trimming of plants to remove dead or injured material, or to control and direct new growth.

R

red wigglers: Worms used in worm composting.

resin: The collection of cannabinoid secretions from trichomes.

rH: Abbreviation for relative humidity; rH is expressed in a percentage and measured with a hygrometer.

root ball: The network of roots along with the attached soil of any given plant.

root bound: A condition that exists when a potted plant has outgrown its container.

roots: The colorless underground part of a vascular plant, which serves to anchor it and convey nourishment.

rot: Rot is the disintegration, discoloration, and decomposition of plant tissue.

Ruderalis: A species of Cannabis that reputedly autoflowers.

rust/rusting: Rust is a plant disease that gives a rusty appearance to the infected surface of the plant.

S

Sativa: A species of cannabis plant.

seed bank: An organization that stores and distributes seed developed by breeders.

sepal: Can mean a leaf or segment of the calyx.

sinsemilla: Refers to non-pollinated female cannabis plants.

skuff: Sifted resin from the cannabis plant.

Skunk: An old strain of cannabis that has a strong smell and sour taste.

stigma: The receptive part of the pistil.

strain: A line of Cannabis pants developed by a breeder.

subdioecious: When monoecious plants sometimes produce dioecious species.

substrate: A surface upon which an organism grows or is attached.

synthetic: Manmade; not produced naturally.

T

tetrahydrocannabinol (THC): The psychoactive cannabinoid in marijuana that is responsible for the high or drug effect.

THC: See Tetrahydrocannabinol

thinning: In gardening, the act of removing some plants to allow sufficient room for the remaining plants to grow.

tilling: To plow soil in preparation for crop cultivation.

toxins: Poisons produced by organisms.

transplanting: The process of moving one plant from its medium to another medium or location.

trichomes: A hairlike or bristlelike outgrowth from the external surface of a plant.

trimonecious: Occurs when male, female and hermaphrodite structures appear on the same plant.

V

vascular: Term applied to a plant tissue or region consisting of conductive tissue.

vegetative growth stage: The stage in the life cycle of the marijuana plant that occurs before flowering and after the seedling stage.

vermiculite: A moisture-holding medium for plant growth or a protective covering for bulbs made from hydrated silicates.

W

whorl: Group of three or more structures of the same kind (generally leaves or flower parts) at the same node.

wilt: Any of various plant diseases characterized by slow or rapid collapse of terminal shoots, branches or entire plants.

Z

Zero Zero: An extremely pure and potent grade of hashish.

++ | Endnotes

Preface
1 Cherry, Paul (2006). "RCMP Make Cyberbust." The Gazette.

Chapter 1
1 The branch of paleontology dealing with fossil plants.
2 Fleming, M. P. and R. C. Clarke (1998). "Physical Evidence for the Antiquity of Cannabis Sativa L." *Journal of The International Hemp Association 5*, 280-293.
3 Pringle, H. (1997) "Ice Age Communities may be Earliest Known Net Hunters." *Science 277*; 5330: 1203–1204.
4 Vavilov, N. I. (1992) "Origin and Geography of Cultivated Plants." Cambridge University Press: Cambridge.
5 Garg, A. (1996) "Palynocontents of Bee-Collected Pollen Loads of Autumn Season in Bhimal, India." *Taiwania 41 (3)*: 197–207.
6 Li, H. L. (1974) "An Archaeological and Historical Account of Cannabis in China." *Econ. Botany 28 (4)*: 437–448.
7 Li, H. L. (1973) "The Origin and Use of Cannabis in Asia: Linguistic and Cultural Implications." *Econ. Botany 28 (3)*: 293–301.
8 Dörfler, W. (1990) "Die geschichte des hanfanbaus in Mitteleuropa aufgrund palynologisch-er untersuchungen und von Großrestnach-weisen." Praehistorische Zeitschrift. 65:218–244.
9 Miotik-Szpiganowicz, G. (1992) "The History of the Vegetation of Bory Tucholskie and the Role of Man in the Light of Palynological Investigations." *Acta Palaeobotanica 32(1)*: 39–122.
10 Ralska-Jasiewiczowa, M. and B. van Geel. (1992) "Early Human Disturbance of the Natural Environment Recorded in Annually Laminated Sediments of Lake Gosciaz, Central Poland." Veget. Hist. Archeobot. *1*: 33–42.
11 Godwin, H. (1967) "Pollen-Analytic Evidence for the Cultivation of Cannabis in

England." Rev. Palaeobot. Palynol. 4: 71–80.

12 Harlan, J. R., (1971) "Agricultural Origins: Centers and Noncenters." *Science, 174,* 468–474.

13 A Glossary of Plant Genetic Resources Terms, IBPGR Secretariat, Rome, 1980.

14 Pistorius, R. (1997) "Scientists, Plants and Politics: A History of the Plant Genetic Resources Movement." International Plant Genetic Resources Institute, Rome.

15 There are exceptions where chemicals compounds, such as growth hormones, are used to manipulate these qualities.

16 Small, E., and A. Cronquist. (1976) "A Practical and Natural Taxonomy for Cannabis." *Taxon 25:* 405–435.

17 Small, E. (1975) "On Toadstool Soup and Legal Species of Marihuana." Plant Science Bulletin. Botanical Society of America. 21: 34–39.

18 "Cannabaceae." (2006) Encyclopædia Britannica.

19 "Species." The American Heritage Stedman's Medical Dictionary.

20 Linnaeus' Species Plantarum 1753 (May 1)

21 Please note that speciation and cannabis is disputed by botanists and the breeding community, although all sides do contribute important points of view for our consideration. Since the term "species" is itself disputed, this criteria may be subject to change or challenge, especially with more immediate genetic research of the cannabis genome.

22 Breistroffer (1948) and Stafieu (1967).

23 Yearbook of the United States Department of Agriculture—1913: Hemp. Lyster H. Dewey, Botanist in Charge of Fiber Plant Investigations, Bureau of Plant Industry.

24 Schultes, R. E., et. al. (1974) "Cannabis: An Example of Taxonomic Neglect." *Harvard University Botanical Museum Leaflets 23:* 337–367.

25 Hillig, K.W. (2005) "Genetic Evidence for Speciation in Cannabis (Cannabaceae)," *Genetic Resources and Crop Evolution 52:* 161–180.

26 Hillig, K.W. (2005) "A Systematic Investigation of Cannabis." Indiana University, Indiana.

27 Richard E. S. and A. Hoffman (1992) "Plants of the Gods—Origin of Hallucinogenic Use." Hutchinson, London.

28 R. E. Schultes and A. Hoffman (1992) "Plants of the Gods—Their Sacred, Healing, and Hallucinogenic Powers." Healing Arts Press, Rochester, VT.

29 Exodus 30:23, meaning reed of balm.

30 The name marijuana, meaning the dried flowers of the female cannabis plant, is hard to etymologize. In excerpts from April 14, 1999, House of Commons Debates on Medicinal Marijuana, it was recorded that

> As for the word marijuana, its etymology is not clear. Some sources say that it is the contraction of two first names that are popular in Mexico, namely Maria and Juana. Others believe that this word comes from the Mexican word mariguano, which means intoxicant, or the Panamanian word managuango, which has the same meaning.

31 Delile, A. R. (1849) "Indexseminumhorti botanici Monspeliensis. Annales des Sciences Naturelles." *Botanique 12:* 365–366.

32 Janischevsky, D. E. (1924) "Formakonopli nasornykhmestakhv Yugo-vostochnoi Rossii." *Uchenye zapiski 2(2):* 3–17. University of Saratov, U.S.S.R.

33 Vavilov, N. I. and D. D. Bukinich. (1929) "Zemledelcheskii Afghanistan: Trudy poprikladnoi botanike, genetike i selektsii." *Prilozhenie 33:* 380–382.

34 Schultes, R. E., et. al. (1974) "Cannabis: an Example of Taxonomic Neglect." *Harvard University Botanical Museum Leaflets 23:* 337–367.

35 Small, E., A. Cronquist. (1976) "A Practical and Natural Taxonomy for Cannabis." *Taxon 25 (4):* 405–435.

36 The remaining terms are "pure ruderalis," "indica x ruderalis hybrid," "sativa x ruderalis" hybrid, "indica/sativa/ruderalis" hybrid, "mostly ruderalis," and "mostly indica/sativa."

37 Since this type of breed is not popular then we can surmise that our main focus should be on the core breeds and not these uncommon types.

38 The American Heritage Dictionary of the English Language, Fourth Edition.

39 The author has not personally had experience with all these strains. These are the ones commonly advertised by seed resellers.

40 ElSohly, M. A. (2002) Quarterly Report #76, University of Mississippi Potency Monitoring Project.

41 Green, G. (2005) "The Cannabis Breeder's Bible: The Definitive Guide to Marijuana Genetics, Cannabis Botany and Creating Strains for The Seed Market." 44–46, 141–144 Green Candy Press, San Francisco.

42 Hirata, K. (1924) "Sex Reversal in Hemp." *Journal of the Society of Agriculture and Forestry 16:* 145–168.

43 Schaffner, J.H. (1931) "The Fluctuation Curve of Sex Reversal in Staminate Hemp Plants Induced by Photoperiodicity." *American Journal of Botany 18 (6):* 424–430.

44 Peil, A., H. Flachowsky, E. Schumann, and W. E. Weber. (2003) "Sex-linked AFl P Markers Indicate a Pseudoautosomal Region in Hemp (Cannabis sativa L.)." *Theoretical and Applied Genetics 107:* 102–109.

45 It is said that you should wait until the plant shows its sex during the flowering stage of the life cycle and then clip away the top 6 to 12 inches of the male plant and remove the leaves. Stems and branches are discarded. The leaves are cured and then sampled.

46 As soon as the plant is flowered it continues to grow rapidly in height again. For Indica, the "vegetative growth to flowering height ratio" is usually around 1:2. Indica plants that are flowered at 2 feet usually finish at 4. For Sativa this ratio can go as high as 1:5. Some Sativa strains that are flowered at 2 feet can finish at 10 feet. Most breeders work on the 1:2 or 1:3 "vegetative growth to flowering" ratio.

Chapter 2

1 In 2000 I estimated this figure based on seed bank product guides. Since then, the figure has increased into the thousands; however, new hybrids take time to stabilize and the facts in this chapter remain the same.

2 Flowering times commence at the start of the photoperiod (12/12) and not at the start of calyx development (pre-flowering). This is covered in detail in Chapter 7.

3 Counterfeit goods are seeds released under a breeder's name which are not originally from the breeder. Instead, they are the result of seeds bred from the breeder's original seeds, which were purchased by the counterfeiter, who used them to make the fakes. These seeds are less stable and are generally non-uniform in growth when compared to the original breeder's line. These counterfeit seeds can also be called F2 seeds, although F2 does not necessarily mean that the line is counterfeit. Breeders now practice sealing their original seeds in breeders' packs to help prevent counterfeiting. Consult Chapter 15 for more information on F2 offspring.

Chapter 3

1 Some germination soils are not suitable for cannabis because they contain higher amounts of P and K than N. Most growers find that ordinary loam soil is just as good for germination as long as the N values are equal to or higher than the P and K values.

2 For more information about soil and NPK, refer to Chapters 5 and 6.

3 Propagation kits can also be used with growing media other than rockwool.

4 The Angiosperm Phylogeny Group. (2003) "An Update of the Angiosperm Phylogeny Group Classification for the Orders and Families of Flowering Plants: APG II." *Botanical Journal of the Linnean Society. 141(4): 399–436.*

5 Harvey, R. (2002) "Growing Ferns from Spores." Australian Government Department of the Environment and Heritage, Australian National Botanic Gardens.

6 Single cotyledons are produced by monocotyledons and gymnosperms may have two or more.

7 W. B. O'Shaughnessy, M.D, notes in his "On the Preparations of the Indian Hemp," or Gunjah that cannabis is oily, and devoid of all narcotic properties.

8 Charles Darwin, simply by using experiments in his back garden, examined the feet of birds and left seeds in water for months to simulate animal trekking and oversea transport. Darwin concluded that these methods allowed fauna to spread from island to island and thus successfully explained how the same fauna species could appear in areas separated by obstructions.

9 Consult Chapter 6 for details on temperature.

10 Seeds take up to 3 weeks to germinate. After this time, if no seeds have germinated, check your seeds and your germination method. Usually seeds germinate together within a few days of one another. If all the seeds fail to germinate and your method was good then report this to the seed bank to see if their batch was faulty. Usually, good seed banks keep records of germination rates and failures.

Chapter 4

1 In most countries, a high electricity bill is not grounds enough for a search warrant. Electric heaters use just as much, if not more, electricity than grow lights. If your grow is well-hidden but the authorities suspect that you grow, then all they can do is look through your trash for evidence of a growing operation. If they find anything it can be used to obtain a search warrant. Do not use your trash for getting rid of growing materials. Find another way to dispose of unwanted growing rubbish. Create a compost heap in your garden for most waste materials.

2 Check to see if your country or state has granted law enforcement officials the legal right to track purchase orders from grow shops. A quick search on the internet will reveal news items about this. In most countries, it is illegal for law enforcement officials to trace purchase orders as a means to track down indoor cannabis cultivation operations.

3 Steiner, R. (1993) "Spiritual Foundations for the Renewal of Agriculture: A Course of Lectures." Bio-Dynamic Farming and Gardening Association. Kimberton, PA.

4 Reganold, J.P., Palmer, A.S., Lockhart, J.C., and A.N. Macgregor. (1994) "Soil Quality and Financial Performance of Biodynamic and Conventional Farms in New Zealand." *Science 6 (2).*

5 Paull, J. (2006) "The Farm as Organism: The Foundational Idea of Organic Agriculture." *Elementals: Journal of Bio-Dynamics Tasmania 80:* 14–19.

6 Organic farming produces the same corn and soybean yields as conventional farms, but consumes less energy and no pesticides. Susan S. Lang. (2002) "Soil Fertility and Biodiversity in Organic Farming." *Science v.296,* n.5573, 31 May.

7 Donaldson, D.J. (1996) *Canadian Chemical News,* January 1. Chemical Institute of Canada. 48. 1 p24; Ocean and Climate Change Institute (OCCI) http://www.whoi.edu/institutes/occi/viewTopic.do?o=read&id=521>; Intergovernmental Panel on Climate Change (IPCC).

8 Burros, M. (2003) "Eating Well: Is Organic Food Provably Better?" *The New York Times.* July 16.

9 On-Farm Composting Handbook. (1992) NRAES (Natural Resource, Agriculture, and Engineering Service). http://www.css.cornell.edu/compost/OnFarmHandbook/apa.taba1.html

Chapter 5

1 Professional growers choose lighting kits with an external ballast because it is easier to move the light and keeps temperatures cooler. Internal ballasts make the light heavier and cause extra unwanted heat on your plants. External ballasts are highly recommended.

2 Fluorescents tend to produce buds that are airy and less dense than buds produced under HID lights.

3 In general, grow bulbs come in the following wattages: 250, 400, 600, and 1,000.

4 Air-cooled kits have openings in the reflector to allow for hot air extraction. Some of them even come with a built-in extractor fan.

5 Most bulbs have a lifespan of approximately 2 to 4 grows. This depends heavily on the bulb type and how long the bulbs are left on for. After the third grow, the bulb's quality tends to reduce overall.

6 Although some growers can manipulate the photoperiod without sexual dysfunctions emerging, it is not worth the risk. Once a dysfunction appears it cannot be reversed. Sexual dysfunctions are covered in Chapter 7.

7 The conversion of electricity to light has been one of the great modern environmental catastrophes because of its inefficiency (imagine that before energy saving bulbs were around or industrial grade lamps, most lights lost around 90% of the energy used in the process). Progress in understanding light and incandescent lamps has helped scientists to reduce this waste factor.

8 Julia Silverman. (2007) "Teachers Press for Ban of Halide Lights after Sight Damage." Associated Press. March 30. http://www.suburbanchicagonews.com/couriernews/business/319820,3_3_EL30_BULBS_S1.article

9 Adjustments are made in the flowering phase of a plant's life by adding different nutrients to your medium.

Chapter 6

1 It usually takes about two to three days to observe a correction in a nutrient disorder. If there has not been a change in three days, then you need to reconsider your diagnosis or treatment.

2 Heat stress can be responsible for sexual dysfunctions. Avoid heat stressing your plants.

3 Transplant shock causes plant stress. If your plant is sexually mature enough to flower (has calyx development) or is flowering, transplant shock can induce sexual dysfunctions to appear (the hermaphrodite condition). Even is your plant survives a transplant in the later stages of its growth, it can cause problems down the line. Avoid transplanting after the second week of vegetative growth if you can. It is during the third week of growth that the plant's sex is usually determined and avoiding stress just before or after this point helps prevent sexual dysfunction. All strains are different in this respect. Some exhibit sexual dysfunction with only a little bit of stress. Others are more resistant and can endure quite a large amount of stress without exhibiting sexual dysfunction. The latter is especially true of strains that are recommended for the novice grower.

Chapter 7

1 Do not confuse a calyx with initial secondary branch development, which occurs in the first to second week of vegetative growth. If you are not sure, initial branch development, or secondary growth, produces two small leaves in a few days. These eventually extend into branches, which form more leaves and node regions.

2 Initial calyx development is not photoperiod responsive. You do not need to change your light photoperiod in order to find calyx development. Calyx development is a natural part of the plant's life cycle and occurs when the plant is mature enough to display sex.

3 If you have a light photoperiod of 24/0 then sexual expression may only be evident in the calyx shape. If you have a light photoperiod of 16/8 then chances are the calyx may display sex very quickly because there is a dark period involved. If you see tiny white hairs (pistils) growing out from the pods then the plant is female. If the pods are very raised and growing in large numbers then it is probably a male.

4 "Feminized" seeds can produce the following sexes if the growing environment is not well maintained: (1) Females, (2) Hermaphrodites, (3) Males. "Feminized" seeds only increase the chances of getting females. They are covered in detail in Chapter 15.

5 Cannabis plants can be flowered as early as June, but this depends on how well the weather was up until then. If the plants were started in March and have sexually matured by June, then they may flower with as little as eight hours darkness. This is very strain dependent.

6 Variations in the photoperiod that cause hermies are mostly disturbances to the 12/12 photoperiod, although early 24/0 or 18/6 photoperiod disturbances can also cause sexual dysfunction to appear later.

7 This hermaphrodite condition depends largely on the strain and how well the environment has been kept. Not all attempts at early-induced flowering will hermaphrodite the plant. If the light regime has not been consistent or was variable, then early-induced flowering may cause the plant to respond by exhibiting the hermaphrodite condition.

8 Not all seed banks provide their strains in packs of 15. The most common amounts sold by seed banks and breeders are packs of 10, 15 and 16. On rare occasions, seed banks release "mix bags" of 30. These lucky mix bags are unidentified seeds that got mixed up by the breeder. They are usually very cheap to buy because of this.

Chapter 8

1 Reverting to vegetative growth or "re-vegging" is covered in detail in Chapter 11.

2 Clones usually take up to three weeks to root properly, but some root in two weeks. This is covered in Chapter 11. You should root your clone before trying to flower them if you want to see the "bud on a small stick" effect.

3 Remember to add for a rooting time of two to three weeks before you begin vegetative growth.

4 Remember that flowering plants require a strict light photoperiod of 12/12 and plants in vegetative growth require a light photoperiod of 24/0 or 18/6. For this reason, plants used in a "perpetual grow" operation must be kept in separate grow rooms or partitioned off from one another.

Chapter 9

1 Mylar is an excellent material to patch light leaks because of its high reflectivity.

Chapter 10

1 Sometimes roots can grow out through the bottom pot pores if there is a vacuum created between the pot and the dish/tray. Pots with small raised bases help prevent this from happening.

Chapter 11

1 F1 hybrids and non-uniform plants tend to exhibit more of this vigor than stable strains and IBL lines.

2 Cannabis plants rarely fail if they have lost 50 percent of their leaves sometime after the seedling phase of growth, but it will stunt them. Most strains will fail if no leaves are left on the plant.

3 Fishing line is also great for keeping those top colas upright. If you find that a top cola is bending over from the weight (and you will after using this book!) simply train it upright by using fishing line.

4 The exceptions to this rule are Ruderalis and other strains that have autoflowering properties. These strains can only be continued with seed and cannot be reverted back to vegetative growth.

5 It does not matter if you regenerate a female that has been seeded or is sinsemilla. The results will be the same.

6 The compromising of the genetic integrity of a rejuvenated plant usually occurs when the plant has reached an age where cellular breakdown occurs, causing death. If seeds are made from this dying plant, then it is possible that DNA repair malfunction may, because of cellular breakdown due to age, be passed on to these offspring. In this case, the genetic integrity of the plant has been compromised. Also, cuttings taken from this dying plant may also express the same problems or be mutated.

Chapter 12

1 Using small amounts of sticky pest tape around your grow will help you to detect if any pests have entered the grow room. Remember, though, that sticky pest tape can still catch friendly pests.

Chapter 14

1 Make sure to store your canned buds in a cool, dry and dark place away from any direct light. Check occasionally for mold, which can build up onto the buds due to humidity or age. If you find mold, just clip it away to prevent it from spreading. Moldy buds should not be smoked.

Chapter 15

1 The phenotype is the expressed genotype, but this can be influenced by the environment.

Remember your growing conditions influence the expressed phenotype. A purple hue in the plant's stem may not be genetic at all but rather the result of a lack of K in the nutrients or cold temperatures.

Chapter 18

1 Cannabis also has medicinal uses for cancer treatment.

2 National Institute on Drug Abuse (NIDA).

3 U.S. Department of Justice, Federal Bureau of Prisons.

4 European Monitoring Centre for Drugs and Drug Addiction (EMCDDA).

5 European Monitoring Centre for Drugs and Drug Addiction (EMCDDA).

++ | Index

A

acidic soil, pH adjustment, 171–73
aerators, 280
aerobic decomposition, 112
aeroponic systems, 251, 281
air circulation, 180–81, 497
air drying, 370–71, 375, 376, 381
air layering, 322
air pruning, 296–97
air purification systems. *see* odor control
alcohol use vs cannabis, 474–77
algae buildup, 272
alkaline soil, pH adjustment, 171–73
aluminum foil, 138–39
anaerobic toxicity, 116
Anderson, Loran, 19, 20, 22
ants, 335, 336, 340
aphids, 120, 335–36, 345, 346

B

ballasts, 123–24, 136, 518n1
    Ballast Efficacy Factor (BEF), 146
bonsai clones, 323
boric acid, 335
boron (B), 161
botrytis, 351–52
breeding considerations, 32–33, 383–423
    backcrossing, 417–19
    pollen collection, 383–84
    seed collection, 384–85

simple hybrid breeding, 385
test crosses, 396–403, 405, 414
true breeding, 398, 412–16
. *see also* genetics; hybrids
Bubble Bag kit, for hash, 445–47
bubbler method, 277–79, 281
buds, 18
    abnormal bud growth, 205–6
    curing, 374–77
    genetic threshold of, 185, 202, 307
    growth increase in, 42
    impact of light on, 127, 301
    plant training, 312–13
    rehydrating, 381
    sample testers, 367
    seeded buds, 31
    THC quantities, and bud mass, 5–8
Bukinich, D. D., 17
butane extraction, for hash oil, 448–51
    safety issues, 450, 451–53

C

cabinet growing, 123, 213, 226–27, 233, 241
calcium (Ca), 161
    deficiencies, 164, 167
calyx development
    and flowering stage, 516n2
    nutrient control, 162
    photoperiod manipulation, 202–3, 206–7,
      519n2

pre-flowering phase, 39, 196–98, 519n1
calyx to leaf ratios, 33, 39
cannabinoids, 5–7, 31–32
cannabis
    and alcohol use, 474–77
    breeders' strain type terminology, 21–29
    cooking with, 470, 471
    driving under the influence, 477–79
    history of, 1–3, 20
    hyper-potent cannabis, 467
    landrace cannabis, 3–5, 458
    legalization, 473–74
    scientific classification debate, 14–21,
      514n30
    scientific taxonomy, 21–29
    speciation, genetic evidence for, 19–21
    street cannabis, adulteration of, 43
    tolerance, 460–61
    vaporization, 471–72
    varieties, strains, subspecies, and hybrids,
      23–24, 26–29
cannabis myths, 456–67
    brain damage myth, 479–80
    gateway drug theory, 485
    potency, increase in, 458–67
cannabis plants
    breeding considerations, 32–33, 383–423
    fan leaves, 9, 301
    flower development, 15
    flowering stage, 35
    genders, 12–13
    germination, 35–37
    grow decision, considerations, 41
    leaf types, 35
    life cycle of, 35–43
    nutrient requirements, 164–65
    plant development, 301
    plant types, 36, 55
    pre-flowering phase, 39
    reproduction, 29, 31
    seedling sub-stage, 37, 38
    sex determination systems, 34
    sinsemilla plants, 13–14, 31–32
    trichomes, 6, 7, 8–9
    vegetative growth stage, 35, 39
    . *see also* indica; ruderalis strains; sativa

cannabis strains by name, 26–29, 425–35
    Arjan's Haze #1, 432
    Arjan's Haze #2, 389
    Arjan's Haze #3, 389
    Arjan's Ultra Haze, 390
    B1, 379
    Big Bang, 235, 391
    Blue Moonshine, 391
    Blue Thunder, 392
    Blueberry, 307, 429
    Brainstorm Haze, 230, 392
    Bubba Kush, 235
    Bubbleberry, 393
    Bubblegum, 18
    Cali O, 467
    Canna Sutra, 230, 393
    Champagne, 467
    Cheese, 235
    Chemdog, 235
    Chemo, 467
    Chronic, 18, 240
    Church, 395, 478
    Dieselryder, 236
    The Doctor, 395
    Double Kush, 395
    Durban Poison, 18, 431
    Durga Mata, 427
    Dutch Dragon, 435
    El Nino, 395
    Euforia, 229, 396
    First Lady, 396
    FOG (Fruit of the Gods), 230, 397
    G-13, 379, 459, 467
    Great White Shark, 397
    Hash Plant, 426
    Hawaiian Snow, 398
    Headband, 233
    Ice Cream, 239
    indica top ten, 426–27
    indica/sativa top ten, 434–35
    Jack Flash, 398
    Jack Herer, 399, 435
    Jack the Ripper, 399
    Jacky White, 71, 238
    Jazz, 433
    Jorge's Diamonds, 229

Juicy Fruit, 379
Khola, 400
Kryptonite, 379
K-Train, 235
Kush, 18
LA Confidential, 232
La Lybella, 400
Lowryder, 237
Magic Bud, 238, 400
Matanuska Tundra, 428
Mazaar, 229
Mekong Haze, 402
Mexican Sativa, 402
Mongolian Indica, 400
mostly indica top ten, 428–29
mostly sativa top ten, 432–33
Mother's Finest, 431
Mr. Nice, 403
MTF, 467
Nebula, 238, 239, 403
Neville's Haze, 12, 430
NL5 Haze, 404
NLx6, 379
Original Cheese, 468
Ortega Indicac, 404
Pamir Gold, 405
Power Plant, 229
Purple #1, 405
Querkle, 406
sativa top ten, 430–31
Sensi Star, 42, 89, 406, 462
Shaman, 407
Sheherazade, 407
Shiva Shanti, 409
Shiva Skunk, 461
SIMM18, 235
Skunk, 18
Skunk #1, 460
Sleestack, 233
Snowbud, 409
Southern Lights, 422
Space Jill, 409
Stonehedge, 241, 409
Strawberry Cough, 411
Strawberry Haze, 390
Super Haze, 411

Super Lemon Haze, 413
Super Silver Haze, 22, 413
Super Star, 231
Swazi, 18
Sweet Purple, 12
Third Dimension, 415
T.N.C., 87
Trainwreck, 235
Twilight, 427
Ultra Violet, 101, 367, 379
Vortex, 415
Washington, 433
White Rhino, 235
White Widow, 434
X-18 Pakistani, 233
Yumbolt, 429
canning method of curing, 377–81
carbon dioxide enrichment, 184–88, 500
    calculating requirements, 186–88
    digital measuring devices, 259
carbon filters, 175
caterpillars, 336–37
cellular necrosis, 104
chemical burns, 355–56
    vs nutrient deficiency symptoms, 356, 357
chlorine (Cl), 161
chlorophyll synthesis, 127
clay, 152
clay pellets/pebbles, 268
    hydroponic systems, 243, 246, 255,
        265–66
climate controllers, 188–91
clones and cloning, 61, 313–23
    aero cloning kits, 318
    air layering, 322
    bonsai clones, 323
    botrytis and, 352
    cabinet growing, 226–27
    clone mothers, generating, 419
    clone mothers, preparing, 213–17
    cutting location, 313–14
    factory cloning, 317, 318
    hormones for, 321
    lighting for, 67
    mother plants, 31, 38, 215–16
    oasis cubes, 318

photoperiod manipulation, 214
process of, 215–16
rockwool cubes, 64–65, 256, 257, 315, 318–19
root development, 519n2 (ch8)
rooting solutions, 318
in Sea of Green (SOG) setups, 217–20
to soil, 316
thinning, 302–4
transplanting, 71–73
in vegetative growth stage, 320–21
water cloning, 317
closet systems, 123, 213, 226–27
suitable strains, 233, 241
cobalt (Co), 161
coconut fiber, 268, 269, 292
color
change as indicator of problem, 334–35
as harvest indicator, 107, 211, 369
impact of light color on plant growth, 124–27
as indicator of finished compost, 114
Color Rendering Index (CRI), 126
compost, 111–14
worm composting, 117, 119
containers. see pots and containers
copper (Cu), 161
Correlated Color Temperature (CCT), 125–26
Cronquist, A., 19, 20, 21
cultigens, nomenclature of, 4
curing, 377–81
cuttings, 38
cleanliness, importance of, 256
labeling, 213, 215
rockwool cubes, 265
cutworms, 336–37, 344

D

Darwin, Charles, 16
deep water culture (DWC), 277–79, 281
dehumidifiers, 181
Delile, A. R., 17, 20
delta blocks, 257, 267
Delta-9 Labs
Brainstorm Haze, 230, 392
Canna Sutra, 230, 393

Double Kush, 395
FOG (Fruit of the Gods), 230, 397
Mekong Haze, 402
Shaman, 407
Super Star, 231
dioecious reproduction, 29, 31, 33
DNA Genetics, 232–33
dominant hereditary traits, 387
genotype determination, 402–3
test crosses, 396–403, 405
dormant oil sprays, 340
Dr Greenthumb
Jazz, 433
Original Cheese, 468
drip irrigation systems, 249–51
drug testing, 479
Dutch Passion, 229
Blue Moonshine, 391
Blueberry, 429
Durban Poison, 431
Euforia, 396
Khola, 400
La Lybella, 400
Ortega Indicac, 404
Pamir Gold, 405
Purple #1, 405
Snowbud, 409
Strawberry Cough, 411
Super Haze, 411
Twilight, 427

E

ebb and flow system, 246–48, 256–63
emergency transplants, 74, 75, 193
and mulch toxicity, 116
Epsom salts, 359
magnesium deficiency, 167–68
extraction fans, 94

F

factory cloning, 317, 318
fan leaves, 9, 301, 371
fans
and air flow, 173, 180–81
extraction fans, 94
ventilation systems, 178–80

female plants, 12–13
  calyxes, 199
  female to male ratio, increasing, 326, 328
  flowering stage, 39, 40, 211
  force-flowering, 199
  height as indicator of sex, 198, 515n46
  plant traits, 200
  sinsemilla condition, 13–14, 42
  THC extraction, 437–38
feminized seeds, 199, 420, 519n4
fertilizers, 499
  compost tea as organic feed, 114–15
  and emergency transplants, 74
  feeding schedules, 168–70
  NPK ratios, 63, 151–52
  nutrient control, 161–64
  organic feeding products, 121
  for outdoor growing systems, 95–96
  overfeeding, 64, 69
  overfeeding vs pest attack symptoms, 334–35
  plant burn, 80, 162, 168–69
  for seedlings, 63, 64–65
  . see also nutrient solutions; plant problems
flood & drain system, 246–48
flowering stage, 35, 40
  bone meal, 169
  delaying, 201–2
  early induced vs force flowering, 206, 519n7
  feeding schedules, 168–70
  and harvest timing, 9, 49, 516n2
  to induce, 202–3
  lighting requirements, 140–41
  nutrient disorders, 165–68, 357–63
  nutrient needs, 106, 152, 162
  outdoor flowering, 297, 299
  perpetual grow cycles, 520n4
  pesticide use and, 332–34
  pre-flowering phase, 39, 195–98, 201–2
  and pruning, 308
  reverting to vegetative stage, 320–21, 325–26, 520n6
  temperature control, 182

  vegetative growth to flowering ratio, 515n46
fluorescent lighting, 128, 518n2
  cabinet growing, 226–27
  fluorescent white tube lights, 129
  for seedlings, 67
Friis-Hansen, Esbern, 3
fungus and fungal diseases, 167, 351–54
  fungicides, 332
  fungus botrytis, 351–52
  mold, 167, 178, 352, 353
  powdery mildew, 354–55
  root rot, 353–54

G

gardening tools, 83
genetics, 386–87, 495
  backcrossing, 417–19
  bad genetics, 363
  F1 generation, 408, 417, 520n1
  F2 generation, 408, 418, 516n3
  gene frequencies, 389–90, 410–12
  gene frequency manipulation, 412–16
  gene migration, 411
  genetic drift, 411
  genetic notation, 387
  genotype, 387, 396–403
  Hardy-Weinberg law of genetic equilibrium, 387, 389–94, 403–5, 410–12
  Mendel's pea experiments, 406–8
  mutations, 410
  natural photoperiods, 299
  natural selection, 412
  non-random mating, 411–12
  phenotype, 521n1 (ch18)
  and plant potential, 7, 185, 202
  Punnet squares, 401
  role of in potency, 458, 462
  test crosses, 396–403, 405, 414
  true breeding, 412–16
  true breeding vs unstable, 398
genotype, 387
  determining, 396–403
  environmental influence on, 419
germination, 35–37, 67–68
  dangers during, 68–70

effect of temperature on, 69
germination rates, 517n12
germination soil, 63, 516n1(ch3)
propagation kits, 64–65
seed quantity to germinate, 59, 61–62
seed towel propagation, 60, 64
techniques, 63–64
Germplasm Resources Information Network
  (GRIN), 21
gibberellic acid, 422
GMOs, and organic farming, 102
gravity system, 253–54
Green House Seed Co., 234–35, 388
  Arjan's Haze #1, 432
  Arjan's Haze #2, 389
  Arjan's Haze #3, 389
  Arjan's Ultra Haze, 390
  Big Bang, 391
  Church, 395, 478
  The Doctor, 395
  El Nino, 395
  Great White Shark, 397
  Hawaiian Snow, 398
  Neville's Haze, 430
  NL5 Haze, 404
  Strawberry Haze, 390
  Super Lemon Haze, 413
  Super Silver Haze, 22, 413
  White Widow, 434
ground covers, 294
grow decision, considerations, 41
grow rocks, 265–66
growing mediums, 497–98
  clay pellets/pebbles, 243, 246, 255,
    265–66, 268
  coconut fiber, 268, 269
  compost, 111–14
  germination soil, 63
  hydroponic systems, 243, 265–69
  oasis cubes, 266
  perlite, 153–54, 269, 270
  rockwool cubes, 64–65, 265, 267
  seed towel propagation, 64
  soil, 150–59
  soilless mixes, 243, 268
  transplant mediums, 79

vermiculite, 153–54, 269, 270
growth rates, and light adjustment, 139, 140–41
guerrilla farming, 86
  concealment of, 88–89
  hanging baskets, 95–96
  security issues, 95–97
  site selection, 89–90

H

halogen lights, 129
hanging baskets, 95–96
Hardy-Weinberg law of genetic equilibrium,
  387, 389–94, 410–12
Harlan, J. R., 3
harvests and harvesting, 365–81
  air drying, 370–71, 375, 376, 381
  breeders' flowering times and, 369
  color as gauge in harvesting, 9, 369
  curing, 377–81, 521n1
  curing fan leaves and trim, 372
  expert indicators, 367–69
  harvest indicators, 365
  indica harvest, 370–71
  labeling, 366, 374–77
  manicuring, 374–77
  multiple tasters, 365–66
  sativa harvest, 371–72
  security issues, 94–95, 97
  timing of, 48–49, 107, 211
  trim matter, 376
  washing line setup, 50
hash (hashish), 437–55
  adulterates in, 465, 468
  advanced screening, 442–46
  Bubble Bag kit, 445–47
  drum machines, 444
  flat metal screening method, 440
  flat silk screening method, 439
  grades of, 454
  Hash Honey Oil, 448–51
  homemade vs street hash, 455
  leaves used in, 372, 377
  multiple screening method, 440–41
  potency and, 465
  resin, pressing into, 453–55
  skuff, 438, 443

supercritical fluid extraction (SFE),
448–51, 451–53
water extraction, 445–47
Zero Zero, 9, 12
health issues, 457
affect on immune system, 480
alcohol use vs cannabis, 474–77
brain damage myth, 479–80
cancer-causing agents, 469–72
carbon monoxide inhalation, 461, 469
human DNA repair malfunction, 481
medicinal uses of cannabis, 482–83
nicotine, 470
pregnancy, 481
sexual dysfunction, 480–81
short-term memory, 485
tolerance, 460–61
heat stress, 182, 188, 359, 518n2 (ch6)
vs pest attack symptoms, 334–35
hemp fiber, 2, 8, 33
herbicides, 332
hermaphrodites, 12–13
early induced flowering, 206, 519n7
flowers, 204
gibberellic acid, 422
heat stress, 142
and photoperiod manipulation, 519n6
and plant stress, 13, 105
reproduction, 29, 31
selfing, 419–22
sinsemilla hermaphrodites, 323–24
stress-related sex problems, 205–6
HID system (high-intensity discharge lights),
129, 146–48
bulb brand comparison, 133
high-pressure sodium lights (HPS), 129,
130
illumination formula, 133–34
lamp efficiency comparison, 137–38
lamp efficiency in lumens, 135–36
mercury vapor (MV), 129
metal halide lights (MH), 129
potency and, 463–64
High Bred Seeds, 236–37
high-pressure sodium lights (HPS), 129, 147,
148–50

in Screen of Green (ScrOG) setups, 225
in Sea of Green (SOG) setups, 225
highs, types of, 47, 458, 468
and harvest timing, 48–49
negative experiences and, 487
from trimmed material, 371
Hillig, K. W., 19–21
honey as healing agent, 312–13
horticultural lighting (HID). see HID system
(high-intensity discharge lights)
humidity issues, 178, 181
botrytis and, 352
digital measuring devices, 259
humus, 121, 152
hybrids
backcrossing, 417–19
F1 generation, 408, 417, 520n1
F2 generation, 408, 418, 516n3
gene frequencies, 389–90, 410–12
gene migration, 411
genetic drift, 411
GMO/non-GMO hybrids, 102
Hardy-Weinberg law of genetic equilibrium, 387, 389–94, 403–5, 410–12
high from, 468
Mendel's pea experiments, 406–8
mutations, 410
natural selection, 412
non-random mating, 411–12
simple hybrid breeding, 385
stability of, 45
strain list, 26–29
taxonomy terminology, 24
test crosses, 396–403, 405, 414
true breeding, 412–16
true breeding vs unstable, 398
. see also genetics
hydrogen peroxide, 266, 354
hydroponic systems, 123, 213, 243–81
about, 243–44
aeroponic systems, 251, 281
algae buildup, 272
automatic hydroponic pots, 255
bubbler method, 277–79, 281
checklist, 495–501
drip irrigation systems, 249–51

ebb and flow system, 246–48, 256–63

flood & drain system, 246–48

gravity system, 253–54

growing mediums, 153–54, 265–69

hard water, 276

manual hydroponic pots, 255

nutrient film technique (NFT), 244–46, 274–75

nutrient solutions, 264–65, 269–72, 273

pH levels, 271

potency and, 462–63

recycle systems, monitoring, 276

reverse osmosis filters, 276

thinning, 302–4

wick system, 252–53

YouTube videos, 260, 280

hyper-potent cannabis, 467

I

imbibing, process of, 67

indica, 19

characteristics of, 34

growth cycle, 42–43

harvesting, 370–71

high from, 47, 458

indica top ten, 426–27

indica/sativa top ten, 434–35

leaf types, 35

mostly indica top ten, 428–29

plant traits, 200

plant types, 36

in Screen of Green (ScrOG) setups, 224

in Sea of Green (SOG) setups, 217

strain list, 26–29

varieties, strains, subspecies, and hybrids, 23–24, 25

vegetative growth to flowering ratio, 515n46

indoor growing systems, 123–59

carbon dioxide enrichment systems, 184–88

checklist, 495–501

climate controllers, 188–91

extraction fans, 94

feeding schedules, 168–70

horticultural lighting (HID), 129

humidity issues, 178, 181

lighting, types of, 128–30

lights and lighting, 124–27

natural light vs artificial, 84–86

nutrient control, 161–68

odor control, 174–81

ozone generators, 94

photoperiod manipulation, 202–3

planning, 84–86

security issues, 92–94

seed selection, 48–49

soil control, 171–73

soil gardens, 104–9

temperature, 181–83

water control, 173–74

Integrated Taxonomic Information System (ITIS), 21

International Federation of Organic Agriculture Movements (IFOAM), 99, 101, 102

ionizers, 176

iron (Fe), 161

nutrient disorders, 357, 359, 360

J

James, Walter (Baron Northbourne), 100

Janischevsky, D. E., 17, 20, 22

K

K.C. Brains, 87, 88

kief, 441

L

labeling

harvests, 366, 374–77

importance of, 213, 215, 500

ladybugs, 120, 336

Lamarck, Jean, 22

Lamarck, Jean-Baptiste, 17, 20

landrace cannabis, 458

leaching, 357

legalization issues, 473–74

alcohol vs cannabis, 474–77

driving under the influence, 477–79

drug testing, 479

light

and bud development, 301

degradation of THC and, 370
as germination initiator, 67
and photosynthesis, 127
light bending (phototropism), 290, 304
lights and lighting, 123–50, 496
advanced systems, 144–50
Ballast Efficacy Factor (BEF), 146
ballasts, 123–24, 136, 518n1
bulb brand comparison, 133
cabinet growing, 226–27
Color Rendering Index (CRI), 126
common types of, 128–30
Correlated Color Temperature (CCT),
125–26
cost issues, 134
domestic lights, 128
electricity usage, 92, 134, 144, 517n1
electromagnetic radiation spectrum,
124–26
fire hazards, 94, 140
fluorescent lighting, 67, 128, 518n2
fluorescent white tube lights, 129
high-pressure sodium lights (HPS), 129,
130, 147, 148–50
horticultural lighting (HID), 129, 133,
146–48
illumination formula, 133–34
impact on temperature, 181
lamp efficiency comparison, 137–38
lamp efficiency in lumens, 135–36
light color, impact on plant growth, 124–27
light height, 139, 140–41
light rails, 143
lighting kits, 123–24, 134–36
mercury vapor lights (MV), 129, 147
metal halide lights (MH), 129, 147
natural light vs artificial, 84–86
potency and, 463–64
reflectors, 123–24, 132, 138–40
in Screen of Green (ScrOG) setups, 225
in Sea of Green (SOG) setups, 225
timer schedules, 123–24, 184
wattage and lumens, calculations for,
130–34
lime, 171
Linnaeus, Carolus, 16–17, 19, 20, 21

loam, 63, 153
low-pressure sodium lights (LPS), 147, 148
lumens, and wattage
calculations for, 130–34
comparison, 138

M

macronutrients, 151–52
nutrient disorders, 165–68
magnesium (Mg), 161
deficiencies, 167–68, 357, 359
effect on taste, 381
as problematic nutrient, 164–65
male plants, 12–13
calyxes, 199
female to male ratio, increasing, 326, 328
flowering, 208, 421
force-flowering, 199
height as indicator of sex, 198, 515n46
irregular photoperiods and, 144
plant traits, 200
and pollen production, 209–11
potency, 35, 515n45
THC extraction, 437
manganese (Mn), 161
nutrient disorders, 357, 360–62
manicuring, 33, 108, 374–77
marijuana factory. see perpetual grow cycles
Maxwell, James Clerk, 145
medicinal cannabis, 33, 235, 452, 482–83
Mendel, Gregor, 406–8
mercury vapor lights (MV), 129, 147
metal halide lights (MH), 129, 147
micronutrients, 63, 161, 164
mold. see fungus and fungal diseases
molybdenum (Mo), 161
monecious reproduction, 29, 31, 33
moss, 154
mother plants, 31, 38, 213–17, 419
mulches, 112, 115–16
mutations, 363, 410
mylar reflectors, 86, 140, 141

N

National Genetic Resources Program, 21
natural lighting vs artificial, 84–86

natural pest control. *see* pest control
nitrogen (N), 63
 nutrient disorders, 165, 167, 357, 359
NPK ratios
 for soil, 151–52
 soil mixture preparation, 155–56
 for starting seeds, 63
 understanding, 156
nutrient control, 161–64, 497
 digital measuring devices, 259
 macronutrients, 151–52
 micronutrients, 63
 nutrient testers, 161
 nutrient types, 163–64
 plant burn, 80, 162, 168–69
nutrient deficiencies, 497
 micronutrient deficiencies, 362
 nutrient disorders, 164, 165–68, 357–63,
  518n1 (ch6)
 nutrient lockout, 163, 168, 172
 vs chemical burn symptoms, 356, 357
 vs pest attack symptoms, 334–35
 . *see also* plant problems
nutrient film technique (NFT), 244–46, 274–75
nutrient solutions
 aerators, 281
 chemical burns, 355–56
 compost tea as organic feed, 114–15
 feeding schedules, 168–70
 grow and bloom, 272
 hydroponic systems, 264–65, 269–72
 mixing charts, 277
 pH levels, 271
 potency and, 464
 ppm readers, 276
 recycle systems, monitoring, 276
 strength of, 273
 total dissolved solids (TDS) meters, 276

O

oasis cubes, 266, 318
odor control, 92–94, 174–81, 259
 activated carbon air filtering, 177–78
 extraction fans, 94
 ionizers, 176
 ozone generators, 94, 176–77

ventilation systems, 178–81
organic farming, 99–101
 drawbacks, 110
 and GMOs, 102
 indoor soil gardens, 104–9
 yields vs artificial cultivation, 101–2
organic growing
 compost, 111–14
 compost tea as organic feed, 114–15
 humus, 121
 mulches, 112, 115–16
 nutrient disorders, 118
 reactive vs proactive organics, 114
 rules for, 121
outdoor growing systems, 86, 283–99
 air pruning, 296–97
 checklist, 495–501
 coconut substrates, 292
 concealment of, 88–89
 feeding schedules, 295
 ground covers, 294
 irrigation techniques, 288, 290
 outdoor soil, 290–92
 photoperiods, 297, 299
 plot preparation, 285–88
 polymer crystals, 290
 ruderalis strains, 34, 46
 sativa harvest, 371–72
 sativa strains, 283
 security issues, 94–95, 290
 seed selection, 48–49
 thinning, 302–4
 watering, 294–96
 weather conditions for transplanting,
  74–75
 weeding, 288, 293–94
overfeeding
 chemical burns, 355–56
 emergency transplants, 74
 plant burn, 80, 162, 168–69, 273
 vs pest attack symptoms, 334–35,
  356–58
overwatering, 157
 root rot and, 354
 vs pest attack symptoms, 334–35
ozone generators, 94, 176–77

P

Paradise Seeds, 40, 46, 47, 238–39, 298, 466
  Durga Mata, 427
  Dutch Dragon, 435
  Ice Cream, 239
  Jacky White, 71, 238
  Magic Bud, 238, 400
  Nebula, 219, 238, 239, 403
  Sensi Star, 42, 89, 406, 462
  Sheherazade, 407
  Sweet Purple, 12
perlite, 153–54, 269, 270
perpetual grow cycles, 226, 228, 520n4
pest control
  ants, 335, 340
  aphids, 120, 335–36, 345, 346
  caterpillars, 336–37
  cutworms, 336–37, 344
  deer, 337
  dormant oil sprays, 340
  fly tape, 338
  gnats, 338
  grasshoppers, 338–39
  groundhogs, 339
  herbicides, 332
  insecticide, pyrethrum-based, 336, 338, 340
  mantis, 345
  mealy bugs, 340
  pest attack symptoms, 334–35
  pest invasion, recovery from, 347–49
  pest predators, 120, 121, 336, 342, 343, 344–47
  pesticides, 332–34
  powder bugs, 348
  rabbits, 340
  rodents, 343
  scale, 340
  slugs, 340, 344
  smoke bombs, 348
  snails, 340, 344
  spider mites, 340–41, 344, 346, 348
  termites, 341–42
  thrips, 342, 344
  vs nutrient deficiency symptoms, 334–35, 356–58
  whitefly, 342–43
  woodchucks, 343
  . see also plant problems
pesticides, 332–34
  Safer's Soap, 336, 343
pH levels, 497
  as germination inhibitor, 68
  hydroponic systems, 271
  of loam, 63
  mulch maintenance, 116
  nutrient lockout, 362–63
  pH meters, 151
  of rockwool cubes, 265
  root rot and, 354
  of soil, 150–51
  of soil, adjusting, 171–73
  vs pest attack symptoms, 334–35
pH up / pH down, 172, 272
phenotype, 387
  environmental influence on, 419, 521n1 (ch18)
phosphorous (P)
  NPK ratios for starting seeds, 63
  nutrient disorders, 165, 357, 359
photoperiods, 499
  abnormal bud growth, 205–6
  manipulation of, 46, 141–44, 202–3, 206–7, 420, 518n6, 519n2
  perpetual grow cycles, 226, 228, 520n4
  reverting to vegetative stage, 320–21, 325–26
  stress-related sex problems, 205–6, 519n3, 519n6
photosynthesis, 127–28, 167
phototropism, 290, 304
Pistorius, Robin, 3–4
plant burn, 80, 162, 168–69, 273
plant care
  bushes, pruning for, 310–11
  female to male ratio, increasing, 326, 328
  FIM technique, 308
  increasing harvest yields, 324–29
  light bending (phototropism), 290, 304
  pruning, 293, 296–97, 305–11
  reverting to vegetative stage, 320–21, 325–26
  sinsemilla hermaphrodites, 323–24

Super Cropping pruning technique, 308–9
thinning, 302–4
topping, 306–8, 309
training, 312–13
plant problems, 496
approach to troubleshooting, 356–63
and bad genetics, 363
chemical burns, 355–56
fungus and fungal diseases, 167, 351–54
heat stress, 182, 188
herbicides, 332
leaf curling, 164, 167–68, 335, 359, 360
leaf discoloring, 164
nutrient deficiencies, 164, 356, 357
nutrient disorders, 165–68, 357–63,
   518n1 (ch6)
nutrient lockout, 163, 168, 172, 362–63
overfeeding, 74, 273
overwatering, 157, 174
pesticides, 332–34
plant burn, 80, 162, 168–69, 273
pot-bound stress, 78, 363
powdery mildew, 354–55
red stems, 167
root damage, 81
root rot, 353–54, 360
rust, 164
stress-related sex problems, 205–6
stunted growth, 81, 164, 165, 167
transplant shock, 64, 76–77, 80–81
under-watering, 174
unveven growth, 302–4
wilt, 167, 341, 360
yellowing, 162, 165–67, 359
. *see also* pest control; problem solver
plant waxes, 312
pollen
collection for breeding, 383–84
pollen production, 209–11
pollination
pollination rooms, 62
selfing, 419–22
potassium (K)
deficiencies, 165, 167
NPK ratios for starting seeds, 63
nutrient disorders, 357, 359, 360

potency
breeding considerations, 32–33
of clone mothers, 214
role of genetics in, 458, 462, 466
sinsemilla plants, 31–32
and THC levels, 8
pots and containers
choosing, 156–57, 498
net pots, 245–46
powdery mildew, 354–55
pre-flowering phase, 39
flowering, to induce, 202–3
identifying, 196–98
lateral branching, 195–96
length of, 201–2
Pringle, H., 2
problem solver, 331–63
troubleshooting steps, 356–63
. *see also* pest control; plant problems
propagation
of cuttings and clones, 38
defined, 59
germination decisions, 59, 61–62
germination techniques, 63–64
propagation kits, 64–65
seed towel propagation, 64
soil propagation, 63
pruning, 293
air pruning, 296–97
botrytis and, 352
bushes, pruning for, 310–11
FIM technique, 308
mother plants, 217
Super Cropping technique, 308–9
topping, 306–8, 309
for yield, 305–11

R

recessive hereditary traits, 387
test crosses, 396–403, 405
recycle systems, monitoring, 276
reflectors
cabinet growing, 226–27
lights and lighting, 123–24, 132
mylar, 86, 140, 141
rejuvenated plants, 320–21, 325–26

resin
    potency of, 8–9
    pressing into hash, 453–55
    sinsemilla condition, 42
    and soapy pesticides, 332–34
    staining ability of, 365
resin glands. see trichomes
reverse osmosis filters, 276
rockwool
    hydroponic systems, 243, 265
    nutrient film technique (NFT), 245
    rockwool cubes, 64–65, 256, 257, 267,
        315, 318–19
    wick system, 252
root rot, 353–54, 360
rooting solutions, 318
    vitamin B1, 321, 354
roots
    clones, root development, 519n2 (ch8)
    in hydroponic systems, 244
    pot-bound stress, 78
    root ball size, estimating, 76, 79
    root mass development, 321
    root pruning, 79–80
    rooting solutions, 321
    substrates, effect of on growth, 76
    vitamin B1 (thiamine), 321, 354
ruderalis strains, 19, 24, 25
    characteristics of, 34, 35, 36, 46

S
safety issues
    butane extraction, for hash oil, 450, 451–53
    faulty HID lights, 148
    fire hazards, 94, 140
    ozone generators, 177
Sagarmatha Seeds, 241
    Blue Thunder, 392
    Bubbleberry, 393
    Matanuska Tundra, 428
    Mongolian Indica, 400
    Stonehedge, 241, 409
salts, 363
sand, 153
sativa, 19
    characteristics of, 34

growth cycle, 42–43
harvesting, 371–72
high from, 47, 458
indica/sativa top ten, 434–35
leaf types, 35
mostly sativa top ten, 432–33
in outdoor growing systems, 283
plant traits, 200
plant types, 36
sativa top ten, 430–31
in Sea of Green (SOG) setups, 217
strain list, 26–29
varieties, strains, subspecies, and hybrids,
    23–24, 25
vegetative growth to flowering ratio, 515n46
Saxena, Sanjeev, 4
Schultes, Richard E., 19, 20, 22
scientific classification debate, 14–21
Screen of Green (ScrOG), 123, 213, 220–25
    advanced setups, 228
    plant density, 220
    screen height, 221–22
    suitable strains, 235
    thinning, 302–4
    variations of, 224
Sea of Green (SOG), 123, 213, 217–20, 231
    advanced setups, 228
    plant density, 217–18
    suitable strains, 231
    thinning, 302–4
security issues, 90–97
    concealment of outdoor grows, 88–89
    electricity usage, 92, 517n1
    fire hazards, 94
    grower communication, 217, 517n2
    indoor growing systems, 92–94
    odor control, 92–94, 174
seed banks
    choosing, 50–53, 57
    customer feedback, 363
    damaged seeds, 53, 57
    delivery time, 53
    Internet review sites, 50, 53
    pricing, 53
    security issues, 92
    as source of strain information, 8

seed banks by name
  Delta-9 Labs, 230–31, 392, 393, 395,
    397, 402, 407
  DNA Genetics, 232–33
  Dr Greenthumb, 433, 468
  Dutch Passion, 229, 391, 396, 400, 404,
    405, 409, 411, 427, 429, 431
  Green House Seed Co., 22, 234–35, 388,
    389, 390, 391, 395, 397, 398, 404,
    413, 430, 432, 434, 478
  High Bred Seeds, 236–37
  K.C. Brains, 87, 88
  Paradise Seeds, 12, 40, 42, 46, 47, 71,
    89, 219, 238–39, 298, 400, 403, 406,
    407, 427, 435, 462, 466
  Sagarmatha Seeds, 241, 392, 393, 400,
    409, 428, 429
  Sensi Seeds, 396, 398, 399, 402, 403,
    409, 426, 431, 435
  Serious Seeds, 240, 423
  Subcool, 399, 406, 409, 415
  Trichome Technologies, 101, 274–75, 367,
    379, 433
seedlings
  fertilizer for, 64
  handling of, 69
  labeling, 71
  lighting for, 67
  nutrient control, 162
  seedling sub-stage, 37, 38
  support for, 69–70
  transplant shock, 64
  transplanting, 71–73
seeds
  collection for breeding, 384–85
  counterfeit goods, 53, 516n3
  determining viability of, 70
  feminized seeds, 199, 420, 519n4
  harvesting, 54
  production, 40, 42
  production of, 62, 209–11
  propagation kits, 64–65
  purchasing, 50
  rockwool cubes, 265
  scuffing, 516n8
  seed coat hardness, 67, 516n8

seed development, 46, 64–65
seed structure, 66–67
selecting, 48–49
storage, 57
transporting, 51
selfing, of hermaphrodite plants, 13, 419–22
Sensi Seeds
  First Lady, 396
  Hash Plant, 426
  Jack Flash, 398
  Jack Herer, 398, 435
  Mexican Sativa, 402
  Mother's Finest, 431
  Mr. Nice, 403
  Shiva Shanti, 409
Serious Seeds, 240, 423
sex determination systems, 34, 196–200,
  518n6
  calyx development, 207
silts, 153
Singh, Anurudh K., 4
sinsemilla, 13–14
  all-female grow room, 62
  flowering stage, 211
  potency in, 31–32
  sinsemilla hermaphrodites, 323–24
skuff, 438, 443
skunk strains, 55
Small, Ernest, 19, 20, 21
smoke-free vaporization, 461, 471–72
smoking accessories
  apple pipe, 489
  bucket bong, 492
  joints, to roll, 488
  light bulb vaporizer, 493
  tinfoil pipe, 490–91
social issues
  alcohol use vs cannabis, 474–77
  driving under the influence, 477–79
  drug testing, 479
  gateway drug theory, 485
  pregnancy, 481
  prohibition arguments, 456–67
soil, 497
  composition of, 152
  factors in selecting, 150–52

germination soil, 63
humus, 121, 152
outdoor soil, 290–92
pH levels, adjusting, 171–73
types of, 152–54
watering problems, 360
soil flushing
emergency transplants, 74
leaching, 357
nutrient lockout, 168, 362–63
overfeeding, 169–70
procedure for, 191–93
soil mixture preparation, 155–56
as germination inhibitor, 68
nutrient control, 161–64
soilless mixes, 243, 268
spider mites, 340–41, 344, 346, 348
Steiner, Rudolf, biodynamic agriculture, 100
stress
avoiding, 500
heat stress, 142, 182, 359, 518n2 (ch6)
and hermaphrodite condition, 13, 105
pot-bound stress, 78, 363
role of in sex reversal, 34
root rot and, 353–54
stress-related sex problems, 205–6,
518n6, 519n3, 519n6
transplant shock, 317, 518n3 (ch6)
Subcool
Jack the Ripper, 398
Querkle, 406
Space Jill, 409
Third Dimension, 415
Vortex, 415
sulfur (S), 161
deficiencies, 167, 357
and spider mites, 341
supercritical fluid extraction (SFE)
for hash oil, 448–51

T

temperature
digital measuring devices, 259
effect on germination, 69
hand heat test, 183
indoor growing systems, 181–83
and photoperiod cycles, 142
and photosynthesis, 127
THC
components of, 7
extraction for hash, 437–38
Federal Potency Monitoring Project, 32
levels, genetic determination of, 5
light degradation of, 370
natural light vs artificial, 84–86
and potency, 8, 465–66
quantities, relation to bud mass, 5–8
in trichome structures, 10
thiamine (vitamin B1), for rooting, 321,
354
thinning, 302–4
thrips, 342, 344
timers, 123–24, 184, 259
top ten strains, 425–35
topping, 306–8, 309
total dissolved solids (TDS) meters, 276
training, 312–13
transplanting
emergency transplants, 74, 75, 116, 193
premeditated, 74–79
root ball size, estimating, 76
root pruning, 79–80
seedlings, 71–73
transplant shock, 64, 76–77, 80–81, 317,
518n3 (ch6)
and weather conditions, 74–75
Trichome Technologies, 379
nutrient film technique (NFT), 274–75
Ultra Violet, 101, 367, 379
Washington, 433
trichomes, 6, 7, 8
and calyx to leaf ratios, 39
gathering for hash, 437–38
and resin production, 8–9
role of genetics in potency, 466
structure of, 10
withering process, 368–69
troubleshooting problems, 331–63
. see also pest control; plant problems

U

USDA Plants Database, 21

V

vaporization of cannabis, 471–72
Vavilov, Nikolai Ivanovich, 2, 17
vegetative growth stage, 35, 39
 blood meal, 169
 clones, taking, 320–21
 feeding schedules, 168–70
 lighting requirements, 140–44
 nitrogen requirements, 165
 nutrient control, 163–64
 nutrient disorders, 357–63
 pre-flowering phase, 195–98, 201–2
 to prolong, 201–2
 reverting to, 320–21, 325–26, 520n6
 solid stems, developing, 70
 topping, 306–8, 309
 vegetative growth to flowering ratio, 515n46
ventilation systems, 178–81, 497
 airflow control, 259
 cabinet growing, 226–27
 components in, 179
 humidity issues, 178
vermicomposting, 117, 119
vermiculite, 153–54, 269, 270
vitamin B1 (thiamine), for rooting, 321, 354

W

water
 hard water, 276
 overwatering, 157
 underwatering vs pest attack symptoms,
  334–35
water cloning, 317
water extraction, for hash, 445–47
watering cycles, adjusting, 173–74
 drip irrigation systems, 249–51
wattage, and lumens
 calculations for, 130–34
 comparison, 138
weed killers, 293
weeding, 121
wick system, 252–53
wilt, 167, 360
window grows, 84–86
worm castings, 344, 346
worm composting, 117, 119

Y

yields, 33
 bushes, pruning for, 310–11
 in hydroponic systems, 243–44
 increasing, 324–29
 lighting overkill, 134
 natural light vs artificial, 84–86
 of organic grows, 109
 organic vs artificial cultivation, 101–2
 and photoperiods, 499
 pruning to increase, 305–6
 Super Cropping pruning technique, 308–9
 supplementary carbon dioxide, effect of,
  185
 topping, 306–8, 309
YouTube videos, 260, 280

Z

Zero Zero (hash), 9, 12
zinc (Zn), 161
 nutrient disorders, 357